WILLA CATHER

Family, Community, and History

(The BYU Symposium)

Willa Cather

Willa Cather

Family, Community, and History

(The BYU Symposium)

Edited by John J. Murphy
with
Linda Hunter Adams and Paul Rawlins

Brigham Young University
Humanities Publications Center

(and Willa Cather Educational Foundation)

Provo, Utah, 1990

Cover photo: The Pavelka family
Courtesy of Nebraska State Historical Society

The Oxbow, pp. 294–95
All rights reserved, The Metropolitan Museum of Art

Library of Congress Catalog Number: 90–085382

ISBN 0–8425–2299–9

Printed in the United States of America

In Memory of Mildred R. Bennett
Mother of Catherians

Table of Contents

Editor's Note

    This volume collects a selection from the sixty presentations given at Brigham Young University's Willa Cather Symposium, 15–17 September 1988. While they represent a significant range of approaches, the essays are held together, loosely at least, by related themes. Sponsored in part by BYU's Center for Family and Community History, perhaps to encourage a local focus, the involvement of historians broadened the theme toward the theoretical and Cather's handling of historical sources. Also, the family topic encouraged speculation in several essays that balance others dwelling more closely on the Cather biography.

    Arranging so many essays into a sensible pattern was an editorial challenge met, I hope, with at least the semblance of a rationale. It was something like a department head doing class scheduling for a faculty of thirty–two—involving sensible judgments in some instances and arbitrary ones in others. The arrangement begins with the biographical, moves to the theoretical, and concludes with the hopes we have for family and community beyond.

    Each of the volume's five sections is prefaced by a summary of what the essays in that section are about. Since few other than reviewers will read this collection from cover to cover in sequence, the prefaces should guide the scholar toward her or his interests. However, the essays must speak for themselves. As the reviewer of Cather criticism for seven years for *American Literary Scholarship*, I can say with some assurance that a number of these essays are among the best of their kind, if not the first of their kind.

—John J. Murphy

Acknowledgments:

We are indebted to Marilyn Arnold for the genesis of a Cather symposium at Brigham Young University, to her secretary Chris Tolman for general helpfulness, to LaMond Tullis for securing publication funding, to Pat Phillips of the Willa Cather Pioneer Memorial and Educational Foundation for help with photos and other things, to BYU English Chair Bert Wilson for valuable time, to Shirley Warren for keeping track, to the student editors at the Humanities Publications Center: Rebecca P. Bennion, Carol S. Oertli, Scott Patrick, Lale L. Anderson, Nancy Gunn, Serena Hansen, Darcy L. Haroldsen, Shauna K. Harris, Valerie Holladay, and Jonathan Langford. My co-editors, Linda Hunter Adams and Paul Rawlins, deserve special thanks for their patience, dedication, and expertise.

J. J. M.

Courtesy of NSHS

Charles, Willa, Jennie, and Douglass Cather

Part One:
Cather's Family and Home Place

Generally biographical, this first group of essays begins with Arnold and Woodress providing factual basis for Willa Cather's deeply felt home connection, which Woodress then applies to the body of fiction, and Baker, Ryder, Burgess, and Wasserman develop in individual works. The final essays concern homecoming as a conflict between security and independence.

In "Poses of the Mind, Paeans of the Heart: Cather's Letters of Life in the Provinces" Marilyn Arnold surveys the early letters Cather wrote from Red Cloud and Pittsburgh, her early "provinces," to uncover beneath her superior pose (occasionally ill-tempered) an abiding love for family and home place. Arnold warns against reading the early letters at face value, especially those to Louise Pound and Mariel Gere, due to their "gamemanship." Arnold comments on some recently uncovered letters from Cather to Helen Stowell and in notes gives extensive treatment to the Pound and Gere letters. Although paraphrasing rather than quoting from the letters, due to the testamentary restrictions against publishing Cather's letters, obscures a good deal of their gamemanship, Arnold manages to communicate the discrepancy between a young artist's lofty posing and poor spelling.

James Woodress concludes at the beginning of "A Dutiful Daughter: Willa Cather and Her Parents" that although Cather's generally happy relationship with her parents did not make her a world-class author, "it did have a lot to do with what she wrote about." He reviews the biographical highlights of this relationship (repeated visits home, anguish over illnesses and death, etc.) and then fictional portraits that emerged from it in "Old Mrs. Harris," "The Best Years," and *The Song of the Lark*. He sees father–daughter relationships in *The Professor's House, Shadows on the Rock, Lucy Gayheart,* and *Sapphira and the Slave Girl* as based on Willa's fond relationship with Charles Cather, whom he suggests as a prototype of Anton Rosicky, who like Charles died of a heart condition.

Bruce P. Baker's " 'Old Mrs. Harris' and the Intergenerational Family" takes up the biographical connection in analyzing this significant story as Cather's personal journey of reconciliation with the family that resided in her childhood home on Cedar Street in Red Cloud, Nebraska. Through the ambivalent perceptions of a Jamesian controlling consciousness, Mrs. Rosen, the Templeton family is explored as a sanctuary as well as a context of suffering.

Cather is able to sympathize here with imperfect people in a fallen world. The oneness of family living, of Mrs. Harris ceasing to be an individual with her grandchildren and becoming "a relationship," is given religious dimension through biblical imagery.

Alarm over loss of the individual is Mary R. Ryder's handle in "Loosing the Tie That Binds: Sisterhood in Cather," a survey of the sister relationships in *The Song of the Lark*, "The Diamond Mine," *The Professor's House*, and *Lucy Gayheart*. Ryder sees Pauline's relationship with Lucy as "perhaps the most complex of [sisterly relationships] depicted in Cather's fiction" and concludes: "For Cather [who had two sisters], then, the bond between sisters was a fragile one, based on blood ties and family loyalties but threatened by the struggle for individuation . . . [that] often cripples women in developing satisfactory unions with any other individuals."

Individuation in conflict with relationship concerns Cheryll Burgess in "Willa Cather's Homecoming: A Meeting of Selves," a comparison of *The Song of the Lark* and "The Best Years" from the perspective of homecoming and the divided self. After having portrayed homecoming as surrender and fantasy in apprenticeship stories, Cather seriously represented her own duality as writer and family member in the characters of Thea Kronborg and Lesley Ferguesson (she gave both her attic room in the Red Cloud home). While Thea's individuality becomes her professional self, Lesley drowns in family. But Cather herself avoided either tragedy by balancing "her individuality and [family] communion" in writing about Nebraska.

The inevitable leavings and returnings to the home place extend beyond the biographical in Loretta Wasserman's "Going Home: 'The Sculptor's Funeral,' 'The Namesake,' and 'Two Friends.' " Wasserman compares the painful return in the first story of the sculptor Harvey Merrick to the grotesque family that indelibly marked his art, and the discovery of home place and family kinship enabling the sculptor Lyon Hartwell in the second story to develop his art. Against these, she discusses the third story, in which the narrator's childhood experience of a special friendship and its death gains cosmic dimension through the years, and occasions her imaginative return to the home place.

J. J. M.

Poses of the Mind, Paeans of the Heart: Cather's Letters of Life in the Provinces*

MARILYN ARNOLD

It is commonly assumed, partly on the basis of her fiction and her defiance of some conventions, that the young Willa Cather was in open rebellion against Nebraska in general and Red Cloud in particular, but that later she made a nostalgic emotional return to the landscape of her youth. This view, while not wholly inaccurate, is misleading. Her rebellion was at least partly a verbal pose, and emotionally she never really left Nebraska. As James Woodress has pointed out, a reading of the early letters can create quite a different impression than a reading of the bleaker early stories (78). Surely, stories such as "On the Divide" and "The Clemency of the Court" are in part affectations of a young mind searching for a potentially dramatic subject. On the other hand, the letters are in part affectations of a young mind seeking to entertain a familiar audience. Cather herself reportedly said in a 1921 interview that "nearly all very young writers write sad stories and very many of them write their first stories in revolt against everything. Humor, kindliness, tolerance come later" (Hinman 2).

The most prominent differences between the stories and the letters of Cather's youth are differences of tone. In the very early Nebraska stories— "Peter," "On the Divide," "Lou, the Prophet," and "The Clemency of the Court"—the narrative voice is angry and ironic; in the slightly later "A Wagner Matinée" it is simultaneously tributary and regretful. But in the existing letters written from and about what young Cather jestingly called "the provinces," that is, Red Cloud and the surrounding countryside, the tone is frequently satirical. Until she leaves Nebraska for Pittsburgh, the would-be sophisticate pretends to expose the follies and foibles of provincial manners and folk, though laughing very tenderly if the folk are family and very jovially if the folk is herself.

The game lasts until Cather moves to Pittsburgh at age twenty-two and falls prey to unexpected homesickness. Then the satirical mask peels away and she shamelessly confesses her love. Actually, she does not give up the game; she merely changes the ground and the ground rules, becoming an exile *away from* home rather than *at* home, a satirist of the newly dubbed

---

*This paper, which for oral presentation quoted from Cather letters, has been revised to conform to testamentary restrictions against publication of the letters.

Pennsylvania provinces and a proclaimed devotee of Nebraska. For Cather's purposes, it appears, the "provinces" could be anywhere she happened to land, so long as it offered material for her satiric posturing.[1]

This gifted youngster, endowed with the fictionist's imagination and the dramatist's love of performance, took whatever materials were at hand and made epistolary productions of them. Moreover, she loved playing the village wit. She had a gift for detecting a community's soft spots and a superb talent for manipulating language to produce humor. It is obvious in the early letters that she is playing with gusto to a knowing audience, one privy to the game. Once she arrived in Pittsburgh, she was no longer writing letters from the home territory, nor journalistic "letters" about that territory for the *Nebraska State Journal*, but she was publishing epistolary satire all the same, fortuitously furnished by an unsuspecting city. This woman who reputedly turned her back on Nebraska, and the sooner the better, nurtured extraordinarily close ties all her life to Red Cloud and the surrounding countryside. Her use of Nebraska materials in drama and in jest before her use of them in love does not mean that her heart found its home on the prairie only after she was sufficiently removed to romanticize it. The letters, even the satirical ones, testify otherwise.

It is true, though, that in spite of angry reactions from friends and family, Cather did not soon back away from the harsh portrayal of Nebraska pioneer life found in "A Wagner Matinée." In response to an apparent inquiry from Witter Bynner about her western sources for the story, Cather supposes that her early experiences had clung to her and that she devoted her first years of awareness largely to discovering the ugliness in her surroundings (7 June 1905). Reacting to the stinging criticism Will Owen Jones, editor of the *Nebraska State Journal*, administered in his column after the 1904 publication of the story, Cather defends the conditions described as so beastly true that her own family took offense at them, insisting that common courtesy should keep one from disclosing them (letter to Jones 6 March 1904). She says essentially the same thing in a letter to Kate McPhelim Cleary of Hubble, Nebraska (13 February [1905?]), who had apparently written to *McClure's* in corroborative appreciation of Cather's story.

Ten years later, however, Cather voices a different view. Writing to Jones again, she confesses that her early stories distorted reality and adds that the distortions were so obvious she wonders how anyone could have been misled by them. If a young person howls in the cornfields because there are no music-dramas for him to hear, she says, it should not be assumed that he has had a falling out with those cornfields. If he is satiated with music and exposed to what the world can offer him, he will be at peace about the corn (29 May 1914). In 1911 Cather had written to Elizabeth Shepley Sergeant that she was glad if Sergeant could like anything in the early stories, written so long ago and now seemingly so distant. To Cather years later they seem mostly to convey the ill-tempered rage of a young person who could not have the things she wanted. Cather granted that the western stories are distorted by the note of personal discomfort.

The warping Cather describes in the laboriously serious early fiction takes a different cast, a comic one, in the early letters. In fact, mock seriousness is their forte, satire is their mode, and the epistolary self is a theatrical persona—often a dual persona who is both satirist and satirized. Cather also interjects sincere feeling into the satirical posturing in these letters and in the process reveals that her true attitude toward Nebraska and Red Cloud is better assayed through them than the early fiction. Caution must be exercised, however. Readers of the letters, especially those to Mariel Gere and Louise Pound, have been tempted to credit isolated statements in them with more meaning than they deserve. Taking such statements as totally serious and loaded with ponderous burdens of truth surely distorts them. Many of these letters are in large measure the gamesmanship of a nimble, restless mind, and a mind that delighted in shocking more conventional minds. In fact, a chronological reading of all the letters suggests that Cather's mature expressions of yearning and appreciation for Nebraska and family reflect not so much a change in feeling as an adjustment in tone, from satire mixed with sentiment (for Cather had always talked lovingly as well as humorously of home and family) to sentiment without satire. It was quite easy to keep up the provincial pose so long as she was securely "trapped" at home among loving family and familiar landscapes. It should be no surprise that she dropped that pose and found another when she was thrust from the nest.

We should remember, too, that Willa Cather could be very funny. Anyone who doubts it should try immersion in her early newspaper columns, letters, and interviews.[2] Although Cather could apply her wit to almost any subject, and did so with abandon, it is the Nebraska "provinces" that provided the very young satirist with her first (and only) materials. And her interest in those materials never waned; she was deeply engaged with the provinces all her life. It is important to remember, too, that in Cather's view conflicts and tensions were a natural part of community and family life.[3] She was keenly aware that she was not unanimously loved in Red Cloud, but her mature letters to Carrie Miner Sherwood and others leave no doubt of her desire to be well regarded there. It is clear from a 1 October [1921?] letter to Will Owen Jones that she was disturbed enough by his "Wagner Matinée" editorial to remember its contents many years later. The editorial had suggested that Red Cloud was not likely to extend a friendly welcome to the author of that story, but Cather pointedly tells Jones that the people of Red Cloud have always treated her as a friend, as one of them, never meeting her with the hostility Jones had suggested. Like hometown folks, she said, they don't fuss over her either, but they indicate their pleasure in her successes.

By a stroke of good fortune, three very early letters from the provinces, and one later one, were acquired by the Cather Foundation in November 1987, the priceless creations of Willa Cather at ages fourteen and fifteen. All four were written to Helen Louise Stevens Stowell, who had moved from Boston to a sheep ranch near Red Cloud, probably in 1881. She and her family eventually left for California, apparently by the end of August 1888, but not before the young Willa Cather had befriended her and her youngest sister Georgie (which name Cather spells "Gorgie"). By the time Cather finds her again, for a 1928 letter, Helen Stowell is once more in Massachusetts.[4] These are extraordinary letters, precocious, badly spelled, newsy, hilarious— in short, absolutely delightful. More important to our purposes here, they are letters in which the youthful writer strikes what would become a characteristically superior pose, the pose of one whose interests are loftier than those of even her older provincial peers. This pose when accompanied by poor spelling creates, of course, humor that Cather did not intend; but the letters also contain a good deal of humor that she did intend. These letters, in tone and manner, are clearly the precursors of the slightly later satirical letters from the provinces, especially those to Mariel Gere.

The first one to Mrs. Stowell, written 31 August 1888 when Cather was fourteen, is full of family and community news, including descriptions of picnics and personal observations. Paraphrase of these letters cannot begin to do them justice, but until the testamentary ban against publishing them is lifted, paraphrase must suffice. The youngster writes that she approaches the beginning of school with nothing that resembles enthusiasm. Her attachment to her office, laboratory, dissecting equipment, and stuffed animals makes leaving them difficult. With characteristic precocity she adds that frail humanity being what it is, she prefers her work place where she governs as Miss Cather to school where she is governed.[5] Later in that letter she observes aloofly that Fred and Suard, that is, Winifred Richardson and Seward Garber, Silas's son, still act as if their loving bliss is unequalled by any except perhaps the heroes of Ouida. In mock disdain she concludes that a romance such as theirs, limited by an annual income of $1200, could scarcely escape an abundance of ennui. She blithely utters the hope that the Stowells will return ere another Christmas has passed and signs off as Wm. Cather.

The next letter, written at the end of her junior year (31 May 1889), when she was fifteen, is the wonderfully posed production of a self-confessed intellectual of the provinces. It is addressed to both Mrs. Stowell and Gorgie.[6] The first sentence is a priceless bit of posed adolescent erudition. She supposes that none of life's various emotional moments exhilarates like a moment of triumph, and by fortune's caprices she writes in one of those moments. Today ends the school year, and she is favored not only to have won the class honors but also to have borne off the prize for producing the best Latin translations, all of which, she confesses, have made her feel more than a little cheerful. Next, she lists her grades and interprets them. Then, she reproduces her teacher's accompanying note, altering her own hand-writing for the citation but revealing by the aberrant spellings that she had reproduced the accolade from memory. The letter is full of news, reported by the town sophisticate who speaks familiarly of Swinburne and is appalled that Mary Miner's piano teacher would have given this sixteen-year-old child the fourteenth "Hungarian Rhapsody" of Franz Lizst. She exclaims at the idea and wonders what next, asserting that one might expect "Moonlight Sonata" or *Requiem* by Mozart rather than a profaning that would make the old masters turn in their graves. And, she says, she does not mean that the composers would turn Mary's music for her. Apparently, Mrs. S— (Sill) is planning to take her best pupils to a Rubinstein recital, but young Willa Cather has decided that rather than go with that group of intellectuals she will play the pilgrim, worshiping in a faraway land. Earlier she had written of being deeply engrossed in Caesar, that wretched veteran, and observed that we certainly have no call to censure Brutus, for in youth we daily perform the awful deed of murdering Caesar. Later she comments with awful precocity that in such degenerate times as these strange fires are built on the gods' altars. At the end of the letter she adds, turning a bit of the satire toward herself, that this epistle's spelling and penmanship are protected by copyright and that all rights are reserved by Wm. Cather, Jr. The last of the three adolescent letters, written 28 August 1889, is equally packed and equally varied, but especially delightful in its superior scorn of spoony provincial lovers.

While attending the university in Lincoln, Cather found in the Charles Gere family (Mr. Gere was Cather's first editor at the *Nebraska State Journal*), and especially in Mariel Gere, the same kind of audience she had earlier found in Mrs. Stowell—loyal, forgiving, and intelligent enough not to take the provincial poser too seriously. By the time Cather wrote her first surviving letter to Mariel on 16 July [18]91, apparently following a visit of the Gere sisters to Red Cloud, she had aged a couple of years and improved her spelling only slightly. This letter, like all of the first letters, is newsy, mock-intellectual, and funny, striking the dramatic posture of the superior exile condemned to the provinces, but at the same time expressing sweet feelings for family members and poetic responses to the prairie. Again, adequate paraphrase is impossible, but perhaps it can suggest something of Cather's witty, intellectual pose. Cather says that as she drove about with Kit (Weston) she used the whip so frequently to emphasize her effusive outpourings that the poor horse's back presented an astonishing amalgamation of punctuation marks—homogeneous in their total effect, heterogeneous in their makeup. There were, she says, not only commas, periods, colons, and semicolons, but also numerous exclamation points as evidence of the rapture of their discussions.

The first overt satire of the provinces appears in a letter dated 1 June [18]93, written while Cather was in Red Cloud for summer vacation. She begs Mariel and her sisters to venture down that summer and experience semi-barbarism's solitude. She supposes that the primitivism of life there is no worse than what the Geres experienced in the Black Hills and promises that the children will not be any more bother than the insects the Geres contended with in camp. This same letter, however, speaks of concern over her grandmother's illness and young Jim's measles, and it describes at some length the endearing antics of the cunning and adorable little Elsie. Here also Cather begins teasing openly about her schoolgirl crush on her somewhat older idol, Louise Pound, and the subject is obviously a standing joke between them. Later, Mariel becomes a trusted confidante. Cather is both the superior exile who laughs at provincial folk and the inferior bumpkin who suffers by comparison with the superior maiden from civilization, in this case, Lincoln. The light, playful tone certainly argues against heavy reliance on the face value of its contents.

The dramatized pose of the exile, of course, carries into that same summer's letters to Louise Pound, which toss off comments about how exciting murders and attempted suicides have made life in the provinces of late. Cather had been hoping that Pound would journey to Red Cloud some time that summer (1893), but by 29 June it was doubtful that her hopes would materialize. Her letter to Pound on that date hyperbolically announces her melancholia as she groans under what she describes as the ages' total accumulation of dense hued sub-marine blue. In language that rivals that of the morbid Emmeline Grangerford in *Huckleberry Finn*, the poser laments that in her sickness and affliction the hard-hearted Pound visited her not. Near the end of this long letter, Cather again adopts the masquerade of biblical language to beseech Pound to travel to Red Cloud and deliver her soul. She clinches her argument with the exaggerated plea that Pound bring along her pistol and perform a kind service for her suffering friend. But despite Cather's affected pose of despondency and her expressed concern that her brothers and sisters would annoy Pound, she adds the genuine comment that she herself is accustomed to the children, and her fondness for them makes them no nuisance to her at all. Again, perceiving the tone of these letters, written with studied hyperbole and self-satire as well as general provincial satire, is critical to understanding what they really say.

Later in the summer of 1893 (1 August), Cather sends a lengthy narrative to Mariel Gere describing not only a visit from Louise Pound but also numerous local activities. Elated because the deific Pound condescended to appear in the provinces after all, Cather writes a sidesplitting letter. The provincial "materials" she uses for this production include her failure to conduct the permanent disappearance of little brother Jim during Pound's visit and an excursion to the home of country relatives who she says journeyed west long ago, just about when the earth was created. Her account of a major social event, a literary affair for country folk, is a real screamer. Still, she admits, the country uncouth have at least as clear an understanding of transcendentalism as any students at the university; in fact, some of them understand it better. Cather laughs at herself, too, in connection with her Aunt Franc, whom she describes as one of humankind's ugliest, smartest, and most eccentric of beings, adding slyly that she is said to be like her aunt in ugliness and eccentricity. Red Cloud, naturally, does not escape the satirical poser's barbs. Life there continues apace, with Lora, the elephant, regularly jumping the fence, Winning Card forever pacing the sidewalks in the company of master and mistress, and the billboard urging all to chew

Spear Head Plug burning forever before the youthful and innocent, guiding them in its lifegiving letters of light.[7]

By the next summer, the adolescent phase of Cather's relationship with Louise Pound is painfully over and the wit of the provinces, though somewhat subdued and wiser, is up to her old tricks. Again the poser is writing epistles to Mariel Gere from the much-maligned territory. Her letter dated 16 June [18]94 opens with the announcement that upon arriving in due time in country that could substitute ably for Africa she found the province's elite all dressed up in new attire as a tribute to her return. Like most of her letters, this one, too, has a double thrust. It speaks lovingly, proudly, and playfully of brothers and sisters, affirming that the ties to both family and place are deep and tender, but then it takes a humorous swipe at the provinces. She reports that the folks wish for rain but that she would regret the loss of the rounding batch of suicides that would accompany a lengthy stretch of dry weather.[8] By contrast, Cather was to write from the heart to Ellen and Frances Gere the following summer (30 July 1895) about returning home from a fun-filled stay in Beatrice. The country looks like a garden, so green and beautiful it belies description; everywhere, she exclaims, the cornfields are like forests.

So long as Cather was spending time at home both before her graduation from the university and after it, the Geres were "blessed" with letters from the provinces. A 2 January [18]96 letter addressed to Mariel, her two sisters, Ellen and Frances, and two friends, Allie and Maysie, rivals Irving in describing a country dance Cather proudly attended with her brother Douglas (she spelled it with one s in those days) as her escort. This letter, by the way, is datelined Siberia. Again, hyperbole abounds as Cather immoderately heaps the dance floor high with wood shavings and chunks of wax so big they had to be leaped or mounted and clambered over with the aid of an alpenstock. So rustic was the affair that ice water was served from a wooden bucket and sandwiches from a bushel potato basket, and all of these amenities paled beside the dancing itself. And this, she snickers, was a dance attended by Red Cloud's upper crust. The satirical poser then pleads pitiful indifference to her fate, sighing that she does not know and does not much care when she will next appear in Lincoln. She observes that one of the charming aspects of the provinces is that here a person can maintain absolute indifference, even toward suicide. She fittingly concludes with a few lines of melancholy verse, sighing audibly that she now has only her youngest brother, Jack, and the cats to whom she can quote poetry. Then she signs off in archaic language. Two months later (12 March [18]96) the pose remains intact as she complains to Mariel Gere that she is languishing in bitter exile and Mariel has not written, not even to tell her about Paderewski. Furthermore, she sighs, the province has ceased its mad festivities, leaving her to family affairs and her own devices. But the poser, after recounting the misadventures of younger siblings when she was left in charge during her parents' absence, adds tender comments about several of them. For example, she says that she and Douglas, a model brother, enjoy wonderfully good, quiet times together. If there was any resentment or jealousy toward younger brothers and sisters (Cather was the eldest of seven children), it is not apparent in the slightest degree in the existing letters.

In May 1896 Cather was still suffering, though not in silence, through the provincial interim between finishing college and receiving a job offer from the *Home Monthly* magazine in Pittsburgh. True to form, she is still indulging in self-drama, this time berating herself as an erstwhile prep with a shaved head, an idiot of monumental proportions, and whatever else comes to mind. Some of her distress is, of course, genuine—her complaint that she is unable to accomplish anything in Red Cloud because she has seen too little of the world, and her sense that since her graduation from the university, her family seems to be waiting expectantly for her to make something of herself. Even so, she takes comfort in her adorable baby brother, Jack, and shakes off her melancholy pose to report another side of life in the provinces. She attended a rather civilized dance in Blue Hill with Douglas, where she met a new and interesting friend, cheerily danced all thirty-five dances, and gladly received the undivided attention of an attractive young man.

And then, *rescue.* In June the exile departs for Pittsburgh and the *Home Monthly.* She writes Mariel Gere (June [July?] 1896) that her spirits began to rise the minute she saw clean streams and hills and the trees planted by the Lord east of Chicago. The thematic switch from western province to eastern province, however, occurs in the twinkling of an eye. Within hours after Cather arrives in Pittsburgh, she begins to satirize certain provincial aspects of what she calls the City of Dreadful Dirt, this time warning Mariel not to take her seriously.

Although she would grow to like Pittsburgh, Cather focuses immediately on what she perceives to be its most vulnerable and provincial aspects—its dyed-in-the-cloth Presbyterianism, its myriad women's clubs, and its flimsy overtures to culture.[9] At the same time, her homesickness for Red Cloud and family now preclude any satire at all on the old provinces. The provincial wit, however, is not without resources, and she takes readily to her new material, stereotyping James Axtell, one of the *Home Monthly* publishers, and his family as narrow, bigoted Pittsburgh Presbyterians. Both parlor and library of the Axtell home are adorned with portraits of Grandpa, Cather writes, and the bedroom, Cather's quarters until she can find lodging, characterizes the Puritan Maid who generally occupies it. That room, Cather says, boasts three Bibles, not counting the three the maid took with her when she went to visit some aunt or other, presumably to escape the contamination of Cather's influence. The room also contains, she claims, ample numbers of amply worn cheap religious novels by E. P. Rowe. The Bibles she can stand, Cather adds; E. P. Rowe is another matter.

A letter from Cather to Mrs. Gere in July (13 July 1896) opens with a plaintive cry from the eastern province, a cry reminiscent in tone of the Red Cloud letters. She calls the Gere sisters heartless for not writing to someone as alone and lonesome as she is. After working hours, she says, her soul yearns for her own kind, especially for little Jack; and she vows that she would pay any price just to have ten minutes with Jack, whose big, gray eyes she dreams of every night. She assures Mrs. Gere, though, that when called upon by three prim female stalwarts of the Presbyterian faith, she demurely conversed with them about flower gardening and church music.

Letters to Mariel Gere continue the witty, satirical pose, as do newspaper columns—another version of letters from the provinces—sent back to the *Journal* and the *Lincoln Courier*. For example, the alleged Presbyterian distrust of classical music and secular literature is satirized in a column that appeared in the *Nebraska State Journal*, 17 January 1897 (13). If it were not for the Germans, Cather says, concert halls and bookstores would be entirely superfluous in Pittsburgh. She notes that the Presbyterian church of Pittsburgh has only slowly become aroused to the terrible iniquity of playing composers like Mozart, Wagner, and Beethoven on Sunday, but when the church is aroused, it can be fearsome. The church is now conducting mass meetings in Pittsburgh and Allegheny, as well as petitioning the board of trustees and piously denouncing advocates of Sunday concerts, along with the flesh and the devil.

Even with Pittsburgh residents George and Helen Seibel, Cather tosses off barbs about Pittsburgh Christians. In one instance, the *Home Monthly* was apparently delinquent in paying what it owed writer George Seibel, and Cather, on vacation in Nebraska, wrote to Helen (23 July 1897), suggesting that George ask Axtell in person for his money, and without delay, for a Christian as good as Axtell is not to be trusted. There is also self-satire in the letters about Pittsburgh, just as there is in those about Nebraska. It should be noted, too, that when Cather writes to the Seibels from Red Cloud, she reverts to the satirical western pose, relishing a new audience for her old materials. She reports, for example, that in the approved manner of provincials she attended a fire the previous night and that in deference to her family she regularly attends services at the Baptist church. She tells Helen Seibel (23 July 1897) that she picked up a gift for the Seibels' small daughter, apologizing for the limited selection in this untamed village where jewelers deal mainly in silver-mounted six-shooters. As she had always done, however, the poser also drops a few paeans of the heart, writing warmly of her pleasure in being home again and adding comments about Jack's rapid growth and an upcoming hunting trip with Roscoe. She indicates later (9 August 1897), taking up the pose again, that she is soon off for her trip to the Wild West (wilder even than Red Cloud) and that she just might return to Pittsburgh sporting six-shooters in her belt.

Wherever she was, the young writer found ample material for posing as the exile. Later, too, in letters to Zoë Akins and Carrie Sherwood, she spoke of New York as godforsaken, and it became the place of exile. But if there is one predominant theme in her letters, early or late, satirical or not, it is the reality of her iron-strong ties to Red Cloud and family. She can boast happily to Mariel Gere (19 September 1897) that five young men met her train when she returned to Pittsburgh, but in the same letter, growing dramatic in the reverse direction, she virtually shouts that she will not absent herself from Nebraska another year, insisting that money and success are useless if one is unhappy, which is what she is when she is far away from home. She wonders, sometimes, if she is the same person who so eagerly yearned for the shine of other lives two years ago. She speaks of a heart once asleep that has awakened and now aches for baby Jack sleeping in his bed so many miles away. Only God, she says, will ever know what Jack has done for her, killing forever every unworthy ambition. Now, she says, money and fame have no appeal at all; she wants only to have her three boys always. This letter contains hyperbole, yes; affectation, possibly; but satire, no.

And later letters, to innumerable correspondents but notably to Carrie Miner Sherwood and her two sisters, Mary and Irene, to Elizabeth Sergeant, Zoë Akins, and Dorothy Canfield Fisher, are full of concern for family and friends in Nebraska, and love for the place where Cather spent her youth. She still jokes about her background on occasion, about growing up in the cornfields and finding she could not entertain cows with her sonnets (letter to Akins, 31 October [ca. 1905]), or about the fact that spending Christmas with a big family such as hers is like living through *War and Peace* (letter to Fisher from Red Cloud, 18 January [1928]). But overriding the humor are her obvious love for family and Nebraska and regret at being separated from them.[10]

Years after she had left Nebraska, Cather was still yearning for home. She writes Mariel Gere from Pittsburgh, 30 September 1905, that she is convinced that she wants to live only in the West and hopes to spend at least a year in Red Cloud soon. She is very fond of many people there, she adds. And she confesses to Carrie Sherwood as she nears fifty (21 September [1922]) that even though she had to learn her art in the proximity of artists, her heart remains west of the Missouri River. She promises almost ten years later (19 June 1931) to go back some day because her heart still lives there, in the soil itself, and she deeply regrets her inability to stop in Red Cloud on her last trip across the continent. It is true that soon after her parents were gone, Cather's visits to Red Cloud ceased, in spite of her intentions. But on 10 November 1931, she is making serious plans to go home. She writes Carrie that she is sacrificing a great deal in order to spend a month in Red Cloud, but more than anything else in the world, just now, she wants time with her old friends. The letters reveal that numerous times, plans were thwarted—by her own illnesses, by the illnesses and deaths of loved ones, by work demands, and by the advent of war. Nevertheless, the bonds remained strong. She writes to Annie Pavelka's boys, Edward and Clement, about their high school commencement (26 June 1931); to Nell McNeny (5 January [1935]) in praise of her grandchildren and her eternally youthful outlook; to Mrs. Lambrecht and her daughters about a certain beloved "little round-topped lilac" tree (19 January [1935]).

Countless letters to others, too—Ferris Greenslet at Houghton Mifflin, Blanche Knopf, Mabel Dodge Luhan, Mary and Sarah Orne Jewett, Harriet Whicher, Viola Roseboro, Josephine Goldmark, and many more—speak of her Nebraska home and family and her fondness for nieces and nephews as well as for parents and brothers and sisters. In short, the mature letters openly show what the immature letters from the provinces disclose beneath their sometimes satirical veneer, that Willa Cather loved Nebraska, and especially her family, with an extraordinary and unabating love.

By contrast, I consider my own indifference toward my hometown, where I lived for nineteen years and my parents lived for fifteen more, and I marvel at Willa Cather. Unlike Cather, who over the years corresponded with many people in Red Cloud, I left Ogden, Utah, and scarcely looked back. I wrote to no one there, ever, except my parents. Cather not only wrote, but all her life she sent gifts and money to beloved old women on farms in the vicinity. Her letters to Carrie Sherwood and others reveal her endless worry over these old friends and their homes and crops. She even saved the farms of some during years of drought and depression by paying the interest on their mortgages. And for years she made contributions to the local Red Cross, the Episcopal church, and Red Cloud projects such as the cemetery tree fund. Not only do I never write to anyone in Ogden, Utah, but I never go there either, and it is only eighty miles away, considerably shorter than the distance between New York and Red Cloud, and much more easily traveled. Furthermore, I have never subscribed to the *Ogden Standard Examiner* and never intend to, but Cather was still subscribing to the Red Cloud *Commercial Advertiser* (formerly, then latterly, the *Red Cloud Chief*) at least as late as 1946, the year before her death.[11]

I could count on one hand the times brothers and nieces and nephews have stayed with me, and yet Cather's letters are full of her stays with brothers, often running to weeks, and their stays with her, and of numerous short and lengthy visits of cherished nieces. Her grief over illnesses and deaths of family members is excruciating, and her sorrow is genuine when the husbands of nieces are called to war and their families divided. I have been awed, even stunned, to realize the depth of Willa Cather's attachment to what she once lightheartedly termed "the provinces" and to the family and friends with whom she shared that most important prairie province. In spite of the satire, which now seems to me largely the entertaining intellectual exercise of a young, creative mind beset with real frustrations at being denied the larger world, the overwhelming message of hundreds of letters from and about the provinces is a message of love. And even the earliest letters are not merely poses of the mind; they are also most assuredly paeans of the heart.

—Brigham Young University

NOTES

1. Even Virginia could become the "provinces," as is evident in a letter to Elizabeth Shepley Sergeant from Virginia, dated 5 September 1913. Cather writes that Winchester is unbearably dull. The food is terrible, and there is scarcely a male to be found. By the time Cather had spent several days in the Virginia mountains, however, she had reversed herself. A letter sent from Gore 22 September has nothing but praise for the area of Cather's birth and early childhood.

2. Several of Cather's interviewers and commentators remark on her wit and sense of humor, though few of her critics do. Rose C. Feld, for example, without using the term, actually describes Cather in 1924 as a satirist, that is, as one whose eyes and lips must be watched carefully, for they "betray her when she seems to be giving voice to a serious concept, but is really poking fun at the world." Her "homespun sense," Feld says, is driven home "with a well-wrought mallet of humor." In H. L. Mencken's view, *The Song of the Lark* is enlivened by "sly touches of humor" (306–07), and Evelyn J. Hinz sees humor in Cather's fiction as "both a stylistic trait and . . . a characterizing device" (55). George Seibel, one of Cather's dearest friends in Pittsburgh, mentions her "precious sense of humor" (11) in his tribute to her after her death in 1947, and Edith Lewis notes it in her memoir.

3. On several occasions Cather has made written comments on group life, in communities and families, and sometimes she has linked the two. Her observations in her essay on Katherine Mansfield about the "double life" in families are well known (*Not Under Forty* 135–37). She speaks of the group life perceived by the neighbors and the passionate private life lived by each individual member of the group as each strives for separate selfhood. In a 7 January 1899 *Courier* column, she had attributed similar observations to a lecturer on Henrik Ibsen's plays. Ibsen, according to Israel Zangwill, dramatizes "the romantic revolt [that] occurs every day in the unit of society, the family," in which secrets, hopes, passions, and indignities long concealed are finally given voice (*World and Parish* 492–93). Cather identifies the blood's claim as a theme in one of Dorothy Canfield Fisher's books (*Her Son's Wife*) and indicates that she has seen it repeatedly in Red Cloud (letter to Fisher, 14 October [1926]). Cather's own supposed "quarrel" with Red Cloud is better understood when we consider that it is perfectly normal for the demands of love and loyalty to conflict with the individual will. These forces are stronger in small towns because in such communities the town is an extension of the family. As Cather says in *Lucy Gayheart*, "In little towns, lives roll along so close to one another; loves and hates beat about, their wings almost touching" (167). Cather states it clearly in a 5 June [1919] letter to Viola Roseboro. Speaking of a Roseboro novel, Cather observes that every town seems like a family, big and quarreling. The intimacy among the people, even those who are enemies, Cather says, is enough to make a person shudder. She adds that in seeing this operating in Roseboro's novel, she has become more consciously aware that the coexistence of love and hate typifies communities.

4. The information about Mrs. Stowell comes from a 5 November 1987 letter to Mildred R. Bennett from Alice E. Woodbridge, granddaughter to Mrs. Stowell.

Alice Woodbridge made a gift of the letters to the Cather Foundation in Red Cloud, and they have been deposited in the Willa Cather Historical Center there.

5. One of the most delightful aspects of these letters that is lost in paraphrase is the spelling and the affectation of expression. It would be worth the trip to Red Cloud just to read these letters in the original.

6. Names were never Cather's long suit. It was years before she consistently spelled the Seibels' name correctly in letters to them, and she addressed one of Mariel Gere's letters to M— Gere, she said, because she did not know how to spell her friend's name.

7. This, incidentally, is the letter that contains the infamous passage about driving-with-one-hand-or-no-hands with Pound. When Cather says things like this, and in this tone, it is well-nigh impossible to separate truth from playful invention. The passage should not be interpreted apart from its immediate context. In that letter Cather tells Mariel Gere that she is now well, except for various bruises acquired while driving with one hand about the country with a certain fair maid, adding that sometimes she drove without any hands. The passage is more playful in tone than any paraphrase can make it, especially in Cather's next comment that Louise Pound apparently did not object to Cather's haphazard driving, even when the buggy plunged off banks and climbed over haystacks. As for herself, Cather adds, with obvious delight, she continues to drive one-handed in her sleep. Hyperbole runs rampant in this letter, along with the buggy. To Cather, during the short period of her infatuation, Pound was something of an untouchable goddess, and she mentions in a later letter (16 June [18]94) her gratitude for Mariel's endless patience with things like Cather's silly rapture on one occasion when she accidentally touched Pound's hand. This incident, by the way, suggests that the driving with one or no hands was either showing off or pure invention. Later Cather was to play the role of rejected peasant lover, and even though it hurt, she threw herself wholeheartedly into the drama. Again, Mariel was her audience and confidante. Interestingly, Cather was to say in a 1918 (13 March) letter to Carrie Sherwood, one expressing appreciation for their precious, sustaining friendship, that a person has to live upwards of forty years before she discovers which things offer merely temporary excitement and which result in affection that endures. It did not take her forty years to recover from the Pound infatuation and disappointment, however.

8. Black humor such as this, of course, is appropriate for the melodramatically grieving heart or for the performer distancing herself from herself and her bleeding heart. In describing her grief, the performer becomes melodramatic, thanking Mariel for saving so worthless a soul as hers and for having faithfully attended the corpse. By the time Cather had been in Pittsburgh a few months and been courted by both the women's clubs and a number of young men, her letters to Mariel Gere certainly indicate a complete cure. In fact, a letter to Pound dated 13 October 1897 carries only a trace of the old hurt, and when a few letters were exchanged in 1911 and 1912, after the death of Pound's father, it is as if the two were simply friendly old acquaintances. Cather's letters contain mainly news of her family.

9. Later Cather found Pittsburgh, especially the home of Isabelle McClung and her parents, conducive to productive writing and refreshing interludes outdoors. After

she moved to New York, she returned often to write and visit. In a letter to
Elizabeth Sergeant she even apologizes for wearying Sergeant with her hymn to
Pittsburgh (5 December [1914]).
10. A good example of Cather's ability to blend the provincial observation with
obvious appreciation is a comment she makes to Elizabeth Sergeant in a 23 June
[1917] letter from Red Cloud. Cather speaks of the patriotism and the bubbling
heat of Red Cloud, asserting that the corn-country dwellers in summer are scourged
as persistently by fire as Dante's sinners. It takes a lot of heat to effect the
germination of corn, she says, and then describes the heat as fire of magnificence
and the air as replete with smells that are hot and sweet. It is possible, too, that
Cather's attachment to Jaffrey, New Hampshire, and Grand Manan Island, which
some might regard as places of exile, may indicate that all her life Cather sought
the solitude and health of "provinces" such as the one she had known as a youngster.
11. Canceled checks in the Cather family papers give evidence of a March 1946
subscription to the *Advertiser*, sizable contributions in December 1945 and 1946
to the Ladies Guild of Grace Episcopal Church, and in September 1946 to the
Red Cloud Hospital Fund. Cather's unflagging interest in keeping up with happen-
ings in Red Cloud is obvious in the fact that a 28 March [1939] letter asks
Carrie Sherwood to arrange with the publisher of the *Advertiser* to make up a new
address label for her. The New York mail carrier, she complains, cannot read
a blurred numeral on the label. She says she has written the *Advertiser* several times
with no result and has missed some papers as a consequence.

BIBLIOGRAPHY

Bohlke, Brent L. *Willa Cather in Person*. Lincoln: U of Nebraska P, 1986.
Cather, Willa. "Katherine Mansfield." *Not Under Forty*. New York: Knopf, 1936.
    123–47.
Curtin, William M., ed. *The World and the Parish: Willa Cather's Articles and
    Reviews, 1893–1902*. 2 vols. Lincoln: U of Nebraska P, 1970.
Feld, Rose C. "Restlessness Such as Ours Does Not Make for Beauty." *New York
    Times Book Review* 21 December 1924: 11. Rpt. Bohlke. 68–72.
Hinman, Eleanor. "Willa Cather, Famous Novelist, Says Pioneer Mother Held Greatest
    Appreciation of Art—Raps Women Who Devote Themselves to Culture Clubs."
    Lincoln Sunday Star 6 November 1921: 1–2. Rpt. Bohlke. 42–49.
Hinz, Evelyn J. "Willa Cather's Technique and the Ideology of Populism."
    Western American Literature 7 (Spring 1972): 47–61.
Lewis, Edith. *Willa Cather Living*. New York: Knopf, 1953.
Mencken, H. L. "Cinderella the Nth." *Smart Set* 48 (January 1916): 306–07. Rpt.
    Schroeter. 7–8.
Schroeter, James C. *Willa Cather and Her Critics*. Ithaca: Cornell UP, 1967.
Seibel, George. "Willa Cather from 'April Twilights' to April Midnight." *Musical
    Forecast*, June 1947, 5, 11.

LETTERS CITED

Letters to Zoë Akins (81 originals) are in the Huntington Memorial Library, San Marino, Calif. (photocopies of 12 housed at the University of Virginia, Charlottesville).

Letters to Witter Bynner, Ferris Greenslet, and Mary and Sarah Orne Jewett are in the Houghton Library, Harvard University, Cambridge, Mass.

Letters to Mary Miner Creighton and Irene Miner Weisz are in the Newberry Library, Chicago.

Letters to Dorothy Canfield Fisher are in the Bailey Library, University of Vermont, Burlington.

Letters to members of the Charles Gere family (including those to Mariel Gere) and to Kate McPhelim Cleary are in the Nebraska State Historical Society Library in Lincoln (photocopies at the Willa Cather Historical Center in Red Cloud).

Letters to Will Owen Jones and Viola Roseboro, plus 3 letters to Louise Pound, 14 letters to Zoë Akins, 2 letters to Mary Miner Creighton, and 1 letter to Carrie Miner Sherwood are in the Alderman Library, University of Virginia.

Letters to Blanche Knopf are in the Ransom Humanities Library at the University of Texas, Austin.

Letters to Mabel Dodge Luhan are in the Beinecke Library, Yale University, New Haven, Conn.

Early Letters to Louise Pound are in the Duke University Library, Durham, N.C.

Letters to Elizabeth Sergeant, Harriet Whicher, and Josephine Goldmark are in the Pierpont-Morgan Library, New York City (photocopies at the Alderman Library, University of Virginia).

Letters to Carrie Miner Sherwood, Helen Louise Stevens Stowell, Edward and Clement Pavelka, Nell McNeny, Lydia Lambrecht, and George and Helen Seibel, plus 1 letter to Mary Miner Creighton are at the Willa Cather Historical Center in Red Cloud.

A Dutiful Daughter:
Willa Cather and Her Parents

JAMES WOODRESS

Willa Cather was fortunate in the selection of her parents. When I began to think about this paper, I had the feeling that Cather was a lot luckier than some of her writing friends and contemporaries, and when I did some investigation of the biographies of these others, I discovered that my hunch was correct. The writers I checked on were Edith Wharton and Ellen Glasgow, two important American women novelists of Cather's era, and Cather's friends, Dorothy Canfield Fisher, Mabel Dodge Luhan, and Mary Austin, all three of minor stature. Among these women only Cather could be said to have had a really happy childhood.

Wharton, as the daughter of a socially prominent New York family, received no encouragement in her intellectual and literary interests and was rushed into making her debut into society at the age of seventeen in an effort to thwart her writing and turn her into a conventional society matron. In her autobiography, *A Backward Glance*, Wharton remembers that she wrote her first story at the age of eleven. It began: " 'Oh, how do you do, Mrs. Brown?' said Mrs. Tompkins. 'If I only had known you were going to call I should have tidied up the drawing-room.' " When young Edith shyly took her story to her mother to read, Lucretia Jones glanced at it and handed it back to her daughter with the chilling comment that "drawing-rooms are always tidy" (73). Edith was so stricken by her mother's rejection of her effort that she dropped for a time her attempts to write stories. This rejection is emblematic of her unhappy relationship with her mother. In addition, her childhood may have been troubled by doubts about her legitimacy: rumors surfaced when she was an adult that her real father was her older brother's English tutor, but there is no proof of this, and her biographer, R. W. B. Lewis, does not think it is true.

Glasgow also was born into a social background in which an intellectual and literary daughter was an embarrassment. Her parents were prominent Virginians from Richmond who expected their female offspring to play the traditional role of Southern belle. To add to Ellen's difficulties, there were psychological problems: her beloved mother from tidewater Virginia suffered a nervous breakdown while Ellen was still a child, for which she always blamed her father, a stern Calvinist from the western part of the state.

Among Cather's literary friends Dorothy Canfield Fisher had the most impossible mother. She was a clubwoman to the point of caricature and a failed artist who left her family for a year at a time while she tried to be a painter, dragging young Dorothy off to Europe. The satiric portrait of Flavia Hamilton in Cather's early story "Flavia and Her Artists" is probably based on Flavia Canfield. Cather's later friend Mabel Dodge Luhan had to break with her socially prominent Buffalo parents in order to become a leader in avant garde literary and aesthetic movements. And Mary Austin, who was Cather's friend for a number of years, suffered the loss of her father, who died when she was ten, and the death of her adored younger sister two months later. To these losses was added the burden of overhearing her mother say she wished Mary had been the one to die. As a result, Austin went through a painful adolescence.

It is quite obvious that native talent and industry are more important than a happy childhood in producing a writer, and that Cather's good fortune in her parentage had little to do with making her a world-class author. Such good fortune did, however, have a lot to do with what she wrote about. If Charles Cather had died when Willa was a child, all the fathers in her fiction certainly would have been different. If Mary Virginia Cather (usually called Jennie) had had a nervous breakdown during Cather's youth, the sense of family and community that gives distinction to Cather's fiction would no doubt be absent. What I want to talk about in this paper, after I deal with the biographical details of Cather's relationship with her parents, is the impact of her parents on her writing.

o   o   o   o   o

Cather's first nine years in Virginia were happy years.[1] She lived the life of a healthy, active child surrounded by a large number of relatives—uncles, aunts, two grandmothers, a grandfather, and after a while two brothers and a baby sister. Charles Cather and Jennie Boak were married in 1872 and Willa was born a year later, the first of eventually seven children. Charles's family stayed with the Union during the Civil War, while Jennie's people supported the Confederacy, but it was Jennie's charm and initiative that later brought the formerly warring families together. While Willa was still an infant, Charles's father and mother migrated to Nebraska and the young parents moved into Willow Shade, the spacious three-story brick house built by Willa's grandfather at Back Creek, a few miles west of Winchester. Charles became a successful sheep farmer who sold his animals in the Washington and Baltimore markets.

Life at Willow Shade was orderly, comfortable, and continuously interesting. It was a stable world for a child to grow up in. The Cathers were better off than many of their neighbors, and there were always household servants and field hands, both black and white, to watch and talk to. There was a three-story sheep barn with a loft above its ground-floor pens, where

children could play. Spinning and quilting, butter-making, preserving, and
candle-making went on regularly. Old women from the mountains came down
to help during the busy seasons. Butchering, sheep-shearing, and tanning were
done on the farm. During the winter evenings the black help sat around the
kitchen fireplace cracking nuts, telling stories, cutting old clothes into strips,
and winding them into balls to send to Mrs. Kearns, a neighbor who made
them into rag rugs. There was a steady stream of guests at Willow Shade.
The tin peddler and the broom-maker came often and were housed overnight in the two-story wing at the back of the house. More important guests,
relatives from all over and friends from Winchester and even Washington,
stayed for visits or stopped over on their way through the area. It was open
house almost all the time. Jennie Cather was a gracious hostess, a real
Virginia lady, and Cather, as Pat Yongue has demonstrated,[2] grew up with
a desire to emulate her mother, her nonconformist tomboy adolescence
notwithstanding.

Jennie Cather, who had taught rural school before marrying, was a woman
of energy and force. Handsome and domineering, she provided the power
that drove her household and often produced sparks. She ruled her family
with a stern hand, exacting strict obedience from her children and punishing
disobedience with a rawhide whip. Her offspring apparently never objected
to her rigorous methods of enforcing good behavior. Jennie also had a great
capacity for enjoying life and for caring about things—whether the coffee was
hot, whether a neighbor's child was well, whether the weather was right for
a picnic. She had the good sense to let her children develop their own personalities. Willa Cather remembered in her old age that her mother kept her
seven children clean and fed them but allowed them to be individuals from
the time they were able to crawl. They were all different, and she let them
be different. She cared for their bodies and kept her hands off their souls.

This was of vast importance for a daughter who was to become a novelist.
Cather probably did not appreciate her mother's hands-off method of childrearing when she was growing up in Red Cloud, cutting her hair short,
dressing as a boy, and refusing to be a girl. Her relations with her mother
were sometimes difficult, although I don't think too much should be made
of this, for there is no evidence that between Jennie and Willa there was
anything like the estrangement between Edith Wharton and Mary Austin and
their mothers. Cather herself once remarked that her mother would much
have preferred that she be like her sister Jessica, who conformed quite
happily to the conventional role of Victorian maiden. Jennie Cather must have
been puzzled to find that she was raising a daughter who wrote in a friend's
album that slicing toads was her hobby, doing fancy work a real misery, and
amputating limbs perfect happiness.

In contrast to Jennie Cather, Charles was soft-spoken and tenderhearted.
He was tall, fair-haired, gentle; he did not at all inherit the inflexible will
and evangelical zeal of his Calvinist-turned-Baptist father. He was handsome
in a boyish Southern way and solicitous of everyone's feelings. Before his

marriage Charles had studied law, and though he never practiced, he often was called on to help his neighbors with legal problems. When he gave up farming to go into real estate and insurance, this legal training was useful, and despite his easygoing ways, he operated his sheep business in Virginia profitably and more than doubled his capital during the eighteen months he farmed in Nebraska. There is no record of any friction ever disturbing the relationship between Charles Cather and his oldest daughter.

When Willa was nine, the family moved to Nebraska. Being taken from the cultivated landscape and established society of Virginia to the flat, raw, open and sparsely settled prairie was a traumatic experience, as Cather later recalled to interviewers. But the shock was far less for Cather than for her fictional creation Jim Burden in *My Ántonia*, who goes to live with his grandparents in Nebraska after the death of his parents. He is accompanied only by Jake the hired man, whereas Willa traveled with her parents, her grandmother, three siblings, two cousins, and the hired girl and her brother. It was a closely knit, supportive group that ventured into the unknown country in April 1883.

The year and a half that they spent on the farm in Webster County, Nebraska, was made up of happy months for Willa despite the culture shock. As an intelligent, energetic child she explored her new prairie world and learned about the Old World from her immigrant neighbors. We know very little about the day-to-day Cather family activities during this period, but Charles was busy farming, and Jennie was busy raising children. Apparently both parents agreed the next year that life in town would be preferable to life on an isolated prairie farm. Charles wanted to go into business, and Jennie wanted the amenities of town life. Thus the Cathers took up residence in Red Cloud in the fall of 1884, and Willa then spent the years from ten to sixteen in the town made famous in her fiction.

Cather left the parental home for good when she went to Lincoln in the fall of 1890, but the ties to home remained strong. During her college years she went home in the summers and for holidays, and during her first year after graduating from the university, she lived at home part of the year. Usually she was happy to return to her parents and brothers and sisters, but during the year following her graduation from the university when she did not have a full-time job and probably went home to Red Cloud to save money, she missed the social life and the theater in Lincoln, and her letters reveal dissatisfaction with home and family. She headed one letter from Red Cloud in January 1896 "Siberia," suggesting both climatic austerity and a sense of banishment. By May she felt that she was growing away from her family and their way of looking at things, that they were no longer much comfort. But this feeling was temporary and vanished when she left Nebraska and settled in Pittsburgh.

During her decade in Pittsburgh she managed to get home nearly every summer. When she returned for the summer of 1899, she wrote an old friend and college classmate that she expected to have to spend all her time with her mother, who was sick, and probably would not get to see her Lincoln friends. She was obviously worrying about her mother and feeling her filial duty strongly. But when she made her first trip to Europe in 1902, she skipped her annual trip to Red Cloud, although this was an exception. During the summer of 1905 she spent a month helping her father get ready to move the family into a new house he had bought.

Then after 1906, when she left Pittsburgh for New York to become an editor of *McClure's Magazine*, she continued to return home nearly every year. She wrote her father sadly in December 1906 that she was bitterly disappointed that she would not be able to return home for Christmas because her boss, S. S. McClure, had given her an important assignment to work on—the life of Mary Baker Eddy that he was serializing. McClure apparently had convinced her that the magazine faced a crisis unless she gave up her Christmas trip. Also, during the years that Cather was working in Pittsburgh and New York, she was sending money home. How often or how much, I don't know, but her letters contain a number of references to these remittances. She accepted willingly her family obligations.

Her returns to Nebraska and home continued during the teens and twenties. When Cather began going to the Southwest in 1912, she combined trips to Arizona and New Mexico with visits to Red Cloud, either going or coming, sometimes both. Family ties were strong, and Red Cloud drew her like a magnet. In 1916 she spent several months there and conceived the idea for *My Ántonia.* On that occasion her mother was sick and Cather took over the duties of housekeeper. The next summer she received her first honorary degree from the University of Nebraska and continued on to Red Cloud. Again in 1918 her mother was ill and Cather took over the task of running the household. From 1918 until 1921, however, she missed going home for three years, but after that she returned nearly every summer. In 1922 she went home for Christmas to help her parents celebrate their fiftieth wedding anniversary, which was a joyous occasion. All the children were there. Then after Christmas she and her parents joined the Episcopal church together.

Both parents were still in good health. Charles Cather was then seventy-five and drove her about the country in his car to visit the immigrant families that she loved. She was terrified of his driving, however, and would much have preferred the old days of the horse and buggy. Her parents were more robust than she, it seems. They could drive a hundred miles a day (no mean feat over the dirt roads of 1922) and be ready to go again the next day. Willa usually retired to her room for a nap after lunch, but her parents never did.

This happy relationship of parents and dutiful daughter who returned to the old homestead regularly ended in March 1928. The previous Christmas she had been home for what was a truly happy time and was surrounded by parents, brothers, sisters, nephews, and nieces. Before leaving in February to return to New York, she took charge of having repairs made on her parents' house. Then on 3 March, one week after she had left Red Cloud, her father had a fatal heart attack.

Cather took the first train west and arrived back in Red Cloud at three in the morning the day after her father died. Friends met her at the station and took her home. Recalling this incident thirteen years later, she told a friend that she had gone to her father's room without waking anyone in the house. He was lying on a couch in the bay window. She spent several unforgettable hours with him before anyone else got up. When the red dawn broke it flushed his face with the rosy color he always had and he looked entirely himself and happy. Later as the body was lying in Grace Church before the funeral, her calm apparently vanished, and friends remembered her pacing frantically back and forth between the house and the church, wringing her hands, overcome with grief.

This was the end of an era for Cather. Her brother took their mother back to California, where he lived, and Cather stayed on in Red Cloud for a month, not wanting to tear herself away from the place her father had lived for so many years. She wrote later that the silence in the old house and in her father's room had done a great deal for her. She felt rested and strong, as if her father himself had restored her soul; yet his death was a heavy blow, for Charles and Willa always had been very close. Before returning to New York, she worked at getting the house ready for her mother's expected return from California. In a letter written at this time she described what she had been having done. There was papering and painting going on; she had put up new curtains and planted some new shrubbery.

After leaving Red Cloud, she stopped off in Lincoln to discuss with her younger sister Elsie her mother's future. They agreed that whenever their mother wanted to come home, one of them would be there with her and they would do everything they could to make her happy. We will put our whole heart into it, Willa wrote. Elsie would request a leave of absence from her high school teaching job, but if she couldn't get it Willa promised to be there.

Jennie Cather, however, never returned to Nebraska. In December 1928 she suffered a stroke that left her paralyzed on one side and almost unable to speak, though her mind was unimpaired. This distressing event blighted the Christmas season, and Cather made plans to go to California in early spring. During the next three years she went to California annually to visit her mother. It was the most difficult time of Cather's life. She wrote a friend during her first visit that she had no time for anything but the grave material difficulties of helping care for a helpless and very sick person stricken away from home. She grieved that the stroke had not occurred in Red Cloud, where her mother would have been surrounded by relatives and friends.

Jennie Cather died in the summer of 1931 while Willa was at her summer cottage on Grand Manan Island in the Bay of Fundy. Willa did not have the strength or energy to attend the funeral in California or return to Nebraska when the body was brought there for burial. She stayed on at her cottage, taking her daily walks along the lonely cliffs of the island and adjusting to her new condition of life. She wrote Blanche Knopf, the wife of her publisher, that she was trying to get used to the strange feeling of having nobody to report to. Helpless as her mother was, she had expected accounts of her children's activities, and Cather was glad that her mother's mind had not dimmed, as it surely would have in time. That Christmas Cather arranged a family reunion in Red Cloud, to which all her brothers and sisters came, and that was the last time she ever visited Nebraska.

o   o   o   o   o

Now let me turn to a discussion of the impact of Cather's parents on her fiction. Cather more than most writers turned the stuff of her life into fiction, and her family played a significant role in her literary creations. It had less impact on her apprentice work, however, for when she was learning her trade, she was trying out various themes and motifs, imitating writers she admired, especially Henry James, and placing her fiction in a wide variety of settings, only some of which were Nebraska. It was only after she "hit the home pasture," as she put it, with *O Pioneers!* that she found her real subject, her memories of Nebraska in the 1880s. With these memories came the memory of family, particularly her parents, and they found their way into her fiction.

When one surveys the entire corpus of Cather's novels and stories, a pattern emerges that might be called the uxorious syndrome. In five of her novels and two of her most important stories there is a male–female relationship that parallels in some measure the Cather parental relationship; that is to say, there is a strong, dominant woman linked to a gentle, good-natured, patient man. Beginning with *O Pioneers!*, there are Alexandra and Carl, whose marriage is projected as the novel ends. In *The Song of the Lark*, Mr. and Mrs. Kronborg repeat the pattern. In *My Mortal Enemy*, Myra and Oswald stand in a similar relationship, and in the Templetons in "Old Mrs. Harris," we have the most explicit fictional re-creation of Cather's parents, replicated to a lesser degree in the Ferguessons in Cather's last story, "The Best Years." In *Lucy Gayheart*, the dominant woman is Jacob Gayheart's older daughter Pauline, who manages the household, and in Cather's last novel, *Sapphira and the Slave Girl*, Sapphira dominates both the action and her more passive husband, the miller.

The most important use of Cather's family in her fiction occurs in *Obscure Destinies*, the story collection she published in 1932. After her father's death and during her mother's long paralysis, Cather's mind turned to home and her youth in and about Red Cloud, and she wrote "Neighbour Rosicky," "Two Friends," and "Old Mrs. Harris." The first to be published, "Neighbour Rosicky," is a sort of sequel to *My Ántonia*, in which the characters are Ántonia and her husband some ten years after we encounter them in the novel. The central incident, created with the utmost poignancy, is the death from a heart attack of the title character. The emotional impact derives from Cather's feelings about her father. Anton Rosicky, who has lived a good life, been a loving father, husband, and a useful citizen of his community, is, I think, Charles Cather transformed. Particularly moving is the relationship between Rosicky and his daughter-in-law Polly, who reflects late in the tale: "It was as if Rosicky had a special gift for loving people" (66). It would be safe to say that all the loving fathers in her fiction owe something to the fondness Cather felt for her father.

"Old Mrs. Harris," my choice for Cather's best story, re-creates the entire Cather family, not only father and mother, at the time Willa was getting ready to go to college. This is a very autobiographical story, though, of course, it is fiction and not strictly autobiography. But in many respects Charles and Jennie Cather play themselves in the tale. Young Mr. Templeton is an easygoing businessman from the South who hates to press his debtors: "His boyish, eager-to-please manner, his fair complexion and blue eyes and young face, made him seem very soft to some of the hard old money-grubbers on Main Street, and the fact that he always said 'Yes, sir' and 'No, sir' to men older than himself furnished a good deal of amusement to by-standers" (112–13). But the main characters in the story are the three women of the family: Victoria, the mother; her daughter Vickie, and the title character, who is drawn from Grandmother Boak. Charles Cather as Mr. Templeton, though he is sympathetically portrayed, plays only a walk-on part.

Much of the tale is seen through the eyes of Mrs. Rosen, a neighbor who observes these Southerners from the perspective of her Jewish, European background. We first see Victoria as "a tall, handsome woman" emerging from her house "dressed in white broadcloth and a hat with white lilacs"; she carries a sunshade and walks "with a free, energetic step, as if she were going out on a pleasant errand" (76). This is Jennie Cather accurately described. She always dressed up to go out and never forgot she was a Virginia lady. Mrs. Rosen does not entirely approve of the Southern manners of the Templetons, as Cather herself didn't approve of some aspects of her own Southernness. (Cather once told an old friend that Southerners, herself included, scorn accurate knowledge and always think they can get by with "pretty near.") But Mrs. Rosen likes to visit the Templetons: "One felt a pleasantness in the human relationships. These people didn't seem to know there were such things as struggle or exactness or competition in the world. They were always genuinely glad to see you, . . . and were usually gay in mood" (111). And she goes on to reflect that "the Templetons were not selfish or scheming. Anyone could take advantage of them, and many people did. Victoria might eat all the cookies her neighbour sent in, but she would give away anything she had. She was always ready to lend her dresses and hats and bits of jewellery for the school theatricals" (112). This again is a good description of Jennie Cather.

Later Mrs. Rosen remembers that when the Templetons arrived in Skyline (Red Cloud once more), they strewed their backyard with packing cases and did not pick them up. But when she first met Mrs. Templeton, she had to admit that "her new neighbour was an attractive woman, and that there was something warm and genuine about her. She wasn't in the least willowy or languishing, as Mrs. Rosen had usually found Southern ladies to be. She was high-spirited and direct; a trifle imperious, but with a shade of diffidence, too, as if she were trying to adjust herself to a new group of people and to do the right thing" (113–14). In a particularly good scene, the ice cream social, Victoria's humanity and concern for others, which are like Jennie Cather's, are demonstrated when she gives the poor Maude children money to buy ice cream and instructs Vickie to be sure they get plenty of it.

We also find that Mrs. Templeton is a good mother. Returning from an afternoon card party, she takes off her dress and corsets, puts on a negligee and begins to nurse the baby, all the while talking about the card party to Mrs. Rosen, whom she had invited in, and laughing about their walk home through the snow. Mrs. Rosen is charmed at this scene of domestic intimacy, at the beautiful baby and Mrs. Templeton's comfortable relationship with it and her other offspring. This too is apparently an accurate evocation of Jennie Cather as mother, and one would also suspect at the end of the story when Mrs. Templeton finds herself pregnant again and takes to her bed (she already has five children and can't bear the thought of another) that this scene has a basis in Cather history. Jennie Cather's seven children were born over a period of nineteen years, the last when she was forty-two. Willa was in college when her youngest brother Jack was born.

Jennie Cather's strict discipline and prickly nature come in for some criticism in the story. The third-person narrator says of Victoria and her children that "when she whipped them, she did it thoroughly" (146), and Mrs. Rosen observes that when she gives a present to old Mrs. Harris, the grandmother must conceal it from her daughter because "Victoria couldn't bear to have anything come into the house that was not for her to dispose of" (95). And Mrs. Harris herself notes at another point, "Victoria had a good heart, but she was terribly proud and could not bear the least criticism" (97–98). This characteristic is consistent with a comment made by Jennie's mother-in-law early in Jennie's pregnancy with Willa. Caroline Cather wrote to her daughter Jennie Ayre in 1873 that she had been to visit Jennie, who thought she was sick and had called the doctor twice: "I went up to see her with your Aunt Sidney, and I think we understand her case as well as the doctor and think he was not needed as much now as he may be after a while, but I did not tell her so, for she is so easily insulted. I knew she would fly right up, for she thinks she is awfully sick. Her mother and Charley have a happy time waiting on her." Cather valued her mother but understood her, and the realistic portrait of her in this story provides tension and dramatic conflict. Cather herself was more like her mother than her father, and the friction in real life resulted from occasional clashes in temperament. Her father, by contrast, complemented rather than clashed with his daughter's personality.

After writing *Obscure Destinies* (1932), Cather did not give major treatment to the family in her fiction until "The Best Years," written in 1945, two years before she died. It was planned as a gift for her brother Roscoe as a reminder of their life together as children. It is an excellent tale, vintage Cather, and evokes the image of Jennie Cather in the character of Mrs. Ferguesson, mother of the story's protagonist. The third-person narrator describes her as a person who could not be overlooked: "All the merchants in MacAlpin [Red Cloud again] admitted that she was a fine figure of a woman. As she came down the little yard and out of the gate, the evening breeze ruffled her wavy auburn hair. Her quick step and alert, upright carriage gave one the impression that she got things done" (93). She is in fact the driving force behind the family, and when the younger children want to bother their sister, who has just returned for the weekend from her rural school, the narrator comments: "Mrs. Ferguesson merely shook her head. She had control in that household, sure enough!" (97). Mr. Ferguesson in this story, however, is not really a portrait of Charles Cather. He is an idealist, something of a dreamer, defers to his wife, has the gentleness and good manners of Cather's father, and a warm relationship with his daughter; but he is also a rather ridiculous figure, laughed at by the townsfolk, and a Populist, which Charles Cather never was.

When Cather discovered her flood subject, to use Emily Dickinson's term, and began to write about the Nebraska of her youth, she produced *O Pioneers!* (1913). This novel begins in the town of Hanover (Red Cloud again), but it immediately moves to the country and deals with Swedes and Bohemians. Cather did not begin putting her family into her fiction until she wrote *The Song of the Lark* (1915). There Moonstone, Colorado, is Red Cloud all over again, and the first two hundred pages are the most sustained piece of autobiographical fiction Cather ever wrote. Jennie and Charles Cather sat for the portraits of Mrs. and Mrs. Kronborg, the parents of the protagonist, Thea Kronborg. The third-person narrator writes that the children "were wholesomely afraid of Mrs. Kronborg's rawhide whip. She did not chastise her children often, but she did it thoroughly. Only a somewhat stern system of discipline could have kept any degree of order and quiet in that over-crowded house" (18). This is, of course, the house at Third and Cedar, which had to shelter father, mother, five children (in the 1880s), grandmother, cousin, and servant girl. We learn from the narrator that "Mrs. Kronborg let her children's minds alone. She did not pry into their thoughts or nag them. She respected them as individuals, and outside of the house they had a great deal of liberty. But their communal life was definitely ordered" (19). So far we have real autobiography. However, the character of Peter Kronborg, Thea's father, is undeveloped and plays a very minor role in the story. He is like Charles Cather only in his mild manner and willingness to leave the domestic decisions to his wife. The demands of the novel required Cather to make Mr. Kronborg a minister because Thea is going to grow up to be a Wagnerian soprano like her prototype Olive Fremstad, whose father was a clergyman. At the end of Book One, Thea leaves for Chicago to study music and is seen off at the station by her parents, much as Cather must have been when she went off to Lincoln following her graduation from high school.

After *The Song of the Lark*, Cather did not create other characters resembling her parents during their lifetimes. In *My Ántonia* (1918) she was preoccupied with Annie Pavelka, her Bohemian friend, and in *One of Ours* (1922) with her cousin, G. P. Cather, who was killed in World War I. *A Lost Lady* (1923) evokes Mrs. Silas Garber, the prototype of Marian Forrester, a woman Cather had admired when she was growing up in Red Cloud. When she came to write *The Professor's House* (1925), she created in the professor a father whose problem was her own mid-life crisis, although I think that there is something of Charles Cather in the warm relationship between Godfrey St. Peter and his daughter Kathleen and in his fond memories of his children when they were little. One can't push this relationship very far, and we have no way to get inside the mind of Charles Cather, but one can imagine that he had thoughts (or so his daughter might have surmised) similar to the professor's thoughts after his children had grown up and married. The professor sits alone in his study at one point and reflects: "Oh, there had been fine times in this old house then [when his girls were little]: family festivals and hospitalities, little girls dancing in and out, Augusta [the sewing woman] coming and going, gay dresses hanging in his study at night. Christmas shopping and secrets and smothered laughter on the stairs. When a man had lovely children in his house, fragrant and happy, full of pretty fancies and generous impulses, why couldn't he keep them?" (125–26).

Cather's next novels, *My Mortal Enemy* (1926) and *Death Comes for the Archbishop* (1927), have little to do with the Cather family, but her Quebec novel, *Shadows on the Rock* (1931), owes a good deal to Cather's memories of her father. After she returned to New York in April 1928 feeling absolutely drained from her father's death, she went up to her summer cottage on Grand Manan Island via train through Montreal and Quebec, a city she never had seen. She remained in Quebec while her traveling companion and friend Edith Lewis recovered from the flu and during this interval discovered French Canada as a prime source of fiction. In constructing her historical novel of seventeenth-century Quebec, she created a widower and his young daughter, Euclide Auclair and Cécile. The relationship between father and daughter suggests strongly the relationship between Willa and Charles Cather. He was much on her mind during the writing of the novel, and she said at the time that it was her refuge and salvation during her mother's long paralysis.

Shadows on the Rock is not one of Cather's best novels, and the character of Auclair tends to be flat and two-dimensional. It reminds me of a Theophrastean character exemplifying perhaps the loyal friend and loving father. Yet, except for the beard, the opening description of Auclair seems to me a pretty good portrait of Charles Cather: "a slender, rather frail man of about fifty, a little stooped, a little grey, with a short beard cut in a point, and a fair complexion delicately flushed with pink about his cheeks and ears.

His blue eyes were warm and interested, even in reflection,—they often had a kindling gleam as if his thoughts were pictures. Except for this lively and inquiring spirit in his glance, everything about him was modest and retiring" (7). But as a fictional character evoking the author's father, Anton Rosicky is a much more successful portrait.

After publishing *Shadows on the Rock*, Cather brought out the three stories (already discussed) in *Obscure Destinies* and then combined her memories of Red Cloud and her interest in music in *Lucy Gayheart* (1935), a novel dealing with a young woman from the provinces who goes off to study music in Chicago. In it we have another father–daughter relationship, that between Jacob Gayheart and Lucy. Gayheart is a widower, like Auclair in *Shadows on the Rock*, and also a loving father who is easygoing, soft-spoken, and dominated by a woman, his older daughter Pauline. There is a poignant paternal scene after Lucy returns from Chicago to recover from the death of the man she loved, when Pauline wants to cut down the orchard and plant it in potatoes and Jacob comforts Lucy.

There are two father–daughter relationships in Cather's last novel, *Sapphira and the Slave Girl* (1940), based on family history from a period before Willa was born. The major loving father–daughter relationship is between Rachel Blake and Henry Colbert, the miller, whose real-life prototypes were Grandmother Boak and her father, Cather's Great-grandfather Siebert. Although Henry is drawn from the maternal side of the family, which was originally German, he does have Charles Cather's dreamy eyes and upright, god-fearing character, and he is the direct opposite of his strong-willed wife. The second father–daughter relationship is between Old Mr. Cartmell and his postmistress daughter, Mrs. Bywaters. What unites them in a strong bond is their mutual hatred of slavery. These are very minor characters, but they were drawn from Cather's paternal great-grandfather, James Cather, and her Great-aunt Sidney Gore. Finally, it ought to be mentioned that Jennie Cather appears in this novel as Rachel Blake's daughter who survives the diphtheria epidemic.

Unfortunately, Cather's relationship with her parents cannot be documented from much correspondence. So far as I know, only three letters from Willa to her mother and two to her father have survived. All the letters that passed between them on both sides presumably were destroyed by Cather herself, whose practice it was to retrieve and burn letters to correspondents who predeceased her and not to save letters she received. But the relationship can be constructed pretty well from her actions, from comments in letters that have survived, and from her fiction. We can conclude that from childhood she adored her father, and though she and her mother often clashed in her youth, she came to value her mother more and more as time went on. She wrote in her old age to a close friend that she had been thoughtless and self-centered when she was young and that she had taken her parents for granted. But haven't we all? What is important about the Cather parental relationship is the use it was put to in fiction. As I have said before, all the loving fathers

in Cather's fiction have something of Charles Cather in them, and I think
it no accident that five of his daughter's novels and two of her most important
stories have male–female relationships that parallel in some measure the family
parental relationship. Henry James wrote in "The Art of Fiction": "A novel
is in its broadest definition a personal, a direct impression of life"; and "As
people feel life, so they will feel the art that is most closely related to it."[3]
Cather's fiction is no exception, as her readers will recognize.

—University of California, Davis

NOTES

1. For biographical details not footnoted, see my *Willa Cather: A Literary Life*
(Lincoln: U of Nebraska P, 1987).
2. See Patricia Lee Yongue's two-part article, "Willa Cather's Aristocrats," in
Southern Humanities Review 14 (Winter and Spring 1980): 43–56, 111–25.
3. "The Art of Fiction" was originally published in *Longman's Magazine* (Sept. 1884)
and first reprinted in *Partial Portraits* (1888), but it appears in nearly every anthology
of American literature.

BIBLIOGRAPHY

Cather, Caroline. Letter to Jennie Ayre, 17 April 1873. Nebraska State Historical
　　Society, Lincoln.
Cather, Willa. "The Best Years." *The Old Beauty and Others*. New York: Knopf,
　　1948. 75–138.
_____. "Neighbour Rosicky." *Obscure Destinies*. New York: Knopf, 1932. 3–71.
_____. "Old Mrs. Harris." *Obscure Destinies*. 75–190.
_____. *The Professor's House*. New York: Knopf, 1925.
_____. *Shadows on the Rock*. New York: Knopf, 1931.
_____. *The Song of the Lark*. Lincoln: U of Nebraska P, Bison, 1978.

"Old Mrs. Harris"
and the Intergenerational Family

BRUCE P. BAKER

Visitors to the restored Cather childhood home in Red Cloud, Nebraska, are often surprised at how accurately the details of that particular physical setting are described in Willa Cather's works. In the opening pages of *The Song of the Lark*, for example, young Thea Kronborg, confined by illness, looks about the parlor in the "red light from the isinglass sides of the hard-coal burner [observing] the nickel trimmings on the stove itself, the pictures on the wall, which she thought very beautiful, the flowers on the Brussels carpet" (10). And later the narrator describes Thea's little bedroom

> upstairs in the half-storey. It was the end room of the wing, and was not plastered, but was snugly lined with soft pine. The ceiling was so low that a grown person could reach it with the palm of the hand, and it sloped on either side. There was only one window, but it was a double one and went to the floor. In October, while the days were still warm, Thea and Tillie papered the room, walls and ceiling in the same paper, small red and brown roses on a yellowish ground. (71)

In "The Best Years," the last story Cather completed, her memory of the physical details and excitement of the children's large attic room is vivid and evocative:

> "Upstairs" was a story in itself, a secret romance. No caller or neighbour had ever been allowed to go up there. All the children loved it—it was their very own world where there were no older people poking about to spoil things. . . . Their upstairs was a long attic which ran the whole length of the house, from the front door downstairs to the kitchen at the back. Its great charm was that it was unlined. . . . The roof shingles were old and had curled under hot summer suns. In a driving snowstorm the frozen flakes sifted in through all those little cracks, sprinkled the beds and the children, melted on their faces, in their hair! That was delightful. The rest of you was snug and warm under blankets and comforters, with a hot brick at one's feet. (130–31)

Such a place is, in short, Cather's symbolic re-creation of the warm sanctuary of childhood, a place apart where one could return through memory to the security and comfort of the child's world.

Then, too, there is the description of her own Grandmother Boak's tiny room in another late story, "Old Mrs. Harris," my concern here:

> It was a queer place to be having coffee, when Mrs. Rosen [the next-door neighbor] liked order and comeliness so much: a hideous, cluttered room, furnished with a rocking-horse, a sewing machine, an empty baby-buggy. . . . There was a wash-stand (two wash-stands, if you counted the oilcloth-covered box as one). A corner of the room was curtained off with some black-and-red striped cotton goods, for a clothes closet. In another corner was the wooden lounge with a thin mattress and a red calico spread which was Grandmother's bed. Beside it was her wooden rocking-chair, and the little splint-bottom chair with the legs sawed short on which her darning-basket usually stood, but which Mrs. Rosen was now using for a tea-table. (80–81)

In my many trips to Red Cloud over the years, I always make it a practice to revisit the Cather house and listen to Cather's words as they are transcribed on a splendid tape played for visitors. As many times as I have gone, I always find myself emotionally affected by the experience. During one of my last visits there, I suddenly became acutely aware of a dimension of that physical setting I had not really considered before: the fact that this small house with its tiny rooms (except for the open attic) was the home of twelve people: Charles and Virginia Cather, their seven children, Grandma Boak (Willa's maternal grandmother), Bess Seymour (Mrs. Cather's cousin), and Margie Anderson (the hired woman the Cathers had brought with them from Virginia to Nebraska). Twelve people and three generations, a crowded space in which moments of privacy must have been few but precious. It is, I believe, a positive commentary on Virginia Cather's awareness and concern for her eldest daughter that she insisted that the little dormer room off the upstairs attic be given to Willa. Virginia seems to have appreciated that Willa's remarkable intelligence and independent nature needed a sanctuary, as much a place apart as the crowded Cather home could provide. It was in this room, papered with the yellow paper she had purchased from her wages earned at Dr. Cook's drugstore, that Willa dreamed many of her dreams, thought her thoughts, and prepared for the career that was to result in international fame and success.

But young Willa was also a part of the world downstairs, a world containing the entry hall with its clothing hooks and piles of boots and papers, the parlor with its impressive stove, her parents' small bedroom just off the parlor, the kitchen to the back of the house, and Grandmother Boak's narrow sleeping space, which also served as the passageway to the kitchen. The location of Grandma Boak's bedroom, Mrs. Harris's as well, made it a place shared by the entire family, all three generations, as they went about their daily business. It was almost literally at the center, a position, symbolic, I would suggest, of the heart of the house—just as old Mrs. Harris often finds herself at the center of the Templetons' family life: cooking meals, caring for the children, protecting Victoria from the criticism that hurt her so deeply; in short, working hard—neighbor Mrs. Rosen calls it "drudging"—"to keep [the Templeton household] going" (112).

In the story itself, the reader is actually introduced to Mrs. Harris through the eyes of Mrs. Rosen; in fact, it is that woman's perception of the old woman as drudge that influences our own first perceptions of her lot. After entering the Templeton kitchen with a poppy seed coffee cake she wants to share with Mrs. Harris in Victoria's absence, Mrs. Rosen sees the old woman in her "cluttered, hideous room . . . washing her hot face and neck at a tin basin . . . her feet wide apart, in an attitude of profound weariness" (77). The image is a powerful one, suggesting in this first scene a soul kindred to those of obscure destiny celebrated in Gray's "Elegy in a Country Churchyard." And in many ways that is precisely who and what she is: a self-effacing woman dedicated to serving others (particularly her beautiful daughter Victoria) with resignation and apparently no trace of bitterness. Even the old woman's eyes, as described by Mrs. Rosen, "seemed to ask nothing and hope for nothing" (81). Marilyn Arnold perceptively describes Mrs. Rosen's function as that of a "controlling consciousness" who "observes and interprets what goes on at the Templeton house," the third of Cather's "Three Women," the title of the story when it first appeared in the September–November 1932 *Ladies' Home Journal* (141). Mrs. Rosen is certainly the key to the ongoing unfolding in the reader's mind of new perceptions, perhaps misperceptions, about other central characters and their relationships.

Mrs. Rosen is a reader's guide, a Jamesian central intelligence through which many of the story's scenes and characters are sifted, but from the first scene Cather suggests that Mrs. Rosen's judgments are not necessarily the full story, not perhaps even the real story. It becomes clear that good friends as they are, Mrs. Harris is not particularly pleased with her neighbor's conscious attempt to avoid Victoria and share the prize coffee cake with the old lady alone: "Grandma looked troubled—at a loss. . . . It was clear that she felt embarrassment" (77–78). There is, in short, a dramatic and revealing contrast between Mrs. Rosen's assumptions and Mrs. Harris's real feelings. When Grandma Harris lets her coffee cool down because she "generally drink[s] it that way," Mrs. Rosen immediately thinks: "Of course she does . . . since she never has her coffee until all the family are done breakfast!" (79). And when this neighbor suggests that the old woman give "those naughty children a cold lunch occasionally," Mrs. Harris replies simply, "I don't mind the heat. . . . I don't feel the stove, I'm accustomed to it" (82). Cather's juxtaposition of such mixed perceptions creates a fascinating ambivalence in the reader's response to the characters and situations, a compelling desire—and need—to read on in order to sort out and judge the actual state of affairs in this intergenerational household. It is on the one hand difficult to accept Mrs. Rosen's characterization of the grand-children as "naughty" when we have learned in the paragraph immediately preceding this dialogue that "whenever Mrs. Harris's grandchildren were about, tumbling all over her, asking for cookies, teasing her to read to them, the old lady looked happy" (82). On the other hand, it may be possible, as Mrs. Rosen insists, that "the real grandmother was on her guard, as always" (83). Much of the story's power and poignance derives, I would suggest, from ambivalent perceptions often instigated by Mrs. Rosen. In actuality, a number of tensions and unresolved conflicts lie within both the Templeton and the Rosen households, and it is the reader's expanding awareness of and often shifting responses to these that make "Old Mrs. Harris" so emotionally and intellectually appealing and complex.

Indeed, Mrs. Rosen herself, while sympathizing with a woman she considers ill-used by her family, is not without personal and household problems. Her jealousy of Victoria Templeton is based partly on the fact that the Rosens have no children, a "bitter sorrow" shared by her husband and a denial of her deepest desire: "There was nothing else in the world she wanted so much" (101). It is little wonder that young Vickie Templeton has become a kind of surrogate daughter whom Mrs. Rosen "mothers" in her own way, encouraging the young woman's intellectual growth and seeing to it that she goes to college. Also, Mrs. Rosen's "tightly corseted figure" and "dark, ruddy, salmon-tinted skin"contrast dramatically with the "tall, handsome" (a word repeated three times in two pages) Victoria, who in spite of her five children maintains her naturally elegant figure and regal bearing. It is apparent that Mr. Rosen admires the lovely Victoria, losing no chance to talk with her and paying her considerable attention at the ice cream social where Mrs. Jackson, another neighbor, expresses her disdain of Victoria by offering her "some of your own cake," which she makes plain has been baked by "somebody" (clearly Mrs. Harris) Victoria ke[eps] . . . in the kitchen to bake [cakes] for [her]" (126). This scene, occurring in part four of the story, associates the querulous and judgmental Mrs. Jackson's opinion with Mrs. Rosen's attitude toward Victoria and serves to create sympathy for Victoria and discredit Mrs. Rosen's judgment of the plight of old Mrs. Harris.

The fact is that Mrs. Harris sees her own life as particularly full and satisfying; she is, quite simply, genuinely happy with herself and her role in the Templeton household. Far from feeling "exploited," as Henry Seidel Canby contends in his early review of *Obscure Destinies* (Murphy 280) and as Mrs. Rosen and her friends believe, Grandma Harris is not only resigned and accepting, she is content and happy. She takes pride in Victoria's good looks, draws great satisfaction from caring for the children and experiencing their love and physical touch: "They had no physical shrinking from her because she was old" (136). In this crowded, intergenerational family she finds her sense of purpose, her work, her integration: "The moment she heard the children running down the uncarpeted back stairs, she forgot to be low. Indeed, she ceased to be an individual, an old woman with aching feet; she became part of a group, became a relationship" (136–37). She becomes, in effect, the embodiment of Jim Burden's definition of the fulfilled life in that famous phrase repeated on Cather's own tombstone: "That is happiness; to be dissolved into something complete and great" (*My Ántonia* 18).

For Mrs. Harris, that something is the family unit, a place where she is both loved and needed, a means by which her own needs are served in serving others. As Mrs. Rosen fails to perceive, there is really nothing to be pitied here; in fact, Mrs. Harris's thought that "to be pitied was the deepest hurt anybody could know" (97) conveys one of Cather's most profound insights into the sensibilities of the aged. Old Mrs. Harris belongs, is busy, needed, touched, loved, which is beautifully evident in the quiet scene where Mandy, the poor servant woman who lives with the Templetons, washes the old woman's feet. David Stouck calls the scene "the most moving image in the story" (Murphy 294), and Susan Rosowski observes that Mandy's action "springs from compassion, from sharing in the suffering of another" (198). The two women are silent, almost asleep as Mandy performs what Cather calls "one of the oldest rites of compassion" (93). Cather's observation, short and simple though it is, is extraordinarily significant because it suggests her central theme, that a life is made meaningful and full, "complete and beautiful" to use Dr. Ed's words at the conclusion of "Neighbour Rosicky," through serving others with love.

Mandy's rite, given so freely from one "who had nothing else to give" (93), is one of a number of religious images and allusions Cather includes to convey more than what is written on the page. Mandy's act of love, reminiscent of Mary's washing of the feet of Christ, who, like Mrs. Harris, will not always be with us, becomes a sacred moment preceding an instinctive awareness of the old woman's illness and impending death. Even the image of the imperial Victoria is softened significantly in a brief but important scene with religious overtones. Upon returning to the Templeton parlor after a party where she first meets Mrs. Rosen, Victoria excuses herself to attend the baby while her new friend looks about the parlor, noting the "warm red glow" of the hard-coal burner and the old paintings of "Hagar and Ishmael in the Wilderness" and "The Light of the World" hanging on the wall. These overt biblical references prepare for Victoria in a white gown nursing her baby, a religious icon of universal significance. Mrs. Rosen thinks of the two as "so comfortable and complete" (the word *complete* is central to the story's major theme of belonging). Her remarks introduce a paean to the child: " 'What a beautiful baby!' she exclaimed from her heart. And he was. A sort of golden baby. His hair was like sunshine, and his long lashes were gold over such gay blue eyes. There seemed to be a gold glow in his soft pink skin, and he had the smile of a cherub" (116). It is another sacred moment in the house of the Templetons, the family confirming its significance as a sanctuary of love and acceptance.

But it is also a place of suffering; this temple reflects the fallen world wherein suffering is present, pettiness sometimes occurs, and death will soon invade. The image of the Madonna and Child is later replaced with the image of Victoria lying "on her bed alone, the room darkened and a handkerchief soaked in camphor tied round her forehead," lamenting (quite understandably but nevertheless with a certain amount of self-pity) that she is to have another baby:

> She wanted to run away, back to Tennessee, and lead a free, gay life, as she had when she was first married. She could do a great deal more with freedom than ever Vickie could. She was still young, and she was still handsome; why must she be for ever shut up in a little cluttered house with children and fresh babies and an old woman and a stupid bound girl and a husband who wasn't very successful? Life hadn't brought her what she expected when she married Hillary Templeton; life hadn't used her right. (178)

Victoria's self-absorption at this particular time has blinded her to what that "stupid bound girl" (Mandy) has quickly perceived: the "old woman" is very ill indeed. This illness provokes from her daughter an "accusing tone": "You ought to be more careful what you eat, Ma. If you're going to have another bilious spell, when everything is so upset anyhow, I don't know what I'll do!" (175). This is Victoria at her worst, but the scene is not altogether condemnatory or judgmental. Rather, Cather views her with understanding and a sensitive ambivalence, aware at once of her strengths and weaknesses in a fallen world wherein pettiness and selfishness frequently surface. Even the likable Hillary Templeton, based partly on Charles Cather, whom daughter Willa so dearly loved, is not without his faults and foibles: immediately after the scene of Victoria's sobbing in her room, section twelve concludes with a brief but significant passage describing his retreats to a German couple's farm out in the country, where he is indulged by Mrs. Heyse's food and attention and can escape the real, everyday world of his uncollected loans and the "awkward" (179) new pregnancy of Victoria. The close juxtaposition of these two scenes conveys vividly the complex ambiguity with which Cather views her characters and situations. "Old Mrs. Harris" is no romanticized return to Eden but rather an attempt to understand—and ultimately to accept— that fallen world in which the Templetons live.

The third generation in that world is represented by the Templeton children, particularly Vickie, the character Mildred Bennett long ago pointed out as based partly on Cather herself (22), Sharon O'Brien recently labeled "a portrait of [Cather's] adolescent self" (27), and David Stouck calls "the 'guilty' perspective" Cather felt "years later" (Murphy 293). However, Vickie embodies admirable, exciting, and positive characteristics: she is intelligent, intent, willing and able to pursue her interests, and wonderfully curious and inquisitive about books, about people and places, about the world in general and her eventual place in it. The scenes in the Rosens' parlor, for example, are revealing in this aspect. When Vickie peruses the illustrated edition of *Faust*, her immediate response is to want to read it in the German, to perceive its splendor for herself—not because Mrs. Rosen calls it "one of the world's masterpieces" but because she feels instinctively that this would be a book that would "t[ake] hold of her" (106). And when Mrs. Rosen asks her how she "g[ot] along with *Wilhelm Meister*," Vickie answers with a simple, "I like it" (105). It is little wonder that Vickie is anxious to tell the Rosens that she has won the scholarship to the state university. But it is unusual that she goes immediately to them rather than to her family, who in the next section she perceives as part of the "enemy" conspiring against the realization of her dreams.

Vickie is, of course, despairing over the fact that in addition to the scholarship she will need some three hundred dollars in order to get her through the first year of college. Nevertheless, it is more than a little disconcerting to hear her speak to the grandmother who has done so much for her "as if she were talking to an enemy" (163). Vickie, like many adolescents, is totally absorbed in self, unaware of her grandmother's illness, her mother's despair, and her father's real though unexpressed anguish at not having the money necessary for college that particular fall. Later, upon learning that Mr. Rosen will lend her the money (Mrs. Harris has secretly asked him to do so), Vickie "brusquely announce[s] her news" to her grandmother and immediately hurries away, worrying about having "no trunk and no clothes" and "only two weeks in which to do everything!" (173). This side of Vickie is hardly flattering—an example of the failure to understand and help those closest to us when we are caught up in our own pursuits and concerns.

Nevertheless, there is within this house of three generations living together enough love and enough bonding to remind a *mature* Willa Cather of what she called in her essay "Katherine Mansfield" "the tragic necessity" of human relationships (109). There are few scenes in Cather's work as genuinely touching as that of little Albert's attempts to minister to his dying grandmother in the same ways she has ministered to her grandchildren. He tidies up the room, brings her a tin of fresh water, and reads to her a favorite book she has often read to him. Juxtaposed with this lovely scene is Vickie's bitter response upon hearing of her grandmother's illness and her mother's pregnancy: "Wasn't it just like them all to go and get sick, when she had now only two weeks to get ready for school, and no trunk and no clothes or anything! Nobody but Mrs. Rosen seemed to take the least interest, 'when my whole life hangs by a thread,' she told herself fiercely. What were families for, anyway?" (185–86).

What are families for? Cather answers her own question in the last paragraph of the story, a kind of coda or epigram which rather than being intrusive seems clearly to have emerged from the characters and the situations of the story that precedes it:

> Thus Mrs. Harris slipped out of the Templetons' story; but Victoria and Vickie had still to go on, to follow the long road that leads through things unguessed at and unforeseeable. When they are old, they will come closer and closer to Grandma Harris. They will think a great deal about her, and

remember things they never noticed; and their lot will be more or less like hers. They will regret that they heeded her so little; but they, too, will look into the eager, unseeing eyes of young people and feel themselves alone. They will say to themselves: "I was heartless, because I was young and strong and wanted things so much. But now I know." (190)

The writing of "Old Mrs. Harris" was, then, for Willa Cather a personal journey of memory, of exploration, of understanding, of reconciliation—a powerful evocation of that intergenerational family that resided on Cedar Street in Red Cloud. For Cather's readers it is more than that, however; it is a reminder of our own journeys and a restatement of the universal need we all have for love, understanding, and acceptance.

—University of Nebraska at Omaha

BIBLIOGRAPHY

Arnold, Marilyn. *Willa Cather's Short Fiction*. Athens: Ohio UP, 1984.
Bennett, Mildred R. *The World of Willa Cather*. Lincoln: U of Nebraska P, 1961.
Canby, Henry Seidel. Rev. of *Obscure Destinites*, by Willa Cather. *Saturday Review of Literature* 6 August 1932: 29. Rpt. in *Critical Essays on Willa Cather*. Ed. John J. Murphy. Boston: Hall, 1984. 280–82.
Cather, Willa. "The Best Years." *Five Stories by Willa Cather*. New York: Vintage, 1956. 112–48.
———. "Katherine Mansfield." *Willa Cather on Writing*. New York: Knopf, 1949. 107–20.
———. *My Ántonia*. Boston: Houghton, 1961.
———. "Old Mrs. Harris." *Obscure Destinies*. New York: Knopf, 1930. 75–190.
———. *The Song of the Lark*. Boston: Houghton, 1983.
O'Brien, Sharon. *Willa Cather: The Emerging Voice*. New York: Oxford UP, 1987.
Rosowski, Susan. *The Voyage Perilous: Willa Cather's Romanticism*. Lincoln: U of Nebraska P, 1986.
Stouck, David. "Willa Cather's Last Four Books." *Novel: A Forum on Fiction* 7 (Fall 1973): 41–53. Rpt. in *Critical Essays on Willa Cather*. 290–303.

Loosing the Tie That Binds: Sisterhood in Cather

MARY R. RYDER

In an 1897 article for the *Home Monthly*, Willa Cather praised George Eliot's *The Mill on the Floss* for its true and beautiful portrayal of family life and cited the relationship between Tom and Maggie Tulliver as "that strongest and most satisfactory relation of human life, the love that sometimes exists between a brother and sister" (*The World and the Parish* 1: 363). Cather admitted that such "perfect love" was rare and, when it did exist, much more than a tie of blood. In her fiction, however, she seldom developed this bond, which she enjoyed most of her life with her brothers Roscoe and Douglass. Instead she preferred a sibling relationship of perhaps more significance in her exploration of family, the sister–sister bond. This bond remains virtually unexamined in Cather criticism, yet sister relationships in Cather's fiction indicate a polarization that, however dividing, defines a deep-seated commitment to family unity.

To acknowledge rivalries with one's sisters is, as Helen Longino and Valerie Miner have noted, a painful experience (1). Writing about the failed sister bond was undoubtedly difficult for Cather because she had experienced its tension firsthand. Jessica Cather, eight years Cather's junior, was, in James Woodress's words, "very different from Willa in temperament, and the two sisters had little to say to each other" (25). Cather knew that Jessica, "who dressed and acted like a lady, was more her mother's idea of a proper daughter than she was" (Woodress 122). In spite of such feelings, Cather was genuinely happy for Jessica, who by 1905 had married a local banker, established her own home, and become pregnant. Thus, to examine sister–sister combinations in Cather's fiction as reflections of her relationship with Jessica would be to misrepresent the thematic importance of this sibling bond. Indeed, considerable objectivity is evident in the early story "The Marriage of Phaedra" (1905), in which Lady Mary's comments about her sister Lady Ellen are not always complimentary but are never delivered spitefully. Ellen does not have a generous nature, but Mary finds this flaw no reason to undermine her sister's plans. Cather reaches beyond personal statement and becomes part of a tradition of women novelists who use sisters "to weave the fabric of family life and to probe the polarities between sisters as a kind of dialectic of women's choices, women's roles and destinies" (Fishel 183).

Not until *The Song of the Lark* (1915) did Cather deal openly with sisters as opposites. Anna and Thea Kronborg are distanced from each other not only in their parental preferences but also in their professed values. Anna, the elder daughter, serves as "her mother's lieutenant," caring for the younger children with a military authoritativeness. Mrs. Kronborg, though, finds Anna's demands sometimes unreasonable and realizes that this daughter is not always fair-minded. Anna's true allegiance is to her father, whose "secret convictions were very much like Anna's" (133). As Cather describes her, Anna "was a harmless girl, mild except where her prejudices were concerned, neat and industrious, with no graver fault than priggishness" (132). As a minister's daughter, she undergoes the expected conversion experience and assumes a sanctimoniousness that Thea admits is "perhaps a good thing for their father" (131). But the distance between the sisters is only heightened by this religious commitment, and when Anna criticizes Thea's playing secular music on Sunday, Mrs. Kronborg sides with Thea, defending her younger daughter's right to follow a different course of life. Indeed, Thea is a spiritual ally of her mother, who recognizes the intelligence and energy that set Thea apart from the rest of the Kronborg children. Peter Kronborg refers to Thea as "your girl" to his wife and, like her, acknowledges the distinctions between his girls. Thea is clearly "not the marrying kind," he remarks, while "Anna will marry before long and make a good wife" (102). Thea readily accedes to this distinction, for in Anna's acquiescence to conventional roles as dutiful daughter and potentially dutiful wife, Thea feels liberated "to make herself independent," a goal Mrs. Kronborg applauds (102). Thea eagerly accepts the position allotted to her by default, making no effort to challenge Anna's position as the one who sits at her father's right at the dinner table (236).

Toni McNaron in her study of competitiveness among sisters argues that "one sister often allows the other to carry certain qualities or behaviors, thereby freeing her to cultivate more fully other qualities or behaviors" (124). Without resentment or anger, Thea allows Anna the role of "good" daughter. What Cather indicates, though, is that this understanding is not always a reciprocal agreement. Whereas Thea pities "Poor Anna" for her prejudices against everyone from Dr. Archie to the Mexicans (133), Anna spites her younger sister for cultivating qualities opposed to her own. When Thea returns from Chicago and flatly refuses to sing at Maggie Evans's funeral, Anna glances at Mrs. Kronborg with vindictiveness as if to say, "This serves you right for treating Thea differently from me." Anna clearly sees Thea's behavior as rejection of an implicit similarity of person, a similarity that carries commitment to a sister's ideals simply because of blood ties. And, in Anna's reaction, Thea, for the first time, "realize[s] that Anna had always disliked her" (222).

This rift between sisters does not occur without pain and sadness. Anna's sense of desertion surfaces later when she criticizes Thea for hobnobbing with the Mexicans and not considering their father's position. After an explosive scene in which Thea provokes Anna into revealing her jealousy, Thea retreats to her room but is no longer able to shut out the hostility (238). Now Thea, too, feels betrayed; in the sudden realization of her sister's animosity, she sees the disintegration of what she calls "a cub loyalty to the other cubs" (239). She must now count Anna as well as her brothers among "her natural enemies" (240). The tears that run down her hot cheeks are more than tears for loss of sibling support. Frowning into her looking glass, she sees the only friend she can now count on—herself. Yet, in that mirror reflection is also a haunting specter of another self, one's sister. As Toni McNaron argues:

> When a girl or young woman looks at her blood sister, she comes very close to seeing herself. Yet her sister is also inescapably other. . . . This paradox lies at the heart of the intensity that usually accompanies relations between sisters. The bond carries the illusion of total connection at the same time that it painfully reinforces the truth that each of us is finally separate from everyone else. If we cannot achieve union with a sister, with whom, then? (129)

Thea, who had "never made fun of Anna's crimpings and curlings and beauty-rites" (239), still cannot totally disregard a desire for union with her and dismisses Tillie's criticism with an apparently magnanimous comment, "Oh, I don't mind her" (241). Even in pursuit of her own separateness, Thea cannot deny essential family unity: "The family was the family, an integral thing" (241). In her final departure from Moonstone, the "something" that breaks inside Thea and the pain she feels stem directly from her awakening to the complexities of a deep and exclusively female connection to family— sisterhood. Thea struggles to find union outside family, merging with her art and finally admitting to having no personal life outside her work (455).

Within a year of the publication of *The Song of the Lark*, Cather released a short story that again showed a successful artist at odds with her family, and particularly with her two sisters. In "The Diamond Mine," Cressida Garnet finds herself exploited by a family that believes it should share her wealth simply because of kinship. Miss Julia and Miss Georgie are unmistakably bound to their sister by "the Garnet look" (68), although they do not possess Cressida's drive. Recognizing themselves as lesser lights, both sisters prey upon Cressida's sense of obligation to family: "They reminded one of two sombre, bumping electrics, rolling about with no visible means of locomotion, always running out of power and lying beached in some inconvenient spot until they received a check or a suggestion from Cressy" (76). Even their use of the diminutive "Cressy" reduces the mature Cressida to a childhood role within the family circle. Though Julia depresses her, Cressida feels obliged to accept her as a traveling companion who has not "much else to expect" from life (73). However, the generosity and pity that Cressida extends to Julia is repaid with jealousy and resentment: "The truth was that all the Garnets, and particularly her two sisters, were consumed by an habitual, bilious, unenterprising envy of Cressy" (77).

Yet, as Cather writes, each sister is bonded to each (75). In spite of grievances that divide them, each is affected by what Elizabeth Fishel calls "the realization of similarity" (154). Miss Georgie "was out to prove to the world . . . that all the Garnets were as like Cressida as two peas," and "what [both sisters] wanted, in the last analysis, was to *be* Cressida" (76–77). Never satisfactorily dealing with her closest female relationships, Cressida has an equally difficult time developing lasting bonds outside her family. David Stouck suggests that the "tragedy of Cressida Garnet's life is her failure to maintain any genuine human relationships" (200). Her unsuccessful marriages and long history of self-sacrifice lead her to conclude, as did Thea Kronborg, that "I've not very much that's personal to give people" (79–80).

Cather's exploration of the ambivalent relationship between sisters surfaces again in *The Professor's House* (1925), a novel of family ties under close scrutiny. Cather had established the pattern for Professor St. Peter's daughters, Rosamond and Kitty, in an earlier story, "Her Boss" (1919), in which sisters are pointedly opposite in both appearance and temperament (even their names—Roma and Florence—echo historical rivalry and antipathy). Studies of *The Professor's House* are unusually silent on the issue of the sister bond, with most critics noting simply that the daughters feel hostility toward one another or have a "poisoned" relationship (Woodress 372). But, in light of Cather's earlier concern with tension between sisters, the novel merits a closer analysis. As in *The Song of the Lark*, the St. Peter sisters identify with opposite parents. Kitty, with her quick wit and artistic skill, is close to her father, sharing "a special kind of affection" (88); even her portrait of him "was the man himself," whereas she "had no luck" in trying to paint her mother's likeness (64). Rosie, on the other hand, is her mother's "second self," as St. Peter declares, and Mrs. St. Peter "always worked things out for Rosamond" (66).

But, in their competitiveness for Tom Outland's affection and in their loyalty to his memory the breach between sisters widens. Cather writes that as little girls "Kathleen adored her older sister" and that "this attachment had lasted even after they were grown" (89). Only after Rosamond becomes engaged to Tom Outland does the idyllic sisterly relationship change. Within a short time, Kathleen announces her engagement to Scott McGregor, and she marries before her older sister. In stepping aside to let Rosamond have Tom, Kathleen acts on contradictory impulses. She preserves the sister bond by reducing competition for Tom's affection and simultaneously exacts vengeance on her sister for being the first to break that bond. When, however, the marriage to Tom does not occur, Kathleen is unprepared for Rosamond's marriage to Louie Marsellus. For her, this act constitutes desertion of Tom and failure to appreciate her own sisterly sacrifice. The rift between sisters manifests itself as Kathleen's apparent envy of the Marselluses' wealth and Rosamond's resentment of her sister's failed affection. Cather aptly nicknames her characters for their confrontation: Kitty has the claws and Rosie the thorns to prick at one another and to do serious emotional injury. Kitty herself admits that her problem with Rosie is much more than simple jealousy for fine furs and jewels: "When we were at home," she says, "Rosamond was a kind of ideal to me. What she thought about anything decided it for me" (86). In Rosamond's alliance with Louie, Kitty finds a betrayal of the values she had shared with her sister, and sister as reflection of self no longer exists.

Cather hints that in failing to maintain connection between themselves, the sisters also fail to establish totally satisfying unions with their husbands. St. Peter early recognizes that Kitty marries Scott McGregor in a willful act of vindictiveness toward her sister and that, in spite of Scott's likeableness, a "more interesting man" with a quicker mind would have made her "happier" (66). That Kitty's relationship with Scott may not be founded on solid ground becomes apparent after the Marselluses announce their plans to visit Europe. In an almost frenzied outcry, Kitty professes her love for Scott, trying to reassure herself that he was "the real one" after all (109–10). Rosamond, too, works to maintain the appearance of a strong commitment to Louie. When Louie mentions the turquoise bracelet from Tom that she used to wear, "a shade of displeasure" occurs in her voice as she turns her back and changes the conversation (107). The bracelet is, of course, a reminder of her commitment to Tom but is also a reminder of the "halcyon days of summer" and childhood in which she and Kitty found delight in and appreciated the same things, like soft blue stones as yet untampered with to make them "look green" (120). Their sisters relationship is now tinged green with envy and corrupted by materialism and a loss of shared values.

The love–hate relationship between sisters remains essentially unchanged in *Lucy Gayheart*, a novel Cather published ten years later. Lucy and Pauline Gayheart, who always dines "opposite her sister" (151) and resents her father's easygoing indulgence of Lucy, are poles apart. Since their mother is deceased, Pauline has no ally in parental affection and thus assumes both a mother and sister role to her younger sibling. In her "clumsy kiss" when Lucy leaves for Chicago (16) and in her "awkward, spasmodic hug" when Lucy cries over the downed apple tree (161), Pauline exhibits a tentative mothering that often characterizes bonding between sisters. But Pauline cannot genuinely serve as surrogate mother for Lucy because she remains the "other," a competitor. When Lucy offers a brief explanation for her aloofness upon returning to Haverford, Pauline means to be kind by reminding Lucy that she "must be plain and outspoken with [her] own folks" (154), yet Pauline cannot bring herself to approach Lucy when she cries in her sleep: "[Pauline] had never gone in to speak to her sister; she was afraid, really" (167). She fears Lucy not as her "child" but as a rival. She resents Lucy's prettiness, which the townspeople constantly contrast with her own levelheadedness. As happens to Kitty McGregor, a greenish tinge of envy colors Pauline's expression when she must acknowledge publicly Lucy's growing beauty (171). Upon learning of Sebastian's death and better comprehending Lucy's emotional trauma, though, Pauline suppresses her anger and reassesses her relationship with Lucy: "She felt sorry for Lucy,—and a little in awe of her, for the first time in her life" (177). Pauline is awed by the mystery of romance, a chapter of her life which she has closed, but she resents that Lucy did not confide in her, either as mother or sister.

Pauline's relationship with her sister is perhaps the most complex of those depicted in Cather's works. Underscoring the love–hate relationship is the devotion to and respect for family that Cather herself experienced. While criticizing Lucy for shielding her innermost feelings from her family, Pauline admires her stubborn sense of privacy and proudly thinks, "Lucy was certainly a Gayheart" (177). Cather's most direct comment on sisters struggling for differentiation appears in Pauline's musings:

> In her own way Pauline loved her sister, though there had been moments when she certainly hated her. Personal hatred and family affection are not incompatible; they often flourish and grow strong together. Everything that was most individual and characteristic in Lucy she resented; but she was loyal to whatever she thought was Gayheart. (168)

Lucy's failure to understand that her older sister could be jealous of her and at the same time care for her (173) makes her unresponsive to Pauline's efforts to reestablish the bond they had shared in earlier years. As Cather points out, Lucy "hadn't the least idea of what Pauline was really like— never considered it" (171–72). The Pauline who had fussed over and adored Lucy as a child now bothers Lucy with her intrusive motherly concern. When Pauline sends Lucy upstairs to rest because "she thought her sister looked tired" (183), Lucy complies only because she wants to be alone to relish her reawakening to life's splendors. Lucy cannot even conceive of her sister's beginning to understand this renewed vitality, and, in fact, mundane Pauline probably could not. But, later, when Lucy's insinuating remarks about her sister's housekeeping nettle Pauline and "really hurt her feelings" (188), Lucy is unaware of this. Lucy, too, is responsible for the strained relationship with her sister. Although Pauline's intention in recruiting piano students for Lucy is not purely selfless, Lucy sees in it only an accusation of familial neglect and little appreciation for her own unique talents. Rather than avoiding a scene as she knows she can do (192), Lucy initiates a confrontation with her sister. Pauline again questions Lucy's refusal to share confidences with "us," meaning of course with her. The scene ends with Lucy's walking off toward the country, marking the final separation from her sister and a declaration of achieved individuation. The few tears Pauline sheds are a mother's tears for the loss of a child she has brought up and worked for. But, more importantly, they are tears of remorse for failing to achieve union with the one person who should be closest to her—her sister.

For Cather, then, the bond between sisters was a fragile one, based on blood ties and family loyalties but threatened by the struggle for individuation. In *The Song of the Lark*, *The Professor's House*, and *Lucy Gayheart*, Cather examines the failure of sisters to accept their dependence and similarity while acknowledging their need for independence and difference. This failure is fraught with sadness and pain and often cripples women in developing satisfying unions with any other individuals. For Cather, though, the confrontation between sisters seems inevitable and necessary. Merely to accept one's sister as a mirror image is to see in a glass darkly. To accept one's sister as separate, as "other," is to see face-to-face.

—South Dakota State University

BIBLIOGRAPHY

Cather, Willa. "The Diamond Mine." *Youth and the Bright Medusa*. New York: Vintage, 1975. 67–120.

———. *Lucy Gayheart*. New York: Knopf, 1935.

———. "The Marriage of Phaedra." *Collected Short Fiction, 1892–1912*. Ed. Virginia Faulkner. Lincoln: U of Nebraska P, 1970. 219–34.

———. *The Professor's House*. New York: Knopf, 1925.

———. *The Song of the Lark*. 1915. Lincoln: U of Nebraska P, Bison, 1978.

———. *The World and the Parish: Willa Cather's Articles and Reviews, 1893–1902*. Ed. William M. Curtin. 2 vols. Lincoln: U of Nebraska P, 1970.

Fishel, Elizabeth. *Sisters: Love and Rivalry Inside the Family and Beyond*. New York: Morrow, 1979.

Longino, Helen E., and Valerie Miner. "A Feminist Taboo?" *Competition: A Feminist Taboo*. Ed. Valerie Miner and Helen E. Longino. New York: Feminist, 1987. 1–7.

McNaron, Toni. "*Little Women* and 'Cinderella': Sisters and Competition." *Competition: A Feminist Taboo*. Ed. Valerie Miner and Helen E. Longino. New York: Feminist, 1987. 121–30.

Stouck, David. *Willa Cather's Imagination*. Lincoln: U of Nebraska P, 1975.

Woodress, James. *Willa Cather: A Literary Life*. Lincoln: U of Nebraska P, 1987.

Willa Cather's Homecomings:
A Meeting of Selves

CHERYLL BURGESS

> *How smoothly the trains run beyond the Missouri;*
> *Even in my sleep I know when I have crossed the river.*
> *The wheels turn as if they were glad to go;*
> *They run like running water,*
> *Like Youth, running away . . .*
> *They spin bright along the bright rails,*
> *Singing and humming,*
> *Singing and humming.*
> *They run remembering,*
> *They run rejoicing,*
> *As if they, too, were going home.*
>   "Going Home (Burlington Route)"

"Who are you? How many selves have you? And which of these selves do you want to be?" demanded D. H. Lawrence of Benjamin Franklin, incensed over Franklin's *Autobiography* for positing a unified and perfectible self (19). Readers of Willa Cather have put the same questions to her, albeit without Lawrence's bluster: Who are you? How many selves have you? And which of these selves do you want to be? Cather might have answered that she had *two* selves but was not always sure which of them to be. She recalls of her early years in New York:

> There I was on the Atlantic coast, surrounded by the great masters and teachers with all their tradition of learning and culture, and yet I was always being pulled back into Nebraska. . . . Whenever I crossed the Missouri river coming into Nebraska the very smell of the soil tore me to pieces. I could not decide which was the real and which the fake "me." I almost decided to settle down on a quarter section of land and let my writing go. . . . I loved the country where I had been a kid, where they still called me "Willie" Cather. (Mahoney 37)

Elizabeth Sergeant also noticed the internal division troubling her friend, observing that Cather "suffered a truly gruelling inner pull between the opposites of East and West. Her restless doubling back and forth across our vast continent . . . did not assure integration and tranquility" (54).

East and West symbolized for Cather entirely different, mutually incompatible indentities. In New York she was above all a writer, an independent adult, dedicated to her art, a city woman. In Nebraska she was a family member, sister, daughter, a kid once again, a prairie girl. If moving to Nebraska meant letting her writing go, living in New York meant "seclusion from [her] family and friends" (Tittle 85). While unwilling to relinquish either self, Cather nevertheless felt unable to integrate these two selves. On the one hand, despite her father's offer to build her a studio there, she was quite sure that she could never write in Red Cloud (Sergeant 61); on the other hand, she never invited her family to live with her in New York.

Perhaps because Cather found it so difficult "to possess psychic wholeness" (the words are Sergeant's, 54) much of her fiction depicts characters searching for a sense of unity or torn between two opposing forces: Jim Burden strives to reconcile his Nebraska past with his New York present; Claude Wheeler wavers between love for his own land and appreciation of French culture; Marian Forrester struggles between loyalty to her invalid husband and a desperate yearning to enjoy her life before she, too, grows old; Lucy Gayheart ricochets back and forth between Chicago, where wonders never seem quite real, and Haverford, where reality is never wonderful.

One motif that recurs throughout Cather's fiction with the rhythmic regularity of a smoothly running train is the motif of homecoming. Leaving home affords a person the opportunity to escape an identity defined in relation to one's family and to make or "find" a new self situated in a new environment; but going back home forces these two identities to confront one another, as self-made adult returns to folks who remember the person that left but do not know the new self that returns. The homecomer has the option of slipping into the childhood self or of insisting that the family at least acknowledge, if not adopt, the adult self. Homecomings in Cather's fiction are sometimes joyful, sometimes painful, often both at once, but they are never bland. To cite just one example, Claude Wheeler in *One of Ours* "never came back without emotion,—try as he would to pass lightly over these departures and returns which were all in the day's work. When he came . . . toward the . . . house . . . something always clutched at his heart. He both loved and hated to come home" (42).

How many selves have you? And which of these selves do you want to be? In other words, how does Cather's fiction reflect or even resolve her own troubling sense of two selves, that internal "tug of war between East and West" (Bennett xviii), artist and person, child and adult, individual and family member? In one of Cather's earliest stories, "The Burglar's Christmas" (1896), a downcast twenty-four-year-old man, who has forgotten his own name and is "hungry and desperate and alone" (73), decides to take his chances as a common thief, having made nothing of himself in the world since taking his life into his own hands twelve years ago when he left home. His attempted robbery turns into an accidental homecoming when his mother discovers him with her jewels—he is unwittingly robbing his parents' new house. Limp in his mother's strong and forgiving embrace, cheek pressed against her warm bosom, the failed thief gratefully returns to his childhood identity as "Willie" (78), "the happy little boy" (81), reassured by his mother that he has not changed a bit and is still "of one blood" (82) with her. This "hastily concocted potboiler," as one critic called the story (Bennett xviii), differs from later fictional patterns of the divided self by portraying a character who *fails* to develop a second self capable of surviving in the outside world (he has no name outside his home), and so is only "Willie," mama's "poor boy" ("Burglar's Christmas" 83). Sharon O'Brien argues that William is a mask for Willa Cather ("Mothers" 274–75). Yet although William draws a sigh of rich contentment to sink back into boyhood under his mother's "refuge and protection" ("Burglar's Christmas" 81), the melodramatic narrative does not mistake such tranquility for triumph but rather depicts it as surrender, hardly a peace that the striving Willa would have accepted for herself.

Another early story, "The Treasure of Far Island" (1902), imagines a more conventional family reunion. Douglass Burnham is returning home to Empire City, Nebraska, for the first time since he left it as a boy twelve years ago (the same amount of time William was away from home, and, incidentally, the same amount of time that elapsed between Cather's leaving home for college in 1890 and the publication of this story [Woodress 156]). Unlike the downcast William, who had failed in the world, Douglass is a successful young playwright, "a man with a man's work done," displaying "that cheerful assurance common to young people whom the world has made much of" ("Treasure of Far Island" 145, 146). Flushed with his own success, Douglass feels "a strange embarrassment" in the presence of his father, an angular gray-whiskered man, who, Douglass feels, "stood somewhat in awe of him" (146). But while Douglass's parents proudly acknowledge the great accomplishments of this "splendid creature" (147), at heart they do not really believe that their son has grown up. When his mother tells him not to get ice from the refrigerator because he always leaves the ice uncovered and it wastes, Douglass knows he is at home: "he was but a boy again in his father's house and must not keep supper waiting" (149). Because Douglass is so happy and secure in his New York life as a successful playwright, returning home for a visit does not precipitate a battle of opposing selves. Being a boy again is a pleasant vacation from his playwright self, never a serious alternative to it. Furthermore, when his childhood playmate Margie Van Dyck agrees to marry him, Douglass's "psychic wholeness" is sealed. With Margie by his side in New York, Douglass will be a fully integrated individual: a dedicated and recognized artist wedded to his own Empire City childhood. As its romantic title, literary allusions, chivalric diction, and moonlight engagement emphasize, "The Treasure of Far Island" is pure fantasy. Even as the story imagines the possibility of a simultaneously satisfying artistic career, warm homecoming, recovered childhood, and perfect match, its fairytale form implies that such harmonious integration does not happen outside of storybooks. Willa Cather's early critical statements likewise warn that Douglass Burnham's happy marriage of home life and artistic success is improbable in the real world. "Domestic and artistic life do not mix well," she insisted (Slote 70). Especially if the artist happened to be female, marriage might satisfy the personal self, but it invariably stifled the artist self.

Let us turn now to two later stories that feature women protagonists and that present a more realistic reflection of Cather's own experience than either of the above male-centered apprenticeship stories. *The Song of the Lark* (1915) and "The Best Years" (1945) are two of Cather's most autobiographical stories, but their protagonists, Thea Kronborg and Lesley Ferguesson, are polar opposites. Thea Kronborg is ruddy, strong, independent, ambitious, determined, defiant, inviolable, specially gifted, and passionately committed to her art. Lesley Ferguesson is pale, weak, childlike, generous, self-sacrificing, obedient, loyal, loving, and ardently devoted to her family. It is as if Cather separated her two selves and put each self into a different character.

Each girl's bedroom is a textual replica of Cather's own attic room in the Red Cloud house, but slight differences in the texts signal vast differences in the temperaments of the girls. Thea wants to be let alone and uses her own money to "fit up a little room for herself" (*Song of the Lark* 71) separate from the other upstairs sleeping rooms. Behind her closed door, Thea is shielded from the "constant turmoil" of her family and can tune into "the voice within herself." Thea begins to live "a double life"; during the day she is "one of the Kronborg children," but at night, upstairs in her room she is "a different person," whose private thoughts are her "companions" and whose own ideas are like "friends" (73). Lesley, in contrast, loves the "undivided loft" where she and her brothers used to sleep in a row, "close enough together to share experiences" ("Best Years" 130–31). Only when Mrs. Ferguesson "exerted her authority and partitioned off a little room . . . for her daughter," insisting that Lesley "must have a room of her own" (131–32), does the dutiful daughter reluctantly sleep by herself. There is even a suggestion that being cut off from her brothers is a kind of death for Lesley; her room is described as "a snug wooden box" (133), a coffin perhaps, and it is a relief to be able to leave the lid, or door, open. (Lesley dies that Christmas when a snowstorm cuts her off from her family.)

Since Thea and Lesley together make one complex person, each of them is a relatively simple character in her own right, and neither is subject to the deep ambivalence that Cather felt toward her family. Sergeant recalls that sometimes a "blind terror" seized Cather, "the fear that she was but a cell in the family blood stream." Yet, at other times, Sergeant continues, Cather was a "plain family woman" who "desired to be of use to her blood-kin, in simple human ways" (143). These two impulses in Cather are reflected in the very different ways in which Thea and Lesley experience homecomings. For Thea, coming home reinforces her sense of difference from the other Kronborgs; for Lesley, coming home is a celebration of connectedness.

As Thea rides the train home to Moonstone after her first winter in Chicago, she thinks of how much she has changed since she left. Her music teacher, Andor Harsanyi, has helped her "to find [her]self, to emerge *as* [her]self" (263) by convincing her to develop her voice, that part of her having most to do with her "sense of wholeness and inner well-being" (272). Thea, by herself, "lack[s] nothing"; she is "all there" (199) and does not need her family to make her feel complete. Nevertheless, as the train crosses the Platte River she is glad to be "coming back to her own land" (276) and to her own kind. And, initially, the ceremonious homecoming rivals a Norman Rockwell painting in family sentiment, as a very creditable number of Kronborg representatives meet Thea, kiss her, and talk to her all at once, while neighbors watch the happy "flock" (278). But Thea's elder sister Anna quickly breaks the spell with a peremptory order that Thea sing at Maggie Evans's funeral. Anna, as Mrs. Kronborg's "lieutenant" and "an obstinate contender for proprieties" (23), is as unlikable as Mrs. Kronborg is likable. While Mrs. Kronborg feels "a great change in Thea" (281) and makes her "feel grown-up" (282), Anna rebukes her as if she were still a rebellious child. Worse yet, Anna makes Thea feel ostracized from the family. She hisses that Thea's all-night revelry with the Mexicans scandalizes the whole family and that they "all" had hoped that going away would have improved Thea (299).

Thea now feels "betrayed," realizing that her grown sisters and brothers are not "of her kind" after all, but "of the Moonstone kind." The "cub loyalty" that she had for her siblings turns sour now that she recognizes them as her "natural enemies." Even the sympathetic Mrs. Kronborg and Aunt Tillie cannot help because they are still "a part of the family" (301), "an integral thing" (303), whereas Thea is not. The house and everything in it now seems hostile, so hostile that it freezes Thea's throat and she finds it difficult to practice at home. Although breaking with her family is painful, the separation is inevitable and irrevocable. In order to develop herself as an artist Thea must escape from this Kronborg desert before it "drink[s] [her] up like a drop of water" (309). When Thea leaves Moonstone for the second time she leaves alone, never to return. As Cather writes in the 1932 preface, *The Song of the Lark* sets out "to tell of an artist's awakening and struggle"; it consistently draws a distinction between Thea's "artistic life" and her "human life," between her "imaginative life" and her "personal life." For Thea, the "artistic life is the only one in which she is happy, or free, or even very real" (vi). The book is appropriately dedicated to Isabelle McClung, the woman who nurtured Cather's own artistic life.

"The Best Years," Cather's last completed story, was written as a gift to her brother Roscoe and was intended to remind him of "the time when he and she and Douglass were all children together" (Lewis 196). In this "portrait of family unity" (Arnold 174) the seventy-one-year-old Cather represents herself not as an aspiring artist but as a "homesick child" ("Best Years" 118). Lesley Ferguesson leaves home at fifteen, not in order to "emerge as herself," as in Thea's case, but in order to ease the family's financial strain. Thus, even while away from home Lesley is emotionally tied to it, asking eagerly for news of "our boys" (118) and saving up her money to buy presents for the family. Moreover, in her life as a school-teacher Lesley displays the same kind of charity and affection that makes her such a beloved sister, so that her profession does not demand that she forge a new self. For Lesley, coming home means returning to "where she wanted to be, where she ought to be" (124). When Miss Knightly delivers her to her family, Lesley responds to the feeling of being at home like a "plant that has been washed out by a rain storm . . . when a kind gardener puts it gently back into its own earth with its own group" (124). Whereas Thea soon discovers that she and her siblings have nothing in common, Lesley and her brothers instantly "become telepathically one" (123). Whereas Thea jealously guards her individuality, Lesley loves the sense that there are *no* boundaries between herself and her brothers. And whereas the cub loyalty that Thea felt for her siblings is betrayed when she comes home, the unspoken "covenant" that binds Lesley and her brothers, giving them a "family complexion" (129), remains steadfast. Lesley relishes the feeling of "being with, and being one with, her brothers," of sharing a consciousness with them; it is a "clan feeling, which mean[s] life or death for the blood, not for the individual" (134).

Whether in opposition to the family or in identification with it, Thea Kronborg and Lesley Ferguesson each achieves an enviable sense of wholeness, a singleness of identity that eluded her creator. As attractive as psychic oneness may appear in theory, however, these stories controvert their own desires, suggesting that there is a grave danger in having a single self; namely, death of the other self. Thea confesses to Dr. Archie that she does not have *any* personal life: "Your work becomes your personal life. . . . It's like being woven into a big web. You can't pull away, because all your little tendrils are woven into the picture. It takes you up, and uses you, and spins you out; and that is your life" (546). If Thea's personal life is sacrificed to her art, Lesley's individuality drowns in the family blood. "*Bound*" to her family (129), Lesley "*gave herself up*" to the feeling of being at home (124), "*sank*" into idleness (133), is overcome by *sleepiness*, almost "*ceased to exist*" (134; emphases added). The *only* future Cather can imagine for her is death.

However painful internal division may have been for Willa Cather personally, conflict at least ensured that both selves were still living. Although Cather, unlike Douglass Burnham, never managed to marry the two sides of herself, neither was she willing to succumb to a wholeness that deprived her of one of her halves. Hence, her lifelong "restless doubling back and forth" across the country by train, escaping to New York "to get away from the folks I love, and work" (Sumner 87); returning to Nebraska for relaxation, where folks "don't care a thing about my books" and where she feels "just like a kid!" (Hinman 44); leaving again to write, when she "need[s] a rest from resting" ("Readers and Writers" 90); going back "home on the range" (Woodress 288) to cook for the family while her mother convalesced from an illness; breaking away once more to follow her all-absorbing passion, "personal, intense, [and] selfish" (Slote 71).

Finally, Willa Cather's two lives were not so divorced from one another as they may appear. Writing about Nebraska *became* a kind of home-coming. Once Cather abandoned her efforts to write like "the great master" Henry James and began writing about the Nebraska of her childhood, the "incalculable distance" (*Lucy Gayheart* 24) between East and West, artist and person, individual and group lives lessened, and, as Sergeant notes, Cather "began to seem and be all of a piece" (54). While her seesawing back and forth across the country did not abate, her two lives at least began to enrich each other rather than to compete against each other. In the West, Cather did not write but she did get "Inspiration" (Hinman 44), renewing herself "at the fountain-head of the life [she wrote] about" (Tittle 85). In the East, Cather worked alone but still considered herself, according to Sumner, "only one of . . . seven brothers and sisters out west who came east part of the time to write about the west" (87). To her great credit, Cather managed what neither of her two fictional heroines could: to live a life balanced between individuality and communion, artistic passion and family love.

—Cornell University

BIBLIOGRAPHY

Arnold, Marilyn. *Willa Cather's Short Fiction*. Athens: Ohio UP, 1984.

Bennett, Mildred R. Introduction. *Willa Cather's Collected Short Fiction, 1892–1912*. Rev. ed. Ed. Virginia Faulkner. Lincoln: U of Nebraska P, 1970. xiii–xli.

Bohlke, L. Brent, ed. *Willa Cather in Person: Interviews, Speeches, and Letters*. Lincoln: U of Nebraska P, 1986.

Cather, Willa. "The Best Years." *Five Stories*. New York: Vintage, 1956. 112–48.

_____. "The Burglar's Christmas." *Willa Cather: 24 Stories*. Ed. Sharon O'Brien. New York: New American Library, 1987. 72–83.

_____. "Going Home (Burlington Route)." *April Twilights and Other Poems*. New York: Knopf, 1923. 66.

_____. *Lucy Gayheart*. New York: Vintage, 1976.

_____. *One of Ours*. New York: Vintage, 1971.

_____. *The Song of the Lark*. Boston: Houghton, 1983. Contains 1932 preface.

_____. "The Treasure of Far Island." *Willa Cather: 24 Stories*. 143–66.

Hinman, Eleanor. "Willa Cather." *Lincoln Sunday Star* 6 November 1921. Rpt. Bohlke. 42–49.

Lawrence, D. H. *Studies in Classic American Literature*. Garden City, N.Y.: Doubleday, 1953.

Lewis, Edith. *Willa Cather Living*. New York: Knopf, 1953.

Mahoney, Eva. "How Willa Cather Found Herself." *Omaha World–Herald* 27 November 1921. Rpt. Bohlke. 33–39.

O'Brien, Sharon. "Mothers, Daughters, and the 'Art Necessity': Willa Cather and the Creative Process." *American Novelists Revisited: Essays in Feminist Criticism*. Ed. Fritz Fleischmann. Boston: Hall, 1982.

_____. *Willa Cather: The Emerging Voice*. New York: Oxford UP, 1987.

"Readers and Writers." *Nebraska State Journal* 5 September 1926. Rpt. Bohlke. 90–91.

Sergeant, Elizabeth Shepley. *Willa Cather: A Memoir*. Lincoln: U of Nebraska P, 1963.

Slote, Bernice. "First Principles: The Kingdom of Art." *The Kingdom of Art: Willa Cather's First Principles and Critical Statements, 1893–1896*. Ed. Bernice Slote. Lincoln: U of Nebraska P, 1966. 31–112.

Sumner, Allene. "Prize Novelist Finds Writing and Eating Kin." *Cleveland Press* 20 November 1925. Rpt. Bohlke. 86–88.

Tittle, Walter. "Glimpses of Interesting Americans: Willa Sibert Cather." *Century Magazine* July 1925. Rpt. Bohlke. 81–85.

Woodress, James. *Willa Cather: A Literary Life*. Lincoln: U of Nebraska P, 1987.

Going Home: "The Sculptor's Funeral," "The Namesake," and "Two Friends"

LORETTA WASSERMAN

Willa Cather ends *The Song of the Lark* (her most expansive novel) with an epic simile representing the relationship between the home community and the youth who leaves to seek a larger world. The simile says that the "little settlements" left behind continue to be energized by their venturesome young people:

> The many naked little sandbars which lie between Venice and the mainland, in the seemingly stagnant water of the lagoons, are made habitable and wholesome only because, every night, a foot and a half of tide creeps in from the sea and winds its fresh brine up through all that network of shining waterways. So, into all the little settlements of quiet people, tidings of what their boys and girls are doing in the world bring refreshment: bring to the old, memories, and to the young, dreams.

Correspondingly, the novel has made clear, the well-being of the youth out in the world depends on memories of home. To cite only one example, the narrative voice tells us that Thea, later in life, will recall with poignant clarity the Wednesday night prayer meetings at the Baptist church, which she found so dreary and from which she would rush to lose herself in *Anna Karenina* as soon as the Doxology was sung:

> Thea would have been astonished if she could have known how, years afterward, when she had need of them, those old faces were to come back to her, long after they were hidden away under the earth; that they would seem to her then as full of meaning, as mysteriously marked by Destiny, as the people who danced the mazurka under the elegant Korsunsky. (165)

Nowhere else in her fiction does Cather present such a happy resolution to the tensions between those who go and those who stay. But clearly for her these opposing pulls were among "the major forces of life" working in "the shadowy realm of personal relationships," to borrow phrases from her essay on Katherine Mansfield (108). The interweaving of these forces appears in two early stories, "The Sculptor's Funeral" and "The Namesake" (in both, a sculptor is the main character), and much later in "Two Friends."

"The Sculptor's Funeral" is a devastating account of the blight cast on a talented youth by a mean-spirited town and oppressive family. Along with "Paul's Case" (especially in its early version, as David Carpenter has stressed), this story insists on the forming—and deforming—power of environment. True, a first reading seems to point another way, to Harvey Merrick's successful escape from "this place of hatred and bitter waters," as his boyhood friend Jim Laird calls their hometown (44). And Laird, who did not succeed in leaving, has comforted himself with thinking of Merrick living "off there in the world, away from all this hog-wallow" (44). But the story makes clear that, whatever his fame as an artist, Merrick as a man never rid himself of "a shame not his, and yet so unescapably his" (39). The world had suspected wine or disappointed love, but Steavens—the sculptor's student, who, out of love and respect, accompanies the body back to Kansas—sees that "the real tragedy of his master's life" lies here in the town, "a desert of newness and ugliness" (39), and in Merrick's appalling family. The mother is a grotesque, driven by violent emotions, her most memorable feature being large, square teeth set far apart, "teeth that could tear" (36)—and we recall the symbolic link of teeth to animality in the lexicon of the naturalists, as noted by Carpenter, 593–94.[1] The father, sister, and mulatto servant appear cowed and weak before such raw power. How had Merrick survived it? The face in the coffin answers. It lacks repose—"the chin was thrust forward defiantly . . . as though the strain of life had been so sharp and bitter that death could not at once wholly relax the tension . . . as though he were still guarding something precious and holy, which might even yet be wrested from him" (36–37).

Most telling, Merrick's art reveals his suffering. Steavens recalls a significant work, the bas-relief of a boy who has caught a butterfly and is trying to show it to a "thin, faded old woman" seated sewing (38). Steavens remembers that he had assumed the woman to be Merrick's mother, a guess that brought a burning flush to the sculptor's face. Here is Merrick's deepest pain—the inability to tell the full truth in his art (the sentimentalized mother) of the boy whose love of beauty is ignored. And perhaps more: the butterfly being an ancient symbol for the soul, the artist may be speaking of the lasting effects of early ignorance and neglect. That Cather wanted to focus on this example of Merrick's work is borne out by the fact that in revising the story she omitted a reference to a second piece, called "Victory," as though to remove a hint that Merrick felt his life a triumph.

But despite rejection by family and town, the artist senses the bond with home as inviolable. On his deathbed, Merrick had asked that his body be returned—"it rather seems as though we ought to go back to the place we came from in the end" (42). Further, the story tells us of another of the town's victims. Laird, like Merrick, had wanted to make the town proud of him. Now an alcoholic and town eccentric, he will die, the narrative voice tells us, of a cold he caught in the Colorado mountains while journeying to help a boy in trouble with the law—a cold reminiscent of the lung congestion that killed Merrick.

This oppressive story must make us wish for alternatives, for escape, for freedom. It provokes an almost visceral desire to be "homeless as the sea . . . a creature of the free wind and waves" (to look ahead to imagery opening "Two Friends"). As though sharing our feelings, Cather wrote some five years later a countering story, "The Namesake," about a sculptor who indeed did grow up free from home. Born abroad and educated in a Jesuit school following the death of his parents, Lyon Hartwell had no knowledge of what he nevertheless called "home" until he was thirty. The story, a Conrad-like tale within a tale, is Hartwell's account to artist friends of his crucial journey. To care for an aged aunt, Hartwell traveled to his father's birthplace in western Pennsylvania, a farm that had been his grandfather's and, before that, the family homestead. Gradually he feels a need to learn about the uncle for whom he was named, who, while yet a boy, enlisted in the Union army and died carrying the colors in battle. He searches out the boy's belongings, clothing and schoolbooks; then, in an extraordinary night in the garden of the farmhouse, he experiences a mystic union with the past. Hartwell describes the night to the listening students in an inchoate rush of language. It was, he says, like "the same feeling that artists know when we, rarely, achieve truth in our work. . . . It was as if the earth under my feet had grasped and rooted me, and were pouring its essence into me. I sat there until the dawn of morning, and all night long my life seemed to be pouring out of me and running into the ground" (146). Only after this induction into "home" does Hartwell create the great works that have made him known as the artist who reveals the essential America, the one who "seemed, almost more than any other living man, to mean all of it—from ocean to ocean" (137).

"The Namesake" says nothing in realistic detail about a home community or family. As such, it is not an answer to "The Sculptor's Funeral." But it does testify to the necessity—at least for the artist—of claiming particular places, particular roots, on the way to full understanding. We may note, in passing, an uncanny instance of Cather's life imitating her art: her near obsession with capturing in *One of Ours* the life and spirit of her cousin Lt. G. P. Cather, who, like the Civil War soldier, died leading men forward in battle in World War I. Woodress states that Cather felt a "blood identity" with her cousin, an identity that lasted the three years she worked on that novel (304).

In the opening paragraph of "Two Friends," the narrative voice, which we sense is Cather's own, speaks figuratively of the unbidden memories of home that, recurring throughout life, unaccountably give courage. In its watery imagery the figure of speech is reminiscent of the simile, mentioned earlier, that closes *The Song of the Lark*. However, here the emphasis is on leaving and returning, not on the community left:

> The sea-gulls, that seem so much creatures of the free wind and waves, that are as homeless as the sea (able to rest upon the tides and ride the storm, needing nothing but water and sky), at certain seasons even they go back to something they have known before; to remote islands and lonely ledges that are their breeding grounds.

"Two Friends" is an infinitely more subtle story than "The Sculptor's Funeral" or "The Namesake," and it invites a number of approaches. Its subject is friendship, one of those affectional bonds in "the shadowy realm of personal relationships" not much explored in modern literature, but one that engaged classical thinkers, as Cather would have known. One may fancy that she remembered Aristotle's discussion of friendship, or Cicero's, and thought of testing their ideas against "my own naked land and the figures scattered upon it" (to quote a well-known phrase from *My Ántonia* [262]). But more particularly in "Two Friends," it is about the effect this friendship had on the youth who observed it and who carries the memory of its dissolution as an "old scar" (230). It is a scar because she had been sure, at age thirteen, that this bond of trust was solid, one of the "unalterable realties, somewhere at the bottom of things," and its break made the world less firm, less predictable (193).

Through their deportment and their conversation, Mr. Dillon, the town banker and store owner, and Mr. Trueman, the cattleman, transmit to the listening adolescent what a community should provide its young—accurate knowledge about the world and the wisdom of experience. She is educated by "the old stories of the early West . . . ; the minute biographies of the farming people; the clear, detailed, illuminating accounts of all that went on in the great crop-growing, cattle-feeding world; and the silence—the strong, rich, out-flowing silence between two friends" (226). She hears ethical judgments: Mr. Dillon defends the Swedish farmers who work their women hard ("It's the old-country way; they're accustomed to it, and they like it"), but Mr. Trueman does not agree ("Maybe. I don't like it" [204]). She learns of the world beyond Singleton, Kansas, as the men talk of St. Joseph, of Chicago. Their journeys "made some of the rest of us feel less shut away and small-townish" (202). She observes the forbearance and trust that make friendship possible: Mr. Dillon curbs his tendency to sharp opinions in Mr. Trueman's presence; Mr. Trueman cautions only quietly against quack social cures ("Mustn't be a reformer, R. E. Nothing in it" [214]).

One particular moment in this delicate relationship—two busy men, a young girl—is held for us, crystallizing its dynamics. In a rough way, the moment is analogous to Hartwell's experience of oneness in the farmhouse garden, a moment out of time. On a summer night, with the dusty street before them "drinking up the moonlight," the three observe an occultation of Venus. As they watch, the planet appears to move toward the moon, to be swallowed, and then to appear on the other side. The scene is described as a tableau—the three watching figures, the intense moonlight making the deep dust of the street silvery, the dust that is like one of the possible answers ("the last residuum of material things,—the soft bottom resting-place" [212]), and above, the mysterious movements of the heavenly bodies, a cosmic pattern enclosing all. But the pattern is one of movement and change, unsettling: not just the eclipse of Venus, which prefigures the end of the friendship, but the swiftness with which it happens, when "everything up there overhead seemed as usual" (212). At the heart of things lies loss and uncertainty, the event suggests. The narrator tells us that ever afterward, when traveling in Southern countries, she feels a sudden sadness at the sight of a dusty road "drinking up the moonlight beside a blind wall"— the old scar (229). Interestingly, a surviving letter of Cather's, written to Edith Lewis from Jaffrey, New Hampshire, tells us that meditating on the night sky was personal for Cather. She writes of watching Venus and Jupiter for an hour and wonders whether indeed their movements may not signal something more than physical and mathematical forces. Mr. Trueman wonders in a similar way. He speaks of the great distances of the moon and stars and tells Mr. Dillon, whose attention has jumped back to immediate problems such as tramps on the railroad, "Maybe the stars will throw some light on all that, if we get the run of them" (214).

Yet what ends the friendship is not, at least not apparently, a stroke of fate. Rather it is a human failing, a burst of ego—Mr. Dillon's irritable temperament breaking through his imperfectly acquired habit of self-control. Though the narrator treats the men as equals, speaking with mild irony of "my heroes" and "my two great men," it is clear that Mr. Dillon is the lesser man. He is more intelligent, the narrator speculates; that is, he knows precise commercial values—the worth of Swede farmers, the mortgage on the home-steader who has a traveling photographer take a picture of his precariously held home, the unacceptable risk of granting a loan to a "foolish, extravagant woman, or a girl he didn't approve of " (206). A man of strong prejudices, a good Catholic and family man, Mr. Dillon had curbed his dislike of poker playing, of questionable women, of Republicanism (all interests of Trueman) out of respect for his friend. But the demagoguery of Bryan's "cross of gold" speech unleashes his temper and local patriotism, and he sacrifices Trueman's friendship.

In contrast, Trueman, slow of speech, moves in a world singularly free of calculation (as his name suggests). He keeps one-hundred-dollar bills in his pocket but leaves his coat hanging in cattle sheds or the barbershop. When he changes banks, he does not know the figure of his account but writes a check for "the amount of my balance" (224). His generosity is of the spirit—a magnanimous man, large-souled; he walks "spaciously, as if he were used to a great deal of room" (203). There is something antique about Trueman, indeed heroic: he moves as though on "the deck of his own ship" (214) and the ring he wears is "the head of a Roman soldier cut in onyx" (199). Unlike Dillon, Trueman knew the worth of friendship. On the sudden death of Dillon, Trueman moves away from Singleton, but before leaving, he gives the young girl a red seal from his watch chain as a keepsake.

And it is Trueman who indicates what our stance should be toward the mysterious shocks and changes of the universe. One of the pleasures of the young observer is hearing her two friends talk of theatrical performances and actors and actresses they have seen. Trueman remembers Edwin Booth in *Richard the Second*, which "made a great impression on [him] at the time."

But now, he says, "that play's a little too tragic. Something very black about it. I think I prefer *Hamlet*" (217). This must be our clue—not the anguish and regret of Richard, but the readiness of Hamlet, the acceptance of a universe where change and loss are part of unalterable reality.

No story is older than journey and return, but none is more American either—the leaving to find oneself, to find a world elsewhere, and the necessary coming back (if only in imagination) to explain, to be comforted, to tell the tale.

—Grand Valley State University

NOTE

1. Unless I am mistaken, Sharon O'Brien unaccountably omits a discussion of this mother in her psychobiography of Cather—*Willa Cather: The Emerging Voice* (Oxford: 1987).

BIBLIOGRAPHY

Carpenter, David A. "Why Willa Cather Revised 'Paul's Case.' "*American Literature* 59 (December 1987): 590–608.
Cather, Willa. "Katherine Mansfield." *Willa Cather on Writing*. New York: Knopf, 1949. 107–20.
_____. Letter to Edith Lewis 10 May 1936, Willa Cather Historical Center, Red Cloud, Nebraska.
_____. *My Ántonia*. Boston: Houghton, Sentry ed., 1961.
_____. "The Namesake." *Willa Cather's Collected Short Fiction, 1892–1912*. Ed. Virginia Faulkner. Lincoln: U of Nebraska P, 1965. 137–46.
_____. "The Sculptor's Funeral." *The Troll Garden*. Ed. James Woodress. Lincoln: U of Nebraska P, 1983. 32–45.
_____. *The Song of the Lark*. Boston: Houghton, 1983.
_____. "Two Friends." *Obscure Destinies*. New York: Vintage, 1974. 193–230.
Woodress, James. *Willa Cather: A Literary Life*. Lincoln: U of Nebraska P, 1987.

Annie (Ántonia) and John (Rosicky) Pavelka Family

Part Two:
The Family Idealized and Explored

These essays expose problematic aspects of family relationships universally rather than biographically. Rosowski offers an overview of Willa Cather's earnest explorations of family, which Skaggs sees redefined in the story of Anton Rosicky. Gelfant associates an idealization of the family with a destructive quest, and Kvasnicka provides a coda to this view. Tanner and Bell concentrate on the troubled St. Peter family, while England addresses the troubled Henshawe marriage and Miller a self-absorbed artist's dependence on family.

Susan J. Rosowski's "Willa Cather's Chosen Family: Fictional Formations and Transformations" concentrates on *O Pioneers!*, *The Song of the Lark*, *The Professor's House*, "Neighbour Rosicky," and "Old Mrs. Harris" in exploring the family as a social unit founded on property, as a personal unit founded upon morality and feeling, as an American romantic ideal corrupted by marketplace values, and as an obstruction to higher calling. Rosowski considers substitutes for the traditional family: the family of humanity, and the religious vision woven into the family living of Anton Rosicky and Mrs. Harris. In "Old Mrs. Harris" disappointed Vickie Templeton asks, "What were families for, anyway?" In a career of answering this, Cather created families we seem to know "as well as our own."

Merrill M. Skaggs, in "Cather's Complex Tale of a Simple Man, 'Neighbour Rosicky,' " sees the story of such a family not only as a model for familial and community bonds but also as a courageous redefinition of the traditional egotistical American way to success. The Christmas Eve and Fourth of July scenes dramatize the definitive blend of independence and responsibility to others that makes Rosicky an exemplary neighbor and father—all this developed against a background of fatal illness.

Blanche H. Gelfant's " 'What Was It . . . ?': The Secret of Family Accord in *One of Ours*" is pessimistic about family in Cather. *One of Ours* is deeply troubling to Gelfant because it traces to inevitable death the hero's quest for illusory happiness associated with family life and because it discovers family in a brotherhood of killing. Gelfant blames Claude's mother for encouraging his idealism regarding the war and then interpreting his death as a "felicitous fate." Claude becomes the most disturbing of a gallery of Cather characters— Jim Burden, Niel Herbert, Tom Outland, Jacques Gaux, etc.—"who feel misplaced in their own homes or have no homes because they are orphans" and "may represent [Cather's] failure to find at home the something she was seeking."

Mellanee Kvasnicka selects two of these characters and adds another in "Fragmented Families, Fragmented Lives in 'Paul's Case,' *My Ántonia*, and *A Lost Lady*," attributing the maladjustments of Paul, Jim and Niel to their lack of conventional family structures. The loneliness of each causes him to fantasize substitute families and prevents him from having his own.

The Professor's House is Cather's most focused extensive study of family, and Stephen L. Tanner and Alice Bell seem opposed about the professor's problems. In "The Deeper Role of Gender Conflict in *The Professor's House*" Tanner tries to transcend gender bickering over this novel by establishing the importance to the professor personally and professionally of his wife and daughters. Tanner views the novel as a struggle with the diminishment of aging and the loneliness of the human condition. Bell concentrates in "The Professor's Marriage" on Cather's technique of allusion to expose the troubled St. Peter family. Anatole France's *Le Mannequin d'Osier*, Shakespeare's *Othello*, a Euripides legend, and the life of Berengaria of Navarre are among sources used to expose and explore manipulation, resentment, and estrangement among the St. Peters.

Eugene England's "Lovers as Mortal Enemies" makes lack of Christian forgiveness the destructive force in Myra Henshawe's marriage and religious reconciliation, which seems an empty form alongside Oswald Henshawe's dutiful service to her. Applying René Girard's theories on imitative desire to Myra's unhappiness and resentments, England sees Cather's references to *King Lear* as ironic, for Myra fails to understand the theme of forgiveness at the play's heart.

Robert K. Miller caps these essays in "What Margie Knew" by exposing Valentine Ramsay's self-absorption, a condition shared by several characters mentioned above. Miller emphasizes even Ramsay's need in "Uncle Valentine" for family, for nurturing by the roses (wife and children) another man has grown and which Ramsay enjoys without the irritating responsibilities of being a husband or father. Miller wonders if Ramsay's handful of sentimental songs is worth his insensitivity toward others.

J. J. M.

Willa Cather's Chosen Family:
Fictional Formations and Transformations

SUSAN J. ROSOWSKI

"There are only two or three human stories, and they go on repeating themselves as fiercely as if they had never happened before," Willa Cather wrote in 1913 (*O Pioneers!* 119). As if continuing the thought years later, she added that one of the oldest of these tells of the quest begun when men "found themselves in an unconscious world . . . the orphan soul trying to find its kin somewhere in the universe" ("Joseph and His Brothers" 97). Indeed, Cather's fiction may be seen as her coming to accept a subject she inherited as surely as she did her midwestern materials—that is, the subject of the family. When I began work on this paper I kept trying to "fix" its subject in one way or another, focusing first upon the importance of property to the family, then on Cather's alternate or surrogate families, and then again on her exploration of gender roles within families. Yet Cather's families kept eluding any such fix: just as I thought I saw one form or idea of family in her fiction, it would change shape and become something else. As I continued to read, I came to accept these changes as the subject that, for me, was asking for attention: the formations and transformations of the family through Cather's fiction. Thus the subtitle of the paper. As for the title, I mean to suggest with it the importance of the family throughout that fiction—that it is "chosen" in at least two senses: in a secular sense as a subject that Cather accepted, then chose as her own; and in a biblical sense of the privileged, even blessed position it came to occupy.

o   o   o   o   o

Cather's early writing gives little indication of the privileged place the family would occupy in her fiction, for during her apprentice period Cather characteristically wrote about individuals living independently. There are exceptions, of course: in "The Treasure of Far Island" the brief scene depicting a successful playwright's return to the small town of his childhood catches well an adult's feeling of being a boy again in his parents' home, and throughout "The Sentimentality of William Tavener" there is authenticity in the story of a couple's recalling their youth, almost forgotten in the press of rearing children. Most often, however, the family in Cather's early fiction is one-dimensionally conventional, with its members serving as a shorthand to depict the central character's predicament: thus preoccupied parents signal Jack-a-Boy's solitude, and a narrowly religious mother signals Eric Hermannson's imprisoned spirit. This was true as late as 1912, for families are strikingly absent from *Alexander's Bridge*. Other than reference to Winifred's aunt, with whom Winifred was living when Bartley met her, there is no mention of any family member—no parents, brothers, sisters, grandparents of any of the characters. It is a modern present that the characters live in, and their individuality is so private that when Bartley's wife remarks that he doesn't remember "what he was really like when he was a boy," Bartley's teacher agrees, explaining, "he was never introspective" (7). In *Alexander's Bridge* boyhood has nothing to do with the communal life of a family, but rather is an internal thing, a matter of energy and imagination.

O Pioneers! is another matter altogether, Cather's first novel in her own voice, a breakthrough for which critics have offered various interpretations. She at last came to terms with her native Nebraska, some would have it; she finally wrote as a woman, others argue. What no one has noted, so far as I know, is that her breakthrough coincided with her choosing the family as her subject. With opening scenes depicting a dying homesteader's passing to his daughter responsibility for the family, Cather announced that ideas of an inherited family were central to her plot. John Bergson recognizes his father's intelligence in Alexandra, and though he would have preferred the likeness in one of his sons, "he had to accept the situation as it was, and to be thankful that there was one among his children to whom he could entrust the future of his family and the possibilities of his hard-won land" (24).

Immediately, then, Cather identifies the fundamental link between the family and property that she would explore for over a decade, in one way or another. By 1925 she specified that marriage and, implicitly, family follow "the laws of society, and they are based on property" (*The Professor's House* 63). The story of the Bergsons unfolds in a series of family discussions, each concerned directly (even exclusively) with property. In the first, the dying John Bergson places Alexandra in charge of his family and his land; in the second, Alexandra proposes that they buy more land; in the third, a family dinner party reverberates with jealousies and ambitions over objects coveted as "reassuring emblems of prosperity" (98); and in the last, Alexandra and her brothers quarrel over property rights. Settings symbolize changes in the family's values: children grouped first about John Bergson's bed and then about the kitchen table give way to a family Sunday dinner in Alexandra's company dining room, which the Hanover furniture dealer "had conscientiously done his best to make . . . look like his display window" (97). The last family meeting takes place against a backdrop of Alexandra's account book. As if an ironic reversal of John Bergson's entrusting to Alexandra responsibility for the family and the land, Lou and Oscar in the end define family responsibility by the most conventional assumptions: "The farms and all that comes out of them belongs to us as a family," Lou argues; "the property of a family really belongs to the men of the family, no matter about the title," Oscar adds (168–69).

While the family remains part of *O Pioneers!*, Alexandra's relationship to it and its importance to the novel change dramatically. Here, as elsewhere, Cather uses the family as a metaphor for social evolution and cultural change. Gender roles are suspended during the brief frontier period, then patriarchal values resume with the second, community period; the themes of the family and the land, so tightly intertwined in the opening of the novel, separate in the later, "Neighboring Fields" section. Alexandra remains with the land while her brothers marry and form their own families, in doing so becoming emblematic of conventional society with the most commercial sense of property. Some of the broadest humor in Cather's fiction occurs with her descriptions of these families, with Lou's blustering political threat to blow up Wall Street, his wife's mindless adaptation of women's fashions, and their concern over the purchase of a bathtub and the acquisition of a piano. In the end, the quarrel over property has divided the family, and Emil's death divides it further, so that Alexandra no longer sees her brothers.

Alexandra's alienation from her family signals one of the central concerns of Cather's subsequent fiction: how to reconcile the family as a social unit founded upon laws of property with the family as a personal unit founded upon ethics, morality, and feeling. Cather sidesteps the question in *O Pioneers!*, however, separating responsibility to the land from responsibility to family: "Suppose I do will my land to their children, what difference will that make?" asks Alexandra. "The land belongs to the future. . . . I might as well try to will the sunset over there to my brother's children" (307–08). Thus the novel ends with a long perspective by which, compared to the constancy of nature, concepts of property seem trivial.

When Cather depicted Alexandra's inheriting responsibility for her family, she might have been describing herself accepting the family as her subject. Surely, she made it central to her next novel, *The Song of the Lark*. In "Friends of Childhood," the novel's longest section, the family is a given, each of its members aware of its public face: Mr. Kronborg has a business-like regard for his family's keeping up appearances; Tillie is foolishly proud and willing to make "an exhibition of herself" (80); Anna preaches "consideration for father's position" (298); and Mrs. Kronborg keeps to herself her conviction that "people talked when they felt like it, and said what they chose, no matter how the minister's family conducted themselves" (159). The sense of the Kronborg's "family face" is heightened by Thea's painfully adolescent sensitivity to precisely that. "As a family, they somehow seemed a little ridiculous," Thea thinks: there are so many of them, for one thing; and she does wish her father would stop cheerily singing a Christmas carol as he marches at their head, the rest of them trooping along in the starlight (80). She thinks of them as "the family band" (302) and reflects that seeing them heading for Sunday school seemed like viewing a military drill.

Again, then, Cather identifies the family as a social unit with comic conventionality; but unlike the broad, almost cartoonish quality of Lou's and Oscar's families, the humor here is gentler, more human, and less socially emblematic. While Lou's and Oscar's families are satiric indictments of American ideas of prosperity, the Kronborgs suggest the comic dimensions of very ordinary human beings living lives we recognize. Not merely an inherited responsibility, the Kronborg family shapes the texture of Thea's childhood. It remains, however, something to escape from. I am hard-pressed to think of any scene in Cather's fiction up to this time in which the family is an ideal, nothing even remotely akin to Jim Burden's descriptions of the Cuzaks. Instead, in *The Song of the Lark* Cather gives particular attention to the idea that underneath the group life are other, private lives of individuals. With the acquisition of her own attic room, Thea begins "to live a double life. During the day, when the hours were full of tasks, she was one of the Kronborg children, but at night she was a different person" (73); her responsibility to that second self means that Thea eventually must leave her family and make her own way in the world.

The talented individual at odds with a conventional family is a common theme in literature. What distinguishes Cather's treatment of it in *The Song of the Lark* is the family's delicate balance between the requirements of the group and the needs of its individuals. More specifically, what distinguishes the Kronborg family is Mrs. Kronborg, Cather's fullest creation of a model (not ideal—that will be Ántonia) mother, one who respects the duality of the family: "Mrs. Kronborg let her children's minds alone. She did not pry into their thoughts or nag them. She respected them as individuals, and outside of the house they had a great deal of liberty. But their communal life was definitely ordered" (23). As she understands it, the function of the family is to provide basic social, communal order; its responsibility is to leave the private, inner lives of its individuals alone. Through Mrs. Kronborg, Cather describes a family strikingly similar to what sociologists have identified as "a traditional model," according to which "the proper performance of family roles was a matter of duty—carrying out tasks properly. If your child was clean and reasonably obedient, you had no cause to look further into his or her psyche" (Skolnick 310).

As in *O Pioneers!*, Cather describes distinct stages in the life of the family. Children grow up and discover themselves outside their families, as in the case of the talented Thea, who realizes that family members had always resented her and that their house, her refuge until then, has become hostile: "Her mother was all right, but her mother was a part of the family, and she was not. In the nature of things, her mother had to be on both sides. Thea felt that she had been betrayed" (301). As Alexandra Bergson had consoled herself by recalling larger obligations to the land, Thea recognizes "older and higher obligations" to art, as if in giving birth to herself as an artist she claims her place in another family—that of the cliff dwellers, from whose caves she is reborn, as if from the womb (383).

Thus families form and disband in their own life and death cycles, a painful inevitability that Cather depicts through the death of Thea's mother. Once the center of the family, then left alone after her children grew up and her husband died, Mrs. Kronborg while dying wanted one thing, "to see her daughter Thea," yet Thea "had to stay [in Germany]—or lose everything" (490–91). " 'Bringing up a family is not all it's cracked up to be,' said Mrs. Kronborg with a flicker of irony," as she read Thea's cablegram reporting that her performance had been well received. " 'I used to feel sorry that you had no family, doctor, but maybe you're as well off' " (492). As for Thea, she ends, as did Alexandra Bergson, successful in worldly terms but lonely; as the diva Kronborg, she has no personal life.

In a sense, *My Ántonia* begins where *The Song of the Lark* leaves off, for Jim Burden at the outset of the one novel is similar to Thea Kronborg at the conclusion of the other: middle-aged, successful in worldly terms, yet without family. The first of Cather's orphan souls seeking their kin, Jim Burden returns in memory to his childhood, then returns in fact to Ántonia, now the mother of a large family. With the final section telling of his homecoming, Cather creates the modern romantic American myth/ideal of the family: "a domain of ideal human relations—a utopia—that compensated for and was in contrast to the tedium, the impersonality, the harassment, the exploitation, the pretension, and the boredom of life in the outside world" (Orr 379–80). Contrasts between Jim and Ántonia, narrator and subject, are those that surround this myth of the family: the individual versus the family appears as progress versus continuity, modern versus primitive, male versus female, sentimental versus realistic, New World versus Old. Jim's nostalgia for his lost childhood, as for a lost golden age, is so fierce, his homecoming to Ántonia's family so golden, that only in retrospect do we remember the harsh details of Ántonia's life. In *My Ántonia* Cather describes what I would call an aesthetic idea of the family—a social unit organized around the creation of art from life.

As if refuting the sentimental potential of Jim Burden's image of the family as protected from change, in her next novels Cather writes of the effect of social change upon the family. Beginning with *One of Ours* and climaxing with *The Professor's House*, she explores the human consequences of such a shift. *One of Ours* tells of Claude Wheeler's search for "something splendid," beginning with his loneliness within the provincial family of his childhood and through his relationships with a series of would-be families: in the longing he feels toward the Erlichs, the pain of his sterile marriage to Enid, the sweetness of his sojourn with the Jouberts, the comradeship of men in his company, the satisfaction of his friendship with David Gerhardt. In *A Lost Lady* families are conspicuous by their absence, appearing only occasionally and then in ruptured forms. The Ogdens, for example, appear as a harshly satiric portrait of parents marketing a girl of marriageable age. The general absence of families reinforces the novel's general theme of a time that is out of joint, during which no family emerges that offers the possibility of renewal.

Up to this point Cather primarily defines the family in standard sociological terms, a social unit composed of persons living together in a household,
related by marriage and blood. *The Professor's House* tells of examining that
conception of the family, finding it inadequate, and seeking another. As she
does so often, Cather begins beyond the endings of standard plots. When
The Professor's House opens, St. Peter has accomplished conventional goals:
he married for love, reared children successfully, completed engaging creative
work, achieved public acclaim, and reaped financial reward. Quest plots of
romantic love and marriage, creative aspiration and achievement exist, then, as
a backdrop to St. Peter's story, which concerns the most basic quest of all—
that for a family. "The moving was over and done. Professor St. Peter was
alone in the dismantled house where he had lived ever since his marriage,
where he had worked out his career and brought up his two daughters"—
with her opening sentences Cather describes the "problem" or dilemma for
the novel, for the family St. Peter had formed with Lillian is as "dismantled"
as his house (11). In withdrawing from the family of his marriage, St. Peter
begins his search for an alternate, "real" family.

The opening introduces, too, the series of houses that will run through
the novel: the dismantled house where the St. Peters had reared their
children; their new house, in which St. Peter feels himself a foreigner; the
Norwegian manor house Rosamond and Louie are building, the abandoned
cliff dwellings Tom Outland discovers. All are symbolic of the family, and
all suggest emptiness, each in its own way. There is no authentic professor's
house at the outset, then, just as there is no authentic professor's family.
Indeed, there will be no actual house that is taken possession of in the sense
of inhabited and made a home; Godfrey St. Peter's quest takes him beyond
such ideas of property and possession.

The novel's three parts depict stages of St. Peter's quest: "The Family"
telling of falling away from modern families, "Tom Outland's Story" of
searching for "ancestors we can all claim," and "The Professor" of finding
kinship in a human community. "The Family" presents the classic life of
a family, begun with a marriage and shaped by the children that result from
it, ending with the departure of children, then repeating the pattern in a
younger generation. But St. Peter's family has a peculiarly American,
democratic form, a fictional depiction of Tocqueville's observations upon the
family as reflecting democratic assumptions of equality: it was formed by
individual affection, then shaped by money and class mobility. The result
is a series of bewildering metamorphoses concealed beneath the apparently
simple idea of the section's title, "The Family." There are the inevitable
changes brought with age: the adolescent Godfrey St. Peter becomes an adult,
then husband, father, and father-in-law; his daughters become wives and will
become mothers. These changes are complicated by shifting relations with
surrogate families—St. Peter's "foster-brothers," the Thierault boys (25);
his "children" born in his den of a study, his "splendid Spanish-adventurer
sons" (165); and most important, Tom Outland appearing in various roles:

for two years "almost a member of the [St. Peters'] family" (173), then St. Peter's younger self, Kathleen and Rosamond's older brother, Kathleen's beloved and Rosamond's fiance. Such changes may be natural enough; what makes them disturbing is that they are reshaping and transforming "the family" along purely economic lines. With the authority conferred by the money he has made marketing Outland's idea, Louie Marsellus has become the most vital force in the family. He has claimed Outland's fiance for his wife, Outland's idea for his product, Outland's name for his property; he would claim Outland himself, it would seem, thinking of him as a brother and posing with Outland's blanket draped about him as a dressing gown. But his conquests extend beyond Outland: Marsellus has become a surrogate lover to Lillian, and he is a would-be benefactor to the McGregors. As St. Peter recognizes when he alludes to James's *The American*, Marsellus is the American writ large, in whom energy, generosity, sympathy, compassion, and even love take the form of an irrepressible instinct for possession.

Thus a family originally formed on the basis of sentiment and ideas is reformed on the basis of marketplace values. Contrasts between past and present demonstrate the nature of that change. St. Peter recalls writing his *Spanish Adventurers in North America*, for example, by the ambition that sprang from the conception of an idea, "the difficulties attending such a project" (25), and the happiness of its harmonious design. As if in ironic echo of St. Peter's creativity, Louie Marsellus appropriates the language of art to describe the difficulties of building a country house, considering it *ambitious* because of its cost and *harmonious* because it is a Norwegian manor in style and set against a forest (albeit of Lake Michigan), then explaining its *flawless conception* in terms of wrought-iron door fittings (39–40).

As ideas of creative inspiration and execution are corrupted by a marketplace mentality, so relationships are corrupted. Again Cather uses appropriated language and displaced metaphor to write of the effect on the family. The most personal family discussions degenerate into discourses of profit and loss, and people as well as purchases are examined and compared, admired and envied: Kathleen remarks upon the cost of her sister's dress, Lillian discusses the extravagant expense of emeralds Louie has purchased for Rosamond, and Louie considers Lillian's distinction "priceless" (160). The reformation of the family by an economic order is verified by the observer, Professor Crane, who reminds St. Peter that he does profit from the Outland patent, "indirectly, if not directly. You cannot shut your eyes to the fact that this money, coming into your family, has strengthened your credit and your general security" (148).

The irony, of course, is that the "credit and general security" of St. Peter's family has been weakened in all but an economic sense. Indeed, Cather's description of changes in St. Peter's family provides a case study of changes in the American family, particularly of a historical shift from families based upon "moral order" (defined as "social units organized around principles of what is 'right' and . . . based on 'sentiments, morality, conscience' ") to those based upon "technical order" (defined as "social units organized around principles of 'mutual usefulness' and . . . based on 'necessity or expediency' " [Stannard 89–90]). It is, as Rosamond says with unintended irony, "only Louie's energy and technical knowledge that ever made Tom's discovery succeed commercially" (60).

Beginning his quest for kinship, St. Peter recalls the story of Tom Outland, Cather's purest orphan. Without birthdate or parents, Tom seeks families that belong "to this country, to the State, and to all the people . . . to boys like you and me, that have no other ancestors to inherit from" (242). Tom's friendship with Rodney Blake is the American surrogate family—parenting displaced into male friendship. Cather depicts it with great sensitivity: As Ántonia was a natural mother, Roddy was a natural father, and as Tom recognizes, "He ought to have had boys of his own to look after" (185–86). And as Ántonia's family was one version of the American utopian family, the "happy family" that Roddy, Tom, and the cook Henry form is its peculiarly Western version, a Garden of Eden without the distraction of women—and appropriately it ends with a snakebite. More basic, however, is Tom's recognition that a surrogate family inevitably falls short, that, as he says, "Nature's full of such substitutions, but they always seem to me sad, even in botany" (186).

Just as the substitute family Tom and Roddy form fails, so does Tom's attempt to claim a legacy by searching in ancient cliff dwellings, retrieving artifacts, and storing them in a museum. In one of the most commercial and yet generous gestures of the novel, Roddy Blake sells the artifacts and then deposits the money in an account for Tom's education. As a marketplace mentality corrupted St. Peter's family, so it corrupts Tom and Roddy's substitute family. Tom accuses Roddy of betraying their trust to "this country, to the State, and to all the people"; the mummy that Tom and Roddy named Mother Eve falls to the canyon depths; and Roddy leaves, never to be heard from again.

In the last section, St. Peter turns to the most elemental quest, possible when one is freed from the press of a domestic family. He now takes the time to think, "bringing up out of himself long-forgotten, unimportant memories of his early childhood," remembering his mother, his father, and his grandfather—"old Napoleon Godfrey, [who] used to go about lost in profound, continuous meditation, sometimes chuckling to himself. . . . There are only a few years, at the last, in which man can consider his estate" (266). The result of these meditations is a revolution, from one order of thought to another. When at the end of his life a man considers "his estate," he considers not the property he possesses but his human condition, and when St. Peter thinks of his house, he thinks neither of his old rented house nor of his newly purchased one, but instead of a house described in poetry, recalled from a volume on his mother's parlor table:

For thee a house was built
Ere thou wast born;
For thee a mould was made
Ere thou of woman camest. (272)

As it has throughout the novel, "house" symbolizes "family," and the revolution in St. Peter's conception of "house" symbolizes his more basic revolution in the meaning of family. St. Peter redefines his dilemma, for he realizes that falling out of love *is* the greatest misfortune—now understood in the broadest of terms: "Falling out, for him, seemed to mean falling out of all domestic and social relations, out of his place in the human family, indeed" (275). His discovery of his human family results from a death (overcome by gas, he falls unconscious in the attic study of his abandoned house) and rebirth (assisted by the sewing woman Augusta as a midwife, he is brought to consciousness). In recognizing the humanity of Augusta, he recognizes his place in the human family. And thus the novel ends, with St. Peter's having withdrawn from one family and discovered another in a sense of obligation toward humanity, "instinctive, escaping definition, but real" (281).

The Professor's House is a watershed book in Cather's depiction of the family, signaling a shift from thinking of it as a social unit of marriage and consanguinity to thinking of it as a philosophic and spiritual human community. As the terms of the family shift, so does the mode by which Cather treats it. Before *The Professor's House* Cather characteristically wrote of the family in a comic mode, most often to criticize social convention. With *The Professor's House* the family resonates with a tragic sense of individuals as the victims of fate, quietly working out their destinies. The flat characters of earlier novels have disappeared, replaced by Lillian, Rosamond, Kathleen, Scott, and Louie—all drawn with individuality that suggests their own stories, all caught within the net that circumstances and their affections have cast (here I am paraphrasing Cather's comments on the family, "Katherine Mansfield" 136).

o   o   o   o   o

Cather characteristically wrote about a theme until she was satisfied with it, then dropped it. Her theme of the modern American orphan's search for a personal or created family began with Jim Burden in *My Ántonia*, continued with Claude Wheeler in *One of Ours* and Niel Herbert in *A Lost Lady*, then climaxed with Tom Outland and Godfrey St. Peter, actual and metaphorical orphans in *The Professor's House*. After telling St. Peter's story of withdrawing from his family by marriage and finding kinship in a more abstract human family, Cather dropped the orphan figure from her fiction. In *My Mortal Enemy* she repeated her theme of characters turning from worldly emotional ties to spiritual ones, this time writing of marriage without children, of a couple who never formed a family. And in *Death Comes for the Archbishop* and *Shadows on the Rock*, Cather avoided families as social units, focusing instead upon a religious sense of community. In *Obscure Destinies* Cather again focused directly upon the human family, weaving together ideas she had identified with it over the previous thirty years and creating two of the finest stories in American literature.

In "Neighbour Rosicky" Cather took the point of view of a patriarch searching for that which he would bequeath to his children, not property he had acquired but wisdom to be retrieved by reflecting upon his life. During his youth Anton Rosicky "was trying to find what he wanted in life for himself; now he was trying to find what he wanted for his boys and why it was he so hungered to be sure they would be here, working this very land, after he was gone" (58). Thus the legal concerns of property, so much a part of *O Pioneers!* and *The Professor's House*, are a given in "Neighbour Rosicky," and Cather establishes at the outset that what Rosicky possesses is that rarest of things, a happy family. "My Lord, Rosicky, you are one of the few men I know who has a family he can get some comfort out of," his doctor observes, then continues: "Happy dispositions, never quarrel among themselves, and they treat you right" (6).

In recalling his past Rosicky provides a vehicle by which Cather reaffirms her long-standing ideas of a happy family: Rosicky married late, and "perhaps the fact that his own youth was well over before he began to have a family was one reason why Rosicky was so fond of his boys. He had almost a grandfather's indulgence for them" (33). United by friendship rather than passion, he and Mary agreed about the important things, and thus "life had gone well with them because, at bottom, they had the same ideas about life" (24). As always in Cather's fiction, culture and class figure in the shape of a family. Czech culture forms the texture of the Rosickys' lives, and a rise in class lies behind their content: Rosicky was the first from his family to own land, and Mary rose from rough farming people to a gentler way of life.

These are familiar ingredients in Cather's happy marriages, all reminiscent of the Cuzaks in *My Ántonia*. What makes "Neighbour Rosicky" different concerns its spiritual—even religious—dimensions. Rosicky's "special gift for loving" has a sacramental quality, and daughter-in-law Polly's choosing his family as hers becomes a secular version of revelation and salvation, depicted in the story's climax. After raking thistles from the field that lies between the home place and that of Rudolph and Polly (the setting and action are symbolic), Rosicky suffers a heart attack. Polly, seeing him bent in pain, runs to him crying "Lean on me, Father, hard! Don't be afraid. We can get to the house all right" (63). Spiritual meanings infuse the scene in the word *father* and in the awakenings or revelations that surround it: Polly reveals first her loving nature and then that she is with child, and she receives the blessing of Rosicky's love. Literary epiphany, spiritual conversion, religious revelation—whatever terms we use—the experience changes Polly's life: "Polly remembered that hour long afterwards; it had been like an awakening to her. It seemed to her that she had never learned so much about life from anything as from old Rosicky's hand. It brought her to herself; it communicated some direct and untranslatable message" (67).

Cather's finest work is, to my mind, "Old Mrs. Harris," the story of the Templeton family, who had moved from Tennessee to Skyline, Colorado, "a snappy little Western democracy" (*Obscure Destinies* 133). Cather tells their story through five points of view—that of a daughter (Vickie Templeton), a mother (Victoria Templeton), a grandmother (Mrs. Harris), a hired girl (Mandy), and a neighbor (Mrs. Rosen). As for the story's action, it is domestic, familiar, and simple: Mrs. Rosen brings a coffee cake to Mrs. Harris; a cat dies; the younger children have a circus; Vickie receives a university scholarship; Mrs. Templeton learns she is pregnant; Mr. Templeton leaves to visit his farm; and Mrs. Harris becomes ill, then dies. What distinguishes the Templetons is that they *are* so ordinary, and as such are the family Cather chose for the question the adolescent Vickie bitterly asks, "What were families for, anyway?" (186).

I wish to make three points in response to Vickie's question. This was the first time that Cather asked it, a quite different question from family concerns implicit in her other fiction: in *O Pioneers!* she had asked what might happen if a pioneer's daughter were placed in charge of his family and his land; in *The Song of the Lark*, how does a family shape the childhood that determines all that a person would ever be. In *My Ántonia* Cather asked what family a middle-aged person would choose to come home to; in *The Professor's House*, what happens when a person can no longer live with his family. And in "Neighbour Rosicky" she asked about the power of a father's love. Only in "Old Mrs. Harris" did Cather ask what are families for, anyway?

The second point I wish to make is that by having Vickie pose the question so directly, Cather invites her reader to answer it, to select an approach to the family, then to follow that approach through the story. So far as I can tell, "Old Mrs. Harris" responds to them all. Mrs. Rosen provides an outsider's view of the family as a social unit; Vickie, Victoria, and Mrs. Harris provide insight into three generations' experiences within a family; the relationship between Mr. Templeton with his wife and her mother invites gender interpretation; and Victoria invites discussion of mothering. The family's move from Tennessee to Colorado calls for historical and sociological interpretations; the interplay of points of view calls for Cather's theories of the group life that conceals the real life. I could go on, as could any reader. Yet after following each approach, we still would not answer Vickie's question. For—and this is my third point—in "Old Mrs. Harris" the family simply is life, in heightened (because more intimate) form.

I began this paper by saying that Cather's families refuse to be "fixed"— that as Cather moved from novel to novel, her idea of the family went through formations and transformations. I end by returning to the same point, but this time about specific families. For when Cather created her families, she created characters in their own right. We customarily identify Cather's fiction by individuals she created—Alexandra, Thea, Ántonia, and the rest, all of whom seem, sometimes, almost to walk off the page. Yet Cather created families that live as fully with their own reality—the Bergsons, the Kronborgs, the Cuzaks, the Harlings, the St. Peters, the Rosickys, the Templetons— families that we know almost as well as our own.

—University of Nebraska–Lincoln

BIBLIOGRAPHY

Cather, Willa. *Alexander's Bridge*. Lincoln: U of Nebraska P, 1977.
———. "Joseph and His Brothers." *Not Under Forty*. New York: Knopf, 1970. 96–122.
———. "Katherine Mansfield." *Not Under Forty*. 123–47.
———. *My Ántonia*. Boston: Houghton, Sentry ed., 1961.
———. "Neighbour Rosicky." *Obscure Destinies*. New York: Vintage, 1974. 3–71.
———. *O Pioneers!* Boston: Houghton, Sentry ed., 1962.
———. "Old Mrs. Harris." *Obscure Destinies*. 75–190.
———. *The Professor's House*. New York: Vintage, 1973.
———. *The Song of the Lark*. Boston: Houghton, 1943. Contains revisions made by Cather in 1937.
Orr, John B. "The Changing Family: A Social Ethical Perspective." *Changing Images of the Family*. Ed. Virginia Tufte and Barbara Myerhoff. New Haven: Yale UP, 1979. 377–88.
Skolnick, Arlene. "Public Images, Private Realities: The American Family in Popular Culture and Social Science." *Changing Images of the Family*. 297–315.
Stannard, David E. "Changes in the American Family: Fiction and Reality." *Changing Images of the Family*. 83–96.
Tocqueville, Alexis de. *Democracy in America*. Vol. 2. Ed. Phillips Bradley. New York: Vintage, 1945. See esp. Book III, chapter 1, "Influence of Democracy on the Family." 202–09.

Cather's Complex Tale of a Simple Man, "Neighbour Rosicky"

MERRILL M. SKAGGS

In "Neighbour Rosicky," one of her best short fictions, Willa Cather characteristically manages to establish plot, character, and theme in the compact scope of her opening sentence. The sentence reads, "When Doctor Burleigh told neighbour Rosicky he had a bad heart, Rosicky protested." We learn here that the story's central concern is a bad heart, that the heart belongs to a man named Rosicky whose neighborliness defines him, and that Rosicky protests the diagnosis, thereby providing an action for the narrative. The story, we are forewarned, will reveal how Rosicky prepares himself and others to cope with bad hearts, and to understand the nature of good ones. We spot in the phrase a *double entendre*. Thus the story begins with the deftly woven and double-stranded intricacies we anticipate in Cather's major work.

The modified name used as title, of course, calls a reader's attention emphatically to the major character. Cather never tired of using realistic names that supplied a wider suggestiveness. She also expected sophisticated readers to catch literary overtones within her texts. Often her names make an important statement about character, and Rosicky's—pronounced in Nebraska with the accent on the second syllable—is no exception. Pronounced as Cather learned it, *Rose-sick-y* suggests the famous Blake poem "The Sick Rose." That poem, in turn, supplies the given conditions of the story by summarizing Rosicky's physical predicament and his reasons for resistance to Doctor Burleigh:

> O Rose, thou art sick.
> The invisible worm
> That flies in the night
> In the howling storm
>
> Has found out thy bed
> Of crimson joy,
> And his dark secret love
> Does thy life destroy.

Rosicky is dying. Having heard the truth in the opening sentence, however, he sets out to prepare all who are important to him for the lives they will live without him. His first act is to put his house in order by making purchases that are of good enough quality to outlast him. His second is to purchase candy for his women to sweeten the moment when he must announce his bad news. The third is to prepare himself for his end by looking carefully, on his way home, at the graveyard in which he will be buried. As snow falls softly "upon all the living and the dead," Rosicky surveys the cemetery. Unlike James Joyce's sadder Gabriel Conroy in "The Dead," Rosicky finds the cemetery to be "snug and homelike, not cramped or mournful"—a good place to lie with "old neighbours . . . , most of them friends." Best of all, "it was a comfort to think that he would never have to go farther than the edge of his own hayfield." Rosicky concludes simply that in connection with his own death, "there was nothing to feel awkward or embarrassed about" (18, 19).

For several reasons, this story can be considered a *tour de force*. For one, it immediately suggests it will end with death, and thereafter keeps readers engrossed in spite of that threatening promise. For another, this consistently upbeat tale continues to hold an admiring public in a century that has associated value with ambiguous and darker shades of irony. A third reason, however, is that Cather creates in her character study of a simple man a story that is *itself* complex and multifaceted in form, without once undercutting a reader's admiration for Rosicky. The feat seems more astonishing the longer you look at it.

By its final sentence, the story has unequivocally established the fact that Rosicky's life has been "complete and beautiful." This life's final stages include a good, affectionate and hardworking wife, a family Rosicky can get some comfort out of, a farm unencumbered by debt, a neighborhood containing people who return his affection. His end appears to be deserved. Rosicky is a man with a gleam of amusement in his triangular eyes, a contented disposition, a gaily reflective quality, "city-bred" and delicate manners, and a clear (though by no means conventional) sense of what a man does and does not do. Significantly, he is known not to be a "pusher" but in fact is characterized by a willingness to indulge himself. He is as considerate of others as of himself. He does not envy and refuses to take hard times hard. He not only remembers his good times but also creates them for himself.

Rosicky seems to love women generally, and his wife Mary specifically. For Mary, he has become an extension of herself: "They had been shipmates on a rough voyage and had stood by each other in trying times. Life had gone well with them because, at bottom, they had the same ideas about life. They agreed, without discussion, as to what was most important and what was secondary" (24). They had agreed "not to hurry through life, not to be always skimping and saving." The key to Mary's enduring affection for Anton, however, is that "he had never touched her without gentleness" (24).

This capacity for loving women gently and well is hinted at when Rosicky goes to the general store. After his fateful doctor's appointment, he waits patiently to be attended by the pretty young clerk who always waits on him and with whom he flirts mildly, for their mutual enjoyment. The small incident is worth noting, especially since no small incidents are trivial in Cather's fiction. The Rosicky marriage holds up so well, we infer, because the husband, fifteen years older than his wife, has known women before her and has learned how to treat them in his youth. In the five happy years he spent in New York as a young man, we read, he was self-indulgent, enjoyed all his favorite pleasures, and never saved money, for "a good deal went to the girls" (27). He obviously learned enough to know that women appreciate receiving special attention. He learned some necessary cautions as well, and concluded, "the only things in his experience he had found terrifying and horrible [were] the look in the eyes of a dishonest and crafty man, of a scheming and rapacious woman" (59).

The delayed marriage shapes Rosicky's attitude to his whole family:

> Perhaps the fact that his own youth was well over before he began to have
> a family was one reason why Rosicky was so fond of his boys. He had almost
> a grandfather's indulgence for them. He had never had to worry about any
> of them—except, just now, a little about Rudolph. (33)

His son Rudolph is a problem partially because he and his wife Polly have married so young that they must do a lot of their life-learning on each other. Yet Rosicky's special sensitivity to women is nowhere better dramatized than in his interactions with his daughter-in-law. He accurately infers that Polly, a town girl, must be lonely and increasingly discontent as an isolated farm wife. So Rosicky tactfully coaches his son about how to keep her happy: "I don't want no trouble to start in Rudolph's family. When it starts, it ain't so easy to stop" (34). He suggests that Rudolph treat Polly as if they were courting, take her to town for a movie and an ice cream, and then he even provides the car and the money the outing requires, while he himself stays to clean up Polly's kitchen after supper. Rosicky knows how to give a treat and why treats are important. Because he is specially attentive, he first guesses that Polly is pregnant, before her husband or mother or mother-in-law know of it—intimate knowledge indeed. But, of course, the experienced capacity for such guesswork partially explains his own happy marriage.

As a member of a communal family, Rosicky enjoys his greatest triumphs. In that context he has also endured his most painful defeat. We are reminded very early that Rosicky has a past (21). That past includes so sore a spot that he has been able to reflect on it only in the last days of his life; for his two years in London were so great a misery that "his mind usually shrank from [it] even after all this while" (42). As a hungry, dirty, harassed, exploited London tailor's apprentice, Rosicky once betrayed a woman's trust in a way that makes him writhe. He tells of the debacle on his last Christmas Eve. The tale emerges as a gesture of trust and concern for Polly and Rudolph, who are experiencing hard times of their own. But the contrasting Christmas Eves thus juxtaposed become one set of the doubled holidays Cather uses as a structuring device.

When young Rosicky lived in London, he subsisted by working for a tailor and sleeping in a curtained-off corner of his employer's apartment. When Christmas approached, his employer's wife arranged a surprise for her household and on Christmas Eve hid a cooked goose under the box in Rosicky's corner; it was the safest place available in her hungry family's quarters. That night Rosicky, hungry himself, followed his nose, found the bird, and characteristically indulged in a small advance bite. He thereafter ended up eating at least half the bird. Distraught with guilt and dismay over his betrayal of trust, he then ran out to the street contemplating suicide. But, accidentally, he heard wealthy patrons talking in Czech as they emerged from a fine restaurant. He approached them and begged them as "fellow countrymen" to give him enough money to replace the goose. Their money not only saved Christmas but also paved the way for Rosicky to get to New York, and to eventual good fortune.

The first point of this episode is that Rosicky's bitterest memory involves his betrayal of an extended family community; for he knows "how hard dat poor woman save to buy dat goose, and how she get some neighbour to cook it dat got more fire, an' how she put it in my corner to keep it away from dem hungry children. . . . An' I know she put it in my corner because she trust me" (53–54). The second point is that he has enough faith left in fellow humans, even after he himself has played Judas, to throw himself, in emotional extremis, on the mercy of strangers. The third point is that it is the ladies of the group who rescue him, feed and comfort him, after which "both of dem ladies give me ten shillings" (55). Thus having sinned by the worst betrayal he can imagine, he finds forgiveness and plenty. Community is re-established and the next day "we all sit down an' eat all we can hold" (56).

Willa Cather had an affinity for doubling effects and used them regularly as part of her techniques to expand the implications of a story. With her Christmases past and present, she suggests both the best and the worst of both past and present. Rosicky tells of his past London memory because of his present gnawing concern for Rudolph and Polly. Yet both Christmases end happily, and Rudolph and Polly run home arm in arm to plan for the first familial New Year's Eve.

In Cather country one pair of doubles deserves another. In contrast to the winter's high holiday is the summer's, and the Fourth of July proves as significant for Rosicky's life as does Christmas. After five happy years in New York, Rosicky remembers sitting miserably on one Fourth, "tormented by a longing to run away" (30). He decides that the trouble with big cities was that "they built you in from the earth itself, cemented you away from any contact with the ground" (31). He resolves to get back to the land and eventually gets to Nebraska and to his own farm. On his second memorable Fourth of July, however, he confronts in Nebraska the worst disaster the land can supply. At this point, he is past running. What Rosicky does in this most dramatic adversity defines him.

In his second summer trial, a heat wave burns up all his crops in a few hours. In the literal heat of this disaster, with no retreat possible, Rosicky suggests fun and frolic. He kills two chickens for supper, spends the afternoon splashing with his sons in the horse tank, and then at sundown takes his family outside for a picnic; his reasoning—"No crop this year. . . . That's why we're havin' a picnic. We might as well enjoy what we got." His wife adds, "An' we enjoyed ourselves that year, poor as we was, an' our neighbours wasn't a bit better off for bein' miserable" (49).

While the two Christmases function to define Rosicky's response to familial and community bonds, his Fourth of July turning points appropriately become his personal Independence Days. In the first, he decides to relinquish one acceptable life in the city for another life near the earth. In the second, he decides when the earth fails him that he will rejoice and be glad. Thus he illustrates what makes him what he is: he loves himself, his family, his life, and his fun. Under the most adverse circumstances, "everything amused him" (28).

What makes "Neighbour Rosicky" great is that the story provides a new set of definitions. Rosicky himself, our definition of a good man, can be summarized best in the phrase he "had a special gift for loving people" (66). The good life is defined almost as succinctly: "You don't owe nobody, you got plenty to eat an' keep warm, an' plenty water to keep clean. When you got them, you can't have it very hard" (45). The good family is depicted as one that can share its pleasures in mutual concern and affection. And the keys to Rosicky's brand of good fortune are as simple: no envy (27); self-indulgence (27); and a "habit of looking interested" (4)—Cather's highest accolade. As a result of having these things, Rosicky can state as a simple fact, "We sleeps easy" (16). But Rosicky is important above all as a "neighbour." His obligations as a neighbor are not defined in this story by what he is rich enough to give; rather, Rosicky becomes the model neighbor because he has made himself a life in which "he had never had to take a cent from anyone in bitter need,—never had to look at the face of a woman become like a wolf's from struggle and famine" (61).

What does this story signify? First, its writer's courage to portray a loving man whole, and lovingly. But its significance also includes that writer's courage to affirm a new route to, or definition of, the American dream of success. With such an appealing definition, we can only hope the story eventually influences a national community.

—Drew University

BIBLIOGRAPHY

Cather, Willa. "Neighbour Rosicky." *Obscure Destinies*. New York: Knopf, 1932. 3–71.

"What Was It . . . ?":
The Secret of Family Accord in *One of Ours**

BLANCHE H. GELFANT

One of Ours has always troubled Willa Cather's critics, who have either dismissed the novel, disparaged it, or discussed its "deficiencies" within a generic framework that allowed them to formulate a "positive interpretation" (Rosowski, Murphy). Described variously as a war novel (Cooperman), a naturalistic novel (Murphy), a social satire (Stouck), or an Arthurian legend (Rosowski), it is either extraordinarily complex, conflating and transcending literary genres, or else inchoate—a troubled text seeking a form for its completion. Whether it deserved the scorn it received in its own time from Edmund Wilson and H. L. Mencken—and, notoriously, from Ernest Hemingway—may now be as difficult to determine as whether it deserved its acclaim (which undoubtedly had exacerbated the scorn). As we know, the novel won Cather a Pulitzer Prize; it also brought her public recognition and money, thus marking a "turning point" in her career (Woodress 334). Though by now critics have discerned involuted sexual themes and gender crossings within its apparently straightforward story (Cooperman, Butler, Rosowski), as well as delicate ironies and allusions (Stouck, Rosowski), they have not refuted a standing claim that it is one of Cather's least interesting novels (Randall 160). Contemporary readers might find the claim tenuous as their interest is engaged by unexpected aesthetic lapses in *One of Ours* that localize its aporias and ambiguities rather than its failures. Interest need not produce a "positive" interpretation of *One of Ours*, but a plausible one that recontextualizes its troubling "deficiencies"— its theatrically staged scenes; bemused characterizations; uncertain, even indefensible, moral tone; and its inert language, inexplicable in a writer renowned for her style.

For all its deficiencies, I read *One of Ours* with disquieting fascination. To me it seems a novel in crisis—not because it is portraying a historically cataclysmic event, but because it cannot reconcile itself to its own representations of ruin and waste. In showing that war—rather than peace, prosperity,

*This essay was presented at the BYU symposium and then appeared in the Cather issue (Spring 1990) of *Modern Fiction Studies*, copyright 1990, by Purdue Research Foundation, West Lafayette, Indiana 47907: Reprinted with permission.

and family life—realized the highest ideals of humanity it attributed a value to violence that it was also impelled to deny, for war led its hero to death, though he believed it was giving him his life. In the novel, Claude Wheeler dies young, happy, and deluded. Because he dies before he can be undeceived about the lies in which he has been enmeshed, he is spared disillusionment. The reader, however, is not, nor are the novel's survivors, those who fought in the war and those, like Claude's mother, who prayed at home. Trying to balance the truth of ideals against the lies necessary to sustain them, Cather created a suspenseful tension in her text, one that holds in almost breathless arrest the moment of crisis when desire for life—for its beauty and passion—turns into a demand for death. Claude must die or relinquish his ideals; but life devoid of ideals does not seem to him worth living. Nevertheless, the rationalizations for his untimely death seem, at least to me, unconscionable. Perhaps they seemed so to Cather, grieving over the cousin killed in the battlefields of France, the cousin whose life she recapitulated in *One of Ours* and whose death she may have been trying to redeem.

One of Ours creates a continuum between personal desire and public life that is markedly uncharacteristic of Cather's fiction, which usually ignores or satirizes historic events shaping the world of its characters. Though social crises woven into a novel's plots might influence a character's destiny, they usually remained peripheral. In *A Lost Lady*, for example, bad times and bank failures affected but did not determine Marian Forrester's fate, just as earlier in *O Pioneers!* a changing economic climate, like the vagarious weather, had been only peripheral to Alexandra Bergson's life. In *One of Ours* the catastrophic war that sweeps through the Western world is central to the plot; it is a crucial determining event that concentrates, though it does not resolve, the novel's disparate and elusive themes. Irresolution, at once disconcerting and interesting, will characterize Cather's subsequent novels which, like *One of Ours*, distance their protagonists from the pioneer period Cather had earlier romanticized. In *The Professor's House*, *Lucy Gayheart*, and *My Mortal Enemy*, idealistically yearning protagonists, old and young, cannot find in their depleted world an object commensurate to their desires.[1] This failure marks the limits of Cather's willingness to imagine possibilities, I believe, rather than an inevitable constriction placed upon her characters by circumstance. When Cather was writing about a heroic past in *My Ántonia* and *O Pioneers!*, or about art in *The Song of the Lark*, she had subjects commensurate with her governing ideals of aspiration, struggle, and creativity. These ideals, she believed, imbued human history with purpose and individual life with meaning. Having set *One of Ours* in the wasteland (as she saw it) of a modern mechanized America—and of a world at war—she faced a formidable problem: how to represent ideals for which she could not find realization except in the death of a hero. The inevitability of this death, which in real life had sorrowed her, brought her art to an impasse that her language reflects. It became vague and strangely inert, as if it were trying to obscure the implications of the moral crisis it had created. Usually considered the novel's deficiency, this vagueness may be purposeful, if not deliberate—a strategy of evasion. Cather could have been incisive, I believe, but she chose to pretend that her language was clear, as though words like *something* and *it* that she needed to leave opaque were translucent. Otherwise, she would have to confront her own devastating nihilism.

In *One of Ours*, *something* signifies a desire for which the character, and the text, cannot find an object; and it appears in questions of definition that confound its hero. What was *it*?, Claude Wheeler asks again and again, implying that if he knew what *it* was, he might reach for *something* he longed for but could not visualize or express. At a moment in the novel that seems to me critical both to Claude's struggle to have *something* splendid in life and Cather's effort to represent the object of Claude's desire, the question "What was *it*?" refers to family life. The specific occasion for the question is Claude's visit to the home of his friends, the Erlichs, a family that he believes has fathomed the secret of "how to live." "What was it," he asks with almost comic bafflement, "that made life seem so much more interesting and attractive here than elsewhere?" (72). "Interesting and attractive" fail to express the heightening of emotions—the charged sense of alertness and accord—that Claude feels in the Erlichs' living room. Nor do the words define qualities in the Erlich family that have evoked his happiness. Seeking to define an amorphous *it*—"What was it . . . ?"—Claude raises a key question complicated by the ambiguity in his—and Cather's—language. *Was* life more interesting and attractive at the Erlichs' or, as the text specifies, did it only *seem* so to Claude, a culturally deprived young man, hungry for "something splendid" he could not define?[2] To him, a room overflowing with "interesting and hard-used" books and cheered with music, pictures on the wall, a bust of Byron, a "big Chinese bowl full of cigarettes" (at home he smoked in the cowshed) seemed splendid; and the constant, contrapuntal, and often controversial flow of family conversation seemed highly romantic, "like talk in a play" (36–37). Having been brought up to a "poisonous reticence" based upon fear, he is astonished at the Erlichs' "fertility of phrase" (38). For the first time he hears a family engage frankly in argument, creating an exciting clash of opinions, a challenge without threat because it is based upon a mutual trust that encourages discussion, difference, disagreement, fun— everything lacking in his own home. But free unafraid speech provides only a clue to the secret of family happiness. Claude remains puzzled as much as enlightened by the Erlichs, for even as he romanticizes them, he knows he is seeing nothing extraordinary: "There was nothing wonderful about this room; a lot of books, a lamp . . . comfortable, hard-used furniture, some people whose lives were in no way remarkable" (72–73, original ellipsis).

Claude's difficulty in defining family accord reflects a crisis that, I am arguing, Cather created and then held in arrest as beyond the powers of representation to resolve. She wanted to express desire for which she could find neither object or words; and she wanted to describe family happiness, a subject novelists usually shun—perhaps because, as Tolstoy has memorably written, happy families resemble each other. Conformity does not create the literary interest of conflict. Nor does it suggest an appealing fulfillment of desire. Moreover, the secret of family happiness, as social theorists indicate, has remained tantalizingly elusive, difficult if not impossible to fathom.[3] Cather was thus compounding her problems in *One of Ours* as she concentrated her hero's desires upon the family, a source of unhappiness in many of her novels, as she believed it was in life.[4] She wanted to make Claude's desire for happiness, for life, immediate and palpable, but she had to mediate it through the family and through words that are necessarily compromised and proximate, suggestive of feelings that she was discovering words could not articulate.[5] Thus, when Claude tries to describe his "sense" of happiness in the Erlich home he resorts to generalities about its "atmosphere": "warm and gracious," "charged with general enthusiasms," and "ennobled by romantic friendships," "new interests," and new "ideas."

Enthusiasms, interests, ideas, friendship, nobility, and romance are, arguably, empty signifiers, evocative but insubstantial general terms waiting to be imbued with specific meanings. When Cather tried to dramatize the terms, she produced, surprisingly, a series of parties: a costume party attended by the oldest brother Henry; an anniversary party given for Mrs. Erlich's cousin, a celebrated singer; signs of party-going left by the dress-tie draped rakishly about Byron's bust. Parties at the Erlichs' are pleasurable because the brothers are "nice boys"—opinionated and argumentative, but not meanly teasing like Mr. Wheeler or envious like Claude's brother Bayliss. They are "cordial" hosts, "easy and agreeable," and as their lolling attitudes suggest, relaxed. Their personalities suit occasions marked by hospitality, companionship, and conversation, by a sharing of time and talk that would return as memories of friendship. Obviously, the secret of a happy family includes gregariousness and a gift for celebration: "The Erlich family loved anniversaries, birthdays, occasions" (51). Mrs. Erlich imbues occasions with "excitement and seriousness," so that baking German Christmas cakes involves "holy traditions" and ingredients "she did not name: the fragrance of old friendships, the glow of early memories, belief in wonder-working rhymes and songs" (41). Old friendships, memories, and music—when these magical ingredients of Cather's art are centered within the home, as in the Erlichs' living room and kitchen, they open life to the romantic possibility of "something splendid."

Even the "rambling" structure of the Erlichs' house suggests openness. The lawn is "unfenced," and a glass door and three full-length windows make the facade unformidable and revealing, as though the house harbored no secrets and was open to passers-by whom the Erlichs could see and invite. People enter and leave easily, and outsiders like Claude quickly become insiders. Inside the house, the living room chairs are "easy," the furniture "comfortable" though "hard-used," the long divan and couches suitable for lounging. The engraving of Napoleon is "rare" but not more highly valued than a portrait of Mrs. Erlich's great-grandfather, one of Napoleon's officers.

Books, piano, guitar, pictures, and a bust of libertine Byron (not Milton, Mrs. Wheeler's choice) suggest an openness to ideas and art alien to Claude's intellectually impoverished home. Even "the heavy brass paper-knife" is suggestive because it had "in its time . . . cut so many interesting pages" (73). In a happy home things are important because they evoke a shared past, are part of one's memories of home, one's feelings. Later, as he packs away things he had selected with "care" and "pride" for his own home, Claude sees that objects are "mournful and ugly" when stripped of "the feeling that had made them precious" (192). Still later, in a secluded French garden, he hears a young woman express what "he [had] been trying to say . . . ever since he was born": that things have little meaning in themselves—"only the feeling matters" (329). Things assume importance to a family because their presence stabilizes the feelings associated with them; things that have remained the same in a home imply a continuity of emotions that time cannot erode.[6] When Claude returned to the Erlichs after a long winter, "he told himself that he must not hope to find things the same. But they were the same" (72)—the mother at the piano playing a Mendelssohn song, the brothers "lounging and smoking," one on his way to a party, and all still engaged in argument.

Claude is seeing the Erlichs as though they are figures on a stage acting out a fantasy of family life. Not only has he set them within the play of his desire: he describes them as a family always at play—going to plays and concerts, talking like characters in a play, re-playing college football games. His friendship with Julius Erlich was initiated at a practice session in which Claude had made a dramatic touchdown; the next season he takes Mrs. Erlich to a football game. As ordinary and innocuous as such play seems, the football games meld into a metaphor of war as a game that young men play.[7] So it seems to an old clergyman who stands watching young soldiers board a troopship that will carry Claude and countless others like him to the battlefields of France: the "howling swarm of brown arms and hats and faces looked like nothing but a crowd of American boys going to a football game somewhere" (235). In a quick series of metaphoric transpositions, these football fans become religious devotees "making vows to a bronze image in the sea" (the Statue of Liberty). They become also sacrificial figures "sailing away to die for an idea, a sentiment, for the mere sound of a phrase . . . (235, original ellipsis). Cather's language subverts the metaphors of play and of human sacrifice as it reduces an ideal to mere sound and then, through ellipsis, to silence. The rapid diminution casts a retrospective doubt upon the play that engaged the Erlichs, play that may have had ominous implications to which Claude was as oblivious as the clergyman watching the soldiers sailing off to war.

While Claude perceives family happiness as a form of play, he sees his own family as characteristically at work. When Mrs. Wheeler cooks, she is not making little cakes fragrant with memories, or dumplings and Wiener-Schnitzel, but breads, pies, and roasting chickens, "plain fare" that feeds a horde of dirty and relentlessly hungry farmers. She does not play romantic lieder or sing plaintive German folk songs in her leisure moments; she reads the Bible and *Paradise Lost*, and withdraws into somber "religious meditation" as an escape from husband, home, and family. While Claude labors on the farm, his brother Bayliss works in town, making money and, like his father, amassing property. The Erlichs, Claude discovers, are poor, though some brothers are "in business" and all are "industrious" and enterprising enough to buy a company they hope to develop (Claude's brother Bayliss gleefully predicts failure). Julius Erlich has gone abroad to study in hopes of becoming a professor.

Thus youthful hope and ambition seem to Claude as integral to the Erlichs' home as the book-lined walls of its living room. But when he tries to penetrate the secret of hope, of its inexhaustibility as well as its elusiveness (since he feels he has lost hope), he remains mystified and floundering. For he is reaching towards the ineffable—an undescribable state of ecstatic supernal being symbolized for him, as for many Cather characters, by the stars. Looking up at stars "whose light travels through space for hundreds of years before it reaches the earth and the human eye" (292), Claude can believe in a lofty eternal order for which the vicissitudes of mundane life make him yearn. Star-gazing suits the romantic disposition, but it distances the gazer from immediate reality and from the object of desire; both begin to seem mysteriously elusive. All Claude can say is that he yearns for "life," and when he feels a sense of accord with the Erlichs, he thinks that they are imbuing him with their capacity for life. The secret of their happiness was, simply but mysteriously, that they "knew how to live."

Knowing how to live implies knowing how to spend money, an odd but significant equation that allows the text to care about materialistic things (like the furnishings of a pleasingly comfortable home) while it criticizes the materialism represented by the Wheeler men. Claude sees that the Erlichs "spent their money on themselves, instead of on machines" (39), rejecting materialism and self-martyrdom, the incongruous combination that determined his parents' depleting way of life.[8] Later, thinking of the money his brother Ralph had dissipated on obsolete or useless machines, Claude calculates that "Julius could go abroad and study for his doctor's degree, and live on less than Ralph wasted every year" (89). Images of waste, associated usually with the basement of the Wheeler house—as though it were its foundational secret—haunt Claude because he believes that his possibilities as a person have also been wasted, and the fault lies with his family. As a boy he "felt bitterly about the way in which he had been brought up" (30). Years later, his bitterness is unabated, though he has escaped the farm and is stationed in France as a lieutenant in the United States Army. Still, he considers himself a product of neglect, someone who should have been cared for but was left unfinished, incomplete as a person and unpolished—"a wooden thing amongst living people" (355–56).

The passivity that underlies his image of himself as inchoate, waiting to be shaped into a man, is reflected in the passive mode of his complaint that he had not been taught anything by his family (355). Yet somehow he has learned that the family should mold a child, nurture him, open him to the possibilities of happiness, even exultation.[9] Claude glimpses his potential self not in his father or his brothers but in strangers—Julius Erlich, a fellow student in Nebraska, and David Gerhardt, a fellow soldier in France. In the Erlich's living room Claude sees brothers he would wish his own, vociferous but "agreeable" companions who contrast with the brothers at home he finds "wholly antipathetic" (16). As in her other novels, Cather quickly establishes an opposition between narrow-minded materialists and characters of sensitivity, passion, and romantic desire. Her sensitive protagonists typically yearn for escape from an uncongenial family. For Claude, however, escape seems impossible.[10] When Mr. Wheeler announces a plan that ends Claude's college career and ties him to the farm, the unhappy young hero feels as though "a trap had been sprung on him" (60)—a trap set by his father, approved by his brothers, and silently accepted by his mother.

The essence of a trap is inescapability, as Claude knows, so that protest seems to him futile, indeed unthinkable. Without realizing how much his family has taught him, Claude has learned from his mother the lesson of resignation and silence, a way of behaving helplessly that constitutes a subtle complicity in his own victimization. Martyrdom is not unappealing to Claude, as his college thesis on Joan of Arc reveals; and by silently acquiescing to his father's arbitrary wishes, he sacrifices his own dreams and becomes a martyr without courage or cause. Submission unsanctified by the religious faith that supports his mother leaves him plaintive and aggrieved. Claude knows how to be unhappy; only when he meets the Erlichs does he see the possibilities of happiness and harmony, of accord, within a family setting. Their fierce but friendly differences enliven Claude, stimulating him to question and think, even to argue. Including him in their bantering disagreements, they shatter his habitual reticence so that he begins to examine and explain his views, rather than merely state them in the laconic style of the Wheeler men.

Mrs. Erlich, in particular, appeals to Claude, for though she has serious responsibilities as the "head" of a large family,[11] she remains hopeful, almost childlike, in her air of happy expectancy: "Her hazel-colored eyes peered expectantly over her nose-glasses, always watching to see things turn out wonderfully well; always looking for some good German fairy in the cupboard or the cake-box, or in the steaming vapor of wash-day" (37). Thus, she transforms daily house chores into pleasures, cooking and laundering into possibilities of fairy-tale delight. Mrs. Erlich sees even in clod-like Claude bright possibilities. On his first visit, as she unstintingly promised him friendship, "she peered up at him with that quaintly hopeful expression, as if—as if even he might turn out wonderfully well! Certainly, nobody had ever looked at him like that before" (39). Expecting its young people to turn out well, a happy family inspires them with self-confidence; it nurtures their hopes and promise. While the Erlichs share Julius's dream of a professorship, to Claude an exalted position, the Wheelers humble their son, so that he "didn't question that the lowest state of mind was the truest, and that the less a man thought of himself, the more likely he was to be correct" (42).

Claude responds to Mrs. Erlich's air of expectancy because it suits his romantic disposition. *One of Ours* begins with Claude waking joyously to the promise of the day. The "broad, smiling face" of the sun beams at him, the waters of Lovely Creek wind "playfully," and the circus is in town: "It was a fine day to go to the circus at Frankfort, a fine day to do anything: the sort of day that must, somehow, turn out well" (3–4). But Claude's expectations are dashed when his father insists he cart grimy farmhands and smelly cowhides to town in the dirty mule-wagon he hated. Mr. Wheeler's order is deliberate: he knows that Claude has washed the car to drive to Frankfort and that he dislikes the mules, the men, the mistreated hides. Whatever his motives in thwarting his son, whether a desire to humiliate him, perhaps for his own good, or an irresistible impulse to bully, Mr. Wheeler maintains a jovial front, demeaning Claude with his jokes and showing him that whatever he plans—to attend a circus or a college—nothing will turn out wonderfully well.

Mrs. Wheeler reinforces this dismal fate by her silence and resignation. Though she is described as sympathetic to her son, indeed sharing his sensitivities, she never defends him, never supports his views, never suggests he should pursue his desires. In her heart, she considers him, as does his wife Enid, wrong-minded and lost because he lacks religious faith. Ironically, because he shares his mother's faith in "miracle" and accepts her piety as a model for women, he discounts his apprehensions about his impending marriage. Telling himself that "women ought to be religious" (111), he tries to dispel his misgivings over Enid's "preoccupations" with "foreign missions," "holy thoughts," and the "incredible" things his mother believed. Just as "his mother believed in the miraculous effects of conversion," Claude "believed in the transforming power of marriage" (151–52); however, even the willfully blind Mrs. Wheeler can foresee that Enid will change for the worst, becoming more like her own rigidly self-centered, eccentric mother. Nevertheless, Mrs. Wheeler remains silent about Enid, conspiring with her husband and with Enid's father to maintain the "lies" about marriage that had trapped them all and will in time ensnare her hapless son. Since, presumably, she understands and loves Claude more than anyone else, Mrs. Wheeler seems most culpable in failing to warn him about the distorted views of women and marriage that she had not undeliberately inspired and that she knows are now determining his mistaken decision.

More to her discredit than her silence, however, is her impassioned advocacy of the war in Europe, which influences Claude to enlist in the army, a crucial and irreversible decision that leads to his untimely death. Mrs. Wheeler prepares Claude for this fate by sharing and yet undermining his belief in a righteous outcome to the war. Telling him that Paris will be saved, despite its wickedness, because its churches were full of women and children praying for their country, she evokes silent assent to her question: "And you believe these prayers will accomplish nothing, son?" (146). Claude and his mother have already disagreed over the efficacy of faith, and if faith rather than works is to save an imperilled civilization, then France seems to him doomed. Choosing action over prayer, Claude enlists in the army, in this way, ironically, fulfilling rather than denying the desire of his parents, both of whom support the war, each for a different reason. Mrs. Wheeler wants prayer and righteousness (as she sees it) to prevail, and Mr. Wheeler wants wheat prices to rise. Congratulating himself on having at long last found his way to the trenches, Claude thinks that his mother "would not have him anywhere else" (310)—a thought intended to show the bond between mother and son, but showing instead the destructive possibilities inherent in family accord based upon shared delusions.

Once on his way to war, Claude finds danger, like happiness, enlivening. The desire for safety seems to him, ultimately, a quest for death, while risk produces energy, life. His perverse view is validated by his dramatic rebirth on his way to combat. The foreign landscape provides an image of his restoration: he sees himself in the cottonwood trees rustling beautifully in the countryside, trees ruthlessly cut down in Frankfort and now newly alive in France. He had been reborn aboard the *Anchises*, a ship named after a wise instructive father, such as Claude had never known: "Here on the *Anchises* he seemed to begin where childhood had left off. The ugly hiatus between had closed up. Years of his life were blotted out in the fog" (259). Though loss of one's past can be a sign of sickness, as Claude realizes when he encounters an amnesiac soldier, for him forgetting, and especially forgetting his wife, seems therapeutic. On the *Anchises*, he considered himself "the least married man on the boat" (260), and the thought made him happy. Now in the countryside of France, temporarily removed from danger, his new life blossoms, and on his twenty-fifth birthday, he feels he is "beginning over again" (349), this time in a family in which he belongs.

In his fellow lieutenant David Gerhardt, "some one whom he could admire" (350), Claude finally finds the brother he has been seeking, as well as the other self he might have become. Claude sees Gerhardt as a "finished product," his potential fully realized: Gerhardt is "young" but "experienced"; "distinguished," "handsome," and "sensitive"; "kindly" though "reserved"; and he is an accomplished violinist. Unlike Claude, Gerhardt speaks French fluently and can transcend cultural differences through his art. Like Claude, he has imbued war with idealistic possibilities and death with the promise of rebirth: "I've sometimes wondered," he says, "whether the young men of our time had to die to bring a new idea into the world . . . something Olympian" (348, original ellipsis). His words recall Claude's solitary musings on life as a process of "ruin and new birth," the "ugly things in the past" making possible "beautiful ones on the horizon" (333). At the end of the novel, these (undefined) beautiful things have disappeared from view, and Claude's simplistic rationale for destruction has been subverted by the pessimism of Cather's epilogue.

For Claude, the value of his brief interlude in France is a gratifying feeling of family accord. He owes this mainly to Gerhardt, who takes him into the homes of French people where he is set at ease with himself and the world. With Mlle. de Courcy, he feels "completely understood, . . . no longer a stranger" (332); and at the Jouberts', he awakens with a "sense of physical well-being" (297) he had not felt since that morning on the farm when the smiling sun had promised a happiness postponed until now. Accepted by Gerhardt, feted by "Papa Joubert," who celebrates his birth-day with a fine old Burgundy, pampered by Madame Joubert, Claude sheds the "nervous tension in which he had lived for years." Life "had after all turned out well for him," he thinks (349), especially at moments of heightened sensuous pleasure created by the comforts of his surrogate homes. In Mlle. de Courcy's "wooden chamber," he luxuriates in the pleasantness of hot water and scented soap, the odor of cleanness (327); and at the Jouberts', he feels "perfect bliss" at the warmth of lavender-scented sheets, "so dry, so clean, so beloved" (343). With this elderly couple, Claude seems to regress to an idyllic stage of childhood when his devoted Mahailey had a fragrant breakfast waiting for him on warm summer mornings. Alone in the Jouberts' bedroom, he momentarily forgets the presence of kindly Papa Joubert and, as though he were once again with his mother and Mahailey, he thinks happily, "It was good to lie again in a house that was cared for by women" (297). Perhaps this is his deepest dream of family happiness, a regression to childhood spent with doting mothers whose destructiveness the child cannot possibly foresee.[12]

Paradoxically, the lessons Claude has learned from the mothers of two utterly different families, his own and the Erlichs', coalesce in the short incandescent interval of happiness that precedes his death. Enjoying a "period of happy 'youth,' about which his old friend Mrs. Erlich used to talk" (349), he learns to live, the lesson of a surrogate mother who had "taught him so much about life" (41). Then he dies, satisfying in a terrible way his mother's dream of his salvation. In the brief epilogue that returns the novel to the Nebraska farm, "two old women," Mrs. Wheeler and faithful, dim-witted Mahailey, agree that Claude's death is a felicitous fate. Mercifully, Mrs. Wheeler thinks, death has saved her son from "some horrible suffering, some horrible end" (390). Mahailey's vision of Claude transported to heaven seems almost a travesty of Mrs. Wheeler's dismal consolation that he has been spared an inevitable and unbearable disillusionment. His mother knows that Claude "died believing his own country better than it is, and France better than any country can ever be. And those were beautiful beliefs to die with" (390). They are the beliefs she had fostered in him and to which she had assented, and now, piously, but for a mother shockingly, she assents to his death: "Perhaps it was as well to see that vision, and then to see no more" (390). Mrs. Wheeler's lugubrious musings at the end mystify her appropriation of her son both during his life and in his death. In her self-righteousness she had assumed that she knew what was best for him when he was on the farm, the "faith" he denied; now she judges according to her view of death, overlooking Claude's fervent desire "to live."

At the end of *One of Ours*, the Wheeler farm is a place of mourning, and even if Claude had lived to return to the homes he had fled, his father's and his own, he would have found only despair—not because of postwar disillusionment, as his mother would like to believe, but more likely, because of his mother, his father, his brothers, his wife. A happy family is always someone else's for Claude, as it is for many other Cather characters who feel misplaced in their own homes or have no homes because they are orphans. Jim Burden's sublime experience of happiness in *My Ántonia*, perhaps the most famous passage in all of Cather's writings, occurs in the garden of his grandmother. In *A Lost Lady*, motherless Niel Herbert feels an exquisite sense of happiness in the bedroom of a lovely neighbor. Both orphaned children learn to expect happiness in a home not their own, and as adults both find such homes. Niel returns to the Forresters for a brief but intensely satisfying vigil, and Jim projects a future with the Cuzaks, a family whose felicitous accord may be his idealized projection. In *The Professor's House*, orphaned Tom Outland finds a surrogate family in the St. Peters, and Godfrey St. Peter gains not only a son but also his own "original self." Cather's variations on the theme of substitute families are ingenious and almost obsessive, tracing through all her works. In *Shadows on the Rock*, for instance, poor fatherless Jacques Gaux is bathed, fed, and instructed by little Cécile Auclair, a surrogate (child) mother. And in "Old Mrs. Harris," young Vickie Templeton finds in her neighbors' living room a quiet privacy in which to dream of the future, while her neighbor, the childless Mrs. Rosen, envies the domestic happiness she sees created in the Templetons' crowded home by busy, noisy children. Even a minor figure like old Mrs. Lee in *O Pioneers!* escapes to a surrogate family, enjoying "liberty" and "her own language" in Alexandra Bergson's house, where she sees only happy accord even though tragedy is imminent. Of all of Cather's circulating characters, each grasping moments of happiness with someone else's family, Claude Wheeler is the most ominous, for he discovers the family he seeks in the muddy trenches of France. There, with the "brave" and "wonderful" men who are his soul-brothers, he finds life worth living, only to die (383). As it turns out, his innocent pursuit of the secret of family accord in a home other than his own has led him ultimately to a foreign land and a landscape of death. This end to his quest seems to me invidious, though Cather tried to justify it with a mother's benediction. But the blessing that Mrs. Wheeler sees in Claude's death represents a moral bankruptcy in Cather's characters, in the families she created, and in the war she romanticized even in her condemnation. It may represent also her failure to find at home something she had been seeking.

According to all accounts of her life, Cather had enjoyed being in homes other than her own from the time she was a child riding her pony out to distant farms where she could visit with immigrant families whose stories widened her vision of the world and provided material for her art. As we know, she fashioned the Erlichs after the Westermann family of Lincoln (significantly killing off the father); she had been happy in their easygoing, gregarious, and intellectually exciting home.[13] Later in Pittsburgh she was happy in the McClung home, where she found, through her friendship with Isabel McClung, an acceptance of herself as a person and a promising writer that may have been crucial to her career. The dynamics of Cather's personal needs remain mysterious, even though recent biographies attempt to understand what the elusive "it" was that impelled her in the directions she took.[14] Her attachment to her family, like her love of the prairies of her childhood, seems undeniable—as does her need to distance herself from both.

Perhaps a necessary distance imbued the family of others with romance; distance permitted imaginative projection, whereas intimacy produced realistic knowledge. In *One of Ours*, Claude imagines the "world" in which Gerhardt must have lived as "a more or less rose-coloured world" that allowed him to belong "over here"—the "here" that for countless young men from midwestern farms was romantically far away and inaccessible, "over there." Claude may be correct when he says that David Gerhardt never knew "the hard moulds and crusts," the "prisons" from which men like Claude could escape only because of an unforeseen event as cataclysmic as war; but David Hochstein, upon whom Cather based her character, came from a family that had seen hardships and injustices beyond Claude's naively unpolitical imagination. In her autobiography, *Living My Life*, Emma Goldman tells of the tragic aftermath of her nephew Hochstein's death, a death that his mother, unlike Mrs. Wheeler, found irreconcilable and could not survive. Goldman's description of her bereaved sister suggests a different epilogue to *One of Ours*, one that would condemn a mother like Mrs. Wheeler for preferring death over disillusionment for her son: "Emaciated to the bone, she was a bent old woman, moving with lifeless steps. Her face was shrunken and ashy, unutterable despair in her hollow eyes" (2: 695).[15] In *One of Ours*, Cather had linked pacifism to narrow-mindedness and greed; the character most despicable to Claude, his brother Bayliss, is unpredictably and for ignominious reasons against the war. For Emma Goldman, pacifism represented an ideal that would challenge any idealization of war and death as an affirmation of life, Claude's final vision: "The sound of the guns had from the first been pleasant to him, had given him a feeling of confidence and safety; tonight he knew why. What they said was, that men could still die for an idea; and would burn all they had made to keep their dreams. . . . Ideals were . . . sources of power among men" (357). Claude Wheeler acquires the power to kill and be killed. David Gerhardt sees his precious violin smashed and accepts destruction as an omen of his fate. His music plays on only in the machines Cather deplored in the novel; and silence, a secret of unhappy families, prevails.

One of Ours is a troublingly nihilistic text in Willa Cather's canon. It describes a quest for an undescribable *something* that ends with *nothing*. At the end of the novel, a war that had dazzled the imagination of its characters and promised to make "something splendid" out of their narrow lives, is condemned by Claude's pious mother who had most glorified it: "nothing . . . has come of it at all but evil" (389). This collapse of *something* into *nothing* signifies more, I believe, than Cather's disillusionment with a war that would disillusion a generation. It signifies also an impasse in her art that, in restrospect, seems inevitable. To avoid this impasse, she would have had to write the same novel again and again—and perhaps fundamentally (like all novelists) she did—or she would have had to accommodate her art to a world crisis she could not conscionably ignore. Having chosen to place her character against the background of war, she thoroughly displaced the idealism inextricable from her art. She affirmed the idealism through a character who found in war the happiness he had been seeking, but she denied the reality of this happiness by affirming also the appropriateness of her hero's death. Indeed, after *One of Ours*, Cather seemed set upon killing off young idealist characters, Tom Outland and Lucy Gayheart, for example; or else she had a young idealistic character like Niel Herbert wish others dead, since death seemed the only way of forfending a terrible realization that the splendid *something* life seemed to promise was illusory and would in time turn to nothing, an eventuality that in another troubling novel, *My Mortal Enemy*, a character lives on to see and show her young disciple.

One of Ours is a courageous novel, perhaps unintentionally, because it pursues the implications of its hero's quest for family happiness. It reached a crisis when it showed this happiness fulfilled by life—and death—in an institution as coercively totalitarian as the army. This displacement of vital family life from the hero's home, to the living room of others, and ultimately to the battlefield of France makes *One of Ours* the least comforting of Willa Cather's novels. It is not, however, her least important or least interesting. For *One of Ours* does reveal a secret—not of what it is that makes family life "interesting and attractive," but of what it was that Willa Cather kept seeking to discover and could not. Her continued quest may be the secret of her art.

—Dartmouth College

NOTES

1. One of Cather's desires was to thematize desire itself, which she considered the source of artistic creativity. In *The Professor's House* Godfrey St. Peter says explicitly, "Desire is creation, is the magical element in that process" (29). St. Peter differentiates art from nature by defining art as the human process of shaping material through selection and arrangement: "The hand, fastidious and bold, which selected and placed—it was that which made the difference. In Nature there is no selection" (75). In *O Pioneers!* Alexandra Bergson is a creative artist because she shapes a "wild land" into a landscape of wheat fields and fruit orchards. Since Cather viewed art as a shaping rather than a substance, the material of art could be the historian's documents, the singer's body and breath, or the land of a still unsettled country, as well as the sculptor's clay.

2. Cather's reiteration of *something* suggests either an inability to define or a certainty of meaning so secure that *something* requires no definition since its referent, however vague, can be immediately intuited. In an interview of 1922, Cather frequently resorted to the word *something* in describing her meetings with David Hochstein, the prototype for her character David Gerhardt. Hochstein, she says, had "found *something*" in army camp life that "he had vaguely felt the lack of all his life"—something "difficult to explain": " 'For me [Hochstein reportedly said] there's *something* in that life just as it is; *something* I've always wanted'. . . . He didn't say what that *something* was, perhaps he couldn't have said." Perhaps Cather also could not have said what she meant by *something,* a word she uses again when she declares Hochstein's statements "mean *something* . . . *something* very revolutionary. . . . I would give a good deal to know what it was." Ironically, Cather comes closest to defining Hochstein's "something" when her memory seems to fail: "I don't remember just what he said; but those of us who were with him understood clearly that what he liked, what he got *something* out of, was his relation to other young men." In this last affirmative conversation, Hochstein seems "very different" from his former dejected self: "*Something* keen and penetrating and confident had come back into his face." Presumably, it is this confident Hochstein who "had been blown to pieces by a shell in the Argonne Forest." Cather's interview, published originally in the *New York Herald* of 24 December 1922, is reproduced by Sergeant (174–80; emphasis added).

3. As R. D. Laing noted when he was conducting his iconoclastic study of families, "the more smoothly they function, the more difficult they are to study" (86). Indeed, modern studies of "strong families" seem vapid when compared with studies in the decline, destructiveness, and "death" of the family. Contrast Stinnett and DeFrain's *Secrets of Strong Families* with Cooper, Pogrebin, or Gordon. Cather's happiest families are those of immigrants, large pioneer families like the Cuzaks of *My Ántonia* and the Rosickys of "Neighbour Rosicky" (essentially the same), who are shaping a country out of wild land to bequeath to their children. These families envision the future of the West as continuous with its past. *One of Ours* says explictly, however, "there was no West . . . any more" (104). Characters who had opened the West for settlement, like Captain Forrester in *A Lost Lady,* and those who transformed its

wild land into prosperous farms, like Alexandra Bergson in *O Pioneers!*, were Cather's heroic figures. Ironically, their efforts helped create the historical discontinuity Cather deplored, for once the railroads made the far prairies accessible (and preempted much of the free land) and enterprising farmers expanded their holdings, the age of the pioneer was over.

4. In a frequently quoted statement from her essay on Katherine Mansfield, Cather warned that appearances of family harmony concealed an "anguish" inseparable from the "sweetness" of close human relationships; family affections wove a net that could ensnare sensitive individuals. "One realizes," she wrote, "that human relationships are the tragic necessity of human life; that they can never be wholly satisfactory" (*On Writing* 109–10). Discord between a married couple could lead to violence in Cather's fiction. In *My Ántonia*, a comically horrific conflict between Mr. and Mrs. Cutter ends in murder and suicide; and an obvious incompatability between Mr. and Mrs. Shimerda contributes to his suicide. Even marriages that begin in love may end badly—if not in violence (the Shabatas in *O Pioneers!*), then in disharmony (the St. Peters in *The Professor's House* and the Henshawes in *My Mortal Enemy*).

5. On Cather's ambivalence towards language as the romantic writer's medium, see Gelfant 117–43.

6. Bennett quotes Cather as saying: "A house can never be beautiful until it has been lived in for a long time. . . . The beauty lies in the associations that cluster around it, the way in which the house has fitted itself to the people" (146). Such associations enhance the Forresters' house in *A Lost Lady*—a house Niel Herbert had loved as a boy and as an adult finds still "beautiful" because its furnishings are the same: "comfortable," "old," and "good." "No other house could take the place of this one in his life" (142), Niel thinks, unconsciously recapitulating his boyhood prediction "that he would probably never be in so nice a place again" (28). In its swift foreclosure of the future, which must bring change, the prediction is ominous. In *The Professor's House*, Cather elaborates on the ugliness and inconvenience of the house the St. Peter family is leaving, but the professor stays on because his crowded little study offers escape from the "drama of domestic life" (26) that interferes with his private inner drama. This interior life requires a "falling out of all domestic and social relations, out of his place in the human family" (275), an "isolation" ultimately indistinguishable from death.

7. Fussell discusses the widespread references to football in writings about World War I (27).

8. How families spend their money provides a clue to harmony or discord. Disagreements over money in *The Professor's House* reveal Godfrey St. Peter's alienation from his family. In *My Mortal Enemy*, lack of money destroys marital love, or so Myra Henshawe believes, though her husband does not share her view. The Rosickys in "Neighbour Rosicky" care more about each other than about money— a view congenial to the Erlichs as a happy family. Thus, Mr. Rosicky agrees with his wife when she says, "I'd rather put some colour into my children's faces than put money into the bank" (*Obscure Destinies* 24–25).

9. Claude believes his family should have taught him how to be happy, but modern sociologists see the family performing diverse and sometimes contradictory educative functions. Because these functions change in response to historical changes, the family resists definition as a stable, definable entity. Even at any given historical period it cannot be restricted either in its educative functions or in its identity, as Elshtain points out in designating the family "a concept, a living reality, a troubled social institution, a metaphor, a nightmare of repressive constraint, and a dream of infinite possibility" (6). Cather's attempt to define an ideal of happy family life locates one site among many of her resistance to historical changes she equated with decline. In *One of Ours* she implies that happy families represent an ideal untouched by time, but she passes the responsibility for defining this ideal to an inarticulate character who lacks critical insight into his expectations. Claude's undefinable expectations may be less impossible to realize than those listed by Pogrebin, who states that "the family is where each of us learns how to become a human being. . . . It is where we learn love, communication, trust, sharing, a sense of humor, a value system, and the control and expression of anger and of sexuality. It is where we experience the consequences of our actions, the limits of egoism, and the pleasures of pleasing others" (30–31).

10. The desire for escape impels mature characters like Godfrey St. Peter and Clement Sebastian, as well as young aspiring artists like Thea Kronberg. Claude shares the desire for "something splendid" that leads Thea Kronberg to leave home in *The Song of the Lark*, but unlike her, he lacks both genius and support (financial and moral). In *Lucy Gayheart*, young Lucy is an accompanist, not a great singer like Thea, but she is talented enough to earn a living and independence from her family.

11. Perhaps one secret of the Erlich's accord is the absence of a father. To Claude, the fatherless family seems exhilaratingly free. No authoritarian figure silences the mother or dominates the sons, as in Claude's home; no parental differences divide the children. The divisiveness in Claude's home may be rooted in Mr. Wheeler's attraction to a prim school principal "because she was so different" from him (9). Different as individuals (though both are New Englanders), Claude's mother and father also represent different views of the family. Evangeline Wheeler personifies a nineteenth-century ideal of the Christian family, while Nat Wheeler represents a twentieth-century economic family. See Scott and Wishy for descriptions of modern families as contrasted with traditional Christian families. When Mr. Wheeler leaves home to manage a ranch in Colorado, mother and son temporarily enjoy a happy intimacy. As though she were sewing a trousseau, Mrs. Wheeler makes dresses out of material Claude chooses: "It's almost like being a bride, keeping house for just you, Claude," she says to him coquettishly (69). Since she behaves like a bride with Claude, he feels "disloyal to her" when he is "so happy with Mrs. Erlich" (74); nevertheless, he "couldn't resist occasionally dropping in at the Erlichs' . . . [when] the boys were away, and he could have Mrs. Erlich to himself" (41). The erotic possibilities in these mother–son relationships become explicit when Mrs. Erlich's cousin proposes Claude as a husband for Mrs. Erlich: "Such things have happened, and will happen again" (54). Thus the absence of a father in Cather's families removes both divisiveness and prohibition against sexual play. Even in an apparently happy family

like the Harlings in *My Ántonia*, the presence of the father is inhibiting (he forbids Ántonia to go to dances), and his absence permits gaiety, noise, and easy social encounters with the appealing Mrs. Harling.

12. Rosowski believes that "Claude is most himself when he is most domestic," that is, creating a home of his own, as he does briefly in the trenches with Gerhardt (111–12). However, the amenities of "home" in Claude's dugout have been created by former occupants; as in Claude's previous surrogate homes, the comforts he now enjoys have been prepared by others and are waiting for him. *One of Ours* may upset "gender conventions," as Rosowski claims, not because Claude is domestic, but rather because he is, as she points out, "most content when lost in the conventionally female and passive dream that marriage will bring happiness . . . and most miserable—and violent—when doing what is expected of him as a man" (111). On Claude's quest for "virility-through-violence," see Cooperman (129–37). Cooperman's introductory chapters provide an illuminating historical and literary context for *One of Ours* as a war novel—though Cather denied that she was writing in this genre.

13. See the description of the Westermann family and other prototypes for Cather's characters in Woodress (82, 326). Bennett's description of Julia Miner suggests to me that Cather's childhood neighbor, the prototype for Mrs. Harling in *My Ántonia*, may have provided some of Mrs. Erlich's characteristics (65). An early account of Cather's sources for *One of Ours* is given by Lewis (117–23). Lewis says that a "strong feeling of kinship and sympathy" existed between Cather and the young cousin who was her prototype for Claude Wheeler (117), a cryptic statement that does not define the basis or nature of the kinship. Rosowski discusses resemblances between Wagner's Parsifal and Claude, and between Tennyson's Geraint and Enid and Cather's Claude and his Enid (95–113). Fussell has described an iconography developed in British literature about World War I that can be traced through *One of Ours*, not only images of mud and trenches but also pastoral settings and homoerotic bathing scenes. Butler concludes that Claude has repressed feelings of sexual attraction to David Gerhardt.

14. Throughout her biography on Cather, O'Brien has defined gender as a formative force in Cather's life as a woman and a writer.

15. When David Hochstein died in 1918, a month before the armistice, Goldman was serving a two-year jail sentence for her pacifist views.

BIBLIOGRAPHY

Bennett, Mildred. *The World of Willa Cather*. New York: Dodd, 1951.

Butler, Ronald. "Sexual Imagery in Willa Cather's *One of Ours*." Presented as a paper to the Western Literature Association in October 1983 at St. Paul, Minn.

Cather, Willa. "Katherine Mansfield." *Willa Cather on Writing*. New York: Knopf, 1942. 107–20.

———. *A Lost Lady*. New York: Vintage, 1972.

———. *Lucy Gayheart*. New York: Vintage, 1976.

_____. *My Ántonia*. Boston: Houghton, Sentry ed., 1961.

_____. *My Mortal Enemy*. New York: Knopf, 1926.

_____. *Not Under Forty*. New York: Knopf, 1936.

_____. *O Pioneers!* New York: Penguin, 1989.

_____. *Obscure Destinies*. New York: Vintage, 1974.

_____. *One of Ours*. New York: Vintage, 1971.

_____. *The Professor's House*. New York: Vintage, 1973.

_____. *The Song of the Lark*. Lincoln: U of Nebraska P, Bison, 1978.

Cooper, David. *The Death of the Family*. New York: Random, 1970.

Cooperman, Stanley. *World War I and the American Novel*. Baltimore: Johns Hopkins UP, 1967. 129–37.

Elshtain, Jean Bethke. "Preface: Political Theory Rediscovers the Family." *The Family in Political Thought*. Ed. Jean Bethke Elshtain. Amherst: U of Massachusetts P, 1982.

Fussell, Paul. *The Great War and Modern Memory*. New York: Oxford UP, 1975.

Gelfant, Blanche H. "Movement and Melody: The Disembodiment of Lucy Gayheart." *Women Writing in America: Voices in Collage*. Hanover, N.H.: UP of New England, 1984. 116–43.

Goldman, Emma. *Living My Life*. Vol. 2. New York: Dover, 1970.

Gordon, Linda. *Heroes of Their Own Lives: The Politics and History of Family Violence in Boston*. New York: Viking, 1988.

Laing, R. D. *The Politics of the Family and Other Essays*. New York: Random, 1971.

Lewis, Edith. *Willa Cather Living: A Personal Record*. New York: Knopf, 1953.

Mencken, H. L. "Portrait of an American Citizen." *Smart Set* 69. 2 (October 1922): 140–42.

Murphy, John J. "*One of Ours* as American Naturalism." *Great Plains Quarterly* 2 (Fall 1982): 232–38.

O'Brien, Sharon. *Willa Cather: The Emerging Voice*. New York: Oxford UP, 1987.

Pogrebin, Letty Cottin. *Family Politics: Love and Power on an Intimate Frontier*. New York: McGraw, 1983.

Randall, John. *The Landscape and the Looking Glass: Willa Cather's Search for Value*. Boston: Houghton, 1960. 160–74.

Rosowski, Susan J. *The Voyage Perilous: Willa Cather's Romanticism*. Lincoln: U of Nebraska P, 1986. 95–113.

Scott, Donald, and Bernard Wishy, eds. *America's Families: A Documentary History*. New York: Harper, 1982.

Sergeant, Elizabeth. *Willa Cather: A Memoir*. Philadelphia: Lippincott, 1953.

Stinnett, Nick, and John DeFrain. *Secrets of Strong Families*. Boston: Little, 1985.

Stouck, David. *Willa Cather's Imagination*. Lincoln: U of Nebraska P, 1975. 82–96.

Wilson, Edmund. *The Shores of Light: A Literary Chronicle of the Twenties and Thirties*. New York: Farrar, 1952.

Woodress, James. *Willa Cather: A Literary Life*. Lincoln: U of Nebraska P, 1987. 323–34.

Fragmented Families, Fragmented Lives
in "Paul's Case," *My Ántonia*, and *A Lost Lady*

MELLANEE KVASNICKA

Having herself come from a large, active family, Cather understood the intimate ties that bind. But she harbored no illusions about families. Homes and the families who dwelt in them could also be cruel and oppressive. Characters love, live in, despise, leave, and return to their families. The strength of Cather's fictional family units usually depends upon a central figure at the helm—Mrs. Harling, Neighbor Rosicky, Ántonia Cuzak. The families that fail are frequently those fragmented by the death of a parent, emotional desertion, or lack of communication. When this fragmentation occurs, the results are often alienation, loss of identity, or spiritual paralysis. In life as in literature we are able to point with satisfaction to close, loving families and read their successes in the lives of the people who live in them; or we can recognize in other families their failure to provide what is needed to survive happily. Sociologists, social workers, and teachers all recognize the connection between family units and the human beings who come from them. "Paul's Case," *My Ántonia*, and *A Lost Lady* demonstrate the dire consequences of physically and emotionally fragmented families.

In "Paul's Case," the fragmentation of the home and family is painfully obvious. Paul's mother is dead, a woman Paul "could not remember" (189). The only trace of her is the sampler she stitched that hangs over his bed, a "Feed My Lambs," ironically descriptive of Paul as emotionally and spiritually starved. The house on Cordelia Street, far from being the sanctuary we romantically envision as home, is a despicable place, physically ugly and emotionally sterile: "The nearer he approached the house, the more absolutely unequal Paul felt to the sight of it all; his ugly sleeping chamber; the cold bath-room with the grimy zinc tub, the cracked mirror, the dripping spiggots" (190). It is desperately empty, inhabited only by a father who demands explanations his son cannot give.

Paul lacks an emotionally satisfying relationship with his father, who has little or no understanding of his son. The man is not deliberately cruel; he is simply insensitive, a hardheaded realist; his solution to Paul's problem is to take him out of high school and make him get a job. Hanging over Paul's bed are portraits of George Washington and John Calvin, hardly attractive role models to a young man who finds great pleasure in the sensuous life of the theater and Carnegie Hall. Paul's father also holds up as an example for his wayward son a dull young businessman from Cordelia Street who was a trifle "dissipated" in his youth but who settled down by "marrying the first woman whom he could persuade to share his fortune" (194). Paul sees only a drudge in the young man, an example to be avoided. It is no wonder that to Paul the idea of marriage and family life is singularly unsatisfying. It is also no surprise that he invents an emotional world far more satisfying than the reality of his home and vanished family.

Because his own life is so fragmented, Paul needs desperately to escape to where he can feel "a sudden zest of life." In the picture gallery at Carnegie Hall, he "sat down before a blue Rico and lost himself" (185), and at the first sound of the music, he is transfixed, transported far beyond Cordelia Street and Pittsburgh to an ideal state of warmth and acceptance and love. It isn't that Paul appreciates or even understands the art and music; they seem to fill an emotional void, to take him away to forgetfulness. Paul's fantasies are far different from his life, and there is a pathetic unreality in his imaginary exploits. When he hears the German soloist, he is entranced, and Cather tells us, significantly, that she was "by no means in her first youth, and the mother of many children; but she wore a satin gown and a tiara, and she had that indefinable air of achievement" (187).

Interpersonal relationships are nonexistent for Paul, except in his dream life. His arrogance antagonizes his teachers. His revulsion at being touched by his English instructor suggests the spiritual and emotional desert in which he dwells. Having rebuffed the people he does know, he seeks to make contact with those who are truly strangers. In this he is predictably unsuccessful; particularly in his relationships with women he is awkward and unrealistic. In fact, the women of the stock company were "vastly amused when some of Paul's stories reached them. . . . They were hard-working women, most of them supporting indolent husbands or brothers, and they laughed rather bitterly at having stirred the boy to such fervid and florid inventions" (199).

When Paul's theft is discovered, the minister implies that the boy's "motherless" state has led to such tragedy. Indeed, the most poignant transformation from fragmented reality to idealized dream of family occurs when he registers at the Waldorf: "He registered from Washington; said his mother and father had been abroad, and that he had come down to await the arrival of their steamer" (200). His pathetic attempt to create a family he does not have suggests how critical for him is this loss. Paul's search for acceptance ends with his death, the ultimate isolation. His suicide does not shock us; it only confirms what his life has suggested, that he has no emotional center, that neither his past nor his present anchors him in reality.

If Paul offers us a case study of adolescence gone wrong, in Jim Burden we see the effects of the fragmented family on an entire life. Jim Burden is always without the traditional family structure. When he is ten, he is sent to Nebraska by his Virginia relatives to live with his grandparents. We never see his parents at all; we only know that he has lost them both within a year.

This loss is partially remedied by his caring grandparents, but they cannot take the place of the real parents he has left behind. After Jim and Ántonia hear the story of the Russian wolves, Jim reveals his loneliness by dreaming of wolves traveling across a landscape that looks "something like Nebraska and something like Virginia" (61). The Virginia landscape and, by association, the people who inhabited it continue to haunt Jim in unexpected ways. When Blind d'Arnault comes to town, his Southern accent and background cause Jim to remark of him, "It was the happiest face I had seen since I left Virginia" (184).

After the move to Black Hawk, Jim quickly outgrows his grandparents and in a typically adolescent way refers to them as "the old people" and sneaks out in defiance of their ban on his dancing at the club. Feeling very much alone, he prowls the winter-dead streets looking for companionship. Unable to find it elsewhere, he seeks solace with the Harlings. He is hungry for warmth, and his nostalgic descriptions of the lively goings-on at the house next door are poignant reminders of the emptiness he deeply feels. Jim is much more content, more complete with this surrogate family than with his own. When Mr. Harling is at home, Jim says, "I did not go in, but turned and walked home by the long way, through the street, wondering what book I should read as I sat down with the two old people" (175).

In Jim's case, such fragmentation leads to uncertainty about the future course of his life. Passivity shows itself in the decisions others make for him; it is assumed he will go away to college, where, Ántonia says, he must "make something of himself" (224); Gaston Cleric presses Jim to continue his education in Boston because, as he says, "You won't do anything here now. You should either quit school and go to work, or change your college and begin again in earnest. You won't recover yourself while you are playing about with this handsome Norwegian" (289).

Like Paul's, Jim's relationships with women are somewhat strained. In his adolescence he champions the hired girls, half falling in love with them, most probably antagonizing the other young people in Black Hawk. When he goes away to school, he seems to fall in love with Lena. On a particularly romantic evening, he takes her to see (what else?) *Camille*. Moved by a second-rate production, they walk home together in the aftermath of a lilac-scented spring shower, protected by Mrs. Harling's graduation-gift umbrella. The past and home are very near. Ironically, Lena wants no part of marriage or family, for as she remembers, home is "a place where there were always too many children, a cross man and work piling up around a sick woman" (291).

It is with Ántonia, not Lena, that Jim's deepest feelings lie. Returning for a visit after the birth of her child he tells her, "I'd have liked to have you for a sweetheart, or a wife, or my mother or my sister—anything that a woman can be to a man" (321). Obviously these feelings are very complicated, and it is not until twenty years later that he begins to understand that what has kept him enchanted is what she stands for: the past and the family, two elements critical in Jim's development. The past is everywhere in the novel's final book—in the violin, the names of Ántonia's children, the photographs, the food, the native tongue. But Ántonia's family is everywhere as well; it is large and close: as Jim says, "In the group about Ántonia I was conscious of a kind of physical harmony. They leaned this way and that, and were not afraid to touch each other" (349). This is what Jim has sought and missed; this is what he so curiously has been unable to attain. It is fitting that on the first night of Jim's visit, Ántonia's husband is absent, for Jim becomes for a moment a kind of father at the center of the family. We are reminded of those warm evenings in the Harling home. We can almost hear the longing in his voice.

But in spite of the nostalgic tone of Book V, there are darker undercurrents. We know that Jim's wife is nothing like Ántonia or Lena; in fact, she is nothing like Jim. As Cather tells us in the Introduction, "She is handsome, energetic, executive, but to me she seems unimpressionable and temperamentally incapable of enthusiasm. Her husband's quiet tastes irritate her. . . . She has her own fortune and lives her own life. For some reason she wishes to remain Mrs. James Burden." Here, then, is Jim Burden— successful, wealthy, educated, but childless and seemingly longing most for family. His life remains fragmented; consequently he still lives much in the past, strangely unfulfilled, looking forward to hunting trips with another man's sons. It is particularly moving when he concludes, "Whatever we had missed, we possessed together the precious, the incommunicable past" (372), for it seems clear the losses are primarily Jim's. He has no real home, only the memories of the past. Whatever Ántonia may have lost, it does not define the person she has become. Jim, however, is defined, sadly, by unfulfillment, a longing to belong.

The effects of a fragmented family take a most curious turn in the character of Niel Herbert in *A Lost Lady*. Niel, like Paul and Jim, is missing a parent. Because his widowed father is as ineffectual in parenting as he is in business, Niel is entrusted to the kindly care of his slatternly cousin Sadie. Like Paul, Niel feels a sense of shame in his home: "Home was not a pleasant place to go to; a frail eggshell set off on the edge of the prairie where people of no consequence lived" (29). Niel's home on the outskirts of town reinforces his peripheral position in Sweet Water society: we are told, "Except for the fact that he was Judge Pommeroy's nephew, Niel would have been one of the boys to whom Mrs. Forrester merely nodded brightly as she passed" (29). When Niel breaks his arm, however, he gets a first glimpse into that society. The lovely woman herself cares for him, in a beautiful room "cool and dusky and quiet. At his house everything was horrid when one was sick. . . . The little boy was thinking he would probably never be in so nice a place again" (28).

Niel never again sees Marian Forrester in quite the same way, and having glimpsed home and family and social order, it is not surprising that he deserts the chaos of his own home situation. When Niel's father loses his business, he goes to Denver, leaving Niel in the welcome custody of his uncle. When his real family is gone (Cather never mentions Niel's father again), Niel is at last admitted into the family that for him has reality. The Forrester place becomes the home he loves, despite his own quarters, where he lived with "monastic severity, glad to be rid of his cousin and her inconsequential housewifery, [resolving] to remain a bachelor, like his uncle" (33). The Forresters are to Niel the parents he has never really had. From the captain he learns the meaning of honesty, integrity, and loyalty. The lessons he learns from Mrs. Forrester are more complex. Like a child who sees his mother as the most beautiful woman in the world, Niel sees Marian Forrester as civilization personified, in her observance of the rituals and graces of home. When Niel is in her company, he has an amazing sense of acceptance, of belonging:

> Niel, who had been so content with a bachelor's life, and who had made up his mind that he would never live in a place that was under the control of women, found himself becoming attached to the comforts of a well-conducted house; to the pleasure of the table, to the soft chairs and soft lights and agreeable human voices at the Forresters. (69)

But Niel's place in the Forrester family is not without its difficulties. Marian's infidelity betrays his trust in marriage and home and family—all of which have come to be central to his identity. The revelation that she is a human being with flaws and faults is a devastating one. Niel had idealized this family and now finds it difficult to accept reality. It falls to the captain to let Niel know that he is aware of his wife's indiscretions and to suggest that in families human beings are always forgiven. As surrogate son, Niel ultimately finds himself assuming responsibility for the care of the Forresters. After the captain's second stroke and his wife's debilitating collapse, Niel stays out of school to keep a kind of vigil in the old place: "He liked being alone with the old things that had seemed so beautiful to him in his childhood" (142). We are reminded of Jim Burden, who was most at home in someone else's house. At the dinner party after the captain's death, Niel has occasion to become the "head of the family," as Jim Burden was briefly during his visit to the Cuzaks. Not only does Niel carve the ducks as the captain had done but he also assumes the captain's role of recalling the past. Unlike the captain, however, he finds it difficult to forgive Mrs. Forrester. When he sees her with Ivy Peters, he is totally disillusioned. His emotional maturity has been impeded by his detachment from any conventional family.

Later, when Niel has grown to a deeper understanding of himself and his past, he has greater charity: "He came to be glad she had had a hand in breaking him in to life" (171). Years afterward when Niel hears of Mrs. Forrester's death, his nostalgia is reminiscent of Jim Burden's at the beginning of *My Ántonia*. He is apparently a man of some wealth and position, a man whose job takes him away from his office, a man whose own family, if indeed there is one, is never mentioned.

Clearly for Paul and Jim and Niel, the fragmentation of the traditional family and home has had important implications. Paul is crippled by lack of security, Jim seeks to complement his own life through another man's family, and Niel is unable to deal effectively with disappointment and disillusionment. All three have difficulty forming close relationships with people their own ages. Perhaps most significantly, none seems to have created a family of his own. Each has experienced an acute sense of being outside the circle. Fragmentation by death or emotional or physical isolation has produced adults whose lives are colored by memories of what they have missed.

—South High School, Omaha

BIBLIOGRAPHY

Cather, Willa. *A Lost Lady.* New York: Vintage, 1972.
_____. *My Ántonia.* Boston: Houghton, Sentry ed., 1961.
_____. "Paul's Case." *Youth and the Bright Medusa.* New York: Vintage, 1975. 181–212.

The Deeper Role of Gender Conflict in *The Professor's House*

STEPHEN L. TANNER

The professor's house has been thoroughly searched. It is as though search warrants had been issued wholesale. The attic study has been exhaustively examined for clues. The dress forms in particular have been subjected to minute laboratory analysis by a variety of forensic experts. Even the garden has been combed for the slightest intimation of evidence. The result is a substantial and surprisingly disparate body of testimony.

I use the metaphor of criminal investigation advisedly, for a dominant pattern in recent critical discussion of this novel is to view Godfrey St. Peter as reprehensible in one measure or another. This negative view has evolved in tandem with the development of feminist criticism. Critics sensitized to gender conflict have turned a suspicious eye on Cather's charming professor, and their scrutiny of his relationships with women has produced rather scandalous discoveries. Professor St. Peter, once considered an admirable and sympathetic character, has now been identified as a frustrated homosexual misogynist.

Margaret Doane asserts that Cather "established an anti-female bias as a dominant aspect of the book," as major a concern as the negative effects of materialism (302, 299). Doane views the professor as "remarkably obtuse and unfair to his wife, who emerges as generally kind, sympathetic, and long ago abandoned by her husband." St. Peter, like the rest of the men in the novel but in greater measure, displays a view of women as "petty, materialistic, and a distinct threat to the higher values of males" (300).

Doris Grumbach is considerably more subtle in attempting to explain the apparent anti-female bias. She claims that the novel is as close as Cather would come to "the question of sexual choice outside accepted social patterns" (338). Her thesis is that Cather transferred her pain at losing Isabelle McClung to St. Peter's loss of Tom. In plainer terms than Grumbach uses, both relationships were homosexual. St. Peter made a mistake in the first place by marrying a woman and has led "a life of marital escape almost from the beginning" (333). His love for Tom has what Grumbach considers a tragic dimension because it was not physically consummated and remained "private, unconfessed, sublimated" (339). Consequently, the professor's problem "lies in his late and blinding realization that the life he had been leading, the life of father and husband, is, and always has been, a false one for him, that his existence within these roles is no longer bearable, and that death is preferable to living any longer in the stifling, elaborately furnished, and *false* (for him) house of women and marriage" (337).

This kind of narrow emphasis on gender conflict prompts obvious and fundamental questions ignored by these critics. For example, why would a female novelist write such an anti-female novel? Why should a character who shares so many characteristics of his female author be portrayed as such an unmitigated misogynist?[1] What is the point or the larger significance of the professor's deteriorating relationship with his wife and family? An inordinate focus on gender conflict spawns distracting ambiguities in a novel already generously supplied with them. This is demonstrated in Thomas F. Strychacz's "The Ambiguities of Escape in Willa Cather's *The Professor's House*." Assuming that the key to the professor's personality is his retreat from "an oppressive domesticity" and "long-standing sexual conflicts with wife and daughters" (51), Strychacz argues that St. Peter indulges in "impossible fantasies of a male paradise" prompted by Tom and the Blue Mesa and that his creativity "depends upon the absence of female and familial ties." He describes the attic study as having "overtones of Gothic horror" and suggests that the dress forms "express the stagnation of his relationships with wife and daughters—even a morbid, repressed sexuality" (53). Such assumptions naturally lead Strychacz to construct ambiguities because they preclude viewing Tom, the mesa, St. Peter's creative work, and St. Peter's very survival at the end as truly positive things. How can they be genuinely positive when they are linked with the anti-feminine?

The fact is that a relevant and potentially useful concern with gender conflict has been myopically applied to this text in a way that distorts and trivializes its larger themes. This novel provides significant, often profound, treatment of universal human problems, such as the perennial tension between solitude and society, the establishing of a proper relationship with nature and the past, coping with the challenges of materialism and technological advancement, and adjusting to the diminishment ineluctably linked with aging. St. Peter's estrangement from his wife and family is obviously a central element of the story, but the degree of that estrangement should not be exaggerated. Marriage and family have been a great deal more satisfying to the professor than the critics mentioned would have us believe. Moreover, this tension in family relations should be recognized as a condition subsidiary to Cather's larger concerns. It is a situation that serves instrumentally to illuminate human problems transcending those of this particular man and his family, including any gender conflicts that might be involved.

Was St. Peter's marriage a mistake from the very beginning, and has his domestic life been a resented and regretted obstacle to his creativity? Not at all. He was "very much in love" with Lillian when they married (31), and as he reflects on their nearly thirty years together, he concludes that "joyful years they had been, nothing could ever change that" (281). On occasions when thoughts of the loneliness of death had oppressed and terrified him—moments that occur in most lives—"he used to feel that if his wife could but lie in the same coffin with him, his body would not be so insensible that the nearness of hers would not give it comfort" (272).

Like any writer he needed solitude in which to work, but

> when he was writing his best, he was conscious of pretty little girls in fresh dresses—of flowers and greens in the comfortable, shabby sitting-room—of his wife's good looks and good taste—even of a better dinner than usual under preparation downstairs. All the while he had been working so fiercely at his eight big volumes, he was not insensible to the domestic drama that went on beneath him. His mind had played delightedly with all those incidents. . . . The most important chapters of his history were interwoven with personal memories. (101)

The drama of domestic life that went on below him while he worked is described as "engaging" and his sense of it as "pleasant" (26). He didn't want to go down for oil because "he would almost surely become interested in what the children were doing" (27).

St. Peter had been deeply attached to his family and they were in his thoughts even during his periods of intensest creativity. This is why he now, returning to his attic, must muster his courage and resignation in order to face the unpleasant awareness "that under his work-room there was a dead, empty house" (15–16). He misses rather than begrudges that past domestic life. It was blended with his creativity not alien to it. This is symbolically reinforced by the way the professor's notebooks and manuscripts share the same box with Augusta's patterns, those "notched charts which followed the changing stature and figures of the Misses St. Peter from early childhood to womanhood" (22). Furthermore, the dress forms—the professor's playful allusion to M. Bergeret in Anatole France's *Le Mannequin D'Osier* notwithstanding[2]—are primarily mementos of a happy domestic past, not symbols of misogyny. Although they subtly intimate the ambiguities of St. Peter's relationship with the women of his family, he is sincere in telling Rosamond, "They remind me of the times when you were little girls, and your first party frocks used to hang on them at night, when I worked" (60).

During those years of writing he did not go to his study at all if someone in the family happened to be ill, but routinely, "Two evenings of the week he spent with his wife and daughters, and one evening he and his wife went out to dinner, or to the theatre or a concert" (28). A contemporary family counselor wouldn't insist on more than this, particularly of a writing scholar and teacher. St. Peter "had burned his candle at both ends": "By eliminations and combinations so many and subtle that it now made his head ache to think of them, he had done full justice to his university lectures, and at the same time carried on an engrossing piece of creative work" (28–29). And his family was not sacrificed in this process. As he tells his wife, "I wasn't willing to slight anything—you, or my desk, or my students. And now I seem to be tremendously tired" (163). This "diminution of ardour" (13) is introduced from the beginning as a central element in the novel. He is confronting the universal question posed in Robert Frost's "The Oven Bird": "What to make of a diminished thing?"—a question that ultimately must be answered by the solitary self in response to "the unpleasant effects of change" (15). He had attempted to balance family, teaching, and writing. Family life had not been a mistake, but rather a vital part of his life, as much a joy as his history. To discount the efforts and satisfactions of this previous domestic life so inextricably linked with those of his creative life is to reduce the significance of his crisis. They are an important part of what he must let go at the end of the novel. His confrontation with a diminished thing loses weight and poignance when his marriage and familial ties are viewed as a mistake from the beginning.

As the professor reflects on past domestic joys—"family festivals and hospitalities, little girls dancing in and out, Augusta coming and going, gay dresses hanging in his study at night, Christmas shopping and secrets and smothered laughter on the stairs"—he asks himself, "When a man had lovely children in his house, fragrant and happy, full of pretty fancies and generous impulses, why couldn't he keep them?" (125–26). The final phrase is the important one and resonates through the novel. The professor is not simply between two houses as the novel begins, he is between two families. One of "the unpleasant effects of change" that plagues him is that family relationships often evolve in unfortunate ways. It is remarkable that Cather, who had no children of her own, could capture so movingly the experience of the professor's confronting his children's adulthood and all the changes this involves. The closeness and dependency of the early years is gone. The children, now independent adults, harden into their own molds, which are seldom exactly what the parent admires or desires. It is an unsettling phase in parent–child relations and affects husband–wife relations as well. Moreover, husband–wife relations evolve in their own right, sometimes in regrettable ways. The professor himself reflects on this: "People who are intensely in love when they marry, and who go on being in love, always meet with something which suddenly or gradually makes a difference" (49).

It is of course Tom who has made a difference in this marriage, both directly and indirectly through the money his invention generates. Husband and wife drift apart, not, as Doane contends, because the professor is "remarkably obtuse and unfair to his wife" and had long ago abandoned her, but because they have reacted differently to change. Godfrey has turned to the past and the values reflected in Tom's mesa adventure. Lillian has adapted to the future (94). She is a woman of "very vehement likes and dislikes which were often quite out of proportion to the trivial object or person that aroused them." For many years her "prejudices" had been "the most interesting things in St. Peter's life" (50). But his interest in the trivial has, largely through the influence of Tom, greatly diminished and the prejudices now strike him as perplexingly materialistic. Since their daughter's marriage to Louie, Lillian has "changed and hardened" and become worldly (160–61).

"With Louie, Lillian seemed to be launching into a new career, and Godfrey began to think that he understood his own wife very little" (78). Louie and Scott, her sons-in-law, have replaced the professor in her affections and with them "she had begun the game of being a woman all over again" (79). Lillian is at the beginning of something, Godfrey at the end. The differences in perspective prevent their understanding each other. She thinks he has become inhuman; he thinks she has hardened. Each finds the other intolerant.

This rift in the family, interesting in itself as a study of the way the human self retains a certain independence and isolation even in the most intimate union with others, corresponds with a rift in American civilization. James Schroeter has observed that Tom is associated with effort and Louie with reward, a pairing that corresponds to two phases in America's history—a noble idealistic past and an ignoble materialistic present (504–05). Effort and reward are both part of the professor's life. He treasures the effort, and his wife and the Marselluses treasure the rewards. The point behind the gender and family conflict is that it encapsulates and illuminates a much larger conflict of values. And, incidentally, the tensions in family relations are not simply a matter of gender—St. Peter against the women of the household. Kathleen is clearly aligned on the side of Tom and her father, and the professor's relationship with Augusta has always been cordial and is ultimately pivotal.

Godfrey and Lillian have a moment of tender understanding at the opera, which prompts him to reflect that "the heart of another is a dark forest, always, no matter how close it has been to one's own" (95). Man and woman remain alone even in the most intimate union. They cannot penetrate each other's innermost center. Each person is ultimately solitary and aware of it. This is the universal predicament Cather explores in this novel. Susan Rosowski notes a pattern of surrogate selves (258): St. Peter lives first through Lillian then through Tom; Lillian lives first through St. Peter and then through her daughters (Rosamond is like her "second self" [66]) and sons-in-law; as children the daughters lived in Tom's stories; Kathleen looked to Rosamond as "a kind of ideal"; and later Rosamond has "become Louie" (86). The St. Peter case makes clear that "the unfortunate effects of change" and "diminution of ardour" ultimately force the reflective mind to recognize its fated solitude and the futility of surrogate selves. As Paul Tillich explains in "Loneliness and Solitude":

> The creation of the woman has not overcome the situation which God describes as not good for man. He remains alone. And the creation of the woman, although it provides a helper for Adam, has only presented to the one human being who is alone another human being who is equally alone, and from their flesh all other men, each of whom will also stand alone. (16)

For Tillich, aloneness, though a burden, is also a blessing, for "it is man's greatness that he is centered within himself" (17). He therefore makes a distinction between "loneliness" and "solitude" and suggests that the former can be conquered only by those who can bear the latter. A person's character is determined by what he or she does with his inevitable aloneness. Cather certainly understood both the pain and the glory of solitude. Her professor rediscovers his primitive child self, his primary or "realest" self, which remains when the effects of chance and change are cleared away. He is tempted to lapse into "eternal solitude" as "a release from every obligation, from every form of effort" (272). But in the end he opts for a wise and courageous solitude among the living, a solitude that distances him from his family but enhances the significance of his humanity and provides a sense of human purpose that endures where career and creativity and even family fail. It involves a principle that Tom discovered too late on the mesa and that Augusta embodies. His family will neither understand his epiphany nor realize he is not the same man. His qualified contentment must remain private and solitary.

—Brigham Young University

NOTES

1. James Woodress provides an extensive list of parallels between Cather and St. Peter in *Willa Cather: A Literary Life* (Lincoln: U of Nebraska P, 1987) 368–69.
2. Alice Bell Salo's "*The Professor's House* and *Le Mannequin D'Osier*: A Note on Willa Cather's Narrative Technique," *Studies in American Fiction* 8 (1980): 229–31, is the most extensive exploration of the allusion. To view M. Bergeret's violent destruction of a dress form as an indication that St. Peter has a repressed violent hatred for his wife, as several critics have done, is to take the playful allusion too solemnly and depreciate the subtlety of Cather's using it. James C. Work provides an entertaining warning against taking the novel's allusions too seriously in "Cather's Confounded Conundrums in *The Professor's House*," *Western American Literature* 18 (1984): 303–12.

BIBLIOGRAPHY

Cather, Willa. *The Professor's House*. New York: Knopf, 1925.
Doane, Margaret. "In Defense of Lillian St. Peter: Men's Perceptions of Women in *The Professor's House*." *Western American Literature* 18 (1984): 299–302.
Grumbach, Doris. "A Study of the Small Room in *The Professor's House*." *Women's Studies* 11 (1984): 327–45.
Rosowski, Susan J. "The Pattern of Willa Cather's Novels." *Western American Literature* 15 (1981): 243–63.
Schroeter, James. "Willa Cather and *The Professor's House*." *Yale Review* 54 (1965): 494–512.

Strychacz, Thomas F. "The Ambiguities of Escape in Willa Cather's *The Professor's House.*" *Studies in American Fiction* 14 (1986): 49–61.

Tillich, Paul. *The Eternal Now.* New York: Scribner's, 1963.

The Professor's Marriage

ALICE BELL

The first book of *The Professor's House* is Cather's most detailed depiction of relationships between members of an extended family. Readers have been quick to acknowledge that tension and discord within the family contribute to St. Peter's crisis, and several have identified in his wife, daughters, and sons-in-law values and characteristics they consider the cause of disharmony. But few critics have analyzed the narrative strategies Cather uses in composing this family portrait to determine what these reveal about the professor's domestic life. Elsewhere I have examined the parallel scenes, historical references, and literary allusions through which Cather pictures St. Peter's interactions with his daughters and sons-in-law.[1] Here I will look at how she uses allusions to define the status of his marriage and incremental repetition to identify a cause of stress within that relationship.

The first allusion that helps describe Godfrey and Lillian's marriage reminds us of the marital relationship in a novel by Anatole France. The professor has often told Augusta that he does not mind having the dressmaker's forms in his attic study: "If they were good enough for *Monsieur Bergeret*, they are certainly good enough for me" (19). Augusta has probably not read *Le Mannequin d'Osier*. But St. Peter knows that M. Bergeret, a professor of Latin at a provincial French university, emphatically objected to sharing his cramped study with the wicker-work woman, "image conjugale." Bergeret's wife customarily left the form in front of the bookcase, ignoring his complaints that each time he wanted to take a book from the shelves he had to embrace the wicker-work woman and carry her off. Moreover, the contrivance set his teeth on edge because it reminded him of a farmer's hen coop or of the idol of woven cane in which ancient Phoenicians were said to have burned their children. Above all, the mannequin reminded him of Madame Bergeret. When M. Bergeret returned home an hour early on New Year's Day, he discovered his wife embracing his favorite student on the sofa in the drawing room. Unable to express his anger openly, the professor withdrew to his study. There he spied the dressmaker's mannequin, which seemed to be none other than Madame Bergeret herself. Flinging himself upon it, he clasped it in his arms and cracked its wicker breast. Overturning the form, he stamped on it, then threw it out the window. After wreaking physical vengeance on the wicker-work mannequin, M. Bergeret punished his wife more subtly: he avoided her presence and he ignored her existence.

Among his friends, M. Bergeret eloquently denounced the cruelty of the penal cell system that kills men by isolation, but at home he relentlessly subjected his wife to silence and solitude. Madame Bergeret, shattered by this punishment, finally announced that she was returning to the home of her aged mother. M. Bergeret secretly rejoiced that she had arrived at the goal toward which, with foresight and firmness, he had been guiding her.

Juxtaposition of Godfrey St. Peter and Lucian Bergeret suggests that the former is deliberately excluding his wife from his attention and affection after a favorite student has come between them. Cather immediately confirms this suggestion of estrangement. On the same page St. Peter says to Augusta:

> "I'm not moving just yet—don't want to disturb all my papers. I'm staying on until I finish a piece of writing. I've seen your uncle about it. I'll work here, and board at the new house. But this is confidential. If it were noised about, people might begin to say that Mrs. St. Peter and I had—how do they put it, parted, separated?" (19–20)

As a matter of fact, St. Peter does not speak to Augusta's uncle, owner of the rented house, until the following day, a conversation that is recorded two chapters later. And Godfrey's pretense of sharing confidential information with Augusta is apparently specious. At any rate, before the end of the fall semester Mrs. Crane knows that he is using the attic study and asks to meet with him there. Because there is no mention of community gossip about his marriage, St. Peter's motive for implying yet denying a marital separation has no significance for the plot. But this narrative strategy has great meaning for the reader because it reinforces the effect of the allusion to *Le Mannequin d'Osier*. Furthermore, St. Peter's appeal to Augusta for the right word and the ruse of confidentiality constitute a subtle maneuver that gains him the support of a person likely to object to domestic irregularity. Thus the professor's first utterance in the novel shows that he skillfully manipulates both facts and people and that he thinks of his marriage in terms of separation.[2]

At the beginning of the third chapter another allusion reinforces the overtone introduced by mention of *Le Mannequin d'Osier*. After the account of a family dinner that reveals some of the tensions between members of the group, this chapter opens:

> St. Peter awoke the next morning with the wish that he could be transported on his mattress from the new house to the old. But it was Sunday, and on that day his wife always breakfasted with him. There was no way out; they would meet at compt. (46)

According to Cather's principles of artistic simplification, the use of the archaic *compt* is justified only if what has been "suppressed and cut away is there to the reader's consciousness as much as if it were in type on the page" ("Art" 102). One who reads Shakespeare as assiduously as Cather did will recognize that what has been excised from this important but unobtrusive allusion is a statement from Othello's speech over Desdemona's body:

> When we shall meet at compt,
> this look of thine will hurl my soul from heaven
> And fiends will snatch at it. (V. ii. 273–75)

Similarities between Lucian Bergeret and Godfrey St. Peter are obvious, but St. Peter and Othello appear to have nothing in common. However, Bergeret and Othello share one attribute: each punishes his wife for infidelity. In the fourth chapter, the professor, like M. Bergeret, comes home earlier than usual and finds Louie showing Lillian the emeralds Louie has bought for Rosamond. This scene is a striking contrast to the one in M. Bergeret's living room, but the professor's banter and his subsequent reverie suggest a similar rift between husband and wife. Although no incident in the novel implies that Lillian has broken her marriage vows, these two allusions suggest that St. Peter is treating his wife as though she has been unfaithful, while—like Desdemona—she is actually innocent.

A third allusion, set in a scene of startling juxtaposition, adds to this theme of infidelity and estrangement. At the beginning of chapter 14, Cather radically shifts the narrative point of view and presents an episode from Lillian's perspective. This gives the reader an intimate picture of Lillian's solicitude for her husband. When Godfrey returns from the shopping trip to Chicago with Rosamond, Lillian hopes that he will take a taxi from the train station, because the weather is raw; but he does not. As he approaches the house, she notices that he looks tired. She opens the door for him and expresses concern that he must be cold because he is wearing his light overcoat. She is perplexed that he did not buy himself a new coat in Chicago as he had planned and is distressed when she learns that he paid his own expenses for the trip. One paragraph in particular shows the depth of her empathy:

> Mrs. St. Peter went swiftly downstairs to make him a cocktail. She sensed an
> unusual weariness in him, and felt, as it were, the bitter taste on his tongue.
> A man, she knew, could get from his daughter a peculiar kind of hurt—one
> of the cruellest that flesh is heir to. Her heart ached for Godfrey. (155)

In the paragraph that follows, the St. Peters are sitting before the hearth after dinner. Lillian notices that Godfrey has let his book drop and that he is smiling quite agreeably. When she asks what he is thinking of, he replies:

> "I was thinking . . . about Euripides; how, when he was an old man, he
> went and lived in a cave by the sea, and it was thought queer, at the time.
> It seems that houses had become insupportable to him. I wonder whether
> it was because he had observed women so closely all his life." (156)

St. Peter's unkind statement about women, coming just after Lillian's expression of concern, is probably the most forceful example of juxtaposition in the novel. In addition, the mention of Euripides suggests a parallel between St. Peter and his cave-like attic study with its distant view of Lake Michigan and the dramatist and his seaside retreat. According to ancient rumor, Euripides sought refuge in the cave because both his first wife and his second wife were unfaithful to him.

These three allusions encourage the reader to search for a motive behind St. Peter's attitude and behavior. In chapter 3 the professor gives a hint about what may have come between the couple. He muses that Lillian had been "fiercely jealous" of Tom Outland, and he goes on to identify his former student as the cause of a change in their marriage relationship. As St. Peter's memories unfold, we gain other glimpses of Lillian's interaction with Tom. In chapter 6, for example, the professor recalls her unpleasant and petty reaction to the young man's manners:

> She could never forgive poor Tom Outland for the angle at which he sometimes held a cigar in his mouth. . . . If Tom, forgetting himself in talk, sometimes dropped back into railroad lunch-counter ways and pushed his plate away from him when he had finished a course, Lillian's face would become positively cruel in its contempt. (78–79)

But when the professor recollects Tom's first visit to their home (chapter 10), we get a different view of Lillian. When Tom eats mashed potatoes with his knife, Rosamond and Kathleen cannot conceal their astonishment, but Lillian talks quietly with him about Indian pottery. Also, she helps Tom get a place to live and some proper summer clothes; during his first months in town, she sees more of him than her husband does. In the last chapter of the first book, St. Peter recalls when—and why—Lillian's attitude toward Tom changed:

> It was not until Outland was a senior that Lillian began to be jealous of him. He had been almost a member of the family for two years, and she had never found fault with the boy. But after the Professor began to take Tom up to the study and talk over his work with him, began to make a companion of him, then Mrs. St. Peter withdrew her favour. (172–73)

St. Peter's recollection that for two years Lillian "had never found fault with the boy" drastically modifies the statement about her distaste for Tom's manners. However, the professor does not acknowledge that his relationship with Tom was the cause of Lillian's change in attitude. Rather he considers her disapproval a flaw in her personality: "She could change like that; friendship was not a matter of habit with her. And when she was through with anyone, she of course found reasons for her fickleness" (173).

Despite Lillian's feelings, Godfrey maintained his relationship with Tom and made the young man his traveling companion. They spent a summer together in the Southwest and another in Mexico. Perhaps St. Peter justifies these trips as necessary for the completion of his history, but the visit to France that he was anticipating at the time Tom left to join the army could have had no such purpose. Noting the mention of separate bedrooms in the new house, some readers have accused Lillian of driving her husband from her bed. But Godfrey is the one who found a more satisfying relationship outside the marriage. Musing that Lillian now lives in the careers of her sons-in-law "as she had once done in his," the professor concludes that "*beaux-fils*, apparently, were meant by Providence to take the husband's place when husbands had ceased to be lovers" (160).

Another reference, in the final book of the novel, supports this overtone of the rejected wife and may also comment on St. Peter's relationship with Tom Outland. Lillian, Rosamond, and Louie return from France on the *Berengaria*, a Cunard Line vessel. In accordance with the principles she sets forth in "The Novel Démeublé," we would not expect Cather to identify the ship just for the sake of "mere verisimilitude." In Book I, for example, she transports the party to Europe in a single short sentence: "Lillian and the Marselluses sailed for France early in May" (171). In contrast, in Book III Cather calls special attention to the *Berengaria* by mentioning it three times, each time in a context charged with greater significance. This repetition suggests that the reference may carry special meaning.

Berengaria of Navarre was the wife of Richard I (to whom Cather referred in her portrayal of Louie Marsellus). The couple were married in Cyprus during the Third Crusade (May 1191), and they went together to the Holy Land where Richard made an unsuccessful attempt to recapture Jerusalem. Traveling separately, they returned to Europe in the autumn of 1192. But Richard was captured and held prisoner for over a year. Meanwhile Berengaria took up residence in Poitou. After his ransom, Richard arranged a second coronation in Winchester Cathedral with his mother, Eleanor of Aquitaine, filling the role of queen. Even after his return to the continent, he did not visit or summon Berengaria. Richard's continued estrangement from his wife led to the report that he had resumed the homosexual relationships he had publicly confessed and renounced before an assemblage of bishops and barons in Messina while on his way to the Holy Land. His subsequent marriage had been regarded as confirmation of his resolution to change his behavior. Early in 1195, however, a hermit warned the king to be mindful of the fate of Sodom and to abstain from unlawful acts, or a vengeance worthy of God would overtake him. Richard paid no heed until, a few months later, he became seriously ill. Then he confessed his sins, received absolution, and sent for Berengaria, who rejoined his household and stayed with him until his death.

Now let us look at how Cather handles this narrative device. The first reference to the ship occurs at the end of a paragraph: "They would sail on the sixteenth, on the *Berengaria*" (273). After a paragraph that contains information necessary to advance the plot, the record of St. Peter's thoughts continues: "They were sailing on the sixteenth, and this was the seventeenth; they were already on the water. The *Berengaria* was a five-day boat." This paragraph closes with a long and significant statement: "There must, he was repeating to himself, there must be some way in which a man who had always tried to live up to his responsibilities could, when the hour of desperation came, avoid meeting his own family" (274). The following paragraphs record St. Peter's reflections during his "hour of desperation." At this time he affirms that he loves his family but that he cannot live with them again: "Especially not with Lillian! Her nature was intense and positive; it was like a chiselled surface, a die, a stamp upon which he could not be beaten out any longer" (274). Readers seem to have accepted this as an objective view of Lillian rather than as St. Peter's distraught vision of her. The third reference to the *Berengaria* occurs in the novel's final statement, which summarizes St. Peter's attitude after his near-death experience: "He thought he knew where he was, and that he could face with fortitude the *Berengaria* and the future" (283). In this context the word should probably be considered a figure of speech (metonymy) used in place of *his family* or, more specifically, *his wife*. In other words, in the final sentence of the book the *Berengaria*, or Berengaria, is directly associated with Lillian. And at the conclusion of the novel, the professor, like Richard I, is contemplating a reunion with his wife after his life has been endangered.

These allusions and the references to Lillian's attitude toward Tom emphasize what is suggested in the narrative: Godfrey's friendship with Tom Outland has strained his marital relationship. Readers have speculated whether this liaison was a platonic or a physical relationship, but these allusions show that the result has been a breach in St. Peter's marriage similar to that caused by sexual infidelity. Lillian has apparently accepted the estrangement with regret. When she comments to Godfrey that it wasn't the children who came between them, "there was something lonely and forgiving in her voice, something that spoke of an old wound, healed and hardened and hopeless" (94). Lillian reveals the pain of this old wound—and suggests its source—in her only ungracious speech in the novel. After hearing St. Peter lecture to his class about science and religion, Scott wonders how the professor "gets by" the Methodists. Lillian asserts:

> "I wish he would get into trouble, Scott. . . . I wish he wouldn't talk to those fat-faced boys as if they were intelligent beings. You cheapen yourself, Godfrey. It makes me a little ashamed. . . . It's hardly dignified to think aloud in such company. It's in rather bad taste." (70)

Analysis of these narrative strategies reveals that St. Peter is a far more complex and less "idealistic" character than readers have usually assumed. In fact, *The Professor's House* may be considered a dramatization of the view of family life Cather expresses in her essay on Katherine Mansfield, published the same year as the novel:

> I doubt whether any contemporary writer has made one feel more keenly the many kinds of personal relations which exist in an everyday "happy family" who are merely going on living their daily lives. . . . Always in his mind each member of these social units is escaping, running away, trying

to break the net which circumstances and his own affections have woven about him. One realizes that human relationships are the tragic necessity of human life; that they can never be wholly satisfactory, that every ego is half the time greedily seeking them, and half the time pulling away from them. (108–09)

Surely Cather is as skillful as her British contemporary in depicting the "secret accords and antipathies that lie under the surface of our lives." By means of narrative techniques such as those we have just looked at, she creates what she describes as "the overtone . . . the verbal mood, the emotional aura . . . that gives high quality to the novel" ("Novel" 41–42).

—Minneapolis

NOTES

1. Bell, Alice. "Through the Professor's Window: Reading Willa Cather's Novel Démeublé." Diss. U of Minnesota, 1986.
2. An earlier version of the France connection appeared in Alice Bell Salo, "*The Professor's House* and *Le Mannequin d'Osier*: A Note on Willa Cather's Narrative Technique," *Studies in American Fiction* 8 (1980): 229–31.

BIBLIOGRAPHY

Cather, Willa. "Katherine Mansfield." *Willa Cather on Writing*. New York: Knopf, 1949. 107–20.
_____. "The Novel Démeublé." *Willa Cather on Writing*. 35–43.
_____. "On the Art of Fiction." *Willa Cather on Writing*. 101–04.
_____. *The Professor's House*. New York: Knopf, 1925.

Lovers as Mortal Enemies

EUGENE ENGLAND

In Willa Cather's spare but powerful novella *My Mortal Enemy*, protagonist Myra Driscoll, a Catholic who eloped with a Protestant and thus rejected the great-uncle who had raised her and the fortune he had offered to dissuade her from the marriage, dies in poverty and resentment, after an attempted reconciliation with her religion. She is cared for in her last illness by her husband of thirty-five years, Oswald Henshawe, and the narrator, Nellie Birdseye, a niece of one of Myra's childhood friends. During an all-night vigil near the end, with Oswald present, Nellie hears Myra exclaim to herself, in a "soft, passionate breath," "I could bear to suffer . . . so many have suffered. But why must it be like this? . . . Why must I die like this, alone with my mortal enemy?" Nellie is horrified at what she calls "a terrible judgment upon all one hopes for" (95), and, long after Myra's death, she continues to hear that "strange complaint . . . like a confession of the soul: 'Why must I die like this, alone with my mortal enemy!' " (105).

Marriage is surely a most difficult human relationship. By its very nature it exposes us to each other in our deepest and most vulnerable parts, where lovers can become mortal enemies—or think they are. Yet it possesses the greatest potential for joy, self-realization, and salvation. It is, in Martin Luther's words, the "school of love," for learning that unconditional love that Christ required of us in order to be saved and about which His "beloved disciple" taught: "If a man say, I love God, and hateth his brother, he is a liar" (1 John 20). Judeo-Christian and humanist traditions both hold to the ideal that the greatest achievement in either divine or human terms is unconditional love, owed equally to all creatures who are in the image of God—to other mortals and to oneself. Even the mystical traditions, which seem to focus on the individual journey to God, have had strong currents of what is called "positive mysticism," the belief that the soul's union with God is completed and evidenced in a return to responsible human relationships.

I can judge Myra only with compassion, indeed with fear and trembling, because I see much of myself in her and recognize in her marriage the incredible dangers and temptations in my own and indeed every marriage. But I must judge her a failure, a negative example of married love, and her death a tragic evasion rather than a triumph or model of return to grace, as some critics would have it (i.e., Murphy 13). Ultimate success involves honesty, realism, and turning from the things of this world—not honesty merely about the failures of *others* and the difficulties of marriage, not realism only about the *deprivations* and obstacles in one's life, and not a final turning away from all *human* commitments. It involves being honest about your own responsibilities, realistic about the possibilities, for good as well as bad, in your present life and in those who love you, and turning away from wealth, vanity, and revenge—none of which Myra is willing to do. Like Myra, some critics would make Oswald—or marriage itself—the villain (i.e., Rosowski 147), rather than holding Myra accountable as one of the free agents who entered the marriage.

Some evidence exists that *My Mortal Enemy* was written at a time, the mid-1920s, when Cather herself was in conflict about human relationships and religion, based on failure or loss in her own loves and faith (Tanner 36). This information lends support to the tendency to see the novel as unresolved and to praise its protagonist for her self-contradictory complexity—even to suggest that the mortal enemy she speaks of dying with is herself or one of her destructive passions or her unfortunate condition.

The evidence of the novel itself, however, as well as certain independent remarks Cather made about it indicate a high degree of certainty of purpose on her part and also some genuine clarity of achievement. On two occasions Cather refused to encourage the growing critical inclination to soften the cruelty of Myra's complaint, in her husband's presence, of dying alone with her mortal enemy. She verified that Myra indeed meant Oswald, not herself or something abstract, and once Cather added, with apparent impatience, "I can't see much in this particular story unless you get the point of it. There is not much to it *but* the point" (Robinson 244). I share the contemporary uneasiness about relying too much on an author's stated intentions, but it seems to me that Cather was generally so perceptive and articulate about the way literature works and so honest and unelusive about what she was trying to do herself that we should get what help we can from these remarks, especially if we can find supportive evidence in her extremely sparsely furnished novella itself.

Stephen Tanner has reviewed the conditions that produce ambiguity in the novel and encourage critical disagreement about its meaning, but he persuasively argues that we can get closer to understanding, even agreement, if we focus on what is clearly the climax of the novel, Myra's religious reconciliation (30). She is in the midst of that conversion when she utters what Nellie calls her "terrible judgment" on Oswald and life. Now, what might Cather, some years later in the very act of insisting that Oswald was indeed the target of Myra's cruel despair, have meant by saying that the story is not much more than its point and implying that the point was fairly clear? Is there an obvious point supported by the textual evidence and what we know of Cather and connected to Myra's resentful identification of her husband as her mortal enemy? I think so.

The context of Myra's judgment includes most prominently the visits of a priest to aid her attempt at reconciliation and her visits to what she calls "Gloucester's cliff," where she finally goes to die. What Cather enables us to make of that conversion and of the associations with Shakespeare's *King Lear* provides sufficient basis for the "point" of the novel. Tanner is certainly right that "Myra's own definition of religion should guide our evaluation of her conversion" (33). She gives that definition immediately before calling her husband her mortal enemy: "Religion is different from everything else; *because in religion seeking is finding*" (94). Nellie tells us that the dying woman "accented the word 'seeking' very strongly, very deeply," and then gives an interpretation: "[Myra] seemed to say that in other searchings it might be the object of the quest that brought satisfaction, or it might be something incidental that one got on the way; but in religion, desire was fulfillment, it was the seeking itself that rewarded" (94). It is immediately after this that Nellie tells of Myra's complaint about suffering beyond what she deserves by dying alone with a husband turned into mortal enemy—but one who is present, nursing Myra, and who bears this insult with perfect patience. Nellie further comments, "I began to understand a little what she meant, to sense how it was with her. Violent natures like hers sometimes turn against themselves . . . against themselves and all their idolatries" (96).

In these few pages Cather reveals a central human process René Girard has since helped elucidate. In his *Violence and the Sacred* (1965) and *Deceit, Desire, and the Novel* (1977), Girard gives convincing evidence, from his thorough study of anthropology, classical mythology and literature, and modern writers like Shakespeare and Dostoevski, that we are motivated largely by imitative desire, wanting things others desire largely *because* they desire them. This defines precisely the romantic love of the young Myra and Oswald, and the mature Myra is right about its terrible deficiencies. Girard's categories are also relevant to Myra's materialistic passion, which she seems to give up for love in leaving her great-uncle's fortune but which actually continues to afflict her to the end, when she blames Oswald for the poverty she has caused in part by her own profligacy and for her frustrated ambitions. Focussed on what others desire, her own desires inevitably lead to envy, jealousy, cruelty, and violence. Those are the evil characteristics Nellie sees in Myra in the first part of the novel, twenty-five years after the elopement, and they continue to afflict her in the second part, ten years later.

Girard demonstrates that all societies learn to survive imitative desire (and the revengeful violence it produces that tends to spread like a plague) by choosing a scapegoat, focusing the blame and violence on *it*, and then masking the process in ritual and rationalization. This very process is revealed in Myra's materialism and jealousy and confirmed by her misunderstanding of religion as pure desire and her turning to ritual rather than repentance when near death. The masking process is perpetuated in critical acceptance of Myra's theological mistakes and human irresponsibility as heroic, even saintly, and a willingness by some critics to join her in scapegoating Oswald.

Two specific examples from the novel support Girard's insight and, on the basis of that insight, help us see more clearly Cather's "point." The first is Myra's imitation of her great-uncle's materialistic desire, which continues to undermine her character and her marriage, playing a direct role in Oswald's "failure" as a provider and her rejection of him as her "enemy." The second is Myra's bitter jealousy, which produces cycles of imitative violence between the two that culminate in Part I in her deserting him and in Part II in her total renunciation of him.

Tanner has pointed out the effective device Cather uses of giving point and richness to her spare novel by paralleling events, people, and memories in the two parts so they comment on each other (38). In Part I, we meet a great-uncle who, while trying to bribe Myra into not marrying the son of a "German free-thinker" he loathes, teaches her, "It's better to be a stray dog in this world than a man without money. . . . A poor man stinks, and God hates him" (15). In Part II, we learn that Myra has continued to desire wealth and to envy the wealthy, even while loathing them. We also learn that the uncle was a man of violent prejudices and was willing to crush an enemy at any cost—and that Myra increasingly identifies with him: "I can feel his savagery stengthen in me" (82).

At the end of Part I, Oswald has the narrator's Aunt Lydia pretend to give him some yellow topaz cuff-buttons, which have actually been given him by a female admirer, so that he can keep them without arousing Myra's jealousy. Myra finds an unfamiliar key on his ring, suspiciously investigates it without satisfaction, and engages with Oswald in imitative recriminations and maliciousness that Nellie perceives very accurately as poison, "evil . . . something malevolent and bottomless" (51). Nellie also gives us some perspective on whose is the greater fault and on the source of continuing energy for such imitative violence between the two. She notices that Oswald, soon after his deception, feels deep remorse, and she comments that "often since I have wondered at his gentle heart" (37). She also reports her later conversation with Myra, who tells her and her aunt that she has left Oswald "to think it over" and says that though it is disgusting in Oswald to lie in such matters, "a woman" might do so for a high enough price—while her mouth "seemed to curl and twist about like a little snake" (54). Thus, in Part I, Nellie clearly suggests that Myra's vindictive jealousy is unfounded, evil, and destructive. In Part II, Cather reinforces this point when she has Nellie suggest, through describing Oswald's kind if somewhat naive and egotistical attentions to a young journalist who admires him, the innocent nature of his earlier relationship with the woman who gave him the cuff-buttons (77–78).

In his most recent book, *Things Hidden since the Foundation of the World* (1987), Girard argues that there is one effective alternative to the plague of imitative desire and violence that tends to destroy both individuals and nations, despite their elaborate techniques for controlling and hiding it. This alternative is found uniquely in the mainstream Judeo-Christian theology and ethics and is epitomized in the life and death of Christ. Girard reads Hebrew history as a progressive effort to reveal the violence mechanism and renounce its basis in scapegoating by taking the side of the victim, and he sees in Christ's clear and persistent refusal to participate in the violence mechanism the potential redemption of all humans and all human history.

The point of Cather's book, which she seemed to think not only the essence of the story but quite obvious, is simply the basic Christian one, which Girard has helped us understand in relation to imitative desire and revengeful violence: To remove rivalry, blame, jealousy, revenge, and scapegoating, it is necessary to renounce desire and do away with the category of enemy. Myra's religion, on the other hand, is mere "seeking," fulfillment through pure desire, form without content, the very antithesis of Christ's "Not my will, but thine, be done" (Luke 22:42) and "Seek, and ye shall find" (Matt. 7:7). She does not find Christ in her "conversion," because finding Christ involves sacrificing the spirit of revenge in favor of forgiveness:

> Love your enemies, do good to them which hate you, bless them that curse you, and pray for them which despitefully use you . . . and ye shall be the children of the Highest: for he is kind unto the unthankful and to the evil. Be ye therefore merciful, as your Father also is merciful. Judge not, and ye shall not be judged: condemn not, and ye shall not be condemned: forgive, and ye shall be forgiven. (Luke 6:27, 28, 35–37)

Myra, whatever she thinks she is seeking in turning to religion, fails to find *any* of these matters of substance. Contrary to Susan Rosowski's claim that Myra "emerges as progressively stronger and more forceful than her husband" (148), Cather carefully parallels events and images to show that there is no detectable change in her basic character. In Part I, after seeing a former friend she has never forgiven for failing to help Oswald in a difficulty, she lets bitterness spoil the rest of her day and finally complains, "It's all very well to tell us to forgive our enemies; our enemies can never hurt us very much. But oh, what about forgiving our friends?" (44). Myra's clever phrasing, apparently based on a passage in Francis Bacon's essay "On Revenge,"[1] cannot hide—and I do not believe Cather meant it to hide—the fact that Myra here fails the fundamental Christian requirement and in Part II continues to do so by identifying her chosen husband as her enemy and refusing to forgive him. If anyone in the story fulfills the requirement of blessing those who curse him and despitefully use him, refusing to judge or condemn but rather forgiving, it is Oswald. With what Nellie calls "indestructible constancy" (103), he stays true to Myra through her desertion in Part I and her rejection in Part II, even when she dismisses him as her enemy.

Cather's central point seems obvious enough: Myra should love, even the one she perceives as her mortal enemy, for any hope of happiness or redemption. But is that asking too much of a human being in the complex, trying circumstances of family bonds? Does Cather give us any basis for thinking Myra *can* give such love? I believe she does, through her many effective devices for fleshing out this spare novel, including symbolic use of gemstones and allusions to religious allegory and to music, especially Bellini's opera *Norma*, which Harry B. Eichorn has shown provides a commentary on Myra's sense of conflict between religion and romantic love and especially on her final failure to resolve that conflict. Eichorn also explores Myra's allusions to Shakespeare—her quoting from *Richard II* and *King John* in ways that suggest comparisons detrimental rather than complimentary to her character (236–38) and her identifying of a majestic coastal promontory as "Gloucester's cliff" in a comparison also negative. Unlike Myra, "Gloucester recovers from his despair and resolves to suffer with patience"; unlike Gloucester, Myra "cares about no one's misery but her own" (235).

I would extend Eichorn's analysis by pointing out that *King Lear* as a whole provides a richly relevant background for the novel and helps make Cather's essential point quite clear through contrast. Gloucester's son, Edgar, even though he has been wrongly identified by his father as his mortal enemy and forced to flee and disguise himself to save his life, tends the blinded old man with indestructible constancy, even finding a way to heal him of his suicidal desires. In addition, Gloucester eventually shows he can learn patience and forgive himself and his supposed enemy, as well as extend pity to his old friend Lear. This subplot is, of course, an imitation of the main plot, where Lear casts off Cordelia, his beloved daughter whom he has come to see as a mortal enemy, just as old John Driscoll casts off Myra and Myra casts off Oswald. However, Cordelia returns to nurse Lear with constancy and unconditional love before their deaths, just as Oswald does Myra.

Again, the contrasts, in Myra's case, are greater than the similarities and must have been clear to Cather, though she ironically shows Myra insensitive to them. Myra tells Nellie, "Perhaps I can't forgive [Oswald] for the harm I did him. . . . In age we lose everything; even the power to love" (88–89). Lear's awareness of the harm he has done in his extreme old age makes it difficult for him either to give or to accept forgiveness, makes it hard even to face Cordelia, "a sovereign shame so elbows him" (4.3.43). But he finally does face himself and then his daughter, and their mutual reconciliation is perhaps the greatest scene in literature—and more, an image of the joy and healing that can occur when those who become enemies in the trying bond of marriage and family can "forgive and forget" (4.7.55). But Myra refuses such a possibility, even in the very process of thinking of Shakespeare's great drama, even while contemplating going to "Gloucester's cliff" at dawn, because "that is always such a forgiving time" (73).

Surely Cather's point is that one who sees religion as personal desire, as form without content, would think only of herself and *being* forgiven as she approaches death, rather than thinking of that loss of self, that sacrifice of will and desire, that willingness to forgive even one's mortal enemy, that makes it possible to *be* forgiven—or to find any happiness in marriage or family life or any kind of life. *That* is Cather's judgment, I believe—not the "terrible judgment on all we hope for" that Nellie fears in Myra's melodramatic complaint about lovers becoming mortal enemies. It is the judgment that even supposed enemies must forgive each other, and, despite her attractive articulateness and honesty and her "hidden richness" that fill us with interest and empathy and her heroic "seeking" at the end, Myra fails.

—Brigham Young University

NOTE

1. " 'You shall read,' saith he, 'that we are commanded to forgive our enemies; but you never read, that we are commanded to forgive our friends.' "

BIBLIOGRAPHY

Cather, Willa. *My Mortal Enemy*. New York: Vintage, 1954.

Eichorn, Harry B. "A Falling Out with Love: *My Mortal Enemy*." *Critical Essays on Willa Cather*. Ed. John J. Murphy. Boston: Hall, 1984. 230–43.

Girard, René. *Things Hidden since the Foundation of the World*. Stanford: Stanford UP, 1987.

Murphy, John J. "The Dantean Journey in Cather's *My Mortal Enemy*." *Willa Cather Pioneer Memorial Newsletter* 30.3 (1986): 11–14.

Robinson, Phyllis C. *Willa: The Life of Willa Cather*. Garden City, N.Y.: Doubleday, 1983.

Rosowski, Susan J. "Narrative Technique in Cather's *My Mortal Enemy*." *Journal of Narrative Technique* 8 (1978): 141–49.

Tanner, Stephen L. "Seeking and Finding in Cather's *My Mortal Enemy*." *Literature and Belief* 8 (1988): 27–38.

What Margie Knew

ROBERT K. MILLER

Although often read as a story about the conflict between "exploitive materialism" and "individual freedom" (Arnold 124), "Uncle Valentine" (1925) is also the story of a troubled marriage—a theme to which Cather turned in many of her works. Recognizing that Valentine Ramsay is a threat to the marriage between Charlotte and Harry Waterford should keep us from altogether sympathizing with the values he seems to represent.

In the opening scene, a talented and intelligent young woman offers enthusiastic praise for the songs of Valentine Ramsay. "I'm crazy about them," she glibly tells her teacher, adding, "I never heard of Valentine Ramsay before" (3). Although the teacher had known Valentine well, she gives her pupil only a brief and general sketch of his career before referring her to a visitor who is at that moment present in the studio: "If you wish to know anything further about him, this American lady can tell you. She knew him in his own country" (3). This "American lady" is the narrator of the story that then unfolds: an account of the "golden year" when she was sixteen and knew Valentine as a neighbor, teacher, and family friend. "Yes," the narrator reflects, "I had known Valentine Ramsay. I knew him in a lovely place, at a lovely time, in a bygone period of American life; just at the incoming of this century which has made all the world so different" (3).

This opening, with the focus initially upon a music student who subsequently plays no role in the long, melancholy story that follows, emphasizes that there are things beyond the understanding of the young. Cather reinforces this opening note by making the narrator recognize early in the story that she did not entirely understand the complexity of the relationships she witnessed during her sixteenth year. "Aunt Charlotte was the person who felt all that went on about her—and all that did not go on—and understood it," she tells us. "I find that I did not know her very well then. It was not until years afterward, not until after her death, indeed, that I began really to know her" (8). By using Marjorie as the narrator, rather than her aunt who knew so much more about what "went on," Cather's strategy is similar to those she used in two other works of this period, *A Lost Lady* (1923) and *My Mortal Enemy* (1926). Like Niel Herbert and Nellie Birdseye, Marjorie only partially understands the mysterious behavior of the adults she thinks she knows. This creates a situation in which readers must listen to her closely and complete the story for themselves. When we do so, it soon becomes clear that there was more than one source of tension in that ostensibly golden year.

I base this reading upon several important scenes, the first of which takes place the afternoon after Valentine has returned to Greenacre after living abroad for many years. The setting is Harry Waterford's study, a room Marjorie describes as "my favorite spot in that house full of lovely places. It was . . . like a little pond off the main currents of the house" (11). When she joins Charlotte and Valentine there for tea, Marjorie detects "just a shade of embarrassment" in her aunt's voice. "Aren't you surprised to find us here?" Charlotte asks—and then unnecessarily explains, "This was Uncle Valentine's choice." Marjorie is always observant, even if she does not always understand what she is observing, and reflects about her aunt: "Curious; though she always looked so at ease, so calm in her matronly figure, a little thing like having tea in an unusual room could make her a trifle self-conscious and apologetic" (11). Valentine, on the other hand, has already made himself thoroughly at home, "sitting in Uncle Harry's big chair, one foot tucked under him" (12).

The conversation that follows is dominated by Valentine's self-justifying account of his unhappy marriage to Janet Oglethorpe and subsequent affair with Louise Ireland, culminating in his often-cited claim that it is more important for a woman to be pure in heart than irreproachable in behavior. But I'd like to draw attention to the way the scene concludes. Uncle Harry returns from his office early, turns on the light, and comments, "Awfully happy I got here before Valentine got away. . . . And, Charlotte, how rosy you are! It takes you to do that to her, Val" (15), when he observes that his wife is blushing. We see too little of Harry Waterford to be certain he is speaking ironically, but we cannot overlook the intriguing reflection Marjorie makes about her uncle's behavior: "He was almost pathetically eager for anything of this sort he could get, and was glad to come in for cold toast and tea" (15). Why, we must ask ourselves, should Harry Waterford be "almost pathetically eager" for "cold toast and tea"? Is his life so bleak? After all, he is not an Oglethorpe, dreaming of bargains in his sleep. He has values that have nothing to do with his business in the city. His study is filled with his "favorite books" (11), and, as we see in the scene I will now consider, he also cultivates roses.

The blooming of these roses, which entirely cover a stone retaining wall, was, according to Marjorie, the "vivid event of our year"—a "great assault, for which we children waited" (27). It was Harry's idea to plant these red rambler roses, and he did so even though his wife laughed at his plan. Marjorie remembers that "nowhere in the valley did ramblers thrive so well and bloom so gorgeously" (27). During the spring of this golden year, the entire family (accompanied by Valentine) walks down the driveway to admire the roses at their height:

Aunt Charlotte admitted that they were very showy, very decorative, but she added under her breath that she couldn't feel much enthusiasm for scentless roses.

"But they are quite another sort of thing," Uncle Harry expostulated. "They go right about their business and bloom. I like their being without an odor; it gives them a kind of frankness and innocence."

In the bright sunlight I could see her dark skin flush a little. "Innocence?" she murmured, "I shouldn't call it just that."

I was wondering what she would call it when our stableman Bill came up from the post office with his leather bag and emptied the contents on the grass. (27–28)

Like Marjorie, I also wonder what Charlotte would have called it. Moreover, why should a woman blush when her husband speaks to her of innocence? She would seem to have taken his remark as a personal rebuke.

What we know of Harry Waterford suggests a man who is both intelligent and civilized. Valentine Ramsay, on the other hand, is a much more dubious character. Even if he was entrapped into marriage with Janet Oglethorpe, there is surely something reprehensible about the way he treats women. The language hs uses to describe his break with Janet is extraordinarily crude: "You can't hurt anybody as beefy as that without being a butcher!" (13) he tells Charlotte. He describes Louise Ireland as "the sacrifice" (14) who enabled him to escape from matrimony, and seems willing to sacrifice Charlotte as well when her needs conflict with his own. Because he is disappointed with the guest list, he breaks a promise to play at a Christmas Eve party Charlotte has arranged on his behalf. And when he fails to encourage Charlotte to join an outing to Blue Run, even the admiring Marjorie is moved to reflect, "He was sometimes quite heartless" (29). Whatever his talent and charm, there is ultimately something bestial about Valentine Ramsay with his "thick, seal-brown hair [that] grew . . . exactly like fur" and his mustache and eyebrows that "had the same furry look" (9). I find myself picturing this furry face when, upon discovering that his ex-wife has bought the land over which he likes to roam, Valentine bitterly declares, "What does it say on the rat-bane bottle; *put the poison along all his runways.* That's the right idea!" (36). The metaphor may be extreme, but it is not entirely inappropriate.

Of course, there is much more to Valentine Ramsay than the unattractive qualities that I have outlined here. If I have focused on Valentine's shortcomings, it is not because I wish to cast him as the story's villain—a mustachioed cad who abandons his wife and child and then attempts to seduce his neighbor's wife. I only want to suggest that he is less than entirely admirable. Although Cather scholars agree that the prototype for Valentine was Ethelbert Nevin, a gifted musician with whom Cather was friendly when she lived in Pittsburgh, the character we see within the story is both selfish and self-indulgent. Characters should not be confused with their prototypes; however agreeable Ethelbert Nevin may have been to Willa Cather, Valentine Ramsay is capable of injuring the people among whom he lives.

There is no evidence to suggest that the injury he does to the marriage between Harry and Charlotte Waterford was intentional; it is simply a consequence of his egocentricity. Before the marriage had even taken place, Valentine had already thrust himself between the couple. Although it is not clear how she could have known this, Marjorie reports that "in the years when Uncle Harry came a-courting, the spoiled neighbor boy was always hanging about and demanding attention" (6). Years later, he is still doing precisely that. By the end of the story, Harry Waterford is running out of patience. The anxiety, which infects two households, over who has purchased the Wakely place springs principally from the effect this sale will have on the walks Valentine enjoys across this land in the company of another man's family. Charlotte immediately divines that Valentine's ex-wife has bought the property, and she knows that Valentine is almost certain to leave the area once he discovers this. When she attempts to voice these fears to her husband, Harry accidentally breaks "the long stem of his pipe." (I am reluctant to explore all the implications of this, but I will observe that a man may be afflicted with more than one type of broken stem.) Harry' s explanation of this pipe breaking is worth noting: " 'There,' he said, throwing it into the fire, 'you and Valentine have got me worked up with your fussing' " (33–34). On the following evening, in the last scene in which he appears, Harry refuses to accompany his wife when she wishes to check on Valentine: "Take Marjorie, won't you?" he suggests. "I really don't want to see the poor chap tonight, Charlotte" (37). What is interesting about these lines is that they seem to be so out of character, and I can only surmise that Harry has grown tired of settling for the cold toast of his wife's affections.

That Charlotte enjoys an intense and intimate bond with Valentine is clear throughout the story; that this bond is stronger than the relationship she has with her husband seems equally clear. Analyzing the relationship between Charlotte and Valentine, Marilyn Arnold has argued that they are close "because the deepest human attachments are aesthetic; a mutual appreciation of the beautiful is the strongest bond possible" (122). If this is the case, then the scene in which Charlotte and Harry respond so differently to the wall where the red roses grow may be taken as a sort of counterpoint to the scene in which Charlotte and Valentine simultaneously murmur, "The Rhinegold!" when they gaze upon a moonlit river (25). Charlotte and her husband do not find beauty in the same things; however, in Valentine, Charlotte has found a sensibility that mirrors her own. Whatever the source that feeds this relationship—be it aesthetic, intuitive, or a sort of "blood-identity" between "spiritual siblings," as another critic suggests (O'Brien 264)—the bond between Charlotte and Valentine should not be viewed as an ideal male–female relationship. However strong it may be, it is not strong enough to sustain Valentine when his ex-wife invades the territory he perceives as his own. And during his remaining weeks at Greenacre, Valentine makes himself so unpleasant that Marjorie confesses, "All of us, except Aunt Charlotte, were eager to have him go" (37).

Although the apparently lovely world of Greenacre is undeniably threatened by the industrial expansion of the nearby city, Greenacre also carries within it the seeds of its own self-destruction. It is a world populated by women, children, and elderly alcoholics who isolate themselves on a hill and vainly try to ignore the passage of time. Within such a world, Valentine may be capable of writing a handful of songs—just as his Uncle Roland is still capable of occasionally shutting himself up in his room and playing the piano brilliantly. Valentine temporarily succeeds because he is sustained not only by the physical loveliness of Greenacre but also because he is nurtured by the affection of the artificial family he has acquired for himself. Without the irritating responsibilities that he once endured as a husband and father, Valentine enjoys several months wandering through a pastoral landscape in the company of a surrogate wife and children who make no demands upon him. In more than one sense, he enjoys the roses another man has grown. Unfortunately, for both Valentine and the family he appropriates, relationships built upon the pursuit of beauty have nowhere to go once beauty is besmeared.

Within the world of Willa Cather, it is easy to choose between the gross materialism of a Janet Oglethorpe and the sensitive cultivation of a Charlotte Waterford. The difficult choice is between the freedom for self-expression and the responsibility one owes to other people. Valentine Ramsay equivocates when faced with this choice. He is a man who cannot even decide the order in which he should read his letters. Lacking the strength to live alone and the patience to live with others, he fails because he needs the comfort of family life but is unwilling to accept any of its cares. We must question the value of Valentine's relationship with Charlotte when we recognize not only its unhappy effect upon Harry Waterford, but also, more sadly, that however intense that relationship may have been during the spring and summer, it leads nowhere for either Valentine or Charlotte once fall descends upon their enchanted hill.

—*University of Wisconsin—Stevens Point*

BIBLIOGRAPHY

Arnold, Marilyn. *Willa Cather's Short Fiction.* Athens: Ohio UP, 1984.

Cather, Willa. "Uncle Valentine." *Uncle Valentine and Other Stories: Willa Cather's Uncollected Short Fiction.* Ed. Bernice Slote. Lincoln: U of Nebraska P, 1973. 3–38.

O'Brien, Sharon. *Willa Cather: The Emerging Voice.* New York: Oxford UP, 1987.

Willa Cather and her nieces: Virginia, Margaret, and Elizabeth

Part Three:
Feminist Perspectives
on Family and Community

This section begins and ends with essays by Yongue and Dollar pitting males against females in matters of family and fulfillment. Romines follows Yongue's argument that war is destructive to women's lives with one about slavery being equally so. Levy and Hallgarth compare Thea Kronborg with the heroines of "The Bohemian Girl" and *Lucy Gayheart*, respectively, to explore dilemmas of artistic calling for women, and Ramonda and Hart appreciate the bonding through fiction of generations of women.

In "For Better and for Worse: At Home and at War in *One of Ours*" Patricia Lee Yongue views the Pulitzer Prize winner as a woman's anti-war novel evaluating life-making over death-making and defends it from Hemingway's dismissal. Yongue locates two voices here, Claude's and Cather's, one glorifying and the other condemning war as man's resentment of woman's birth power, as his preference for blood shed in battle over blood shed in birth. Cather attempts to redefine history as more than military deeds, as a domestic record of family-making. It is ironic Claude never realizes that family is the antithesis of war, that war does nothing but oppose the ideal familial life he discovers in France.

Another male institution challenges female survival in Cather's last novel, argues Ann Romines in "*Sapphira and the Slave Girl*: The Daughters' Plot." She shows an older Cather in touch with her female heritage, including the concerns of Stowe's *Uncle Tom's Cabin*, a novel Cather disparaged in youth. These concerns involve the slavery woven into Southern domestic life, an evil destructive to families and reducing women to powerlessness and silence. Once Sapphira Colbert's daughter Rachel Blake learns the truth about ownership and Till's daughter Nancy's vulnerability as a slave, she develops a revolutionary language and shapes it into a plot to effect the slave's freedom. Although this language severs Rachel's communication with her mother, in Nancy's happy return in the epilogue the narrator (Cather herself as a child) attempts to link the female generations. Just as Till's domestic skills provided Nancy with a profession in freedom, and Rachel's soup-making saved her own daughter Mary's life, Cather as a writer depends on the inherited gift of the lives of her family's women.

Reconciliation of the female generations becomes a priority in Helen Fiddyment Levy's comparison of Thea Kronborg and Clara Vavrika, "Mothers and Daughters in 'The Bohemian Girl' and *The Song of the Lark*." Levy sees Thea rather than Clara as reflecting a mature Cather's creativity and difficult leave-taking. Cather respected traditional nurturing roles for women, and in Thea's story a nurturing mother gives birth to an artist daughter who then celebrates her mother. Cather saw the female generations in harmony rather than in conflict, as in Clara's story.

In "The Woman Who Would Be Artist in *The Song of the Lark* and *Lucy Gayheart*" Susan Hallgarth concentrates on individual freedom as a woman's birthright in paralleling Thea's and Lucy's stories. Cather argues in the later novel that even the conventionally feminine woman like Lucy is capable of escaping the restricted role society tries to impose on her, the group life of families and small town communities, and capable too of discovering the kingdom of art as not exclusively male.

We return to the theme of female kinship in Karen Stevens Ramonda's "Three in One Woman in 'Old Mrs. Harris.'" Having lived through the trials presently suffered by her daughter and granddaughter, the title character is sympathetic to them. They, in turn, will have sympathy for her when they are old. The three women in the story are thus interchangeable—or, as Susan Gubar notes, "nurturing grandmother, anxiously pregnant mother, imaginative daughter" make a woman. But this truth is complicated in Cather's story by progress, for Grandma Harris's last project allows her granddaughter to transcend the restrictions of the Southern belle tradition.

Sue Hart's "My Great-Grandmother in Cather's Pages" is an example of how fiction can serve female kinship. Hart juxtaposes the stories of Cather's Western heroines and the life of her maternal relative, who left little written record, and appreciates through Cather the hardships of her own pioneering women forebears: "I find the history of my own family in Nebraska woven into Cather's pages."

J. Gerald Dollar's "Community and Connectedness in *A Lost Lady*," the only essay in this group by a male, will serve to close the frame. Dollar detects in Cather's cameo portrait of Marian Forrester threatening masculine forces. Frank Ellinger and Ivy Peters would disconnect Marian from the captain's society for their satisfaction, while Niel would sacrifice her sexual nature for his idealization of her. Marian is torn between her need of security with the captain and her need to satisfy the feminine energy for which there is no outlet in the feudal brotherhood of railroad aristocracy. The three men are in various ways disconnectors and reflective of the social decline paralleling Marian's fall.

J. J. M.

For Better and for Worse:
At Home and at War in *One of Ours*

PATRICIA LEE YONGUE

I

Ernest Hemingway not only inveighed against Willa Cather's portrayal of soldiers and war in *One of Ours* (1922), he also insinuated that women are in fact impoverished by their general exclusion from the heightened experience of war. In a swaggering letter to Edmund Wilson, Hemingway was brutal and accusing:

> E. E. Cummings' *Enormous Room* was the best book published last year that I read. Somebody told me it was a flop. Then look at *One of Ours*. Prize, big sale, people taking it seriously. You were in the war weren't you? Wasn't that last scene in the lines wonderful? Do you know where it came from? The battle scene in *Birth of a Nation*. I identified episode after episode, Catherized. Poor woman she had to get her war experience somewhere. (105)

Although Hemingway himself would philosophically reject militarism for its conformity and war for its absurdity and declare convincingly that the words *honor* and *patriotism* and *courage* used to defend acts of war were "obscene," he nonetheless reckoned "dirty war" to be central to the achievement and understanding of manhood. He accepted war—its physical violence and death dealing—as an inevitable human situation that mirrored life's biological consequences, yet, for all that, offered a boy his best chance to become "a man." The twisted bedsteads, crumbled walls of houses, mangled flesh, and human screams that would make the Hemingway hero "sick" of war are impressive as imprints on his consciousness. They are the indelible, concrete proof of the absurdity of war. But they do not evoke a compassion for who and what are destroyed or a concern for civilization; they are, instead, an imprimatur that compels him "straight" into a manly stoicism that is primarily a narcissism.

Hemingway went out of his way to contend that love, marriage, and family life—the domain of woman—were not war's equals in making a man. Quite the contrary, vis-a-vis a suspiciously Aristotelian assertion, he presents such family affiliations as deleterious to that process. The home, because of the menacing woman (mother or wife), is a dire threat to manhood. War, then, like its derivatives hunting and athletics, evolves an inherent positive function in Hemingway's stories—that of making man stronger in the broken place—a function that Willa Cather, like any "poor woman," could neither comprehend nor reproduce.

Perhaps the most unappreciative implication in Hemingway's censure of Cather for invading the male realm of war is that, like F. Scott Fitzgerald, who felt his exclusion from World War I threatened his power to write "like the big boys," Cather herself perceived war as a developmental experience in which she needed to share as a writer. Its corollary, that she did not share at all in the experience, is the point of Hemingway's invective. Unhappily, tradition largely supports Hemingway's assumptions, for war has been represented to us as the epicenter of human history and the preserver of civilization; and, to be a part of all that, even in America, one must wield a lance or gun. For example, in Francis Parkman's *The Oregon Trail*, a text Cather said she liked, it is difficult to decide what activity Parkman more pleasurably describes: exploration and discovery, or fighting and controlling man and animal alike with gun, knife, and bow and arrow.[1]

Society has learned to define itself according to martial occupations. Our concept of "heroic death" issues from a soldier's death in war, so society awards more medals for dying or being wounded in war than for any other human "achievement." In *One of Ours*, it is the sight of his "wonderful men" mutilated and bloody that stirs a bleeding Claude Wheeler, just before his own death from "three clean bullet holes—one through his heart," to profess that "they were mortal, but they were unconquerable" (453). A large portion of our culture's vocabulary and imagery of power and right is martial (my own use of *invading*, for example, in the previous paragraph). Henry Colbert in Cather's *Sapphira and the Slave Girl* (1940) reads Bunyan's *Holy War* and is actually comforted by the allegory.

In light of this, there is indeed an oddity—or irony—in the fact that Willa Cather won a Pulitzer Prize for *One of Ours*, and for its presumed patriotism—its war setting and Claude's "heroic death" in battle. The truth is that *One of Ours* is an anti-war novel and a woman's novel. I would, moreover, go so far as to recommend that it is an anti-war novel because it is a woman's novel, and that it is a woman's novel because it supremely values making life, marriage, and the home and family, and not at all making death—the end to all these things.

For Willa Cather, the woman's primary mode is bearing life, providing nurture, and organizing and preserving the disparate aspects of living in whatever environment she exists, usually the home; the woman's own imagination and physicality are not natively induced to develop a logic or myth/mythology that justifies elimination and death, especially that attendant upon killing. She recoils, at last, even from hunting. The land itself, particularly the garden, which mirrors the life-giving and nurturing and beautifying nature of woman (and woman's blood) and where her children must live and on which her home must rest, is desecrated by blood from a kill spilled upon it. The title character in Cather's *My Ántonia* (1918) tells Jim Burden, "Ever since I've had children, I don't like to kill anything. . . . Ain't that strange, Jim?" (342).

But Cather had not always presented it this way. In her second novel, *O Pioneers!* (1913), Alexandra Bergson, for all of her splendid, special love of life, land, and family, espouses several conventional attitudes that are worrisome, perhaps even to Willa Cather. For example, she encourages her young brother Emil to tell the story of a matador killed in the bull ring and to tell it for the benefit of Mrs. Xavier Chevalier, mother of twenty, who liked "bloody" stories (218). When Emil and Marie Shabata are murdered by Marie's husband, and Marie, ripped apart by bullet wounds, sheds a trail of blood as she drags herself across the field to return to Emil, Alexandra herself does not reflect upon the brutality and the horror, or upon Marie's agony. Only the narrator does. Likewise, though Alexandra grows grim and bent from her grief, she priggishly blames her brother and Marie more for adultery than she blames Frank Shabata for murder. She tells Frank that she does not "feel hard toward" him; Emil and Marie "were more to blame than you" (293). Alexandra hopes she and Frank can be "friendly." In her way, she endorses the conventional paradigm: man is frustrated with wife/woman and his frustration leads him to kill, for which act he will somehow be exonerated. It is a simple and anti-woman pattern that Cather will expose in its ultimate destructive form in *One of Ours*. Alexandra has no honest sympathy for the woman who, in Marie's case, expresses her own frustration with her marriage in adultery rather than in murder. Alexandra's bitterest feelings are for Marie.

Conventionally, too, however, Alexandra finds a sentimental compensation and logic in the deaths of the lovers:

> The moment she had reached them in the orchard that morning, everything was clear to her. There was something about those two lying in the grass, something in the way Marie had settled her cheek on Emil's shoulder, that told her everything. She wondered then how they could have helped loving each other; how she could have helped knowing that they must. (285)

Although her marriage to Carl Linstrum, following upon the forgiving of Frank Shabata, ameliorates the brutality of the murders and particularly Marie's physical and emotional pain, Alexandra's generous nature—sometimes a little too generous, I think—is paradoxically not generous enough, not in a woman's way, at any rate.

In 1913, Cather was as yet unexposed to war and to killing except via stories. She was born just a decade after the Civil War and had heard numerous stories about it. She even had a young uncle who was killed in it. But that was not enough to bring her to full consciousness about war and its effects on people, their family life, and the land. She could intellectually deduce from her reading of classical literature alone—"*Arma virumque cano*," begins her favorite epic—that war and killing were anti-woman and anti-family, but there was not the force of seeing and feeling that pushed the subject to the forefront of her consciousness and stirred her. By 1917, when she was writing *My Ántonia*, the Western world was swallowed up in war and in the vortex of verbal and pictorial messages that accompanies war. Her many references to masculine violence and killing (most of them anti-marriage and anti-family acts) in that novel set mainly in rural Nebraska are the domestic links to the stories of the violence in war-ruined Europe that families were hearing on a daily, sometimes hourly, basis.

By 1921, Cather's personal loss of her cousin G. P. Cather in the war, her touring of the battlefields, trashed homefields, and cemeteries in France, and her considerable reflections about all this would bring her round to writing directly about one of humanity's most inhumane acts. Contrary to having no right or knowledge to write about war, Cather had every right and, more important, every obligation to write about it from a thinking and articulate woman's perspective; for, despite Hemingway's opinions, war tremendously affects women and the people to whom they give birth. How women feel war and feel about war ought, from a human and moral viewpoint, to matter as much as how men feel it and feel about it. It would have been, I think, inhumane, immoral, and unwomanly of Cather, who preferred to avoid writing directly about current affairs, not to write about the war and not to oppose war, somewhat in Martha Nussbaum's sense in *The Fragility of Goodness*, for its despoiling of life/beauty/goodness. That *One of Ours* is Willa Cather's only novel to address a contemporary social "problem" directly and analytically is evidence of the enormity of the issue, and the evil, in her eyes.

I cannot speak to the realism, the veracity, of the troopship scenes ("The Voyage of the Anchises") or the battle scenes, which several male readers have criticized harshly, or to her inauthentic intrusion upon a male sphere of action. (Hemingway [the most censorious of these readers], I might point out, seemed himself to have no misgivings about describing what women go through when they give birth.) I will say that it is apparent that Cather aspired to accuracy of detail in the troopship episodes and in her descriptions of a ravaged France, decimated families, and mutilated bodies but did not aspire to compete with a man's experience.[2] She did, however, want to compete with a man's story and with a man's voice. It is also apparent, as I will explain later in this essay, that at least two noninterchangeable narrative points of view and two styles are represented in these sections, just as they are in other sections. Sometimes, then, the "words" are Cather's and are intended, interestingly enough, as the more objective and woman's view; sometimes they are Claude's and are intended to represent his—a man's— partial view and vocabulary of war. Cather sets this divergence up elementally, in a conventional dialogue between Claude and his mother.

Mrs. Wheeler has been asking about "every detail of Claude's life in [boot] camp": "She asked about the mess, the cooks, the laundry, as well as about his own duties. She made him describe the bayonet drill and explain the operation of machine guns and automatic rifles." Then she expresses her fear, a womanly fear, for the safety of the "thousands of young men" who will sail overseas on troopships in waters menaced by German submarines. Stupidly, though, she cannot or will not go farther than that, and she says "thoughtfully, 'If they can once get you over there, I am not afraid; I believe our boys are as good as any in the world.' " To her question, "How do you boys feel about it?" Claude responds:

> "About what, Mother? Oh, the transportation! We don't worry about that. It's the Government's job to get us across. A soldier mustn't worry about anything except what he's directly responsible for. If the Germans should sink a few troop ships, it should be unfortunate, certainly,—but it wouldn't cut any figure in the long run. The British are perfecting an enormous dirigible, built to carry passengers. If our transports are sunk, it will only mean delay. In another year the Yankees will be flying over. They can't stop us."

Mrs. Wheeler replies, "That must be boy's talk, Claude. Surely you don't believe such a thing could be practicable?" (256–57).

Of course, Mrs. Wheeler's thinking is limited, but it makes a start at distinguishing between a woman's perspective (which tends to be integrative) and "a boy's" (which in Cather's view is also the perspective the American man has been trained to have) in terms of the regard for individual life and family. Mrs. Wheeler's argument is never seriously considered by her son, however, for two reasons: it is an argument she herself aborts and, as such, embodies one repercussion of the history of woman's enforced silence and subservience in society; and, related to this, Claude as a male automatically demotes the importance of what a female has to say and "feel," especially about "male" activities like war. Women have learned to treat their own outlook as less comprehensive and comprehending than men's; they learn to speak mainly as a background against which the male voice is showcased. Claude will talk to his mother out of a narcissism, in order to give himself an opportunity to speak, not in order to listen to and reflect upon what she has to say. Like his father, he clearly sees her function, and the function of any woman he encounters, as that of servant to his needs and mind. Her point of view, therefore, does not register as influential. If it were, Cather implies, society might not be so quick, so enthusiastic, to violate the home by sending its boys to war.

I realize that one of the first arguments against what I have just said is that the family life Claude Wheeler experiences in Nebraska with his parents and brothers and the life he tries to make with his wife Enid are anything but warm and nurturing. His father is a bully, and his mother is her husband's submissive collaborator. Mrs. Wheeler has the right impulses, but they have lost their power in her conditioned subservience; they are like her "sensitive hands" that "seemed to have nothing to do with sense, to be almost like groping fingers of a spirit" (256). Mahailey, the housekeeper, seems to show Claude real care and rallies to his defense, but she has even less power to make him happy than his mother because he allows her less power. Gladys Farmer, a young music teacher, loves him dearly and as he wishes to be loved, but Claude does not love her and relegates her to the cellar of the powerless along with Mahailey and his father's superannuated machinery.

Instead, Claude marries Enid Royce, who refuses to sleep with him on their wedding night and thereafter, and whose obsession with the cleanliness and "perfect order" of her house projects her inner sterility and frigidity. Even her father tries to tell Claude that Enid, like her mother, cannot make a man happy. Enid wears crisp white clothes and white shoes when she tends the house; she cooks vegetarian meals; she breeds chickens with "not a dark feather among them"; she drives two thousand miles in her electric coupe for the Anti-Saloon League; she is a "scrupulous" practitioner of Christian ideals; her farming methods, honed by the latest technology, outdo those of her father; her flower gardens are the most beautiful; she and her mother bake the best bread in town. Her voice is the dominant one. It seems clear that she is a Mother Earth and Mother Goddess run amok.

When Enid decides to go to China to help her ill missionary sister and by so doing fulfill a lifelong ambition to nurse and serve a ministry outside the home, Claude boards up the house he has designed and built "for her" and moves back in with his mother and father. As soon as America enters the war, he enlists in the army. War is his escape from the battleground of family life, and in his relationships with the men in his outfit he finds an emotional satisfaction he has never known "at home." It would thus seem that Willa Cather herself is using a pattern that implicitly endorses war in the mode of a Hemingway.

While there is no question about the unhappiness of Claude's family situation, there is a question about point of view regarding the nature and validity of war as the antidote, even the ironic antidote, for his affliction. There is also the question of the source of the unhealthiness of his family and marital life that sends him seeking to rehabilitate himself in war. With respect to the latter, Willa Cather (as I mentioned earlier) integrates into *One of Ours* a complex argument about the status of war as an anti-woman and anti-family act. She proposes that by limiting the sphere of influence and action of the female, man-centered society has forced the integrative woman (Gladys Farmer), whom man/society rejects as dangerously "extravagant," to extremes of subservient (Mrs. Wheeler) or autocratic (Enid)—but respectable—behavior, and that this then makes man equally unhappy in the resulting "unnatural" home environment while feeding the stereotype of woman as either "trivial" or, in Cather's own word, "Enid-y."

Our tendency has been to blame Enid alone, and maybe Claude's romantic notions, for the unhappiness of her husband and his distress with the home he has supposedly lovingly built for her. We forget, however, that, like Enid's father, Claude rejects every ambition Enid has, including intellectual ones, and presumes, like critic Richard Giannone, that being married to a man and serving as a homemaker to him is ambition or "cause" enough for a woman (Giannone 132). Claude has not even given Enid her say in designing the house; he decides for her what rooms should be emphasized and how. He designs the structure upon which their life together will be based. He expects her to do the decorating and cleaning of the inside, with the attitude that those are necessary but lesser tasks for the lesser being. Small wonder, then, that Enid (though unlike Mrs. Wheeler she has perfected housekeeping and cooking) does not thrill to the house the way Claude does when he is building it as "their" home and dreaming of Enid inside it.

This vicious cycle has the effect of condoning escape, physically and/or psychologically, from the female and home to either all-male worlds or worlds in which males are deferred to. In this context, war in *One of Ours* symbolizes the apogee of man's destructive repudiation of woman's autonomy and his undermining of the home that he recognizes as her place. In his frustration with his wife's and his home's failure to satisfy him, Claude goes off to destroy someone else's home life, to kill some other woman's son, husband, father, brother. It is a process—a dynamic—that Claude engages in unconsciously, but he engages in it nevertheless. It is a dangerous process, engineered publicly in the name of patriotism. It is the subtext of war, and Cather handily exposes it.

Although I cannot take time here to argue the point effectively, I believe that Willa Cather shares with feminist writers the conclusion that, at some point before the Common Era, man used war and embellished warriors to usurp from woman the quintessential power she represented by her capacity to give birth.[3] Respect for the blood she shed in behalf of mothering was replaced by respect for the blood man sheds in war. Fathering a country— giving birth to nations—became synonymous with exploring, appropriating land, and going to war. Subsequently, in later generations of society in which war grew less frequent, what men do became in the public eye more important than what women do. This is conceded in the most mundane of our interactions. For example, when Enid announces her plans to go to China to help her sister Carrie who is very "ill . . . among strangers," Claude retorts meanly that he will let go of the farm animals and the house. "If you've no feeling for the place," he declares, "you can hardly expect me to hang around and take care of it. All the time you were campaigning [in behalf of Prohibition], I played housekeeper here" (221). In *My Ántonia*, unindustrious Anton Cuzak enumerates the many achievements of his wife in the business of sustaining and expanding their farm and family, and Jim Burden gloriously describes her virtues as a homemaker. But all Anton concludes is that Ántonia has given him an "ain't so bad" life for a man; and Jim commits the exemplary sin in entitling the final book of his "My Ántonia" narrative "Cuzak's Boys." In the very section of his text in which he purports to honor Ántonia Shimerda Cuzak as Reproductive Force, the mother of many children (several of them girls), he downgrades maternity and femaleness. Giving birth to boys and feeding them are perceived as the major acts of the "rich mine of life" that is Ántonia. And her husband's name is more important than hers in identifying her progeny.

Willa Cather's woman-centeredness is very modern in the sense that she does not disavow home as the woman's special place or nurturing and ordering and beautifying civilization from within as her special activities. Cather seems not at all anti-marriage in terms of a social and human ideal, although she feared what marriage had become for many women and men. Her fiction is testimony to that outlook; it is very much home and family oriented, as woman's fiction must be in order to reestablish the significance of marriage, the home, and family in the history of civilization that has been undermined by the narrow definition of textbook history as the deeds of men, especially war. She did not want to see women denying the substance of their femininity, even if, like herself, they chose not to marry or have children or "keep house" in the traditional way. Joan of Arc, who is the subject of Claude Wheeler's history thesis, is in Cather's text no real heroine for this very reason. Dressed in her manly armor, tried and convicted of treason, Joan is truly treasonous, not in political terms, but in terms of her betrayal of woman's nature and cause by taking up man's cause, by going to war.

In *Sapphira and the Slave Girl*, Cather's final novel, there is no emphasis on the Civil War or war stories as there easily could have been. The war, *the* event in Southern history that even Abraham Lincoln elevated to greatness, is dealt with summarily (275–77). What is important to the narrator of *Sapphira* in her own development as a woman writer is the memory of afternoons she spent as a child with the returned slave girl Nancy, Nancy's mother Till, and Mrs. Blake, listening to their stories that seemed to cast a "spell" on her. The women gathered in the kitchen after the dinner dishes were done and took their chairs near "the west window where the sunlight poured in. They took out their sewing or knitting . . . and while the pound cake or the marble cake was baking in the slow oven, they talked about old times" (287). Just before this, the narrator describes as inviting but realistic a kitchen as one could imagine:

> We had three kitchen tables: one for kneading bread, another for making cakes and pastry, and a third with a zinc top, for dismembering fowls and rabbits and stuffing turkeys. The tall cupboards stored sugar and spices and groceries. . . . Behind the doors of a very special cupboard stood all the jars of brandied fruit, and glass jars of ginger and orange peel soaking in whisky. Canned vegetables, and the preserved fruits not put down in alcohol, were kept in a very cold cellar: a stream ran through it, actually! (287)

What Cather does recognize and reject is the degradation of woman, the limiting of her powers and her activities to routine housekeeping and cooking, and the demeaning of giving birth and keeping up a home and family as routine activities. For Cather, the home, not the marketplace or the museum and certainly not the battlefield, is ideally the place of great beauty and life, the garden-like center of the spirit of human living, where one ought to feel and learn the major accesses of life. Although it has become a trap for her, woman's domestic, wifely, and maternal art is still the supreme civilizing force in society, in history. One of my favorite lines in *The Song of the Lark* (1915) occurs in the "Ancient People" section, in Thea Kronborg's reverence for the Cliff Dweller women who crafted the jars that held their community's water and food: "They had not only expressed their desire, but they had expressed it as beautifully as they could" (305). Thea's "heart [goes] out to those ancient potters" for the "care" they had "expended upon vessels that could not hold food or water any better for the additional labor put upon them" (305). This, not war, is the true activity Cather wished to share in as a woman and as a woman artist. Like all other successful human endeavors, making a home requires a "desire" for life, skill, understanding, a sense of design and order, a sense of balance, a capacity to integrate, physical and moral courage, endurance, love. In *The Professor's House* (1925), Cather is not just talking about interior design when she says that "the hand, fastidious and bold, which selected and placed" the flowers and furnishings in the wonderfully warm drawing-room that delights the professor is a hand more creative than Nature. That "fastidious and bold" hand belongs to a woman whose work, if valued properly, is the work "that made the difference" (75).

II

A major point to be made in terms of the topic of this essay, however, is that Cather describes war as a crime not only against woman but also against society. War, in addition to its specific characteristics and consequences, its literal blowing up of homes, gardens, and family members, is in *One of Ours* the metaphor for an anti-woman and anti-home society. It is the other side of the picture, or it is a Dorian Grey picture. And it is ghastly. What Hemingway and the traditional eye never saw, were not prepared to see, in *One of Ours* is this denunciation of war, of the rhetoric and rationale and spectacle of killing to prove one's worth and power, and particularly of the assault upon woman and the family and society that war is.

Cather portrays too many fine women and too many fine family situations in *One of Ours* to be accused herself of using the war dynamic as the plot structure. There are women like Gladys and Mrs. Farmer at home; there is Mrs. Erlich in the city. Mlle. de Courcy and the Jouberts await Claude in France. What Cather does is offset with her own the "plot" or scenario Claude drafts. She carefully structures and narrates Claude's experiences in France (" 'Bidding the Eagles of the West Fly On' ") to make very clear that war is an outrageous attack first on woman, then on the family, and thus on civilization, whose basic unit is the family, where principles and values are learned. She anticipates this in the attack "at home" of the Frankfort boys on Mrs. Voigt, the German woman who has been selling "dem candy since dey was babies" and who runs the local restaurant. She feeds Claude, who will seek out her tormentors, "a pot-pie . . . und green peas, chust a few, out of my own garden" (245). In France, Claude encounters a "woman, ill and wretched looking, [who] sat on a fallen log at the end of the marsh, a baby in her lap and three children hanging about her. She was far gone in consumption. . . . Draggled, mud to the knees, she was trying to nurse her baby, half hidden under an old black shawl. She didn't look like a tramp woman, but like one who had once been able to take proper care of herself, and she was still young. The children were tired and discouraged" (359–60).

With the same material Cather also makes very clear that the means for a man to overcome his feeling of being castrated by his own family is not to go to war to kill other people's families. Claude is the one who finds elation and fulfillment in being a part of war; he thinks he has arrived at manhood. He glories, it is true, in the family life he is shown in France in the home of the Jouberts. But he cannot see, as Cather does, his real failure in perception. He does not comprehend that glorious family life is the antithesis of war. To the end, he sees the two facets of his experience in France only as ego-bolstering and thus compatible.

The combination of war and French family life exhilarate Claude. In France, wounded and attended to beautifully, Claude is in his glory at the Jouberts'. This older couple, who have lost their own sons in the war, minister to him and David Gerhardt as if they were their sons. Mrs. Joubert, whom Claude first sees sitting under a cherry tree sewing, quickly discovers that Claude likes his meat and potatoes served together instead of separately and just as quickly accommodates his preference. Like the land Cather so often describes, Mrs. Joubert is loving and generous and a source of life and beauty. Her first act, repeating many such acts performed by women for "their" men in Cather's fiction, is to cut one of the "cream-coloured, pink-tipped roses" from the vine that ran over the wall near the kitchen and stick it in Claude's buttonhole (349), surely a greater gesture of care and dignity than that of putting a bullet through his heart. This act itself repeats and is repeated by Nature. "Poppies and cornflowers ran over" the many, many graves of French and German soldiers (393) at the cemetery Claude stops at en route from Mlle. de Courcy's to the front. Days later, when Claude is back at the Jouberts' recuperating from his ankle wound, "clad in clean pyjamas," he feels "perfect bliss." Papa Joubert has brought him a platter with "an omelette made of twelve eggs and stuffed with bacon and fried potatoes," warm coffee, and brandy. The "chill of the sheets grew warm round his body, and he sniffed in the pillow the old smell of lavender. To be so warm, so dry, so clean, so beloved!" (403).

Claude's problem—the lameness suggested by his name—is his inclination to move from the experience of perfect domesticity at the Jouberts' to a romantic view of war in which there is continuity and contiguity between homefront and battlefield.[4] Claude, remember, does not even detect any grief or anything "sharp and definite like sorrow" in Mrs. Joubert's face when first he sees her; he prefers instead to see in the face of this woman who has recently lost all her sons "an old, quiet, impersonal sadness,—sweet in its expression, like the sadness of music" (349). He had made the same mistake in evaluating the spirituality of Enid Royce's disposition when she came to nurse him after he got erysipelas, and he fell in love with what he thought he saw in her. Now, lying blissfully in bed, he reminisces on the landscape:

> The journey down, reviewed from here, seemed beautiful. As soon as they had got out of the region of martyred trees, they found the land of France turning gold. All along the river valleys the poplars and cottonwoods had changed from green to yellow,—evenly coloured, looking like candle-flames in the mist and rain. Across the fields, along the horizon they ran, like torches passed from hand to hand, and all the willows by the little streams had become silver. The vineyards were green still, thickly spotted with curly, blood-red branches. (403)

The picture is almost perfect, and very close to the striking visual performance that enriches Cather's fiction. But this is Claude's performance, and it diminishes the horrors of war that Claude had seen and acknowledged earlier, for example, in the town where Mlle. de Courcy lives that is now "mounds of burned brick and broken stone, heaps of rusty, twisted iron, splintered beams and rafters, stagnant pools, cellar holes full of muddy water," where an American soldier was known to have drowned (380).

Claude's self-indulgence notwithstanding, Cather's picture of domestic life in France is splendid, and the women he meets are not docile like his mother or cold like Enid. Even the men understand the conduct of a genteel household, from the cooking of marvelous food to the washing and cleaning up. Husband and wife, at least during the circumstances of wartime, share a life and the rituals that give a dignity and beauty and warmth to it. Papa Joubert does not demean housekeeping as Claude had seen it sneered at and himself had sneered at it at home. One gets the sense that, even if it were not wartime, Papa Joubert would not regard the performing of the rites of domestic life degrading or intrinsically unimportant.

Mlle. Olive de Courcy likewise cares for her home, and the people who come to stay, with the devotion of a lady who takes care of the altar and sacerdotal vestments in a church. Her garden is important too, and, "lying flattened in the sun," it is the final thing Claude sees and, literally, "would never find again" as he leaves the woman who speaks with such great reverence about humanity and her country: "three stone arches, the dahlias and marigolds, the glistening boxwood wall" (392). Back in Nebraska, Gladys Farmer might have made this kind of home for Claude, but his American eyes have been trained to evaluate woman and wifeliness in a dysfunctional sort of way.

Cather continues to contrast Claude's lovely experiences of family life and maternity with the molestation of that life by war. A blonde little girl eating chocolate is shot, "blood and brains oozing out in her yellow hair" (428). The Jouberts' sons are dead. Mlle. de Courcy's brother died from shelling that "tore" the arm off Louis, his orderly (388). Gardens and farms are ravaged. There is the woman with the three children we have already mentioned, that "pitiful group of humanity, bemired" (359). Even "the infant Jesus had been shot away" from the arms of the statue of the Virgin Mary guarding the door of a ruined church (382). These fragments of a once whole life are a transmogrification of the "fragments of their desire" that are the shards of clay vessels made by the ancient Indian women in Thea Kronborg's *Panther Canyon* (*The Song of Lark* 321).

The little Belgian girl who acts as a maid to the Jouberts reminds us pointedly of the origination and effect on woman and civilization of man's embracing of war. When Claude first sees the frightened, pale girl, she has a "lap full of baby kittens" (349). Then he sees her carrying "a pile of heavy plates" that she "rested against her stomach and leaned back as she walked, to balance them" (355), mimicking pregnancy and the fragility, obligatory in war, of the life woman carries and nurtures. Afterwards, at dinner, she must be told repeatedly to fetch the requisite items, which she did "with dull eyes" that "never seemed to look" and "with manifest reluctance,—sullenly, as if she were being forced to do something wrong" (356). Finally, when Claude reached for one of the kittens, the little girl "uttered a shrill scream, a really terrible scream, and squatted down, covering her face with her hands." Mrs. Joubert, in a word that says it all, tells Claude that the child has been "terrorized" (357).

For Willa Cather, I think, civilization has been terrorized by war. The woman—the wife, the mother, the daughter, the sister, the aunt, the writer— who is at least half of that civilization, has from the childhood of human history been "bemired" in marriage and in the home. Because she and her "place" have been rendered powerless in terms of having an influential voice in the establishment of society's vital processes and outlook and language of strength, man's earliest societal task, to go to war, has overwhelmed her more humane role and has effected an imbalance in human living—for the worse. Every woman must shrink in terror, her voice demobilized into a shrill scream, at the thought of war and what it will do to the family she loves. War, and its virtual celebration by our society and by Claude Wheeler— well-meaning and "sensitive" though we and he think we are—is the great monster that threatens woman, that threatens civilization.

—*University of Houston*

NOTES

1. It seems to me that Cather would not be impressed by Parkman's text as history per se; in addition to glorifying men who kill (his one instance of an Indian squaw butchering a puppy is narrated with revulsion and condemns her), Parkman's attitudes

toward women indicate he gives them no importance in the "real" business of living. Cather would, however, enjoy his truly delightful renderings of the land and the vagaries of nature, some of which she may even have borrowed.

2. Cather's biographers refer to her sources for "The Voyage of the Anchises" and " 'Bidding the Eagles of the West Fly On' ": letters from the young violinist David Hochstein, who was killed in the Argonne in 1918, to his mother; letters home of her cousin, G. P. Cather, who was killed at Cantigny in 1918; and the diary of a doctor in New Hampshire who had tended to the passengers aboard a troopship when an epidemic of influenza broke out. James Woodress summarizes the major reactions of male critics to what was viewed as Cather's "war story" (330–34). The core of Woodress's response to these critics, that Cather was using a woman's point of view while writing primarily through Claude's imagination, comes closer to the reality of the novel.

3. Marilyn French has provided the most thorough historical outline of this process in *Beyond Power*.

4. E. K. Brown, Cather's earliest biographer, reports that Cather was impressed by "the intellectual and emotional maturity" evident in the letters of her cousin G. P. Cather and of David Hochstein, for whom war had brought about an immense and rapid change in their outlook (215–16). James Woodress includes a much more detailed evaluation of Cather's relationship with her cousin and his influence on her conception of Claude Wheeler (303–04). My sense of Claude is that his outlook does not change at all; his war experiences merely elicit responses typical of the mind and imagination we have seen all along.

BIBLIOGRAPHY

Brown, E. K. *Willa Cather: A Critical Biography*. New York: Knopf, 1953.

Cather, Willa. *My Ántonia*. Boston: Houghton, 1926.

_____. *O Pioneers!* Boston: Houghton, 1913.

_____. *One of Ours*. New York: Knopf, 1922.

_____. *The Professor's House*. New York: Knopf, 1925.

_____. *Sapphira and the Slave Girl*. New York: Knopf, 1940.

_____. *The Song of the Lark*. Boston: Houghton, 1915.

French, Marilyn. *Beyond Power: On Women, Men, and Morals*. New York: Summit, 1985.

Giannone, Richard. *Music in Willa Cather's Fiction*. Lincoln: U of Nebraska P, 1968.

Hemingway, Ernest. *Selected Letters 1917–1961*. Ed. Carlos Baker. New York: Scribner's, 1981.

Nussbaum, Martha C. *The Fragility of Goodness: Luck and Ethics in Greek Tragedy and Philosophy*. Cambridge: Cambridge UP, 1986.

Woodress, James. *Willa Cather: A Literary Life*. Lincoln: U of Nebraska P, 1987.

Sapphira and the Slave Girl:
The Daughters' Plot

ANN ROMINES

As a young woman, Willa Cather romanticized her Southern male ancestors, writing that the "proud blood" of a Confederate soldier–uncle would "burn and bite" forever in her veins (*April Twilights* [1903] 26). But what actually seems to have burned most persistently in Cather's consciousness was the Southern female relationships that dominated her early childhood. That heritage finally became the center of her last major work, *Sapphira and the Slave Girl* (1940).

As a young critic, Cather had railed against *Uncle Tom's Cabin* (1852) as a Northern woman's failed attempt to write about the South, "one of the warmest, richest civilizations the world has ever known" (*The Kingdom of Art* 270). Cather had found few nineteenth-century American women writers to admire, and she never expressed admiration for Harriet Beecher Stowe. Nevertheless, in *Sapphira* she took on many of the concerns addressed in *Uncle Tom's Cabin*. As much as Sarah Orne Jewett, Stowe is a foremother of *Sapphira*. In both novels, the actual and symbolic exigencies of slavery give special urgency to the work of traditional plot. And the plots themselves are similar, turning on a woman's escape by the Underground Railroad. In the conclusions, both escapees, Eliza and Nancy, are reunited with their mothers, Cassy and Till. Both books also exalt domestic life and see slavery's most insidious evil in the destruction of families. The most effective opposition to slavery comes from women, and both books present versions of a matriarchal domestic utopia, exploring the relation between women's domestic power and their political powerlessness. In *Sapphira*, Cather was drawn, as Stowe, to a central problem and enigma of Southern history: the relationship of women and slavery.

Cather's novel has at its center the plot of a white woman, Sapphira Colbert, to dispose of her slave girl, Nancy. Although Sapphira decides to sell Nancy, she is stopped by the veto of her husband, Henry, who disapproves of slavery. Immobilized by dropsy, bloated and pale, Sapphira is like a grotesque image of the white mistress with only her household to rule. So she decides to invite the rake Martin Colbert for a visit to facilitate the rape of Nancy, moving the girl's bed to the hallway. The effective antagonist in this domestic plot is Sapphira's grown daughter, Rachel Blake, who engineers

Nancy's escape by the Underground Railroad. At the novel's center, then, is the conjunction of Sapphira's enormous power and her humiliating helplessness as a woman. Historian Deborah Gray White reminds us that, like Sapphira, slave women were forced to learn covert ways to seize power. They came to understand "the value of silence and secrecy. . . . Women, like slaves and servants, deliberately dissemble their objective reality. . . . They hide their real sentiments and turn toward [the master] a changeless smile or an enigmatic impassivity" (24).

To be a Southern-born woman, as Willa Cather was, is almost inevitably to be connected with a history of slavery and with such dissembling.[1] Cather might have fantasized, as in *Shadows on the Rock*, that one could turn one's back on the ugliness and abuse of one's history while retaining the enhancing, nurturing qualities of one's hereditary culture, which for her were often epitomized in domestic life. But as she wrote her last novel, she had to acknowledge that such fantasies of selective escape were impossible. In the Virginia of *Sapphira and the Slave Girl*, domestic ritual, the very fabric of family life, is interwoven inextricably with slavery. Although the novel is full of close and affectionate observation of Virginia domestic life in the 1850s, every household detail is weighted with complicity.

Because of this complicity, Rachel Blake grew up at odds with her mother's household. A turning point of her childhood came when Rachel overheard the local postmistress decline her father's offer to buy her a slave. That a parent and child could speak of such matters is a revelation to Rachel: "She had never heard the thing said before, never heard it put into words. It was the *owning* that was wrong, the relation itself. . . . It was the thing that made her unhappy at home, and came between her and her mother" (137). As a grown woman, widowed, Rachel tries to shape an independent life, working as a philanthropic nurse and making friends who share her abolitionist sentiments. Such friends give her access to a language of conviction, in which one can *speak* of freedom and thus *effect* it. In the tradition of *Uncle Tom's Cabin*, Cather's last novel shows how women and slaves may develop language and plot its use as an instrument of freedom.

Rachel's father silently shares her antislavery sentiments. But the daughter is effective where her father cannot be, because he remains tied to conventional ideas about the plots possible for women, respecting Sapphira's "Southern hospitality" to Martin and refusing to hear about Nancy's terror of rape. Instead he pores over his Bible and his Bunyan for solutions. In *Pilgrim's Progress* he has found a role for Nancy that pleases him; he sees her as Mercy, a perpetually chaste domestic handmaiden. As the honorable husband of a slaveholding woman, Henry is himself enslaved—and he is further bound by his inability to articulate a plot worthy of an independent woman like his daughter.

Thus Nancy puts her life in Rachel's hands because there is no one else who can help her. Since her mother, Till, is Sapphira's housekeeper and most loyal slave, Nancy, like Rachel, has grown up with no one to hear her story.

Reasons for this silence lead back to the crucial event of Till's childhood: the little girl watched her mother burn to death and was "struck dumb" at the sight. If her mother, the center of her child's world, could expire as quickly as rags could burn, what could have meaning and substance? The white English housekeeper, capable Mrs. Matchem, adopted Till and taught her a new language, impressing the precepts of housekeeping upon the traumatized child, who took them "devoutly to heart" (71). Matchem's lesson is that domestic order gives our lives beauty, security, and meaning and is central to civilization. Till is an apt pupil, but the civilization she preserves conceives of her as one of the household objects she puts in order. Like many traditional women, Till adopts housekeeping as her primary language. Matchem never taught her a speakable, liberating vocabulary of feeling and action. Thus it is understandable that Till cannot talk with her daughter about the most pressing feelings of their lives. She does not even tell Nancy who her white father was, and the girl never asks. Like the other daughters and mothers in this book, the two are separated by silence.

According to White, the daughter's adolescence was a particularly stressful period for a slave mother, when she became even more intensely aware of her limited capacity to care for her child: "In the long run . . . a mother could do little but hope that her daughter made it through adolescence and young womanhood unscathed by sexual abuse" (95–96).[2] Till does what she can; she teaches Nancy her domestic arts. The most intimate and touching scene between the two occurs as they clean Sapphira's house together. Till tries to tell Nancy how to get back in Sapphira's good graces, urging the only plot she knows, domestic servitude:

> "Make a nice eggnog . . . carry it to the mistress . . . on the small silvah
> salvah, with a white napkin and some cold biscuit. . . . Smile, an' look happy
> to serve her, an' she'll smile back."
>
> Nancy shook her head. Her slender hands dropped limp at her sides.
> "No she won't, Mudder." (44–45)

Such recipes can no longer keep Till's daughter safe. As Rachel is appalled by her mother's power, Nancy is appalled by her mother's powerlessness. Rachel becomes an effective protector for Nancy partly because, although she has two daughters, she is not entirely boxed into a domestic system. When Nancy is afraid to go into the woods alone, Rachel accompanies her, even though her bread is ready to bake. Nancy can voice her suicidal fears to Rachel, and Rachel can reply with a hitherto unspeakable question: "I think I can get you away. Would you go?" (218).

Twenty-five years after Nancy's escape, she and her mother are reunited in the epilogue of *Sapphira*, as Eliza and Cassy, mother and daughter, are reunited at the climax of *Uncle Tom's Cabin*. Stowe's women are "successful" mothers who have defied slavery and executed spectacular maternal escapes, rescuing imperiled children. By contrast, some of Till's most perceptive recent critics suggest that she is a failed mother. Minrose Gwin, for example, claims that "it is difficult to take Till seriously as a black woman" because of her treatment of Nancy (140).[3] Yet when Till hears from Rachel that Nancy is en route to Canada, she responds with love and concern. Suppressing tears, Till says, "If she's up there with the English folks, she'll have some chance" (249). In Canada, Nancy becomes a professional housekeeper, and on her return, Till delights in her daughter's speech: "Nancy, darlin', you talks just like Mrs. Matchem. . . . I loves to hear you" (286). When Till hears Matchem's accents in her daughter's voice, it is as if Nancy has become the English housekeeper's descendant. The unsafe, combustible slave mother is supplanted, and in her place is the only reliable maternal figure Till has ever known. To listen to Nancy and to hear about her success as a house-keeper vindicate Till's own domestic plot, letting her feel that she is a good mother.

Nancy left Virginia and her life as a slave with great reluctance; she loved her mother's housekeeping and longed to stay home and live a plantation version of the domestic romance. But she was caught between that compelling fantasy and a world of truths that she was loath to admit, the terrors of a slave woman trapped in a dark hall.[4] Nancy was made especially vulnerable by her budding sexuality. For example, when she went cherrypicking and began to enjoy her sensuality, she was seized by the predatory Martin. Thus Nancy found herself at a terrible impasse—her love for her mother, her sexuality, her self-respect, her longing for security and continuity, and her love of place and housekeeping were all at war; and the inner and outer combat were so intense that the only solution she could imagine was suicide.

To continue her life, Nancy had to find a new and honorable plot, one which would let her become fully human. Peter Brooks reminds us that plot is "a form of thinking," an "engagement with human memory and desire" (319). Many of the memories Nancy must ponder are tales of Southern women. Like *Uncle Tom's Cabin*, this novel teems with such stories, most of them germinated in Cather's own girlhood memories. For example, one stunning "inset story" is devoted to Nancy's great-grandmother, Jezebel, a spirited African who is dying at ninety-five. When Sapphira reads her slave a psalm and counsels resignation, Jezebel acquiesces weakly, "Yes'm, I'se resigned" (87). But in fact she is taking her death into her own hands by refusing to eat. When Sapphira offers whatever food the slave desires, Jezebel replies "with a flash of grim humor, 'No'm, I cain't think of nuthin' I could relish, lessen maybe it was a l'il pickaninny's hand'" (89). Nancy, standing by, is shocked by her voracious kinswoman, but Sapphira comprehends Jezebel's response. Both older women are fuelled by hungry energy that resists bondage, although it may seem to Nancy that such old women really do devour their young. As Nancy takes up her adult life in freedom, however, she is potentially an heir to Jezebel, Till, Sapphira, and—as were all daughters of the nineteenth century, including Willa Cather—the oblique language of such women.

Sapphira is the novel in which Cather most fully acknowledges the complexity of that inheritance and her own connections to Nancy's story. The epilogue, viewed through her own five-year-old consciousness, focuses on the moment in which Nancy's story meets her own. There, two kinds of female plots converge, one traditional and one revolutionary. In the Cather kitchen, the mothers' traditional plot of domestic continuance proceeds. Till and Rachel, both now grandmothers, conspire in cooking, sewing, and storytelling, while the girl Willa sits by, listening and silently working at her patchwork, the domestic apprenticework of her own evolving language.[5] The daughters' revolutionary plot of liberation and discovery has been enacted by Nancy in her escape. Yet, by her choice of housekeeping as a profession, Nancy seems to suggest that a woman can—and perhaps *must*—claim both these plots. Rachel too participates in both plots and suggests the same conclusion. Young Willa has been schooled to think of Nancy as an archetypal heroine of song and story. The older women conspire so that the girl can witness the climax of Nancy's story, her reunion with Till, which dramatizes the convergence of the mothers' and the daughters' plots. This reunion is a seductively utopian scene.

In *Uncle Tom's Cabin*, Stowe presents a domestic utopia in her picture of the Quaker household, a free-state oasis. There, such everyday domestic chores as the preparation of breakfast demonstrate the workings of an ideal community, egalitarian but ruled by the righteous authority of a Quaker matriarch who welcomes Eliza as "daughter." The epilogue of *Sapphira* may seem similarly utopian. Abolition is accomplished, and Nancy returns as an honored, storied guest. The house is ordered by female domestic authority and, as in Stowe's scene, a benignly antipatriarchal father is nearby.

Through her Quaker household, Stowe would like to persuade her readers that domestic ritual can be the medium and model for an ideal life. Perhaps Willa's elders would like to impress the same lesson on this child, through the medium of Nancy's "happy ending." But as the little girl sits listening, soaking up the lore and ambiance of her family, she also picks up other clues about mothers and daughters. "Aunt Till," however welcoming she now seems, did not help Nancy escape; that help came from Rachel, who thus opposed her own mother. The completed plot of Nancy's departure and return is counterpointed by a cycle of troubling questions about what mothers and dauthers can and cannot say and be to each other.

With such a multiple perspective, this scene becomes too complexly human to be utopian. The truly utopian scene in *Sapphira* occurs earlier, when Rachel's young daughters fall ill with diptheria. Rachel and the minister are nursing the children; she prepares chicken broth for him and leaves it to cool on the kitchen table. The minister sees Mary enter the room and drink the bowl of broth, in a "solemn" scene that resembles "a Communion service" (259). Later, the doctor tells him that the nourishing soup was the ill child's "chance" (264); by taking it, she saved her own life. This scene has a powerfully sacramental quality, with the "mysterious significance" of dream (259). Sleepwalking, Mary is acting out of her deepest unconscious self—claiming her life. The nourishment she needs is available because her mother is a good housekeeper; even in the upheaval of an epidemic, Rachel has accomplished the time-consuming task of simmering stock. But Mary must find the soup and drink it herself, becoming the central actor in her own plot.

In *The Song of the Lark*, Thea Kronborg, Cather's autobiographical protagonist, is told by her wisest teacher, Harsanyi,

> "Every artist makes himself born. It is very much harder than the other time, and longer. Your mother did not bring anything into the world to play piano. That you must bring into the world yourself."
>
> This comforted Thea . . . for it seemed to give her a chance. (175–76)

Perhaps the most any mother can wish for her daughter is "a chance"—it is what Till hopes Nancy will find in Canada; it is what Thea strains to discover through her art, and it is what Mary swallows with her mother's broth. In the earlier novel, Cather conceives of this process as a second birth, a further separation from the mother. In *Sapphira*, Mary too is working to claim her life. But, although she acts alone, Mary is abetted by her mother's domestic care, by the intuitive sympathy of the observing minister, and by the novelist herself, who is both the creator and the daughter of this character. Such a continuum of support, collaboration, and independence suggests what the relation of mother, daughter, and community might be in a true utopia. And it is a matter of life and death; Rachel's other daughter, who cannot feed herself, dies.

All the women in this novel, including young Willa Cather, struggle to get themselves born in a world that is far from utopian—a world that could extinguish and enslave them. They all wrestle with a central problem: how can a Southern girl come to selfhood, as woman and artist? How can she find the plot that will be her chance?

That was Willa Cather's question, as she turned at last to her Virginia memories.[6] Like the sleepwalking Mary, Cather found waiting for her, in the family kitchen,[7] a sustaining meal prepared by her mother and grandmother. And as the artist explored that material, she claimed another part of her heritage as an American woman writer, learning how to approach Stowe's materials in ways entirely her own. She confronts some of the most continually disturbing questions of American women's history and shows us how they were woven into her own life. In *Sapphira and the Slave Girl*, a Southern daughter found her plot.

—*George Washington University*

NOTES

1. Critics have traditionally emphasized Cather's Nebraska years more than her Southern background. But it is interesting that in *The Eye of the Story* Eudora Welty, another Southern-born writer, takes for granted the importance of Cather's "Southern origin," compares her with Faulkner, and suggests that Cather's sense of history was shaped by her Virginia birth (45–47).

2. Jacqueline Jones also discusses this issue of responsibility in historical terms; she says that "family responsibilities revealed the limited extent to which black women (and men) could control their own lives" (29).

3. See also Marilyn Arnold on Till (332).

4. In *The Voyage Perilous* (236–39), Susan J. Rosowski discusses the gothic implications of this situation.

5. Traditionally, patchwork was one of the first skills a nineteenth-century girl was taught. Five, young Willa's age, was a usual age for such lessons (see Ferrero, Hedges, and Silber 16–19).

6. Both Sharon O'Brien and James Woodress provide indispensable information about those years.

7. The Cather kitchen is vividly evoked in the epilogue of *Sapphira*. Rosowski sketches the significance of kitchen scenes in Cather's fiction in the Foreword to the Welsches' *Cather's Kitchens* ix–xv.

BIBLIOGRAPHY

Arnold, Marilyn. " 'Of Human Bondage,': Cather's Subnarrative in *Sapphira and the Slave Girl*." *Mississippi Quarterly* 40 (1987): 323–38.

Brooks, Peter. *Reading for the Plot*. New York: Vintage, 1985.

Cather, Willa. *April Twilights (1903)*. Ed. Bernice Slote. Lincoln: U of Nebraska P, 1968.

———. *The Kingdom of Art: Willa Cather's First Principles and Critical Statements, 1893–1896*. Ed. Bernice Slote. Lincoln: U of Nebraska P, 1966.

———. *Sapphira and the Slave Girl*. New York: Knopf, 1941.

———. *The Song of the Lark*. Lincoln: U of Nebraska P, Bison, 1978.

Ferrero, Pat, Elaine Hedges, and Julie Silber. *Hearts and Hands: The Influence of Women and Quilts on American Society*. San Francisco: Quilt Digest P, 1987.

Gwin, Minrose C. *Black and White Women of the Old South*. Knoxville: U of Tennessee P, 1985.

Jones, Jacqueline. *Labor of Love, Labor of Sorrow: Black Women, Work, and the Family from Slavery to the Present*. New York: Basic, 1985.

O'Brien, Sharon. *Willa Cather: The Emerging Voice*. New York: Oxford UP, 1987.

Rosowski, Susan J. *The Voyage Perilous: Willa Cather's Romanticism*. Lincoln: U of Nebraska P, 1986.

Stowe, Harriet Beecher. *Uncle Tom's Cabin*. New York: Penguin, 1986.

Welsch, Roger L., and Linda K. Welsch. *Cather's Kitchens*. Lincoln: U of Nebraska P, 1987.

Welty, Eudora. *The Eye of the Story*. New York: Random, 1978.

White, Deborah Gray. *Ar'n't I a Woman? Female Slaves in the Plantation South*. New York: Norton, 1985.

Woodress, James. *Willa Cather: A Literary Life*. Lincoln: U of Nebraska P, 1987.

Mothers and Daughters in "The Bohemian Girl" and *The Song of the Lark*

HELEN FIDDYMENT LEVY

> *Then Willa got up and wandered about the room. To be free, to work at her table—that* was *all in all. What could be more beautiful, if you had it in you, than to be the wife of a farmer and raise a big family in Nebraska? There were fates and fates but one could not live them all. Some would call hers servitude but she called it liberation.*
>
> Elizabeth Shepley Sergeant

The recent critical biography of Willa Cather by Sharon O'Brien has focused attention on Cather's development as an individual, introspective artist. O'Brien's psychological approach is by its nature an ahistorical one, yet the relation of history and art was always crucial to Willa Cather. The record of the fiction itself suggests that in the early years of her career Cather's female cultural heritage troubled her more consistently and urgently than did her sexual orientation. Moreover, the clash between traditional cultural expectations for women, which Cather shared, and her own romantic belief in the nature of the autonomous individual woman artist underwent a drastic change between the writing of "The Bohemian Girl" (1912) and *The Song of the Lark* (1915).

Feminist historian Mary Ryan notes in *The Empire of the Mother* that, surprisingly enough, the settlers who moved westward held views of women's domestic roles fully as conservative as those who remained in the East (22–23). Cather's Virginia background, as portrayed in the fiction, memoirs, and biographies, centered on traditional social roles for women, roles that persisted despite transplantation to the prairies. Despite her well-known rebellion against the traditional roles assigned women in nineteenth-century Red Cloud, Cather felt compelled to justify her repudiation of them. Indeed, the extent of her role refusal suggests the power and persistence of traditional examples. No significant forward movement was possible until she resolved her place in the life of her family and community.

Throughout her career Cather celebrated female biological identity and cultural memory as the forces that directly create a new, vital civilization. Also, she discussed the relation of the prairie mother to the artist in explicit terms:

The farmer's wife who raises a large family and cooks for them and makes their clothes and keeps house and on the side runs a truck garden and a chicken farm and a canning establishment, and thoroughly enjoys doing it all, and doing it well, contributes more to art than all the culture clubs. Often you find such a woman with all the appreciation of the beautiful bodies of her children, of the odor and harmony of her kitchen, of the real creative joy of all her activities, which marks the great artist.

Most of the women artists I have known—the prima donnas, novelists, poets, sculptors—have been women of the same type. The very best cooks I have known have been prima donnas. (Bohlke 47)

The nurturing, conserving mother present throughout Cather's work from Grandmother Ericson in "The Bohemian Girl" and Mrs. Kronborg in *The Song of the Lark* to Ántonia Shimerda of *My Ántonia*, Cécile Auclair in *Shadows on the Rock*, Old Mrs. Harris, and, oddly enough, spinster Alexandra Bergson in *O Pioneers!* share certain similarities: They are vital, calm, guardians of "our ways," sensuous, stubborn, unimaginative, self-satisfied, industrious, and unconventional in matters of fashion. In effect, often, they possess a noble completeness that transcends the temporal and thus death, draws strength from the group and the earth, and stands against the forces of modernity.

That Cather found this model of womanhood heroic, even epic, is beyond question. Although influenced by the female models of her own childhood, she chose to follow the different path her interests and career demanded. How could she, the daughter of a community whose women married and raised families, justify her choices? How could Cather remain faithful to the family and its traditions and at the same time rescue herself from drowning in the stream of time? At the time of "The Bohemian Girl," she had not yet found a model for female endeavor freed from biological and cultural reproductive tasks. Against immigrant mothers like Grandmother Ericson, Cather juxtaposes the Bohemian girl, not woman, Clara Vavrika. At the end of the painterly barn-raising scene celebrating such immigrant mothers, the observing Nils reflects, "No, . . . she'd never be like them, not if she lived here a hundred years. She'd only grow more bitter. You can't tame a wild thing; you can only chain it" (29).

O'Brien considers this long story of Clara's romantic flight to be a representation of Cather's reaction to her own creativity and leave-taking. O'Brien's reading goes against several factors that taken together suggest the story does not offer Cather's portrayal of the reconciliation of her female gender and individual art. Clara may be a female protagonist, but she is not a Cather heroine. Clara despises the housewifely arts, absents herself from the woman's community, spites her husband and his dour family to amuse herself, and exploits the labor of her simple aunt, Johanna Vavrika, who anticipates other foolish, but ultimately wise, attendants like Tillie Kronborg in *The Song of the Lark*. Despite some positive components of her personality,

Clara Vavrika's wild, passionate nature is ultimately destructive. Further, to validate O'Brien's critical reading, one must diminish the importance of the figure of Mrs. Ericson and finesse the implications of the ending that dismisses Nils and Clara from the story. One must also ignore the fates of women similar to Clara in Cather's other works.

Nowhere else in Cather's mature work is the escape through romantic passion presented positively. To the argument that Clara's bitterness will be purged by Nils's love, one must remember that Nils is really stealing his brother's wife and his mother's daughter-in-law, that Clara is fleeing her past and the soil, and that Cather would disapprove of both. Choosing momentary satisfaction over the larger commitment, whether it be parenting or art, Clara and her lover vanish from the life of their people without a trace. In character and, in some cases, appearance, Clara resembles other romantically passionate Cather women, like Marie Shabata, Myra Henshawe, and Lucy Gayheart, sacrificed to the emotional present.

To underscore her intent to portray this sexual escapade as negative, Cather appends the story of Nils's younger brother Eric, who plans to flee because of his loss of favor with his family over his suspected part in the lovers' escape. However, Eric returns to the maternally founded family that the adulterous, almost incestuous, relationship of the lovers threatened to tear apart. O'Brien portrays Mother Ericson offering a "problematic maternal embrace" and describes the twining of the mother's fingers in her son's hair as "almost frightening." O'Brien characterizes the ending thus, "She risks the future, he finds safety in the past" (395–99). But David Stouck writes, "We cannot help feeling that [Eric's] choice involves the author's deepest sympathies and emotional preferences" (22). Rather than showing Cather gaining the confidence of her own female artistry, this story suggests that she had yet to find the rationale for her own leave-taking from women's roles and from her own past, and may in fact have doubted the morality of it.

Such a rationale will be found in *The Song of the Lark*, dedicated to Isabelle McClung, the Muse who gave Cather the confidence to stand outside her early socially conservative background. Here Cather accepts the challenge of the woman artist's choices in much more direct and confident fashion. Whereas Mother Ericson contrasts with the self-determined, somewhat androgynous Clara Vavrika in the earlier story, the female generations are reconciled in the novel, Mrs. Kronborg being a double to her opera singer daughter, Thea. Ray Kennedy's observation makes the connection explicit:

> Mrs. Kronborg had in her face the same serious look that Thea had; only hers was calm and satisfied, and Thea's was intense and questioning. But in both it was a large kind of look, that was not all the time being broken up and convulsed by trivial things. They both carried their heads like Indian women, with a kind of noble unconsciousness. (121)

Mother and daughter share the tie to the Nebraska earth, the same cultural experiences, and indeed the same blood and the same memories. Both women, then, live beyond self and fashion, but one lives unconsciously, through the body, and accepts tradition and homeland; whereas the other must separate from family and home to give birth to the eternal within her self, recover her past, and reach eternity through the soul. Cather explicitly connects the two female creations by Thea's two births.

The first section of the novel centers on Mrs. Kronborg almost as much as on Thea, the two often appearing together so Cather can stress the similarities and attachments between them. Mrs. Kronborg is repeatedly observed in positive terms by such characters as Dr. Archie and Ray Kennedy. Mrs. Kronborg understands Thea's difference instinctively, seeking to nurture Thea's individual talent, protecting her against those in the family and in the town who would force her into conventional behavior. In her turn, Thea accepts and expresses her first birth, her heritage. Unlike the passionate Clara, Thea shares the calm, stubborn, culturally conservative personality of the mother–creator. Here the mother gives birth to the female artist who, in her turn, by giving birth to her art, celebrates her mother's contribution. In *The Song of the Lark*, the female generations of women are in harmony, the strength of mother and daughter increasing by contact with each other.

During these early pages we see the child in relation to her town, her family, and her church. Like Cather herself, Thea finds no place among the available small-town female roles. Like Cather, Thea understands she must leave, yet never really leave behind her home place. The sophisticated Fred Ottenburg observes that Thea as a mature artist never loses the values that fit the Moonstone scale and that this quality has given her the perspective, the rich cultural heritage that underlies her art; so too with Willa Cather.

When Thea returns to Moonstone for the second and final time, she realizes she and her mother have chosen different fates; her mother is a part of the family in an abiding, physical way she can never be. As her train pulls out of the depot, Thea, like Willa Cather herself, knows she cannot return to live with her kin and her earth. All through the night she sobs uncontrollably, but in the morning, she understands that she has left forever. In contrast to Clara Vavrika's instinctive hesitation and her own first, childish homesickness, Thea knows that she has permanently lost daily contact with her people, and especially regrets this regarding her mother. She now prepares to give birth to Kronborg, the artist whose self-determination draws its strength, as Cather tells us repeatedly, from the group, which inspires her art. As she prepares to go to Germany, Thea tells her lover Fred Ottenburg, "Harsanyi said once . . . that if one became an artist one had to be born again, and that one owed nothing to anybody." Fred replies, "Exactly. And when I see you again I shall not see you, but your daughter" (378).

This prepares us for the death of Mrs. Kronborg, which occurs as Thea sings her first major role and gives birth to the artist called Kronborg. On Dr. Archie's last visit to Mrs. Kronborg, she sums up the essence of motherhood, that she raises her children to make their way in the world and understands Thea's absence. As Mrs. Kronborg talks of her daughter, the doctor notes "the same fierce, defiant kind of pride that he had heard often in Thea's voice" (407). As Mrs. Kronborg lies on her deathbed, Kronborg has her triumphant European debut. Dr. Archie, who serves as pallbearer, muses, "she was so serene and queenly that he went back to Denver feeling almost as if he had helped bury Thea Kronborg herself. The handsome head in the coffin seemed to him much more really Thea than the radiant young woman in the picture, looking about at the Gothic vaultings and greeting the Hall of Song" (408). Indeed! With the birth of the soul, the artistic voice that is Kronborg, the female body in its biological, personal sense is transcended. Mrs. Kronborg's death makes this explicit, if we have misunderstood the symbolism of the matrix finding its reflection in the Indian women's pottery and the shape of Thea's mouth and throat. Because of the tie of family and shared experience, Mrs. Kronborg and her daughter will never be separated. Mrs. Kronborg is carried in the flesh and in the emotions of Thea, who, in the depth of her music, gives eternal life to her people, to her mother's experience.

Critical commentary from the beginning has agreed on the specific autobiographical content of the Moonstone section of the novel, despite Cather's use of Wagnerian soprano Olive Fremstad as a prototype. Through the mother's and daughter's contrasting commitments in *The Song of the Lark*, Cather arrived at a justification for her own personal journey away from her close-knit family and her beloved prairie. Cather came to understand how her work fits into the history of her family, her country, and her sex. By all accounts, we know how close and how necessary was the beloved older daughter to her family and to the prairies. Through this profoundly personal book, Cather justified her leave-taking and acknowledged her "use" of her own past. Unlike Clara Vavrika, who quickly leaves behind her identity for a personal passion, Thea Kronborg (and her creator) discovers how to bring her mother's past and her own female experience to bear on her art, to commemorate that past and give birth to the history of her patria as a female artist, and to take her place in the female generations. The mother of the homeland and the daughter of the prairies give birth and nourishment to each other's creativity.

From this time forward, Cather wrote with increased artistry and confidence. Elizabeth Sergeant recounts that Cather considered Thea "as if [she] lived in her own right, objectively," and that at publication, "when the close inner tie was severed, [Cather] felt the pang and emptiness of one deserted" (137). The statement by Sergeant at the beginning of this paper suggests how closely the ideal of the prairie mother and Cather's own artistic fate were linked during the composition of *The Song of the Lark*.

—George Mason University

BIBLIOGRAPHY

Cather, Willa. "The Bohemian Girl." *Willa Cather's Collected Short Stories, 1892–1912*. Ed. Virginia Faulkner. Lincoln: U of Nebraska P, 1965. 3–46.
———. *The Song of the Lark*. Lincoln: U of Nebraska P, Bison, 1978.
———. *Willa Cather in Person: Interviews, Speeches, and Letters*. Ed. L. Brent Bohlke. Lincoln: U of Nebraska P, 1986.
O'Brien, Sharon. *Willa Cather: The Emerging Voice*. New York: Oxford UP, 1987.
Ryan, Mary P. *The Empire of the Mother: American Writing about Domesticity, 1830–1860*. Women and History Series, no. 213. New York: Haworth, 1982.
Sergeant, Elizabeth Shepley. *Willa Cather: A Memoir*. Lincoln: U of Nebraska P, 1963.
Stouck, David. *Willa Cather's Imagination*. Lincoln: U of Nebraska P, 1975.

The Woman Who Would Be Artist
in *The Song of the Lark* and *Lucy Gayheart*

SUSAN A. HALLGARTH

Using different angles of vision and fictional forms, Willa Cather returned again and again to previous settings and subjects to mine their rich complexities. How many fictional communities came, for instance, from Red Cloud, Nebraska? Sandtown, Riverbend, Hanover, Sweet Water, Black Hawk, Moonstone, Frankfort, Haverford—and these are not all. How many pioneers? How many singers? Five opera stars appear in *Youth and the Bright Medusa* alone. These patterns establish key themes in Cather's fiction. Chief among them is her idea of the artist. Cather's thematic treatment of the artist is pervasive: her engineers, pioneers, mothers, soldiers, scholars, and builders are all either closely associated with artists from whom they learn or are themselves representatives of the artist.

In a recently discovered letter to Dorothy Canfield Fisher, Cather makes it clear that the artist was the organizing principle for her first collection of stories, *The Troll Garden* (1905). By her second, the 1920 *Youth and the Bright Medusa*, which retains four of the early tales and adds four others, she had narrowed her focus to the female as artist. Cather had already raised the issue of gender and the artist in *The Troll Garden*, and the development of the female artist is the subject of the 1915 *The Song of the Lark* and of its 1935 tragic counterpart, *Lucy Gayheart*. Repeated treatments like these invite comparison. Reading *Lucy Gayheart* in the context of its predecessors, we learn how Cather refined and enlarged her portrait of the female who would be artist.

In the satiric "Flavia and Her Artists," the first story in *The Troll Garden*, Cather asks what must have been a question of central concern for her own life: can a girl, especially one from America's heartland, become a great artist? With Thea Kronborg in *The Song of the Lark*, Cather's answer would be a resounding yes. But among the victimized women in the harsh heartland of *The Troll Garden*, no female gains the autonomy necessary to assert herself, and the answer delivered by Cather's satiric version of the male artist as stuffed shirt is an ironic no. According to Monsieur Roux, art is the province of male intellect. Women are simply not meant to be great artists. He has searched and found none qualified. In Flavia's world, he explains, women appreciate and absorb—they do not produce. Only men rise out of obscurity because only men take themselves seriously and possess the necessary independence of intellect. Were a woman to do so, Roux claims, she would be unwomanly and monstrous, a Medusa who would "transmute us all into stone" (18–19). Thea Kronborg and the Medusas in *Youth and the Bright Medusa* would certainly transfix Monsieur Roux. Yet their characters suggest that ironically he might have reflected at least partially Cather's own concept of the female artist by assuming that only "mannish" women need apply, women with guts and the strength of self to reject socially defined and limiting stereotypes of conventional heterosexual femininity.

Cather returned to the gender issue with Lucy Gayheart, whose innocence and "phantom love" remind us of Imogen Willard, the naive main character in Flavia's story. But where Flavia's second cousin, the actress and youthful New Woman, "Jimmy" Broadwood, did not test the limits of Roux's smug assumptions about gender and art, Lucy Gayheart does. Cather makes it clear with Lucy that even when pitted against all odds, the most stereotypically feminine of women can learn to take herself seriously and choose to pursue the "fugitive gleam."

Lucy is also anticipated in other *Troll Garden* stories. "The Garden Lodge" and "A Death in the Desert" record ecstatic and profound but transitory unions between female and male artists, similar to Lucy's experience with Clement Sebastian. Raymond d'Esquerré and Adriance Hilgarde are great artists; Caroline Noble and Katharine Gaylord are not. Muses more than artists, they manage to acquire memories of great art, but they have no sustained creative life. Nor does the title character of "The Joy of Nelly Deane," published separately in 1911. Both Nelly and her daughter Margaret are characterized by an evanescence and gaiety like Lucy's—and Margaret's hat and comforter prefigure Lucy's cap and jaunty red feather—but Nelly literally succumbs to small town values when she marries her local beau, an early version of Harry Gordon, and then dies giving birth to his son. Like Henry James's Isabel Archer and the women of *The Troll Garden*, Nelly sacrifices her potential to become what is expected of her. These are poignant, noble victims, but not heroic like Thea or tragic like Lucy.

To grasp Cather's thematic development of the female artist, by far the most interesting comparison is between *The Song of the Lark* and *Lucy Gayheart*. Thea Kronborg becomes a great artist; Lucy Gayheart—who has great desire, experiences her own awakening, and succeeds as a human being—does not. Instead, her potential arrested when she drowns in the icy turbulence of Haverford's river, Lucy escapes through art into the images of star and frieze, ironic symbols of artistic inspiration and immortality. Artistic achievement is rare. Even rarer, Cather's fictional portraits suggest, is the woman with enough self-knowledge, honesty, energy, and courage to escape from culturally defined roles and emotional ties, to break free of deadening ordinariness and deliver herself into art.

Escape is a key word for understanding Cather's concept of the artist and, for that matter, of the wise human being. As Cather describes the challenge in her essay on Katherine Mansfield, escape means breaking free from the constraints imposed by human relationships, from the web woven by circumstance and affection, from the need to be accepted, to be part of the "group life" of families or communities. Truly to escape, as Cather describes it, means to unleash the potential of our "real" selves, those parts of us that in the course of our normal, everyday lives remain subterranean, "secret and passionate and intense." Most of us never fully escape. We remain caught, suspended always in the act of "running away" ("Katherine Mansfield" 109). The true artist, like Thea, begins like the rest of us, but where we remain in this "double life," struggling between the personal and social, she frees her "real" self from it. Once she delivers herself entirely into art, she seems changed, to the rest of us perhaps even lost, as does Thea to Dr. Archie. That is because, as Thea explains, the artist undergoes a kind of sea change or second birth, and having labored long for her own deliverance, she protects her new inner life, her work, with a public mask. In *Lucy Gayheart*, the mask that conceals Sebastian's inner life also creates his aura of grandeur and mystery so that Lucy is drawn to him as much by his tragic look as she is by the rich emotional response she has to his voice.

That a young, impressionable woman like Lucy would be attracted to a sophisticated and worldly artist like Clement Sebastian comes as no surprise. The epitome of the Byronic or Gothic hero, he is older, alien, mysterious, gloomy, and cynical, both sated and haunted by experience. But while his prototypes in "The Garden Lodge" and "A Death in the Desert" may have primed us for Sebastian, nothing in *The Troll Garden, Youth and the Bright Medusa*, or *The Song of the Lark* has quite prepared us for Lucy. As a lively young woman perfectly suited to Monsieur Roux's assumptions about what women should do, Lucy is supposed to survive her "phantom love affair" with Sebastian and settle into the obscurity of Haverford family life as prescribed by Harry Gordon. What she is not supposed to do is aspire to Thea's world of the artist for herself. For Lucy is Thea's antithesis. Shifting from Thea to Lucy means turning from singer to accompanist, from the robust Wagnerian opera to the quiet Schubert lieder, and from the vitality, vigor and gusto of the Valkyrie to its opposite, the stereotypically feminine energy of evanescence and gaiety.

Both Thea and Lucy leave small midwestern towns for musical training in Chicago, but where Moonstone defines and encourages Thea's talent and inner strength, Haverford diffuses and discourages Lucy. Lucy has neither mother nor mentor, and her headlong, joyous dash toward freedom, beauty, and finally toward life brings her ironically to permanent stasis in death. The long list of those who recognize and encourage Thea, on the other hand, begins in Moonstone with her mother and her aunt Tillie and includes Ray Kennedy, Professor Wunsch, and Dr. Archie and continues in Chicago with Harsanyi, Bowers, and her lover Fred Ottenburg. Ray Kennedy tells Thea, there are "a lot of halfway people in this world," people foreordained either to help others on or push them down (*The Song of the Lark* 156). Thea quickly learns to identify and ignore her "natural enemies"—her sister Anna, for instance, and many other people in Moonstone—as those who would hold her down (301). This is an important lesson, for if Thea is to fulfill her destiny, she must break free from Moonstone and familial ties. Even more important, she must free her mind and spirit from stereotypes that would link art and aspiration only to male intellect and drive. Professionals in Chicago and Germany may teach her her craft, but Moonstone and Panther Canyon offer her more fundamental lessons, those of fortitude and of the female in art and aspiration. In Moonstone, where Thea develops her perspective and values, the land itself adds to her self-confidence by giving her its own New World Symphony, conveying a sense of honesty, optimism, and the "childlike power to love" (277). Later, in the symbolic womb of Panther Canyon, where Thea births herself, she discovers that women have always been artists. There Thea realizes that whether it is an ancient jar created by female Indian potters to catch water from the stream, a sculpture in the Chicago Art Institute, or the throat of an opera singer, art is womblike, a "vessel" designed to catch life in "a flash of arrested motion," life that is always "hurrying past us and running away, too strong to stop, too sweet to lose" (378).

Lucy Gayheart shares Thea's joy and desire for escape. However, she lacks the self-confidence and sense of direction that fortify Thea's resistance to Moonstone's provincial attitudes toward women. Where Thea's return to Moonstone acts as a turning point in her career by unleashing the fierceness in her determination to break free, Lucy returns to Haverford to mourn Sebastian's death and, with it, her own aborted awakening. Lucy's associations with Chicago and Sebastian—her first, tentative joy in experiencing freedom and autonomy and her emotional, sensual, and even spiritual responses to beauty and the splendor of art—all of these seem transitory, lost. Exiled, hopeless, Lucy no longer distinguishes friend from foe, and no "halfway people" in Haverford or Chicago emerge to empower her. Those who should help her most—Auerbach, Pauline, and Harry—actually precipitate her death. Where Harsanyi helped Thea to articulate her goals, Auerbach constricts Lucy's, telling her to marry Harry and settle for family life in a small town no matter how deadly she thinks it. And when she writes him on Christmas day, reborn and ready to try even harder, he puts her off, delaying by several months her escape from Haverford. Where Thea can ignore her sister Anna and listen instead to her mother, Lucy's sister Pauline's conformity and insensitivity help to send Lucy toward her death. And finally, where Thea's career is furthered by Ray Kennedy's death, Lucy and her dream die with Harry Gordon's refusal to acknowledge even her simple request for warmth and human kindness.

Although Lucy's tragic fate seems determined from the outset, she experiences a late epiphany and rebirth that parallel Thea's in the canyon. When a Denver touring company performs "The Bohemian Girl," Lucy is almost saved by the worn voice of an old soprano whose "sympathy," "tolerant understanding," and intelligent phrasing give fresh meaning to the "humdrum" opera (*Lucy Gayheart* 181). In this ancient woman's voice, Lucy hears again from the world that "strives after excellence" (181)—and, significantly, this time the artist is female. Later that night Lucy feels an inner "purpose" begin to beat in her like a second heart, and on Christmas Eve, the "time of miracles," she learns through a mystical vision that her "real sweetheart" is not Sebastian but Life itself and that alone she can seek for herself all the "splendours" of the world (182–85). Despite feeling trapped by winter and Haverford, Lucy sees new beauty in the world about her, and in the seconds before her death, she vows again to escape the cruel, stupid propriety of people in this "frozen country," to return to the world of "light and freedom" such as Pauline and Harry "could never know" (198). Ironically, when the tree branch catches her racing feet and the ice lets her down to drown in the freezing stream, they achieve what Haverford's "frozen people" could not, by dragging her down as surely as Mockford's grip had drowned Sebastian in the cold of a Switzerland lake.

Lucy's fate may be tragic, but Lucy is victorious. Stereotypically feminine, the opposite of Thea, and trapped in a heartland as repressive as any in *The Troll Garden*, Lucy is nonetheless triumphant. She never achieves fame or even returns to Chicago, but she had already escaped from life as Haverford defines it the moment she discovered the female in art and then affirmed Life and her own autonomous self. Twenty-five years later, recalling Lucy in the weeks before her death, Harry Gordon could as easily be describing Thea Kronborg. Lucy had already acquired the "brooding" mask to conceal and protect her new inner life and, like all of Cather's artists, she seemed already to be "gathered up and sustained by something that never let her drop into the common world" (215). And where Flavia and the women of the early stories helped to define Cather's concept of the artist only through their failures, Lucy's triumph adds new dimension to Cather's portrait of the woman who would be artist. More important, with *Lucy Gayheart* Cather reminds us that for her the kingdom of art is not, as Monsieur Roux presumed, the exclusive province of male intellect. It is in fact no *king*-dom at all . . .

—*Empire State College*/SUNY

BIBLIOGRAPHY

Cather, Willa. Letter to Dorothy Canfield Fisher 29 March 1903. University of Vermont Collection, Burlington.

_____. *Lucy Gayheart*. New York: Vintage, 1976.

_____. *The Song of the Lark*. Boston: Houghton, 1983.

_____. *The Troll Garden*. New York: New American Library, 1984.

_____. "Katherine Mansfield." *Willa Cather on Writing*. Lincoln: U of Nebraska P, 1988. 107–20.

Three in One Woman in "Old Mrs. Harris"

KAREN STEVENS RAMONDA

> *We must make it evident that maturity is the fulfillment*
> *of childhood and adolescence, not a diminishing; that*
> *it is an affirmation of life, not a denial; that it is*
> *entering fully into our essential selves.*
> Madeleine L'Engle

"Old Mrs. Harris" is the kind of story that sticks in the mind because the old woman is strikingly lifelike and reflects the human condition so unerringly. Although Mrs. Harris has quiet strength and dignity, her nature is initially puzzling: she seems like a drudge by the community's standards, but other evidence points to an autonomous personality. David Daiches calls "Old Mrs. Harris" a mystery (108). Since the story has a generational structure, the reader, who joins the neighbor, Mrs. Rosen, in her quest "to get past the others to the real grandmother" ("Old Mrs. Harris" 83), must also examine the familial context within which Mrs. Harris operates. To evoke the fullness and richness of Mrs. Harris's character, Willa Cather superimposes on it the selves of the daughter and granddaughter, challenging the reader to solve the enigma and comprehend the source of Mrs. Harris's strength and magnetism. To get to know Mrs. Harris, one must examine her sense of selfhood from a generational point of view.

Cather wrote the story around the time of her mother's death (Lewis 157), and it is both a tribute to her family in general and to her Grandma Boak. The story not only creates an unforgettable character, it also describes the various stages of women's lives in those days. When it first appeared in the September–November 1932 issues of the *Ladies Home Journal*, it was called, significantly, "Three Women." Marilyn Arnold believes that the early title refers to Grandma Harris, Victoria, and Mrs. Rosen (141): more likely it refers to Grandma Harris, Victoria, and Vickie, which is evident in the generational continuity in the story's last paragraph:

> Thus Mrs. Harris slipped out of the Templetons' story; but Victoria and
> Vickie had still to go on, to follow the long road that leads through things
> unguessed at and unforeseeable. When they are old, they will come closer
> and closer to Grandma Harris. They will think a great deal about her, and

remember things they never noticed; and their lot will be more or less like
hers. (190)

These lines not only identify the mother, daughter, and granddaughter, they
also point to generational infrastructure as a source of meaning.

In her essay "The Birth of the Artist as Heroine" Susan Gubar quotes
from Elizabeth Stuart Phelps Ward's novel *The Story of Avis* (1877) that
"we have been told that it takes three generations to make a gentleman: we
may believe that it will take as much, or more to make A WOMAN" (33). Discussing what she calls "different versions of the self" in Katherine Mansfield's
short story "Prelude" (33–35), Gubar refers specifically to Cather's story
as "strikingly similar to Mansfield's New Zealand stories . . . [in describing]
the three generations it takes to make A WOMAN—nurturing grandmother,
anxiously pregnant mother, imaginative daughter" (43). Interestingly, Cather's
naming of her characters may reinforce Gubar's notion of individual characters
constituting "an anatomy of female development" (34). Both Victoria and
Vickie have the same name, and Grandma Harris's first name is never
mentioned, causing one to wonder if her name might have been Victoria
also. The overall generational construct not only allows Cather to move
backward and forward in time, but it also enriches her characterization of
Grandma Harris by making it threefold.

In *The Emerging Goddess* Albert Rothenberg talks specifically about the
forming of characters by superimposing images of three generations through
a process he calls homospatial thinking:

> One author, for instance, was consciously aware of modeling a character
> after his own son. As he constructed scenes involving the character's
> interaction with the father in the novel, the author also thought about feelings
> and impressions pertaining to his own father. In writing the scenes, he
> brought together images of his son and himself, and images of himself with
> his own father. (314)

Rothenberg defines homospatial thinking as "actively conceiving two or more
discrete entities occupying the same space, a conception leading to the
articulation of new identities" (69). When this process is applied to Cather's
story, the identity of Grandma Harris emerges more clearly because the
reader sees versions of her as a youth full of inarticulate longings and as
a mature woman with a family to raise.

Superimposing the selves of the three women illuminates for us the story's
antithetical tensions. Cather gives life to her story by constantly juxtaposing
South and West, old and young, and the Rosen and the Templeton households. In fact, Cather's use of this technique generates the central question
of the story: What is the real Grandma Harris like? Is she selfless, thereby

allowing her family to take advantage of her, or does she have a strong self? The reader entertains both possibilities simultaneously, and Cather heightens this effect whenever possible. For instance, Grandma Harris has so few meager possessions that she clings to an old, cast-off sweater for comfort (94–95), leading the reader to think she might be neglected, when in actuality her grandsons love her so much that they care for her tenderly without being bidden (181–85). Rothenberg calls this Janusian thinking (55) and claims that "one of the important functions of homospatial thinking is to integrate Janusian thoughts" (70).

The story formulates an awareness of both the contrast between the experiences of each generation and the continuity of spirit that the generations share. For instance, Vickie and her grandmother are both avid readers who enjoy reading aloud to the family. Both Vickie and her mother like to keep their possessions to themselves. Referring to Vickie's claim to ownership of the cat, Mrs. Rosen says, "Dat Vickie is her mother over again" (84). In addition, all three have a sincere interest in children. Upon returning home, Victoria "stopped by the picket fence to smile at the children playing in the backyard,—and it was a real smile, she was glad to see them" (87). That same morning when Mrs. Rosen asks where the baby is, Grandma Harris says, "Vickie took Hughie in his cart over to Mr. Holliday's yard, where she studies. She's right good about minding him" (86). In the same way, during Mrs. Rosen's visit, after Victoria has nursed the baby, Grandma Harris says proudly when she holds him, "He never frets with his grandma" (117). The grandmother's devotion to her grandchildren permeates the whole story.

Cather reveals the authenticity the three women share: they are without guile. She says of Victoria, "There was something warm and genuine about her" (113). Mrs. Rosen notices that "Vickie never paid compliments, absolutely never: but if she really admired anyone, something in her voice betrayed it so convincingly that one felt flattered" (108). And when Mrs. Rosen ponders why Mrs. Harris is so special, she notes that "there was a kind of nobility about her head that there is about an old lion's: an absence of self-consciousness, vanity, preoccupation—something absolute" (81). These qualities lead to what Mrs. Rosen calls "a pleasantness in the human relationships" of these women (111) and to her observation that "their feelings were so much finer than their way of living" (110).

From the vantage point of mature middle age, Cather understood what her grandmother's life meant. Like Mrs. Harris, Rachel Boak moved with her daughter's family to Nebraska when she was an older woman. She had been an accomplished person within the restrctions set for women then. E. K. Brown notes that "Mrs. Boak had gone to a good school in Baltimore, she had read much and carefully, and she had an alert mind" (20). Grandma Boak was Cather's first teacher. She shared with Cather her love of the written and spoken word. James Woodress says, "Rachel Boak was a remarkable woman who left an indelible impression on her granddaughter" (21). Willa Cather and her grandmother shared a basic, indestructible relatedness that especially flowered in Cather's writing.

So it is not surprising that given the distance of half a lifetime, Cather was able to use her grandmother as the prototype for such a lifelike and loving portrait. Cather reached back to the early years of her grandmother's life. Rachel Boak was married at fourteen and widowed at thirty-eight, during which time she had five children. Her husband, William, was a member of the Virginia House of Delegates and later an official of the Interior Department (Brown 14–15). The family lived in Richmond and Washington, D. C., because of his positions, but at his death Rachel returned to Back Creek, Virginia, where her father gave her a house. She must have had some conviction and nerve because she delivered a slave woman to the Underground Railroad across the Potomac (Woodress 21–25). Although the lives of the fictional character and her prototype differed in some ways, the flavor of the times and the Southern traditions were the same. But Cather's story is much more than a portrait; it is a scenario of the social, biological, economic, emotional, familial pressures and rewards of womanhood in that time and place. It records graphically the struggles and traumas that older women experienced to keep an inner self intact against the onslaught of time and change in a male-dominated society.

The Southern belle tradition that suffuses all of Mrs. Harris's values and identity divides a woman's life into three distinct phases, each with a prescribed role. In a passage similar to Gubar's comments, Cather describes the system in human terms:

> Young girls in the South were supposed to be carefree and foolish; the fault grandmother found in Vickie was that she wasn't foolish enough. When the foolish girl married and began to have children, everything else must give way to that. She must be humoured and given the best of everything, because having children was hard on a woman, and it was the most important thing in the world. In Tennessee every young married woman in good circumstances had an older woman in the house, a mother or mother-in-law or an old aunt, who managed the household economies and directed the help. (130)

At its worst, this system diminished women because it encouraged them to suppress their individuality and assertiveness and to conform to an idealized role (Bartlett and Cambor 20–21). Because they are removed from the rigid demands of plantation life, the women in the story preserve their strength of character, although the traditional values are so ingrained in them that they do not know any other way to live.

If we are to think of grandmother, daughter, and granddaughter as "different versions of the self" (Gubar 35), then we must ascertain how their lives relate to the belle cycle. Because the three women have been transplanted from their feudal society to what Cather calls a "snappy little Western democracy" (133), they are in a transitional phase, still clinging to the old ways while feeling pressure to be different. The only ostensible advantage for a woman to be a belle was financial security. However, because Hillary Templeton is a poor manager with a weak personality, Mrs. Harris, Victoria, and Vickie never feel secure, although he retains certain powers by virtue of his maleness. Consequently, the women struggle with inadequate resources to maintain their sense of propriety, thus creating a confusing allocation of power.

Back in Tennessee, Mrs. Harris owned land, and the family lived in her house, an arrangement from which she derived considerable power. We are told that Hillary "never so much as mended one of the steps to the front porch without consulting Mrs. Harris" (132). When Mrs. Harris agreed to sell her property and turn the profits over to her son-in-law so the family could move West, she lost status in the family and the option of controlling her own money. When her son-in-law denies her her own money to use for Vickie's education, Mrs. Harris, knowing that she had been robbed of her money and her options, provides Cather with a strong feminist statement: "Invested; that was a word men always held over women, Mrs. Harris thought, and it always meant they could have none of their own money" (165). Because of Hillary's decision to relocate and his mismanagement, the family must live in reduced circumstances in Colorado, with Mrs. Harris taking the brunt of the deprivation so they can keep up appearances that mean so much to her. Her insistence on perpetuating the Southern way of life is actually a sign of her power, since it would be natural for younger people to conform gradually to local values. As a result of a series of choices, Mrs. Harris works hard, has little, but never complains.

She is careful not to upstage Victoria, who makes many routine decisions as mistress of the household and mother of the children. Grandma Harris usually defers to Victoria unless she strongly disagrees, as she does in the matter of the cat's burial, when she quietly countermands her daughter's orders. The old woman follows this pattern when her granddaughter needs money to realize her dream of studying at the university. While it is probably true that he does not have the money, neither does Hillary take his daughter's dream seriously or make any effort to arrange to get money. Earlier he told Mrs. Rosen, "I want to keep my little daughter as long as I can" (109). So, Grandma Harris steps in and asks the Rosens to make Vickie a loan, thereby allowing her granddaughter to transcend the belle tradition. This is Grandma Harris's last loving project before she lapses into the final hours of her life.

Towards the end of the story Victoria and Vickie, besieged by problems, become frantic, desperate, and turn inward, illustrating Grandma Harris's philosophical dictum that "everything that's alive has got to suffer" (141). Distraught and alone, Victoria faces another unwanted pregnancy, while Vickie fears that no one will help her get away to college. Cather accentuates the separateness of each, allowing her to show the frustration and alienation from family life that she wrote about in her essay on Mansfield: "Always in his mind each member of these social units is escaping, running away, trying to break the net which circumstances and his own affections have woven about him" (109). These difficulties remind the reader that each generation of a woman's life brings its hardships. Mrs. Harris herself had eight children and also must have felt the strain of "dragging this chain of life that never let her rest" (178). That part of Mrs. Harris's life is not specifically part of the story, but when we read of Victoria's anguish, we can imagine the similar experiences that make Mrs. Harris the sympathetic person she is near the end of her life.

Cather's dominant metaphor is of life's road. Mr. Rosen writes a quotation attributed to Michelet on a slip of paper for Vickie, "*Le but n'est rien: le chemin, c'est tout*" (158). An earlier explanation of Mrs. Harris's following her daughter's family to Colorado contains a version of this metaphor: "But the road had led westward, and Mrs. Harris didn't believe that women, especially old women, could say when or where they would stop" (97). And again in the final paragraph the road is mentioned: "But Victoria and Vickie had still to go on, to follow the long road that leads through things unguessed at and unforseeable" (190). The metaphor of the road implies that life is never static, but that it involves constant changes and movement that generate meaning. The reproductive metaphor "this chain of life" (178) also echoes the road metaphor. During the time span of the story, we see the selves of the three women superimposed, but Cather also has drawn invisible roads leading up to and beyond Skyline, Colorado. "Old Mrs. Harris" really begins with the grandmother's birth and will end with Vickie's death.

Cather fuses the three generations in the last paragraph when she says of Victoria and Vickie that "their lot will be more or less like [Grandma Harris's]" (190). Although each woman has a separate self that is inviolate, a thread of continuity runs from one to the other. Mrs. Harris has experienced most of the joys and sorrows that will come to her daughter and granddaughter. Somehow the road and the suffering translate into growth. Characteristically, since the end is nothing, Grandma Harris fades out of the family's lives quietly, but not without a final reminder of how deeply Cather perceives their relatedness. While Mrs. Harris was unconscious, she "was hastily carried out of the play-room and laid in Victoria's bed, put into one of Victoria's best nightgowns" (189). Victoria and her mother become interchangeable.

—*San Joaquin Delta College*

BIBLIOGRAPHY

Arnold, Marilyn. *Willa Cather's Short Fiction*. Athens: Ohio UP, 1984.

Bartlett, Irving H., and Glenn C. Cambor. "The History and Psychodynamics of Southern Womanhood." *Women's Studies* 2 (1974): 9–24.

Brown, E. K. *Willa Cather: A Critical Biography*. New York: Avon, 1980.

Cather, Willa. "Katherine Mansfield." *Willa Cather on Writing*. Lincoln: U of Nebraska P, 1988. 107–20.

———. "Old Mrs. Harris." *Obscure Destinies*. New York: Vintage, 1974. 75–190.

Daiches, David. *Willa Cather: A Critical Introduction*. New York: Collier, 1951.

Gubar, Susan. "The Birth of the Artist as Heroine." *The Representation of Women in Fiction*. Ed. Carolyn G. Heilburn and Margaret Higonnet. Baltimore: Johns Hopkins UP, 1983. 19–59.

Lewis, Edith. *Willa Cather Living*. New York: Knopf, 1953.

Rothenberg, Albert. *The Emerging Goddess*. Chicago: U of Chicago P, 1979.

Woodress, James. *Willa Cather: Her Life and Art*. New York: Pegasus, 1970.

My Great-Grandmother in Cather's Pages*

SUE HART

Great literature, of course, needs no verification or validation; its truth is what sets it apart from all the other books published in a given year and what makes it endure through generations of readers. I would be foolish indeed to suggest that the life of my great-grandmother validates the stories told by Willa Cather of Nebraska life at the turn of the century. Yet there are the many instances in the life of Mary Anne Toohey—a life lived out for the most part in Cather's Nebraska—that capture, as Cather's stories do, the happiness and heartbreak experienced by those hearty (and sometimes hapless) souls who settled the West. I "discovered" Cather and my great-grandmother at approximately the same time, and as I journeyed into Cather's fiction and into her Nebraska to search out the places and periods of my great-grandmother's life, the paths kept crossing. Beyond her name on a few census sheets, my great-grandmother left nothing in the way of a written record to document her having been here at all. But what I have been able to find out about her life has been expanded and enriched for me in the characters created by Willa Cather.

Mary Anne was born in New York City to Irish immigrant parents and married, one month past her sixteenth birthday, to Patrick Toohey, an Irish immigrant twenty-three years her senior. Despite the age difference, she died twelve years before he did, at the age of fifty-two, worn out, I suspect, by the rigors of frontier life, by years of childbearing, childrearing, hard work, and loss. In my imaginings—for I have no pictures of her—my great-grandmother becomes, in her later years, "a stalwart, brown woman, flat-chested, her curly brown hair a little grizzled . . . battered but not diminished" (*My Ántonia* 331–32). The description is Cather's, of course, of the Ántonia that Jim Burden discovers when he returns to Black Hawk, his childhood home, after years away. The comparison is not so farfetched, either. At the end of their first year of marriage, Mary Anne and her husband—and the first of their eight children—moved west from a farm in Wisconsin to newly opened territory in Webster County, Nebraska. For five years they farmed outside Red Cloud, the community immortalized by Cather as Black Hawk

---

*This essay is dedicated to John B. Toohey (1910–1989), my uncle, who was influential in my "re-discovery" of Cather.

(in *My Ántonia*), Sweet Water (in *A Lost Lady*), Haverford (in *Lucy Gayheart*), MacAlpin (in "The Best Years"), Frankfort (in *One of Ours*), Skyline (in "Old Mrs. Harris"), Hanover (in *O Pioneers!*), and Moonstone (in *The Song of the Lark*). As Catholics, they no doubt helped build—and attended—St. Juliana's, the church where Annie Pavelka, the prototype for Ántonia, was married. They were among the congregation called to Sunday service not by a church bell— for none was ever hung in the bell tower—but by the whistle of the eastbound train bringing the priest to this corner of his far-flung prairie parish. (His "home church" was in Orleans— fifty-some miles from the white frame church erected by the faithful in Red Cloud.)

For Mary Anne and her family, trains and their music apparently had the same romantic quality they held for Cather and so many of the characters she created. No matter where the Tooheys lived in Nebraska, they were always within whistle-distance of the depot, close enough for them to hear— as the children do in "The Best Years"—trains as they "whistled in. . . . Then came the heavy pants of the locomotive in the frosty air. Then a hissing— then silence. . . . Sometimes the great locomotive used to sweep in armoured in ice and snow, breathing fire like a dragon, its great red eye shooting a blinding beam along the white roadbed and shining wet rails. . . . They were grand old warriors, those towering locomotives of other days. . . . They set children's hearts beating from Chicago to Los Angeles. They were the awakeners of many a dream" (109–10). Certainly they awakened dreams in Mary Anne's children; all four of her sons went to work for the Burlington line as soon as they were old enough, following in the footsteps of one of Cather's most heroic characters, Captain Daniel Forrester, "himself a railroad man, a contractor, who had built hundreds of miles of road for the Burlington,—over the sage brush and cattle country, and on up into the Black Hills" (*A Lost Lady* 10). He was of a kind that Cather held in great esteem, one of the "dreamers, great-hearted adventurers" (106) who had settled the West. In Captain Forrester's own words: "All our great West has been developed from such dreams; the homesteader's and the prospector's and the contractor's. We dreamed the railroads across the mountains" (55).

But such dreams were not without cost. The realities as well as the romance of railroading were known both to Cather and to the Toohey family. Ray Kennedy, Thea's Moonstone suitor in *The Song of the Lark*, is the victim of a railroad accident, thus fulfilling the prophecy of his brakeman, Giddy, who tells Thea's mother that "the trains must be operated by fellows the Lord has it in for. . . . They figure it out that a railroad man's only due to last eleven years; then it's his turn to be smashed" (153). And for some railroaders, like Johnnie Toohey, who didn't live long enough to grow into the man's shorter version of his name, not even eleven years were granted. Johnnie died at twenty-two, while on a railroad job somewhere in Utah. His mother was spared this loss; she died two years before he did.

She had known in her lifetime, though, the human cost extracted by a land that was being tamed, first by the plow and then by the railroad. The family had grown to include two daughters by the time Mary Anne and Patrick moved further west, to Stamford, Nebraska. There four more children were born, but two of the girls, Maud and Ellen, died. My great-grandparents were not the only parents to lose children in infancy: Annie and John Pavelka buried three of their children in the cemetery where they themselves now lie, the cemetery described so feelingly in "Neighbour Rosicky" as "all overgrown with long red grass. . . . [and] sort of snug and homelike, not cramped or mournful,—a big sweep all around it" (18).

There are no headstones marking the graves of the Toohey sisters; we surmise they were buried on the family land, but we have yet to find their graves. And chances are that Mary Anne felt like Mrs. Ferguesson, the mother of the young teacher who dies of pneumonia contracted during a blizzard in "The Best Years," when she complained to Lesley's former superintendent, now Mrs. Thorndike: "Seems so many have forgot her, but I know you haven't. . . . And there's nothing in all my life so precious to me to remember and think about as my Lesley. I'm no soft woman, either" (133–34). Mary Anne Toohey must have been "no soft woman" herself to have survived the harshness of life as a farmer's wife, but we know this more from what she didn't say than what she did. Her youngest son, born nearly fifteen years after the deaths of his sisters, never heard his mother mention them. By the time he was born, the family had moved again, this time to Grant, Nebraska, and the land where we suspect the graves were dug had been sold to another family. But it is hard to believe that Mary Anne, like Lesley's mother, did not harbor her own memories of and sorrows over the daughters she had lost.

Like so many of Cather's heroines—Mrs. Rosicky, Alexandra Bergson, Ántonia—Mary Anne Toohey raised livestock as well as worked the land to help the family's income. The 1885 census reports a profit for "Farm Products Sold" by the Toohey household in the amount of $300. The goods produced that year included 100 pounds of butter and 100 dozen eggs. Twenty-four chickens were sold, and the document notes that twelve cows were milked daily—almost certainly the responsibility of the woman and children. So many activities and so few hours in which to accomplish them! In the fall of 1987, my youngest daughter and I stood at the corner of the property my great-grandparents farmed in Harlan County. We looked out over wheat fields, over orchards, down to where a creek ran through a corner of their land. It was a beautiful evening and a beautiful sight. I wondered, though, how often my great-grandmother had the leisure to enjoy that view, or whether—especially after the earth had received two of her children—she could take much pleasure in it.

Again, I turn to Cather for a vision of what life must have been like on that Nebraska homestead, especially for a woman who found herself far removed from the life she had been prepared for and had expected to live. The New York City that Mary Anne left when she married and moved to the newly opened territories of Nebraska (and, indeed, my grandfather, her oldest son, claimed that the family continued to move ever westward as the Indian population was moved away to make room for more settlers, so they were among the first in the communities where they lived) was even then a bustling, busy city. In exchange, she found the stark, lonely realities of prairie life. The narrator of "A Wagner Matinée" sums up his aunt's daily routine in a passage that suggests not only the physical chores the city-bred frontier woman performed, but also her role as teacher, entertainer, bringer of culture to her new community:

> My aunt, after cooking the three meals—the first of which was ready at six o'clock in the morning—and putting the six children to bed, would often stand until midnight at her ironing-board, with me at the kitchen table beside her, hearing me recite Latin declensions and conjugations, gently shaking me when my drowsy head sank down over a page of irregular verbs. It was to her, at her ironing or mending, that I read my first Shakespeare, and her old textbook on mythology was the first that ever came into my empty hands. She taught me my scales and exercises, too—on the little parlor organ which her husband had bought after fifteen years, during which she had not so much as seen any instrument. . . . She would sit beside me by the hour, darning and counting while I struggled with the "Joyous Farmer." (96)

At the end of the story, Aunt Georgiana, her youth long since gone (given up to the struggle to settle and tame the land of south-central Nebraska), tells her nephew that she does not want to leave the music hall where he has taken her when she makes a trip back East after years away: "I don't want to go, Clark, I don't want to go!" (101). Clark understands her struggle; after all, he too had lived for a time on that farm outside the "little Nebraska village" (94). "For her," he knows, "just outside the door of the concert hall, lay the black pond with the cattle-tracked bluffs; the tall, unpainted house, with the weather-curled boards; naked as a tower, the crook-backed ash seedlings where the dish-cloths hung to dry; the gaunt, moulting turkeys picking up refuse about the kitchen door" (101).

Music was important as entertainment on the Western frontier, and training in classical music was not necessarily a prerequisite for being considered "musical" any more than having a college degree was necessary to serve as a teacher. One accomplishment my grandfather was very proud of was his ability to read and write, and since he seldom had time to attend the schools that were available—he was, after all, listed as a "farmer" on the census taken when he was fourteen—I have no trouble envisioning him practicing his lessons late at night with his mother, much as Aunt Georgiana is portrayed listening to Clark. And, while I have no proof that my great-grandmother was musical—no record of her having sung in the church choir, no piano or parlor organ passed down from her generation to mine—I suspect that she sang to her children. Some of my most vivid memories of my grandfather are of the times he asked my mother to "play the old songs" for him. His eyes would often fill with tears as he listened—and I can well imagine that he was recalling the lilting Irish voice of his mother as it filled whatever frame or sod house the family was living in at the time.

Certainly there were times when there was nothing much to sing about— months and years of hard work, little return, loss, and isolation. What strength the women who made the West a home must have had, what a vision of the promise of the land, what courage to renounce the less challenging life of established communities and risk all on the mental and physical stamina of oneself and one's spouse. When I think of the sacrifices my great-grandmother made to the settling of the West, I find it hard to answer the question posed on a Landscape/Graphics notecard: "If we had lived then, would the strength of our dreams have brought us west with the pioneers?" (Perry). The strength of those dreams, the lure of the land and open space, is expressed by Cather through Anton Rosicky, who realizes that "the trouble with big cities" was that

> they built you in from the earth itself, cemented you away from any contact with the ground. . . . He began to think seriously about the articles he had read in Bohemian papers, describing prosperous Czech farming communities in the West. He believed he would like to go out there as a farm hand; it was hardly possible that he could ever have land of his own. . . . Nobody in his family had ever owned any land,—that belonged to a different station of life altogether. . . . To work on another man's farm would be all he asked; to see the sun rise and set and plant things and watch them grow. He was a very simple man. He was like a tree that has not many roots, but one tap-root that goes down deep. (*Obscure Destinies* 31–32)

For many, like Rosicky and my great-grandparents, Nebraska offered the opportunity of the landed gentry in the "old countries" of owning one's own property, but of earning it by hard work and devotion, by setting one's roots in the soil, and making one's life out of both the good times and the hard times.

My great-grandmother did not end her life farming on the prairies. In 1889, she moved a little farther west, to Grant, where her last child was born when she was forty-two. At that time the family was keeping a hotel. Isolation was now no longer a problem, but the work load was probably no lighter than it had been on the homesteads near Red Cloud and Stamford. I am reminded of Cather's Mrs. Gardener, who runs the Boys' Home Hotel in *My Ántonia*: "It was Mrs. Gardener who ran the business and looked after everything. Her husband stood at the desk and welcomed incoming travellers. He was a popular fellow, but no manager" (182). My uncle confirms the sisterhood between my great-grandmother and Mrs. Gardener in a letter: "It is true that my grandfather was an 'Innkeeper' of sorts," he writes, "but I think he devoted little time to it, leaving the management of the hotel to my grandmother" (Toohey).

It was a hard life, certainly, for those who came West to carve out a new life for themselves and their children; but I think of Mrs. Ferguesson, in "The Best Years," the last short story Willa Cather wrote, saying to her visitor, "our best years are when we're working hardest and going right ahead when we can hardly see our way out" (136). I think of Ántonia, "a battered woman now, not a lovely girl; but she still had that something which fires the imagination, could still stop one's breath for a moment by a look or gesture that somehow revealed the meaning in common things" (353). I think of Alexandra, in *O Pioneers!*, who set her face toward the land of the Divide "with love and yearning" (65) and who succeeded in bending that land and its spirit to her will. I think of Cather's observation that "the history of every country begins in the heart of a man or a woman" (*O Pioneers!* 65). And I recall her final blessing, if you will, for Alexandra, and I apply it as well to my great-grandmother, for in the absence of pictures in a family album, or journals preserved, I find the history of my own family in Nebraska woven into Cather's pages. "Fortunate country," she wrote, "that is one day to receive hearts like Alexandra's into its bosom, to give them out again in the yellow wheat, in the rustling corn, in the shining eyes of youth!" (309).

—*Eastern Montana College*

BIBLIOGRAPHY

Cather, Willa. "The Best Years." *The Old Beauty and Others.* New York: Knopf, 1948. 75–138.
———. *A Lost Lady.* New York: Knopf, 1923.
———. *My Ántonia.* Boston: Houghton, 1918.
———. "Neighbour Rosicky." *Obscure Destinies.* New York: Knopf, 1932. 3–71.
———. *O Pioneers!* Boston: Houghton, 1913.
———. *The Song of the Lark.* Boston: Houghton, 1983.
———. "A Wagner Matinée." *The Troll Garden.* Ed. James Woodress. Lincoln: U of Nebraska P, 1983. 94–101.
Perry, Stephen M. Landscape/Graphics[TM], Wichita, Kansas, 1977.
Toohey, John B. Letter to author, May 1988.

Community and Connectedness in *A Lost Lady*

J. GERARD DOLLAR

Discussions of Willa Cather's *A Lost Lady* often begin with the author's well-known observation in her prefatory note to *Not Under Forty* that in 1922—the year she wrote the novel—"the world broke in two" (v). I would also begin with this quotation because—although on a smaller scale than, say, T. S. Eliot's 1922 "The Waste Land," which presents a fragmented Europe and a Western tradition in ruins—Cather demonstrates in *A Lost Lady* a concern for the breaking of connections on the level of friendship, marriage, and community. To a large extent, this novel is about connectedness and disconnectedness, with the latter, negative force winning out. Images of breaking, severing, and disconnecting are evident throughout, from Niel's breaking his arm to Marian her legs, from Ivy Peters's cruel incision into the woodpecker's eyes to Frank Ellinger's fierce chopping down of the cedar boughs, and from Niel's cutting of the wild roses to his timely severing of a telephone wire. The novel presents an opposition between the will to connect that Cather associates with community, and the divisive, isolating forces which threaten and ultimately defeat community.

The "loss" announced in the novel's title is not merely Niel's loss of his ideal lady to the recognition of her sexual nature, but the loss of community, of human interconnectedness. An important passage in the middle of the novel tells us that Niel's fascination is not with Mrs. Forrester herself, but with "her relation [and loyalty] to her husband," the railroad builder (78). Niel's youthful preoccupation is not simply with an ideal woman but with an ideal relationship founded on trust and self-sacrifice, and, in a broader context, with community. Cather's novel is in fact based on a dialectic of community and egotism, of sacrifice and selfishness, and of connectedness and breaking. Niel Herbert, the young man disconnected from his own parents and birthplace, tries to affirm an ideal community with Marian Forrester at its center, only to see that community succumb to forces from both without and within.

Cather announces her theme of connectedness on the very first page, when she speaks of the Burlington Railroad, the great force and symbol of connectedness in the late nineteenth-century prairie world. The railroad obviously connects places—Omaha and Denver, Chicago and California, East and West—but it also links people in a vast social and economic network.

It represents human as well as geographical interconnectedness and has generated an entire society—from the directors down to the freight agents and departmental assistants—of those " 'connected' with the Road" (9). Association with the railroad, Cather tells us in her first paragraph, confers identity and a sense of belonging: "In those days it was enough to say of a man that he was 'connected with the Burlington' " (9). The Burlington Railroad forged a hierarchical community with a "railroad aristocracy" at the top (9).

Captain Daniel Forrester epitomizes the inner circle of the elite while connecting to the larger community created by the railroad. Nowhere is this more clearly seen than in the episode near the end of Part One in which the Denver bank fails, threatening the life savings of working men who trusted the bank because they trusted Daniel Forrester. The captain rushes off to Denver, nobly sacrifices his investments so that his men will lose nothing, and returns a relatively poor and greatly shaken man. Almost immediately he suffers a debilitating stroke, but he has acted honorably, in sharp contrast to the younger, self-serving bank directors whose only concerns are their own interests. (Judge Pommeroy, narrating the story of the Denver bank failure to Marian and Niel, speaks sarcastically of the "bright fellows, well thought of in the community," to whom trust and honor count for very little [91].) The captain's heroic behavior contributes significantly to his mythic stature as the pioneer leader of men and impresses Niel, who later emulates him in sacrificing a year of his education to prove true to his community—Captain and Mrs. Forrester.

What Cather is underscoring in the bank episode, however, is not so much an ideal of individual heroism as of community interconnectedness. The captain recognizes that there is no "fire-break" between the wealthy and the humble in times of crisis. He feels for his men and appreciates the dreams represented by those threatened savings: "As he tried to explain to the directors, those deposits were above price; money saved to buy a home, or to take care of a man in sickness, or to send a boy to school" (91). Community for him is founded on sympathy, loyalty, trust, and the willingness and opportunity to sacrifice. Acknowledging such responsibilities means being weighed down, and as the major figure of connectedness in the novel, the captain is also a weighty figure, likened to a mountain and an old tree, surrounded by heavy walnut furniture, and constantly growing heavier.

The heaviness of the captain represents a positive value, whereas Marian Forrester's life reveals, at least at times, what Milan Kundera calls "the unbearable lightness of being." Marian is frequently described in terms of her lightness, as when Niel scoops her up when she is lying in the hammock, and this quality suggests her dangerous tendency to free herself from connections, her readiness to escape binding, yet defining relations and flee the community. One might say that her energy is centrifugal—away from the center formed by community; whereas the captain's is inward or centripetal—towards his small circle of close friends, his home, his wife. The early adventure in the mountains of California, when the captain rescued

Marian and thus won her hand, is paradigmatic. Marian's reckless flight away from the others—to descend Eagle Cliff with the mountain climber Fred Harney—nearly resulted in her death. The captain had to bring her back to safety and did so by exhibiting communal values of loyalty, responsibility, and a selflessness that would have extended to self-sacrifice. "I knew that if we fell," Marian tells the young men at her dinner party, "we'd go together; he would never drop me" (165–66). Hearing this story for the first time at the very end of the novel, the reader recognizes it as pivotal in explaining Marian's frequent need to escape community to pursue her own pleasure and sexual gratification.

Marian's impulse to escape the Sweet Water house—and the rootedness that it represents—appears many times throughout the novel. In the first scene she makes a point of leaving to bring fresh-baked cookies to the local boys playing down by the Sweet Water. This is a typical gesture of kindness and hospitality on her part, but it also reflects her desire to witness and vicariously enjoy the boys' freedom from conventionality and constraint. She tells the boys that she too loves to wade in the river: "I wade down there myself sometimes, when I go down to get flowers. I can't resist it. I pull off my stockings and pick up my skirts, and in I go!" (18). Marian's need for unconventional and sensual experience evidently can be satisfied only away from the house and outside the pale of her marriage.

A more significant escape, years later, occurs when Marian and Frank Ellinger go off in a sleigh to cut cedar boughs for Christmas decorations; the outing in fact takes them to a deep, dark Coleridgean ravine where they are able to continue their presumably longstanding affair (in Marian's case, however, the "demon lover" ultimately proves to be quite prosaic). The scene again illustrates the novel's concern with connectedness and disconnection, and especially Marian's equivocal position between these two poles. Her impulsive and risky flight, like the adventure with Fred Harney, represents an attempted break with community, followed by a necessary return—in this case to house and husband. But Marian's break with community to express her hidden, sexual self never really succeeds, and even during this tryst the community is present—in the form of the watchful, unseen Adolph Blum. And with Adolph Blum, the narrator reports, "her secrets were safe. His mind was feudal; the rich and fortunate were also the privileged" (68). This winter outing with Ellinger, we note, ends with an image of disconnection, as Ellinger cuts the nearly forgotten evergreen boughs and the sounds of his hatchet ring through the ravine and send "soft shivers" through Marian's body (67).

A later episode that might be entitled "the end of the affair" offers some interesting parallels to the previous scene. Again, Marian's passion inspires her to escape the house—the house that is becoming more and more her prison—now it is rage rather than desire that provokes her reckless flight to Niel's office on a tempestuous night. As she has scorned the community in the earlier scene, she again does so in venting her anger—despite the listening ears of the town operator, Mrs. Beasley—against the cowardly and mercenary Ellinger, who has just married the wealthy Constance Ogden. Again the community is present as Marian's passionate self surfaces, although the feudally minded Adolph Blum is now replaced by the gossipy, iconoclastic Beasley—another representative of the new, debased community in which betrayal has replaced trust—with whom Marian's secrets are definitely not safe. Once more, a major scene ends with a gesture of disconnection as the quick-thinking Niel cuts the telephone wire as Marian begins to reveal her true feelings toward her lover. Niel tries to disconnect Marian from her illicit passion, so that he can reconnect her to her husband and the community. He is, in short, dedicated to bringing Marian "home," as the captain had earlier brought her home from near death in the mountains; and we see that as the old man weakens and nears death Niel takes on his role as connector, devoted to holding together a community based on loyalty, trust, and honor.

Any discussion of the threat to community in *A Lost Lady* must, of course, take into account the role of Ivy Peters, who is certainly the principal "disconnector" in the novel. Peters in fact represents so many different threats—economic, sexual, aesthetic—that one hardly knows where to begin. But the scene in which he cruelly and gratuitously blinds the female woodpecker is an obvious starting point. It establishes Peters as an aggressive loner and shows his disconnectedness from the natural world. In severing the woodpecker from its sight and therefore from its environment, Peters shows us not just his love of power but also the obvious pleasure he takes in the powerlessness of his victim. The scene clearly foreshadows his later "violence" against Marian, when his sexual and financial appropriation of her disconnects her from her long-standing ties to Niel and the captain's friends and makes her as helpless and directionless as the blinded bird.

It is not only the natural order that Peters disrupts in this revealing scene but also the social order. The idyll of the boys playing down by the river on a summer's day represents a celebration of nature and community. Even though they come from the different social strata of Sweet Water—with Niel and George Adams representing the upper levels of this society—they can enjoy nature together in harmony. But the intrusion of Ivy Peters—rather like the appearance of the ugly dwarf Alberich among the joyful Rhine maidens in the first scene of Wagner's *Das Rheingold*—breaks up this little community, just as Peters will eventually disrupt the harmonious Forrester circle.

Cather again associates Peters with cutting and disconnecting at the beginning of Part Two, when Niel is returning to Sweet Water after two years at MIT. He meets Ivy Peters on the train, learns that he has triumphantly drained the Forrester marsh in order to grow wheat, and then meditates on the symbolism of Peters's actions. Men like Ivy Peters, Niel sorrowfully acknowledges, "would drink up the mirage, dispel the morning freshness, root out the great brooding spirit of freedom, the generous, easy life of the great land-holders. The space, the colour, the princely carelessness of the pioneer they would destroy and cut up into profitable bits, as the match factory splinters the primeval forest" (106). Cather thus links him with Ellinger, who cuts down the primeval woods, and opposes both of these economic and sexual predators to the captain, himself like a great tree, whose name—Forrester—associates him with the primeval forest and affirms the importance of his putting down roots when he builds his Sweet Water house. One recalls that the willow stake the young captain drove into the ground to mark the spot of his future home "had rooted and grown into a tree" (54) by the time he returned.

A *Lost Lady* can therefore be viewed as the struggle between connectedness and community on the one hand and the selfish impulse to disconnect—to isolate and fragment—on the other. Marian Forrester, the central character, is caught in the middle; her affinity for the captain, Judge Pommeroy, and Niel pulls her towards a sheltering and defining community, while her sexual energy leads her, self-destructively, toward the "disconnectors"—the two men who ultimately, and for purely selfish reasons, detach themselves from her. Marian becomes a "lost lady," at least in Niel's mind, because she fails the community—she cannot live up to the standards of loyalty and self-sacrifice of the "courteous brotherhood" whose time is passing (106).

But in fact the community also fails her. Niel's ideal community, centered on the captain, is very much a "brotherhood," with no place for the feminine energy, sexuality, and passion that is so much a part of Marian's nature. If we look once more at images of breaking and severing we see that Niel, like his rivals Ellinger and Peters, also functions, albeit on a subconscious level, as a "disconnector," even while he is consciously trying to reconnect Marian to her husband. In one central episode, when Niel tries to pay chivalric tribute to Marian on a beautiful summer morning, only to find her in bed with Frank Ellinger, he takes out his knife and cuts the stiff stems of wild roses. He clearly associates these beautiful flowers—"only half awake, in the defencelessness of utter beauty" (85)—with Marian, but in detaching them from the earth, from their life source, he reveals his subconscious desire to detach Marian from her passion and her earthiness. In later severing the telephone wire, he again attempts to cut her off from her passionate self, which he sees as pulling down and polluting an aesthetic ideal.[1] Cather has therefore created something of a paradox: Niel would follow in the captain's footsteps in rejoining Marian to a community, but in doing so he would "break her in two," detaching her sexual self from her "exquisiteness." She must paradoxically break with her community to be whole. The regrettable "victory" of disconnectedness at the end results not only from Marian's rejecting the community but from a community unable to accommodate her sexual self.

The novel ends with a general dispersal and fragmentation. Once the center created by Captain Forrester no longer holds, Marian and then Niel drift out of their familiar orbits. Marian begins a degrading liaison with Peters, and Niel, observing this, makes "the final break with everything that had been dear to him in his boyhood" (168). Marian's final flight takes her all the way to South America, from where she will never return. Niel, at the very end of the work, seems to be a rootless and lonely wanderer, as his work takes him to Europe and then to Chicago, where he meets up with the equally itinerant Ed Elliot. When Niel learns from Ed the whereabouts of his lost lady, he declares that he would "almost make the trip to see her" (174). And of course he would too, in one final attempt to "bring her home." But in death, as in life, Marian eludes him. The only connections with which Niel is ultimately left are based on memory, for in this poignant story of uprootedness and disconnection, only memory furnishes the "roots that clutch."

—Siena College

NOTE

1. Kathleen L. Nichols, in "The Celibate Male in *A Lost Lady*: The Unreliable Center of Consciousness," *Critical Essays on Willa Cather*, ed. John J. Murphy (Boston: Hall, 1984), views these two gestures as acts of "symbolic castration" (193–94); I would argue that Niel is here attempting to deny Marian's sexuality rather than his own, although I agree with Nichols's thesis that Niel's story represents that of "a sexually-repressed young man's inability to accept change, growth, and adult sexuality" (188). Along similar lines, Blanche H. Gelfant, in "The Forgotten Reaping-Hook: Sex in *My Ántonia*," *Willa Cather: Modern Critical Views*, ed. Harold Bloom (New York: Chelsea House, 1985), argues that "Cather's heroes have a strong intuitive aversion to sex which they reveal furtively through enigmatic gestures" (104); according to Gelfant, when Niel cuts the telephone wire he "vents his infantile jealousy and rage the only way he can—symbolically" and attempts to "sever a relationship he cannot abide" (104).

BIBLIOGRAPHY

Cather, Willa. *A Lost Lady*. New York: Vintage, 1972.
_____. *Not Under Forty*. New York: Knopf, 1936.

Willa Cather at Mesa Verde

Part Four:
Issues of History and
Fictional Communities

These essays address Willa Cather's developing view of history and use of historical sources in her renderings of Nebraska, the Southwest, and Quebec. Stouck concentrates on *The Professor's House* to consider the growing pessimism in Cather's changing attitudes toward history, attitudes that are then applied to *My Ántonia* by Murphy and Fisher-Wirth. Cherny surveys the Nebraska history instrumental in shaping these attitudes, while Jacobs, Warner, and Larsen compare Cather's fiction to its historical sources and take her to task where demands of fiction led her to distort fact.

The interest of Cather characters in ancestry reflects a desire for the aboriginal experience of the earth missing in our American Calvinistic tradition, notes David Stouck at the beginning of *"The Professor's House and the Issues of History."* He then explains Cather's rejection of the progressive vision glorifying modern materialism and her nostalgia for the cyclical rhythms of classical and pre-Renaissance Christian civilization. *The Professor's House* is a working out of these concerns: Tom Outland is the quintessential modern man in search of ancestry and a community of security, order, ritual; Louie Marsellus represents Henry Adams's concept of the Dynamo, while Augusta becomes something like the Virgin. Godfrey St. Peter conceives of death as a way of reverting to a world uncorrupted by modern science and technology and is appropriately rescued by Augusta.

In Joseph Murphy's "Cather's Re-Vision of American Typology in *My Ántonia*" Jim Burden's vision of history is seen as progressive, a flawed New World concept of perfection achieved through time. Opposed to this Emersonian vision and challenging it are Ántonia's sacramental approach to reality and her Old World cyclical vision of history. Ann W. Fisher-Wirth's "Womanhood and Art in *My Ántonia*" nicely complements Murphy's essay in placing Jim within masculine linear time and Ántonia in feminine cyclical time to explain their separation and Cather's attempt in this novel to reconcile female sexuality and creativity, womanhood and art, Ántonia's body and Jim's mind.

In "Nebraska, 1883–1925: Cather's Version and History's," Robert W. Cherny provides historical background to explain Cather's changing attitudes toward Nebraska. The hardship and narrow-mindedness of the 1880s and 90s are evident in the bitterness of stories like "On the Divide" and "The Sculptor's Funeral." Ethnic diversity and the prosperity at the beginning of the new century are evident in *O Pioneers!*, *The Song of the Lark*, and *My Ántonia*. Prejudice against immigrants and the surge of enforced Americanization accompanying the First World War, and the postwar depressed economy, are reflected in *One of Ours*, *A Lost Lady*, and *The Professor's House*. Cather's attitudes during the 1920s coincide with those of intellectuals like Oswald Spengler, Henry Adams, and William Butler Yeats. Spengler rejected the progressive for a cyclical concept of history; Adams saw the late Middle Ages as the apex of Western civilization, and Yeats predicted the end of that civilization's cycle.

Wilbur R. Jacobs explores Cather's debt in *Shadows on the Rock* to Parkman's *France and England in North America* series of history and biography and compares the two writers' portraits of the heroes and Indians of New France in "Willa Cather and Francis Parkman: Novelistic Portrayals of Colonial New France." Cather was faithful to the Brahmin historian's chronology and selection of personalities; she exaggerated history for effect, as he had, and her descriptions resemble his in employing stylistic techniques to involve the reader in an otherwise remote historical panorama. Cather accepted Parkman's theory of environmental determinism, seeing the wilderness as character-forming, especially in producing the *coureurs de bois*. But Cather was less responsible to fact than Parkman, allowing the environmental factor to dismiss whole peoples, like the Woodland Indians, as barbarian. In creating her Laval and Frontenac, Cather played off Parkman's more historically accurate characterizations.

Ted J. Warner blames Cather for making free with biography in "*Death Comes for the Archbishop*: A Novel Way of Making History." He blames her for creating a negative Martinez myth and a positive Lamy myth through distortion of historical fact. Recent scholarship has attempted to correct distortions of Padre José Martinez's character (enhanced by Cather) perpetrated by Anglo-Protestants bent on justifying the reforms of the occupation and by Catholics bent on justifying the reforms of Bishop Lamy. Erna Fergusson, Rudolfo Acuña and other historians of New Mexico depict Martinez as brilliant, forward-looking, a pioneer educator and socially conscious leader who championed a devout native church and clergy misunderstood by the imported French bishop. Warner finds no evidence in the archives of the Santa Fe archdiocese to support the charge that Martinez was a lustful man and says that his excommunication resulted from a tithing dispute with Lamy.

In "Cather's Controversial Portrayal of Martinez" Lance Larsen juxtaposes the fictional portrait of Father Martinez against the portrait of that controversial priest in W. J. Howlett's biography of Bishop Joseph Machebeuf, Cather's primary source. Larsen argues that Cather's distortions, while blameworthy, contribute to a Dantean portrait of evil serving as a foil for the novel's virtuous protagonists, Latour and Vaillant.

In a coda to these essays, "The Family Affair at Mesa Verde," David Harrell speculates on the contributions to "Tom Outland's Story" of the Rickner and Jeep families who explored and guided visitors in the early days of Mesa Verde National Park. Perhaps Oddie Jeep, daughter of Superintendent Thomas Rickner and wife of Fred Jeep, Cather's guide at the park, inspired the character of cook Henry Atkins. Fred Jeep, like Tom Outland, had discovered a ruin (in this case Daniels house), and with his brother-in-law James Rickner might complete the prototype of the little family made up of Outland, Atkins, and Roddy Blake, a family replaced for Outland by the mesa itself.

J. J. M.

The Professor's House and the Issues of History

DAVID STOUCK

In most of her novels and stories, Willa Cather gives ancestry to her characters. In *O Pioneers!* there is a portrait of Alexandra's grandfather who lost his fortune to a young wife. In *My Ántonia* the narrator's grandparents are central figures in the first half of the book, and we have there as well a portrait of Ántonia's paternal grandmother, a proud woman, wellborn, class conscious. Lineage is important in *Sapphira and the Slave Girl* to both the black families and the white, encompassing four generations. And if we were to draw up a genealogy for Godfrey St. Peter in *The Professor's House*, we could designate seven generations, for we are told something about St. Peter's "remote grandfather" (his grandfather's grandfather) who trekked across Europe into Russia with Napoleon's army.

This contrasts strikingly with most American writers: the protagonists of Dreiser, Hemingway, or Dos Passos very often have no specified ancestry, not even parents being named. The American protagonist is archetypally a new Adam; the idea of ancestry is antithetical to the concept of a Natty Bumppo, an Ishmael, or even a Huckleberry Finn, who is orphaned early in his story. In F. Scott Fitzgerald's famous novel *The Great Gatsby*, shabby and inadequate parents are discarded by Jay Gatsby in favor of heroic and mythic ones—figures like Dan Cody, the Kaiser; finally we are told Gatsby is the child of his own imagination, the son of God. Cather, of course, is not unique in giving her characters ancestry: Hawthorne and Faulkner place their characters in a complex setting of personal and community history. But for the narrator of *The Scarlet Letter* and for characters like the Compsons and McCaslins, history is tragic and memory is a mode in which the sins of the fathers are visited on the succeeding generations.

The evoking of ancestral voices marks Cather's art. Characters typically remember the words and gestures of their forebears, and Cather's narrators frequently quote classic and favorite authors. This intertextual weaving together of voices embodies a dialogue with the past that is both emotionally and intellectually at the center of Cather's art. Cather wrote historical novels—*Death Comes for the Archbishop* and *Shadows on the Rock* are among the finest American fictions in this genre, and we know at the time of her death she was working on another historical novel set in medieval France—but the book in which she most attentively auditions voices from the past and directly confronts the meaning of history is a story of a family. In *The Professor's House*, a "wasteland" novel of the 1920s, Willa Cather extends the meaning of family and community to a comprehensive vision of human history.

I

Godfrey St. Peter in *The Professor's House* is not a historian by accident—this *is* a book about history. The first question we must ask is from what philosophical premise did Cather view history? Her first recorded statement on the subject can be found in her high school graduation speech. There she said: "All human history is a record of an emigration, an exodus from barbarism to civilization" (Bohlke 141). James Woodress points out that Cather was voicing the "conventional wisdom" of her day, that behind her words is the optimistic nineteenth-century view of history with its unlimited faith in the idea of human progress (247). American historians like George Bancroft and John Motley saw humanity advancing on an irreversible path of progress, whereon tyranny inevitably gave way to freedom, monarchies yielded to democracies, and class-structure gave way to equality and material well-being. This was the Romantic view of history, grounded philosophically in Hegel's argument that human history is the progress of reason. It was also a biblical version of history, advancing from Genesis to Revelation, from humankind's fall from Eden to restoration in the New Jerusalem.

Cather may have believed in this philosophy of history when she was sixteen, but as she grew older she would have recognized this view as inimical to her imagination, for as Harry B. Henderson points out, the aim of the progressive view in nineteenth-century America was to organize "the imaginative and emotional resources of people to accept and advance social change" (37). Cather, to the contrary, was a staunch defender of the status quo. Even as a young woman she felt about Nebraska that the Golden Age had passed and that the age succeeding was a greatly diminished one.

As a classics student at university, reading in the history, philosophy, and literature of the ancient civilizations, Cather adopted a cyclical approach to history. She viewed the rise and fall of Greece and Rome not as a progressive drama of human advancement, but as history repeating itself. The title and the epigraph of *The Troll Garden* refer to the cycles of decaying civilizations and the reconquering of nature. This view of history is voiced by Carl Linstrum in *O Pioneers!* when he looks at the little graveyard on the prairie and says to Alexandra: "Now the old story has begun to write itself over. . . . Isn't it queer: there are only two or three human stories, and they go on repeating themselves as fiercely as if they had never happened before" (119). Accordingly, Cather's great plains joins a universal geography that includes the steppes of Russia, the grainfields of Virgil's *patria*. A civilization may decline, but another will be born in which humankind's energies are renewed: Troy and Athens will be succeeded by Rome, and the garden of the Roman trolls will be taken over by the Teutonic forest children. This view of history allowed Cather to celebrate the beginnings of a new country in Nebraska and to ignore the randomness of history and some of its harsher realities, such as the displacement of the region's native peoples. It also allowed her to accept the inevitable tarnishing of the pioneer ideals: in *A Lost Lady* there is an ironic acceptance of the decline of Marian Forrester and the emergence of Ivy Peters in the drama of Nebraska history. In spite of the downward path, this was a reassuring view of history for Cather.

But in 1922 or thereabouts "the world broke in two" for Cather, or so it seemed to her by 1936 (Woodress 240). What this statement may have meant in personal terms we cannot know, but in *The Professor's House*, the first novel written after this break, Cather's view of history has altered. She presents us with a despairing view of history after the Renaissance, a rejection of the age of progress dependent on science and technology, with no reassurance any longer that history is cyclical. In this novel we come to recognize that Cather is a conservative in a historically profound sense of the word. In *The Professor's House*, she holds up a classical view (the Greek view) of human experience, one in which philosophical truths derive from natural right, free of all dependence on the events of history. It is an ideal of contemplation as the highest form of civilized activity, expanded after the advent of Christianity to include charity—love for one's fellow human beings.

The great difference after the Renaissance, with the advent of modern science in the age of Newton and Locke, was that humankind no longer saw itself as part of nature, but for the first time as the controller of nature in a way that established radically new priorities and values for human life. Human beings were no longer content to adjust to the rhythms of the natural world; the goal of living was no longer to be in comfortable harmony with nature, but to master and control its energies. The drive to technology became an end in itself—production and consumption became the goal of living, replacing the ideals of contemplation and charity as the highest good. From this "progressive" course of history Willa Cather withdrew. Significantly, there runs through *The Professor's House* an endorsement of classical and medieval civilizations—their philosophies, literature, and art.

II

A central imaginative preoccupation in *The Professor's House* and in Cather's work as a whole stems from the fact that as North Americans we belong to a civilization with no history before the age of science and progress. When the European settlers crossed the Atlantic Ocean, they entered an alien land and conquered it with their technology. These were the people who had broken with the Greek and Christian ideals; these were the Calvinist Protestants, northern Europeans who brought with them the new physical and moral science—what we describe as the capitalist work ethic. We have then, as North Americans of European origin, no history that goes back before conscious memory. We have no experience of our land that can be called aboriginal, because in all regions there is some consciousness of our making the land our own. Unless we have native Indian ancestry, there can be nothing immemorial for us because we ourselves have made what is here—the farms, the towns and cities—all the encampments on the road to economic mastery. From the outset, on this continent we have lived divided from the earth.

Cather's own yearning for an aboriginal relation to the land emerges in many passages in her writing. In the conclusion to *O Pioneers!*, Alexandra Bergson, though not born in Nebraska, will be happy at her death to become part of the earth she has cultivated. Thea Kronborg, in *The Song of the Lark*, discovers the meaning of art in an Arizona canyon when she surrenders herself to the elements (the earth, sun, water, sky). In *My Ántonia*, Cather suggests that perhaps non-Protestant Europeans could relate to the land in the old primal way. When Jim Burden first sees the Shimerdas, they are coming out of their cave—out of the earth—and, as Susan Rosowski has noted, they are animal forms (78), a suggestion of human evolution. One of Ántonia's brothers has webbed fingers and makes sounds like a rooster crowing; another is foxlike; the cave itself is "warm like a badger hole" (75). This vision is repeated at the end of the book when Ántonia and her children emerge out of the fruit cellar in the earth, a veritable explosion of life.

Other figures in Cather's fiction, less certain of purpose or direction, are cut off from this relationship to place but are haunted by a desire to be reconnected, to be grounded, as it were. One thinks of Carl Linstrum in *O Pioneers!*, Niel Herbert in *A Lost Lady*, and, of course, Jim Burden. There broods over these figures an unmistakable feeling of pathos and loss. They respond sensitively to complex human situations, but more urgently they seek to recover, in the very movement of nature's seasons, a sense of humanity's lost relationship to itself. They are characters who travel the country, are lost, deracinated, cannot locate themselves in a landscape or create a home. Their return to the Nebraska country of their family and childhood is an attempt to return to self and the elusive promise of happiness.

Cather's landscapes are colored emotionally by this search for a people and a culture rooted in place. The peasant immigrants of her early fictions seem to enjoy that intimate relation to their land, yet a melancholy attaches to these figures because they have been uprooted from their homelands and some, like Mr. Shimerda, do not survive. As Cather grew increasingly disenchanted with American life in the 1920s, with the machines and money-grubbing that beset Claude Wheeler in *One of Ours*, she looked to the oldest cultures of North America, those of the pueblo Indians in the Southwest, to locate that lost world where a people lived in an aboriginal relationship to place. Also, in the cultures of the Navajo and Mexicans described in *Death Comes for the Archbishop* she celebrates a continuous, living tradition of people and place that is immemorial. Cather turned to Quebec in *Shadows in the Rock* because the way of life she found there—language and religion bound to the land—had not changed for three hundred years.

The importance of the land, the emotional value of home and family, the despair over technological destruction and waste, the wholeness of the classical and Catholic visions of life—these become the familiar and repeated themes in Cather's later works, articulated with special urgency in *The Professor's House*. Historically, what Cather envisions in this unhappy novel is technology as a comprehensive fate for the modern world, a fate that tragically cuts people off from their ability to know and love what is intrinsically good.

III

Willa Cather dramatizes this vision in terms of a man's home, his family, and the academic community in which he works. The novel opens with Godfrey St. Peter having to leave his house, the place in which he has worked and which has given his life meaning. He resists this rupture with the past and holds on to his old study and to his garden, where he has actually lived close to the earth. But St. Peter has never known continuity or wholeness to his life; he has always been a man divided against himself, living two lives, a division rooted in his ancestry. Although this is a novel about family and the professor's meditation on his past, there are almost no memories of Godfrey St. Peter's parents. We are told simply (but it is significant) that his mother was a practical, "strong-willed Methodist," his father a "gentle, weaned-away Catholic" (30). His mother's family, English-speaking Protestants, represent progressive modern civilization, while his father's family, French Canadians, come from a Catholic peasant culture with its roots in pre-technological society.

What does family mean for Willa Cather? In its ideal form it represents wholeness, the earthly unity celebrated in the last section of *My Ántonia*, the heavenly ideal imaged in the Holy Family in *Shadows on the Rock*. What is a child? A child is a measure of the gaps, a product of the tensions that exist in the family. Godfrey St. Peter has been reared a Methodist but is nostalgic for a Catholic past. His radical inner division symbolizes the dilemma of modern humanity. He is a man of the twentieth century, but he yearns for the more meaningful life of the Middle Ages; he is a man adrift between the Dynamo and the Virgin. He carries within himself the natural desire for worldly activity and accomplishments, but also the deep instinct to give first place to imaginative thought and contemplation. This is why he continues to rent his old house—"to have room to think," he tells his old landlord. The old German appreciates his tenant's sentiments, for he too has "so many t'ings to t'ink about" (52).

The professor's harsh judgments of the world around him are generated by his rejection of modern science and what he believes is an unthinking technology. "No . . . I don't myself think much of science as a phase of human development," he says to Tod Miller, one of the few gifted students in his class. "It has given us a lot of ingenious toys," he says, but they simply "take our attention away from the real problems" (67–68), namely the meaning of human existence. St. Peter identifies the Middle Ages and early Renaissance, the high period of Catholicism, as the time in Western civilization when the individual's life was most meaningful. He says to his students: "As long as every man and woman who crowded into the cathedrals on Easter Sunday was a principal in a gorgeous drama with God, glittering angels on one side and the shadows of evil coming and going on the other, life was a rich thing. . . . And that's what makes men happy, believing in the mystery and importance of their own little individual lives" (68). Religion is what gives human lives meaning and purpose and creates community. St. Peter cites the medieval cathedral-builders, the sculptors, painters, and glass-workers, whose works of art testify to the strength of vision and purpose in their age.

The professor concludes his lecture by asking Miller to tell him next week what science has done for humankind besides bringing great comfort. Earlier in his talk, St. Peter complained that the "laboratory, not the Lamb of God," has taken "away the sins of the world." By this he means that humankind, in controlling nature, has reduced the mystery in life, become oblivious of God and knowledge of evil and good, and eliminated the need for "miracles and great temptations and revelations" (68). The professor accordingly still values what we can't control or fully understand. If human-kind were to eliminate or ignore this realm, then nothing could happen that we hadn't chosen, and so there would be no standard higher than our wills. Excellence depends on encounters with meaning beyond our control. St. Peter (who would be horrified by genetic engineering, artificial intelligence, etc.) reflects that "the most important things in his life had been determined by chance" (257). The coming of Tom Outland to his door, for instance, was a fantastic stroke of chance, perhaps the most important event in his life.

The professor's yearning for a more deeply meaningful and morally coherent world fixes on the Middle Ages and early Renaissance. He admires not only its art but also the wholeness and the enterprise of the Catholic faith. His histories of the Spanish Adventurers concern the transfer of a Catholic culture to the New World. When the first three volumes are reviewed with little real interest, it is recommended that he adopt the more even and genial style of John Fiske. This is a significant allusion because Fiske was the New England historian and philosopher who popularized scientific evolutionary theory in the United States, adapting it to an optimistic theory of human progress. His vision would have been an anathema to the professor because it scientifically endorsed the course of free enterprise liberalism and the spirit of moral relativism. St. Peter's profound conservatism, on the other hand, is indicated in the writers that his son-in-law, Louie Marsellus, envisions entertaining him with in Paris. One of these is Paul Bourget, a novelist who urged a traditional morality against modern scientific theory. (Bourget's 1889 novel, *Le Disciple*, portrays the pernicious influence of a highly regarded Positivist philosopher on an impressionable young man.) Louie also wants the professor to dine with Emile Faguet, a deeply conservative French literary critic. Louie regrets that Gaston Paris, the eminent medievalist, is now dead. When Louie suggests dining with Anatole France, a socialist, the professor replies that he has never made his acquaintance, implying that he has known the others personally.

All these French writers believed that science and the spirit of relativism have brought human society to a moral crisis. This is apparent to the professor in the life of his own family and community, although in their frenetic pursuit of wealth and social status, the people around him seem scarcely aware of the unsatisfactory nature of their lives. The ideal of wholeness, of thoughtful action, which the professor carries within him as a moral measure, is at every turn betrayed in his family. His two daughters, Rosamond and Kathleen, are filled with envy and hatred for each other, as they focus their energies on competitively acquiring material possessions—new houses, furnishings, clothes, jewelry. His sons-in-law are drawn into this rivalry. The professor recognizes they are both good men but corrupted by the values of their society. Scott McGregor so envies Louie Marsellus's good fortune, he mean-spiritedly blackballs Marsellus's application to join the Arts and Letters Club.

Marsellus, electrical engineer turned entrepreneur, embodies much of the professor's moral dilemma. Leaving for New York on a business trip, Louie kisses his hand to the family again and again from the platform of the "Twentieth Century observation car" (152). Louie stands identified with the energy and spirit of the modern era, what Henry Adams meant by the Dynamo, but when the train has pulled away, the professor feels the distinct loss of this man's warm energies and generosity. However, Louie represents everything that troubles the professor—technological expertise, business acumen, pursuit of learning and the arts for status and ornament; his Jewishness is merely the social occasion for deeper strife in this family. Mrs. St. Peter is also actively involved in the family's pursuit of wealth and status, and the professor feels sharply estranged from her. As his wife and the Marselluses plan a trip to Europe, for another "orgy of acquisition," he recognizes that he can no longer be part of this group.

The academic community in which he lives and works also fails to sustain the professor during his crisis. Like his family, it is eroded by the liberal values of a scientific and commercial age. During his career he has fought for the importance of the humanities, for the idea of a university education grounded in cultural studies. But the vulgarizing of education has proceeded inexorably, with top appointments going to those who worked with the regents to turn the university into a trade school, those willing "to give the taxpayers what they wanted" (140). There is no one in Hamilton with whom the professor can share a community of ideas and values. The only unspoiled things left for him at the close of Book One are those that predate the modern world: the lake where he swam as a boy, his garden where he is close to the earth, the curiosity and desire of a gifted student for knowledge and wisdom.

IV

The most curious and gifted of his students was Tom Outland, whose story of youthful adventure and disappointment mirrors the professor's own idealistic quest and defeat. Tom was an orphan and homeless, the quintessential modern man, completely detached from a sense of origins. But in contrast to the stories of Natty Bumppo, Ishmael, or Jake Barnes, the discovery of ancestors is an important part of Tom Outland's experience. Tom's story is of an American boy finding a symbolic home in an aboriginal premodern culture and discovering as well a nurturing relationship with the elements—the rock and sun and water and air that are each so important to life on the Blue Mesa. He finds ancestors—specifically Mother Eve—in what the Belgian priest, Father Duchene, describes as "a provident and rather *thoughtful* people" (220; emphasis added).

The priest's description of the Indian Cliff City echoes the classical ideal of a civil society that achieves its order and purpose through natural right. From the symmetry and design of the buildings, the shapes and decorations of the pottery, and the evidence of some astronomy, the priest concludes that the Indians lived in this city for something more than food and shelter:

> "I see them here, isolated, cut off from other tribes, working out their destiny, making their mesa more and more worthy to be a home for man, purifying life by religious ceremonies and observances, caring respectfully for their dead, protecting the children, doubtless entertaining some feelings of affection and sentiment for this stronghold where they were at once so safe and so comfortable." (220)

There is a vision here of community similar to the Greek idea of the *polis*, the small city-state where individual actions counted, where daily tasks brought people together, where life had an element of ceremony. Suggested here, too, is the idea of autochthony: the strong feeling for a place where one is rooted and has one's being. Father Duchene says there is something sacred about such a place—a place where, over the generations, humanity has lifted itself out of mere brutality to create a civilization. Most importantly, this happened on the mesa "without the influence of example or emulation, with no incentive but some natural yearning for order and security" (221).

The Greek ideal of a civilization that fulfills the natural yearning of humanity for order and security, and the soul's longing for goodness, is a crucial concept here. Looking at it from a mythic frame of reference, John N. Swift writes that the passage "suggests that human experience is neither fragmentary nor random," because without any kind of model, the Indians have built a city that expresses a universal human desire for order, security, and love. The prehistoric city, says Swift, is a mythic paradigm by which all "historical existence can be measured" (303). St. Peter sees the modern world as much less noble, preoccupied with food and shelter and comfort, and without a religious feeling for nature or a transcendent ideal.

The professor sees the members of his family and community wholly motivated by emulation and greed, by the desire for wealth and social status. The Marselluses are building an expensive country house that will proclaim their superior wealth to all the community. It will not be of the community, nor will it be indigenous in design and materials; instead it will be a Norwegian manor house in the Middle West, a source of pride and an object of envy. It would have no place in a civilization envisioned by the ancient philosophers nor in that deduced by Father Duchene as having once existed on the Blue Mesa.

For Tom Outland, the tragic fact is that the Indian civilization has disappeared and modern men and women can value it only in terms of its commercial possibilities (the selling of artifacts) or as a means to acquire promotions and status in a bureaucratic society. After he has been sorely disillusioned in Washington and has found most of the artifacts sold by his friend Roddy Blake, Tom spends a summer on the mesa alone where he comes to understand "possession," not in a material sense but in terms of contemplation. He says, "For me the mesa was no longer an adventure, but a religious emotion. I had read of filial piety in the Latin poets, and I knew that was what I felt for this place" (251). For Tom the mesa is a place of origins, and accordingly what he feels is a religious response to its ancestral and timeless character, something he had intuited almost from the first when he looked up through the falling snow and saw the city looking down into the canyon "with the calmness of eternity" (201).

When Tom takes his place in the modern world he becomes a scientist; he develops a theory of space that leads to the invention of the Outland engine. Then he is killed in a war that is the product of modern technology and dubious morality, and his memory is defiled in the moral miasma in technology's wake, for his invention brings much misery over inheritance.

In the final section of the novel the professor, living alone, has shed his secondary, social self and returned to the boy, his primitive, original being. We are told, "He was only interested in earth and woods and water. . . . He was earth and would return to earth" (265). He has become like his father's father, the old French Canadian in his eighties who so often was lost in profound, continuous meditation. He remembers his own personal ancestors (it is in this section we are given a glimpse of his great-great-grandfather and the emigration to Canada), but he also hears the ancestral voices of writers and great men of history. He finds something curiously comforting in the lines Longfellow translated from the Anglo-Saxon poem "The Grave":

> For thee a house was built
> Ere thou wast born;
> For thee a mould was made
> Ere thou of woman camest. (272)

He probably recalls reading with Tom the only surviving piece by the Latin poet Lucretius, the *De Rerum Natura* (*The Nature of Things*), a poetical rendering of the philosophy of Epicurus (176). Although its central argument is an atomic theory of life, it decries earthly ambitions ("what vanity . . . the discovery of gold . . . the craving of power and fame"), speaks in one of the most moving passages against the fear of dying, and extols the private life of withdrawal to the garden, the life of quiet study and companionship. St. Peter's desire to escape his family—the squabbling and envy and hatred that surrounds him—makes him think of the legend of Euripides' living in a cave by the sea in old age. (In a similar way perhaps, the looting of the Cliff City for its commercially valuable artifacts made Tom remember most keenly those lines from the *Aeneid* where Aeneas is asked to describe the sack of Troy, his ancestral city [113].)

The professor's death wish is not only suicidal in a personal way, but a wish to return human culture to its simplest elements, to revert to a world before modern science and technology corrupted humanity's finest instincts for contemplation and charity. Saving the professor from extinction is surely the meaning of the dressmaker's role in the novel. Augusta represents a vestige of that Catholic world of his paternal forebears whose values pre-date the age of progress, a world where faith and love still provide guideposts to the search for life's meaning, the world of the Virgin as opposed to the Dynamo. It is through Augusta, another instance of chance in his life, that Godfrey St. Peter feels he can resume living, be outward bound, and once again feel "the ground under his feet" (283).

Willa Cather believed with her professor in truths freed from historical contingency. She believed with classical man in trying to rise above one's earthly passions, to enthrone virtue and reason, with medieval man in the preeminent Christian value of charity. She was not a modern; she thought outside of modern assumptions, and from that vantage she saw twentieth-century life sapped by moral relativism and epistemological skepticism. The family, that primal experience of wholeness, was one of the moral absolutes to which she clung. She has been labelled nostalgic and antiquarian, but Cather never reviews the past for purely antiquarian reasons or ancestor worship; instead she looks to see if in its thought and art there are things lost that we need here today, to see if it is possible to glimpse the moving image of eternity.

—Simon Fraser University

BIBLIOGRAPHY

Bohlke, L. Brent, ed. *Willa Cather in Person: Interviews, Speeches, and Letters.* Lincoln: U of Nebraska P, 1986.

Cather, Willa. *My Ántonia.* Boston: Houghton, Sentry ed., 1961.

_____. *O Pioneers!* Boston: Houghton, Sentry ed., 1962.

_____. *The Professor's House.* New York: Knopf, 1925.

Henderson, Harry B., III. *Versions of the Past: The Historical Imagination in American Fiction*. New York: Oxford UP, 1974.

Murphy, John J. "Willa Cather and Religion: Highway to the World and Beyond." *Literature and Belief* 4 (1984): 49–68.

Rosowski, Susan. *The Voyage Perilous: Willa Cather's Romanticism*. Lincoln: U of Nebraska P, 1986.

Swift, John N. "Memory, Myth, and *The Professor's House*." *Western American Literature* 20 (1985–86): 301–14.

Woodress, James. "Willa Cather and History." *Arizona Quarterly* 34 (1978): 239–54.

Cather's Re-Vision of American Typology in *My Ántonia*

JOSEPH MURPHY

My Ántonia might best be approached through two terms from medieval criticism: *symbolism* and *typology*. The first defines the discovery of spiritual significance in the things of the world; the second involves an application of the first to the Bible. Typology restricts symbolism by focusing on intrinsic relationships between biblical occurrences. For example, the Paschal Lamb and the blood Moses sprinkled on the Chosen People set in motion a historical process completed in Christ's Passion and the New Testament covenant. When applied more generally than their medieval context, these terms bear a revealing correspondence to Ántonia Shimerda and Jim Burden. Ántonia's perspective is symbolic, her belief dependent on her unmediated relationship to things; however, Jim's perspective is a flawed typological one, a peculiarly American typology that draws a correspondence between experience in the New World and the Jewish experience in the Old Testament. Unlike its medieval counterpart, Jim's typology results in a redemptive vision of history, which forces historical connections in order to achieve perfection through time. Ántonia, whose experience turns more on the moment than on history, stands in opposition to Jim; her symbolic vision is closely associated with a *providential* or cyclical conception of time. As a text, *My Ántonia* is a struggle between Ántonia's symbolic, providential outlook and Jim's flawed typological, redemptive one.

Sacvan Bercovitch's *The Puritan Origins of the American Self* is instructive in laying the groundwork for Jim's vision. Bercovitch traces the origins of America's obsession with national destiny from Cotton Mather through the Transcendentalists. From the beginning, Bercovitch argues, Americans broke from traditional biblical meanings and interpreted scripture to support a private view of current affairs: "They were not only spiritual Israelites, with Luther, Foxe, and all Christians," writes Bercovitch, "they were also, uniquely, American Israelites, the sole reliable exegetes of a new, last book of scripture" (113). In other words, the Puritans and their descendants transferred, for their own purposes, the *symbolic* significance of the Israelites, well established in the Christian tradition, into a typological significance that revealed a divine plan in the American project.

By Emerson's time, Bercovitch argues, the role of the individual imagination was liberated by the Great Awakening and less restrained by religious institutions. Emerson himself was increasingly occupied with the individual: "His every appeal to *self*-perfection stems from and leads into his vision of the New World future" (Bercovitch 169; emphasis added). To the Romantic tenet that "there is properly no history, only biography" (Emerson 2: 10), Emerson added that "all biography is autobiography" (8: 387) and that the American idea did not belong to historical specifics, which "would make of America another Europe," but to "the simplest and purest minds" only (5: 287). Because it persisted as idea rather than as historical fact, American typology allowed Emerson to overlook the shortcomings in his national and personal history. However, Bercovitch notes "an enormous private anxiety" underlying this affirmation of national destiny, one that Emerson recorded in his diaries (Bercovitch 178–79). Jim Burden's biography of Ántonia, which is really autobiography, also attempts to forsake fact for idea, but ultimately cannot. Underneath the Emersonian surface of Jim's auto (American) biography emerges the reality of his un-American subject, Ántonia; and here dwells a considerable anxiety that imbues the novel with its darker tones but eventually gives way to truth in its finest moments.

The opening chapters establish the uniquely American perspective of Jim's account. Jim has come to Nebraska from Virginia to live with his grandparents, having lost both his mother and father within a year. Many details suggest an association between Jim's journey west and the original Puritan migration across the Atlantic. Jim speaks of himself and his guide Jake Marpole setting out "to try our fortunes in a new world" (3). The baptismal waters of the Atlantic are in Jim's experience the moving prairie grass that is "the colour . . . of certain seaweeds" or, like Homer's sea, "of wine-stains" (15). In the midst of it Jim feels obliterated, forgets he even has a grandmother. Trying one's fortunes here seems to mean resigning oneself to fortune, for "here . . . what would be would be" (8). In an Edenic scene in his grandparents' garden, Jim experiences total resignation, the feeling of being "dissolved into something complete and great" (18).

Although Jim's childhood experience of transcendence seems beyond time and space, he increasingly depicts the supernatural as temporal, spacial, and personal. It becomes temporal when he and Ántonia attribute to the stars an influence "upon what is and what is not to be" (52); it becomes spacial and personal when in looking into the "deep-seeing" eyes of Mr. Shimerda Jim "felt as if [the old man] were looking far ahead into the future for me, down the road I would have to travel" (87); it is also spacial when Jim equates America's destiny with expanding cornfields, which "were far apart in those times, with miles of wild grazing land between. It took a clear, meditative eye like my grandfather's to foresee that they would enlarge and multiply until they would be . . . the world's cornfields . . . one of the great economic facts" (137). Jim's rhetoric is typological because it reads into present conditions a belief in the future, and it is uniquely American because, through biblical echoes and reference to meditation, it yokes spiritual, material, and economic progress.

The development of Jim's corporate sense of destiny is matched by his growing understanding of what this destiny means for him personally; as Emerson would have it, national and personal identity are inextricable. For Jake Marpole and Otto Fuchs, who might be hearing the call of Thoreau, for whom "Westward is heaven, or rather heavenward is the west" (qtd. in Fussell 180), destiny means heading west on a prospecting journey from which they never return. Jim hears the same call, but answers it in a way that presents more challenge to his intellect and considerably less risk to his body. He becomes a railroad lawyer whose faith in and personal passion for the West figure significantly in its development; his heaven is reduced to the physical realm, a bleak eternity extending over a personal country whose heroic age has passed.

From this disappointing perspective Jim tells us the story of his life, seeking redemption in the telling. If his typology is a rhetoric of historical redemption, then it is not surprising that his account reveals a hunger for historical connection. Nor is it surprising that many of the historical connections he suggests are, like his national typology, imposed rather than epiphanic. His narrative is littered with pseudo-historical associations based on wishful thinking rather than truth: Fuchs's story about the Mormons planting Nebraska's sunflowers on their way to Utah; Nina's belief that Christ was born quite recently in Bohemia; Anna's grandmother thinking she is home in Norway. His own association of the snake with evil Wick Cutter in reading its coil as the letter "W" and his final allusion to Shimerda's suicide when Ántonia's boys fall silent in the haymow "as if they had been shot" (352) are equally gratuitous. His anxiety for significance runs haywire in the account of meeting Ántonia before their twenty-year separation. Jim frames the landscape with the moon on the east and the sun on the west, as if to suggest that his destiny as a forward-looking American and hers as a backwards immigrant are irreconcilable. The irony, of course, is that Jim is the one leaving the West to mastermind its development from an office in New York and from fast-moving rail cars, while Ántonia will maintain an immediate relationship with it. Jim's private typology excuses his abandonment of her because it places his destiny elsewhere while allowing him to wish that the "inevitable" might have been otherwise.

Ántonia and her kind stand in opposition to the typological perspective through which Jim explains himself. Their challenge to him is evident from the first line of his account: "I first heard of Ántonia on what seemed to me an interminable journey across the great midland plain of North America" (3). Ántonia emerges as a foreign sound in the midst of the horizontal motion integral to Jim's national and personal identity. Her name comes as an interruption, an exception, a mystery like the word *Selah* his grandfather reads from Psalms. She presents a challenge to progress both here and when Jim visits her farm in his adulthood, an account he prefaces with, "I *broke* my journey at Hastings " (329; emphasis added). Earlier Jim tells us that his affair with Lena Lingard, another immigrant, had "*broken up* my serious mood" (288; emphasis added), and the chapter bearing Lena's name and describing their relationship cuts the novel in two. One might read Jim's anxiety about mutilation—evident in his dream of Lena with the reaping hook, the story of the tramp falling into the thresher, Tiny Soderball's loss of three toes, the county coroner's empty sleeve, and Ántonia's missing teeth—as connected to such interference as well as an extension of the American fear of physical imperfection.

In addition to offering an alternative relationship to progress in space, the immigrants also challenge Jim's concept of time. According to Jim's typology, time is the broker of eternity, the process at the end of which is redemption. As traditional Catholics, however, the Cuzaks locate the source of redemption elsewhere; time itself does not bear the same burden and thus allows for a fuller experience of the present. For Jim, then, years are "long" (331), but for Cuzak "it don't seem like I am away from [Bohemia] twenty-six year" (367). Cuzak's way of living in Vienna—"day by day and night by night, sharing in the excitement of the crowd" (366)—is similar to his experience of family life on the prairie. For Jim, however, it is the years that are "crowded" (328); day-to-day life is lonely and transient. The Bohemians view time not in terms of progress, as Jim, but in cycles. When Jim asks the age of Ántonia's son Leo, for example, he learns not only that the boy is twelve but that he was "an Easter baby" (333).

These different concepts correspond to underlying differences in the way Jim and the immigrants *believe*. Whereas Jim's belief is the product of an imagined personal/national destiny, Ántonia's belief is consistently wound up with what she sees. She rejects the theory that prairie dogs take water from the depths of the earth, which she cannot see, in favor of her own: that they lap dew from the surface. In fact, she causes Jim's confrontation with the snake when she suggests they excavate one of the prairie dog holes to find out "whether they had underground connections" (44); seeing Jim kill a big snake is "enough for Ántonia" (50) to make her treat him maturely. "Seeing is believing" (and believing as seeing) is the sacramental aspect of Catholicism, evident in Mr. Shimerda's sign of the cross before the Christmas tree, which Grandfather answers with a Protestantizing bow, and in Anton Jalinek's belief in the power of the Eucharist and in prayer for the dead because he has "seen too much" (106).

This dependence on sight for belief, partly due to their unfamiliarity with English, can lead to a kind of naiveté that makes the immigrants dependent on others and unable to penetrate the surface of things. Ántonia looks to Jim for knowledge that goes beyond what she can see: knowledge of words, of ideas, of where her father went after he died. Because she loves Jim, she is oblivious to his flaws, as she is to Larry Donovan's, and even after his insincere, past-conditional "proposal" to her at the end of Book IV, she regards Jim with "bright, believing eyes" (321). Nevertheless, Ántonia deepens in her perception of things, achieving a perspective that is impossible for Jim insofar as he ignores the world as it is. At first Ántonia takes consolation in Jim's belief that her father's spirit has traveled back to Bohemia, but eventually she develops an ability to communicate vertically with her father—as if through the surface of the earth—while Jim remains obsessed with the progress of Shimerda's spirit away from the grave and the position of the crossroads above it. Above all, Ántonia develops a sense of purpose based not on an idea, but on where she finds herself.

The immigrant challenge to the American order of things becomes institutionalized in the Italians' weekly dances Jim secretly attends with the hired girls, and it stays with him after he leaves Black Hawk for the university. Jim's crisis in Lincoln can be seen as a conflict between the two views of history represented by Ántonia and himself: providential (associated with the Old World) and redemptive (associated with America). According to the first, civilization moves westward, from Greece to Rome to Western Europe and finally to the New World, but repeats itself in cycles in which civilizations rise to prominence but eventually fall into obscurity. Americans, of course, had to revise this idea in order to escape the inevitability of decline; redemptive history, which progresses invariably toward ultimate perfection, thus replaces cyclical, enabling America to play a salvific role in the last chapter of history.

At the university Jim sits squarely between these two philosophies of history. He studies under Gaston Cleric, a New England scholar who came to Nebraska direct from Italy, where, like Virgil, he lay ill. Unlike Virgil, however, who looked back on his life's work from his deathbed, Cleric recovered from his illness long enough to become the purveyor of culture to a new *patria*. That Jim is the vessel for the providential tradition Cleric guards is clear from their intimate friendship and from the wall-hangings in Jim's study: "a photograph of the Tragic Theatre at Pompeii" and "a large map of ancient Rome, the work of some German scholar" (259). However, Jim's study table looks out over the prairie, suggesting the strong influence of his personal participation as a child in the American triumph over providential history. Jim tells us he could "never be a scholar" like Cleric because "I could never lose myself for long among impersonal things. Mental excitement was apt to send me with a rush back to my own naked land and the figures scattered upon it" (262).

Unable to be a scholar in the tradition of providential history, Jim is equally incapable of rejecting the knowledge of the Old World in favor of New World tradition. His description of being sent "with a rush" back to prairie life recalls the opening of Emerson's essay "The American Scholar": "The millions that around us are rushing into life, cannot always be fed on the sere remains of foreign harvests." Emerson continues, "Who can doubt, that poetry will revive and lead in a new age, as the star in the constellation Harp, which now flames in our zenith . . . shall one day be a pole-star for a thousand years? In this hope I accept the topic . . . [of] the AMERICAN SCHOLAR" (I: 81–82). Declining to follow Cleric's footsteps as a classical scholar, Jim might be expected to conform to Emerson's American alternative, but he does not. Although he shares Emerson's millennialism, Jim is hardly a cultural purist. Classical influences pervade the novel, and the play that moves Jim to tears with Lena in Lincoln is French, not American. Even before his education Jim was open to the culture of the Old World. The most striking example of this is his belief that Mr. Shimerda's spirit moved, horizontally yes, but *eastward*, back to the old country, a clear challenge to Thoreau's association of heaven with the westward.

Jim's predicament is that while his identity and experience are American, the cultural tradition that satisfies his *aesthetic* yearnings is classical and European. His passion for American literature does not seem to go beyond a "Life of Jesse James," which, he says, "I remember as one of the most satisfactory books I have ever read" (4). As for America, its "[places and people] were all I had for an answer to the new appeal" (262) of the classics. Thus, Jim finds himself with culture on one side and experience on the other. He cannot give himself to culture because it is too removed from his experience; yet his experience, though rich in the past, is spiritually limited in the present, dominated by a national and personal identity that confines him to material fulfillment. Declining, perhaps rejecting, Emerson's appeal for a pure American culture, Jim turns from scholarship to the railroad as an answer to his national obsession.

The conflict between providential and redemptive history is resolved, aesthetically at least, in the most memorable scene in *My Ántonia*: Jim's prairie picnic with the hired girls before he leaves for college. The girls are discussing the hardships of life in the New World when Ántonia asks Jim to tell the story of how the Spanish first came to Nebraska. Jim tells them what he can about Coronado's search for the Seven Golden Cities:

> At school we were taught that he had not got so far north as Nebraska, but had given up his quest and turned back somewhere in Kansas. But Charley Harling and I had a strong belief that he had been along this very river. A farmer in the county north of ours, when he was breaking sod, had turned up a metal stirrup of fine workmanship, and a sword with a Spanish inscription on the blade. . . . Father Kelly, the priest, had found the name of the Spanish maker on the sword and an abbreviation that stood for the city of Cordova. (243–44)

The girls wonder what became of Coronado, but Jim can only give them the schoolbook line that he "died in the wilderness, of a broken heart" (244). To this Ántonia adds, referring to her father's suicide, "More than him has done that" (244).

The scene is unique because it avoids both the pseudohistoricity of Jim's American typology and the naiveté of Ántonia's Old World symbolism. Jim makes an objectively verifiable connection between the historical figure Coronado and the American experience on the Nebraska prairie, particularly that of Mr. Shimerda. The proof lies in the relics that establish a Spanish presence in that very place. Thus Jim's "strong belief" arises—like that of

Ántonia, who declares triumphantly of the sword, "And that I saw with my own eyes" (244)—from the ground of experience, not from a private scheme. Yet at the same time his belief does not, like Ántonia's, turn on momentary observation; his knowledge and belief embrace centuries. The epiphany that results from this typological association is the plow magnified by the setting sun, an image whose natural occurrence creates another legitimate typological connection, for the idea of a plow developing from a weapon of war— Coronado's sword—is firmly rooted in Isaiah: "They shall beat their swords into mattocks and their spears into pruning knives; nation shall not lift sword against nation nor ever again be trained for war" (2:4 NEB). The transition from sword to plow and the plow's return to obscurity on the prairie reveal the truth of the American experience—that, like any human experience, it runs in cycles and is not a self-sustaining eternity.

The power of the Coronado scene subsists in its resolution of the novel's central tensions: the plow, successor of the sword and symbol of American progress, is framed in the providential circle of the setting sun. This is the same circle that frames Jim at the end of the novel when, after stumbling upon a piece of the original road north from Black Hawk, he realizes "what a little circle man's experience is" (372). The unearthed relics of Coronado and the old road Jim discovers function with the emergence of Ántonia's children from the fruit cellar in Book V to counteract the submergence of Shimerda's body in the grave. These internal connections of physical things seen, the novel's own legitimate typology, contribute to the actual resurrection of Jim Burden's life.

—University of Pennsylvania

BIBLIOGRAPHY

Bercovitch, Sacvan. *The Puritan Origins of the American Self.* New Haven: Yale UP, 1975.
Cather, Willa. *My Ántonia.* Boston: Houghton, Sentry ed., 1961.
Emerson, Ralph Waldo. *Complete Works.* Ed. E. W. Emerson. 12 vols. Boston: Houghton, 1904.
Fussell, Edwin. *Frontier: American Literature and the American West.* Princeton: Princeton UP, 1965.

Womanhood and Art in *My Ántonia*

ANN W. FISHER-WIRTH

Jim Burden and Ántonia Shimerda meet as children, when the same train bears them to the tiny prairie town of Black Hawk, Nebraska. Jim is an orphan boy come to live with his grandparents from Willa Cather's own birthplace near Winchester, Virginia; Ántonia is the oldest daughter of a Bohemian immigrant family. Jim is ten, just the age Willa Cather was when her own family moved to Nebraska; Ántonia is fourteen. The relationship that ensues is central to both their lives, but difficult to define. Childhood friends, spiritual kin, would-be lover and beloved: for a time they seem as close as "the yolk and white of the one shell," but then inexorably they begin to grow apart. Jim goes to school, and Ántonia to the fields, where she labors like a man to help her family. Jim moves with his grandparents from the farm to Black Hawk, where he becomes one of the town's well-bred, restlessly respectable scions; when Ántonia comes to live in town, she comes as a hired girl. Jim goes off to university, first at Lincoln, then at Harvard; Ántonia goes to Denver to marry her railroad sweetheart, the ne'er-do-well Larry Donovan, and, when he jilts her, returns to the family farm to bear an illegitimate daughter. Briefly they meet again, on Jim's final visit home before law school. In a scene filled with longing and nostalgia, they walk in the fields and he tells her, "I'd have liked to have you for a sweetheart, or a wife, or my mother or my sister—anything that a woman can be to a man" (321). Instead, however, they part, and though he tells her, "I'll come back" (322)—and in fact his eventual career as a lawyer for one of the big railroads causes him to traverse and retraverse the continent—he does not choose to see her for twenty years.

At a famous moment in *Wuthering Heights*, Cathy cries out to Nelly Dean, "Nelly, I *am* Heathcliff—he's always, always in my mind." Calmer but no less earnest, Jim tells Ántonia, "You really are a part of me. . . . The idea of you is a part of my mind" (321). Why, then, does he leave her? Why does he not marry Ántonia? Though his speech occurs near the end of the novel, he is not near the end of his life; he is twenty, and she is twenty-four. She is, furthermore, more accessible than she has ever been. Though she is not ashamed at being an unwed mother, she is sad and very lonely—she needs him. Nor does he explicitly disqualify her because of her sexual experience. Why, then, this tug toward dispossession, so that Jim Burden couches things in the past tense; why the tense of nostalgia and regret about what could lie in the future, if he would only reach out his hand to take it?

There are several answers. Partly, as Blanche Gelfant has argued in her important essay "The Forgotten Reaping-Hook," Jim Burden is incapacitated by an infantile and morbid fear of sexuality and therefore backs away from any real chance to become involved with a woman, either Lena Lingard (Gelfant's main example) or Ántonia. This, Gelfant maintains, reveals Cather's own terror of surrendering her autonomy—her own fear of sexuality as threatening the precarious boundaries of selfhood. It may be, too, as other critics have argued, that Cather creates Jim Burden in order to cast her own lesbian desires in a socially acceptable heterosexual guise (for instance O'Brien, "The Thing Not Named," and Lambert). In this case, Ántonia becomes the beloved of a lover who dares not speak her own name. But though this interpretation helps to account for Cather's use of a male narrator, it does not account for Jim's failure to marry Ántonia. Cather herself had long, intimate, marriage-like relationships with both Isabelle McClung and Edith Lewis;[1] surely, then, she could envision her persona's union with a woman. Nor does it account for the particular quality and nature of Jim's feelings for Ántonia. Near the end of the novel he tells her sons, "I was very much in love with your mother once." However, one of them replies, "She never told us that" (346)—and this reply speaks for the reader, too. For no matter what Jim says, he simply does not seem to be in love with Ántonia. He is in love with Lena for a while; he dates her in Lincoln, makes love to her, and dreams recurrently of lying "in a harvest-field full of shocks." In this dream, "Lena Lingard came across the stubble barefoot, in a short skirt, with a curved reaping-hook in her hand, and she was flushed like the dawn, with a kind of luminous rosiness all about her. She sat down beside me, turned to me with a soft sigh and said, 'Now they are all gone, and I can kiss you as much as I like' " (225–26). He remarks, "I used to wish I could have this flattering dream about Ántonia, but I never did" (226). His feelings for Ántonia are too close for that; she has, not the allure of the object of desire, but the dear familiarity of one's own body. Nor was Cather herself in love with Annie Sadilek, from whom Ántonia derives.

Shortly after Jim tells Ántonia that she is "a part of [his] mind," they walk home across the fields. Jim describes the sunset:

> The sun dropped and lay like a great golden globe in the low west. While it hung there, the moon rose in the east, as big as a cart-wheel, pale silver and streaked with rose colour, thin as a bubble or a ghost-moon. For five, perhaps ten minutes, the two luminaries confronted each other across the level land, resting on opposite edges of the world.
>
> In that singular light every little tree and shock of wheat, every sunflower stalk and clump of snow-on-the-mountain, drew itself up high and pointed; the very clods and furrows in the fields seemed to stand up sharply. I felt the old pull of the earth, the solemn magic that comes out of these fields

at nightfall. I wished I could be a little boy again, and that my way could end there. (322)

These lines suggest the deepest reason for Jim's failure to marry Ántonia. Despite both his putative occupation as a lawyer and his insistence, in the Introduction, that *My Ántonia* is an artless narrative, Jim's real vocation is art. He exists as the (fictive) creator of a highly artful novel. Though the brief biographical information given in the Introduction (which is about Jim but not by him) might seem at first to contradict this assertion, in reality it confirms it, for it shows us that, apart from the act of writing the pages that attempt to embody what he calls "*my* Ántonia," Jim belongs to the world of death. Childless, trapped in a sterile and unloving marriage, a practitioner of the law that helps the railroads develop—that is to say, annihilate—the open prairies, he is something like the shadows in Hades in the *Odyssey*, who, drinking the hot, rich, living blood, take on substance just long enough to tell their stories. Apart from Ántonia, Jim has no story; of the twenty years that intervene between Parts Four and Five of the novel—years during which he ages from twenty to forty, marries, becomes a lawyer, settles in New York—he says not a word at all.

Yet, as the lines about the sunset suggest, Jim would not have a story to tell were he *with* Ántonia. Art, for him—as for Cather herself, as, indeed, for many of the great Modernists—is the testament of loss. The epiphanic moment is the moment of farewell; briefly the meaning flares forth, and there is potency in "every sunflower stalk and clump of snow-on-the-mountain." The sun gives way to the moon in the sky, the imagination comes into its own, and the beloved actual, or the actual beloved, is on the point of vanishing. Only childhood and death are states of wholeness. In between, Jim is an exile, constantly traveling between West and East in a restless search for wholeness, alive only in the act of narration marking his fall from wholeness, impelled toward an empty future, borne back toward a vanished past.

Jim's fate suggests Cather's in two important ways. First, throughout her adult life, she experienced great ambivalence concerning place. She moved to the East in 1896, shortly after graduating from college, accurately realizing that in the Eastern cities—Pittsburgh and later New York—lay her chances for professional, intellectual, and artistic development, first as a journalist, later as a novelist. But she realized too that the deepest, truest sources of her fiction lay in the West, specifically the prairie West, the setting of her first three major novels (*O Pioneers!*, *The Song of the Lark*, and *My Ántonia*). Like Jim, she traveled restlessly, longing for home and family when she was in the East, but when she was in Nebraska, chafing under the confines of small town life, she was terrified of dying in a cornfield. "If there were no girls like them in the world," Jim remarks of the hired girls, "there would be no poetry" (270); by and large, Cather's stories of the art world and artists reveal that for her, as for Jim, the New York life (wife) was a sterile Muse.

But the early story "Peter" suggests what would have happened had Cather stayed in the West. Written while Cather was in college, it gives the earliest version of Mr. Shimerda's suicide; in it, the girl who was to become unforgettably Ántonia is nameless and faceless, just one of "countless smaller Sadelacks" (*Short Fiction* 541). Simply put, if there were no New York City, and if Cather had not moved there, there would have been no fictional hired girls.

Willa Cather also experienced great ambivalence concerning sexuality, gender, the body. Sharon O'Brien argues that, though Cather felt severe conflict between her feminine identity and her artistic vocation during her twenties and thirties, she largely overcame this conflict by the time she wrote her major fiction (in "Mothers, Daughters, and the 'Art Necessity' " and *The Emerging Voice*). I find this view far too sanguine. As an adolescent, of course, she adopted a male identity; she championed vivisection, showed up for college sporting a one-inch crewcut, and signed her early work William Cather, M.D. She later dropped this male persona, outside her fiction. But the major novels that precede *My Ántonia* are about women—Alexandra Bergson, Thea Kronborg—whose sexuality constitutes the main threat to their creativity, and whose creativity blossoms at the price of their sexuality.[2] The books that follow *My Ántonia* are either about women—Marian Forrester, Myra Henshawe—whose sexuality flares forth in a brilliant but lethal fire, and who themselves do not create anything but serve as Muse figures for young narrator-observers, Niel Herbert and Nellie Birdseye, or they are about pairs of men—Godfrey St. Peter and Tom Outland, Father Latour and Father Vaillant—who are bound together in celibate companionship. *My Ántonia*, coming right in the middle, represents Cather's attempt to unite female sexuality with creativity, or Ántonia's body with Jim Burden's mind, in a relationship that would signify the union, in Cather's own life, of womanhood and art.

In order to reconcile the conflict between art and womanhood, Cather attempts first to separate and embody its component elements. This, I take it, is the significance of the Introduction. In the first sentence of the novel, Cather creates Jim Burden—"Last summer, in a season of intense heat, Jim Burden and I happened to be crossing Iowa on the same train," she writes—and within three pages, she has turned her own narrative over to him. Creating Jim enables him, in turn, to create Ántonia. "More than any other person we remembered," Cather comments, "this girl seemed to mean to us the country, the conditions, the whole adventure of our childhood. I had lost sight of her altogether, but Jim had found her again after long years, and had renewed a friendship that meant a great deal to him. His mind was full of her that day. He made me see her again, feel her presence, revived all my old affection for her." *He made me see her again*. Discovering Jim within herself enables Cather to feel the longing for Ántonia that he represents—to get in touch with the split in the self, the mind longing for renewed connection with the rooted, fruitful body, the body having been sacrificed to the restless, aspiring mind.[3]

But, of course, Jim and Ántonia can never unite, for they represent incommensurate modes of being, incommensurate attitudes toward experience. Jim's story takes place in what Julia Kristeva calls the "time of history," a "temporality [which] renders explicit a rupture, an expectation, or an anguish." This linear time, she adds, "is that of language considered as the enunciation of sentences . . . and . . . rests on its own stumbling block, which is also the stumbling block of that enunciation—death" (35). Jim's story reenacts the Judeo-Christian myth which dominates our culture, that of the Garden and the Fall. For a few moments, on his first morning in Nebraska, he soars above time and bereavement; he sits in the middle of his grandmother's garden with his back against a pumpkin, centered, at the *omphalos*, and becomes "entirely happy." "Nothing happened," he says. "I did not expect anything to happen. I was something that lay under the sun and felt it, like the pumpkins, and I did not want to be anything more" (18). But his life forever after is a journey away from that moment: from the garden at the outer edge of the settled prairie, he travels to Black Hawk, to Lincoln, to New York; from childhood he passes to the indecisions and repressions of adolescence, to the bleakness of adulthood. He has what seem at first to be two other Edenic moments, but one—that with the hired girls down by the river, just before he leaves Black Hawk for Lincoln—is marred by thoughts and talk of death, sadness, and sexual confusion; and the other— that with Ántonia and her children in the orchard—is marred by the keen knowledge that the garden he stands in, rich with apples in its triple enclosure, is not his home, not his creation, not his resting place, but Ántonia's.

Ántonia, of course, comes to us through Jim's language; her story too is told in linear time. Yet she continually surpasses the sentences that endeavor to contain her. As Jim Burden comes to realize, that which expresses her best is not the sentence but the image. "In my memory," he writes,

> there was a succession of . . . pictures, fixed there like the old woodcuts of one's first primer: Ántonia kicking her bare legs against the sides of my pony when we came home in triumph with our snake; Ántonia in her black shawl and fur cap, as she stood by her father's grave in the snow-storm; Ántonia coming in with her work-team along the evening sky-line. (353)

Made of language, she leaps free from "the stumbling block of that enunciation." Though she ages, though she becomes believably battered and withered, time does not diminish her, for from beginning to end she lends herself "to immemorial human attitudes which we recognize by instinct as universal and true" (353). She does this because she is the grace of the body—*our* body, which we experience immediately, as presence and continuity, but which, rendered in language, becomes for that reason finally "incommunicable" (372), as the penultimate word of this novel suggests.

Ántonia dwells in what Julia Kristeva calls "women's time," a modality of "*repetition* and *eternity*," of "cycles, gestation, the eternal recurrence of a biological rhythm which conforms to that of nature and imposes a temporality . . . whose regularity and unison with what is experienced as extrasubjective time, cosmic time, occasion vertiginous visions and unnameable *jouissance*" (34). She is just a peasant girl, with sunburnt arms and throat, and a neck like the bole of a tree; she sweats, laughs, clatters about the kitchen, runs with a heavy footfall, bears her babies like a cat. Jim fears at one point that she will turn into an animal—and indeed, she lives in her time as one envisions the animals:

> Fulfilling themselves without pain
>
> At the cycle's center,
> They tremble, they walk
> Under the tree,
> They fall, they are torn,
> They rise, they walk again.
> (Dickey 91–92)

Just as we look through Jim to see Ántonia, so too perhaps we look through the myth of the Garden and the Fall to see the older myth, Ántonia's myth, the Eleusinian mysteries of the grain, the earth, the woman, "planting and tending and harvesting" (353) in the abiding Garden.

—University of Mississippi

NOTES

1. The degree to which these relationships were sexually intimate is not and cannot be known.

2. It is true that Thea's narcissistic sexuality blossoms in Panther Canyon and gives new life to her art, but—with due respect to Fred—Thea forfeits the realm of sexuality as it involves relations with other people. I disagree with critics such as Judith Fetterley who find this a satisfactory resolution to the conflict between sexuality and creativity ("Cather and the Fiction of Development," paper presented at the 1989 Santa Fe Cather conference).

3. The first version of the Introduction, which Cather later revised, emphasizes Cather's dependence on Jim Burden for access to Ántonia's story. In this version, both Cather (or her fictive "I") and Jim Burden agree to write down their memories of Ántonia, but when Jim calls on Cather some months later, with his manuscript complete, she has not been able to progress beyond a few pages of notes.

See E. K. Brown and Leon Edel, *Willa Cather: A Critical Biography* (New York: Knopf, 1953), 200.

BIBLIOGRAPHY

Cather, Willa. *My Ántonia*. Boston: Houghton, 1918.

———. "Peter." *Willa Cather's Collected Short Fiction, 1892–1912*. Rev. ed. Ed. Virginia Faulkner. Lincoln: U of Nebraska P, 1970. 541–43.

Dickey, James. "The Heaven of Animals." *Contemporary American Poetry.* Ed. A. Poulin, Jr. Boston: Houghton, 1980. 91–92.

Gelfant, Blanche. "The Forgotten Reaping-Hook: Sex in *My Ántonia*." *American Literature* 43 (1971): 61–82.

Kristeva, Julia. "Women's Time." *Feminist Theory: A Critique of Ideology*. Ed. N. Keohane, M. Rosaldo, and B. Gelpi. Chicago: U of Chicago P, 1982.

Lambert, Deborah. "The Defeat of a Hero: Autonomy and Sexuality in *My Ántonia*." *American Literature* 53 (1982): 676–88.

O'Brien, Sharon. "Mothers, Daughters, and the 'Art Necessity': Willa Cather and the Creative Process." *American Novelists Revisited: Essays in Feminist Criticism*. Ed. Fritz Fleischmann. Boston: Hall, 1982. 265–98.

———. "The Thing Not Named: Willa Cather as a Lesbian Writer." *Signs* 9.4 (Summer 1984): 576–99.

———. *Willa Cather: The Emerging Voice*. New York: Oxford UP, 1987.

Nebraska, 1883–1925:
Cather's Version and History's[1]

ROBERT W. CHERNY

Many themes in Willa Cather's fiction derive closely from her experiences in Nebraska. While an examination of Nebraska social patterns underscores Cather's perceptiveness as a social historian, it also adds important dimensions to an understanding of her shift from a bleakly negative view of life in Nebraska in work published before 1913, to a more optimistic view characteristic of work published between 1913 and 1918, and then to pessimistic views in works published between 1922 and 1925. These changes reflect not just transitions in Cather's own life but also her perceptions of real changes in the state's society and economy. Cather's misgivings concerning social and economic changes in Nebraska, together with the concurrent emergence of a view among many intellectuals that Western civilization was in decline, may have led Cather to use the American West as a metaphor for the decline of Western culture in general.

In 1883, when Cather was nine years old, her parents brought their four children from their native Virginia to a new home in Webster County, in south-central Nebraska. Cather lived in Nebraska for the next dozen years, and her experiences there exactly parallel Jim Burden's in *My Ántonia*: coming as a child to Nebraska, living briefly on a farm, residing in town for a longer time, attending the university in Lincoln, moving East to pursue a career, and returning to Nebraska periodically to visit.[2]

In 1870, census takers counted only 16 people in Webster County. Ten years later, three years before the Cathers' arrival, they found more than 7,000. By 1890, the county had more than 11,000 residents, most of them living on farms (U.S. Census Office, *Eleventh Census: 1890*, 1: 30). Rapid population growth transformed the region. Farmers plowed the plains, planted crops, and hoped that the harvest would suffice to repay their loans. Land was cheap or free, and many came to the plains with little capital. The high cost of lumber forced many pioneers to make homes by cutting the tough prairie sod into blocks and using them to construct dwellings, often dug into the side of a hill to minimize the number of walls that had to be built. Such dwellings, nicknamed "soddies," were common throughout the central plains, but few people considered them satisfactory homes. Distances added to the difficulties faced by early settlers; the closest neighbor sometimes lived several miles away, and many early settlers felt a sharp sense of isolation. Also, low prices for farm products in the late 1880s and early 1890s compounded by drought in the mid-1890s deprived most farmers in central Nebraska of material success until 1900 or so.[3]

Whether they lived in a rural dugout or an elegant house in town, most central Nebraska settlers brought with them a set of expectations that placed the family as the cornerstone of community life.[4] Individuals related to the community through the family, and the community classified individuals in terms of the family. Community members looked askance at a single adult without family ties. For a young lawyer or schoolteacher, the status of single adult was considered only temporary, pending marriage and family life. A young man or woman with neither family ties nor an occupation was almost automatically classified as "not of the better sort," unless he or she quickly manifested exemplary character and a strong desire to marry and settle down.

Whether on the farm or in town, the family portioned out work by sex and age. In a farm family, the father–husband worked the fields, sold crops and livestock, tended the large livestock (hogs, cattle, and horses), butchered hogs and cattle, and looked after the equipment and farm buildings. In town, the family's father–husband followed a profession, labored at a trade, tended a store or business, or worked for the railroad. Most heads of families were self-employed; aside from the railroad, few jobs paid sufficient wages to support a family. Whether on a farm or in town, the wife–mother faced much the same set of tasks: preparing meals; keeping the house clean; doing laundry; tending the poultry and the garden; preserving fruit, vegetables, and meat; sewing for her family; and supervising the children. Younger children of both sexes and older girls assisted their mother. Older boys worked under the father's direction.

All members of the community understood these gender-determined work roles, but also recognized exceptions. On the farm, everyone pitched in to help when needed—to save new-born calves from an unexpected spring storm, to assist with farrowing, or to pick ripe fruit for canning. By the 1890s, many young women worked outside the home before marriage, most often as domestic servants or schoolteachers. Aside from teaching, most female occupations outside the home were extensions of homemaking, notably those of domestic servant, laundress, cook, waitress, boardinghouse keeper, dressmaker, seamstress, or milliner. In smaller numbers, women filled a wider range of occupations. Women who became heads of families through the death or incapacity of a husband or father often took on what the community considered the work of a man, either running a farm (as did Alexandra Bergson) or taking charge of a store or other business in town. Some men and women never conformed to social expectations, and the bachelor farmer or spinster schoolteacher were commonplace in most communities.

Children above the age of twelve or fourteen might hire themselves out to other members of the community—the boys to work in the fields or do day labor in town, the girls to do housework or sewing. Census data for Nebraska in 1890 indicate that three-quarters of female domestics were under the age of twenty-five and that foreign-born women worked as domestic servants more than twice as often as women whose parents were born in the United States (U.S. Census Office, *Eleventh Census: 1890*, 2: 348–51), a situation mirrored in Cather's portrayal of the hired girls in *My Ántonia*. For some young wage earners, the family of their employer became a surrogate family: they sometimes ate at the family table, slept in the family home, and related to the larger community as the family's hired help. Thus, when Ántonia worked as the Harlings' hired girl, townspeople saw her behavior as a reflection on that family.

For the most part, family members took part in the community's social institutions and activities as part of a family unit; they went together to church, school activities, band concerts, or Fourth of July festivities. Lodges like the Masons and Odd Fellows limited membership to men, but they usually had auxiliaries for women and often for children too, so lodge was generally a family activity.

Despite the community's emphasis on family, however, women were excluded from some community activities. Politics formed a male preserve; only men ventured into saloons, and few women risked their reputation by entering a barbershop or livery stable. Women had a counterpart of sorts in the Women's Christian Temperance Union, and they dominated most of the activities of the Protestant churches and the schools. Although women might be excluded from politics or relegated to second place in most business matters, few denied women precedence in promoting cultural activities or maintaining the moral order.

Throughout much of the Middle West, when it came to the moral order, the community's values tended to mirror those of the leading American Protestant churches: Methodist, Baptist, Presbyterian, Congregational. Not all members of the community were church members; in fact, only two out of five adult Nebraskans were church members as late as 1906, and women outnumbered men among communicants by a ratio of nine to seven (U.S. Bureau of the Census, *Religious Bodies: 1906*, 1: 226–31). The influence of the major Protestant denominations, however, extended well beyond the limits of their membership rolls.

The largest Protestant body in Nebraska, as in much of the nation, was the Methodists, and the Methodists' approach to cleansing sin from the life of the individual had long since come to characterize the attitudes, if not the formal theology, of other Protestant groups (Smith chs. 3–5, 8–9). The *Doctrines and Discipline of the Methodist Episcopal Church: 1896* provides a list of *un*acceptable social behavior:

> indulging sinful tempers or words, the buying, selling, or using intoxicating liquors as a beverage, signing petitions in favor of granting license for the sale of intoxicating liquors, becoming bondsmen for persons engaged in

such traffic, renting property as a place in or on which to manufacture or sell intoxicating liquors, dancing, playing at games of chance, attending theaters, horse races, circuses, dancing parties, or patronizing dancing schools, or taking such other amusements as are obviously of misleading or questionable moral tendency. (136–37)

   Not all community residents accepted such a restricted definition of acceptable social behavior. Definitions of acceptable social behavior varied somewhat by social class. For most people, however, attitudes towards such things as liquor and dancing ranged along a spectrum defined by religion and ethnicity rather than by social class. At one end of the spectrum stood Methodists and, near them, Baptists, adhering to attitudes similar to those just cited. Some immigrant groups shared this world view as well, including many Norwegian and Swedish Lutherans, Dutch Calvinists, and Scotch–Irish Presbyterians. At the same end of the spectrum, but tending more toward the center, were the Congregationalists and other Presbyterians. At the opposite end of the spectrum appeared Catholics, most of whom, in Nebraska, traced their ancestry to Bohemia, Germany, Ireland, or Poland. Similar to the Catholics in their definition of acceptable social behavior were German Lutherans and Calvinists, some Danish Lutherans, and Czech free thinkers. (Cather often referred to Czechs as Bohemians, the commonly used name before the creation of Czechoslovakia in 1918.) Most Czech, Danish, German, and Irish immigrants found no sin in a glass of beer, nor in dancing, nor in the theater, so long as one practiced moderation. Catholics might even raise money for church activities through a lottery, something most American Protestants considered gambling and hence sinful (Kleppner 69–91; Luebke 16–32).

   In the late nineteenth century and early twentieth century, alcohol became an important symbol of conflicting cultural values. Agitation to restrict the liquor trade roiled Nebraska politics from the 1880s until 1916, when voters finally approved a statewide referendum to enact prohibition. Throughout this time, prohibition advocates often explicitly connected immigrants, liquor, and immorality. In 1890, for example, one prominent prohibitionist explicitly accused "foreigners" of "leading our sons to destruction" through alcohol (Parsons 111).[5]

   Cather usually portrays her immigrant characters with more sympathy. Immigrants from Europe play major roles in several of her works, especially those published before 1922. Her portrait of ethnic diversity on the Great Plains reflects emigration patterns in the 1870s and 1880s, when the opportunity to acquire a farm with a minimum of capital brought people to the plains from throughout western and central Europe as well as from the eastern parts of the United States and Canada. In 1890, only 29 percent of the state's population had been born in Nebraska, and many of those were under twenty years of age. Forty-three percent of all Nebraskans in 1890 were either foreign born or of foreign parentage; Germans were most numerous, followed by Swedes, Irish, Czechs, English, and Danes.

The years from the influx of immigrants in the 1870s and 1880s to World War I marked the high point in Nebraska for both ethnic heterogeneity and the institutionalization of ethnic identity. Immigrants and their children created a variety of institutions that defined life in the state's ethnic communities, including churches, newspapers, businesses, and a wide variety of voluntary organizations, all conducted in the language of the community's dominant group. Cather, writing of her youth, said, "On Sunday we could drive to a Norwegian church and listen to a sermon in that language, or to a Danish or a Swedish church. We could go to the French Catholic settlement in the next county and hear a sermon in French, or into the Bohemian township and hear one in Czech, or we could go to church with the German Lutherans." In some communities, as Cather wrote of Wilber, a small town that was largely Czech, it was possible to spend "a whole day without hearing a word of English spoken" ("Nebraska" 237). Political appeals were often printed in German, Swedish, and Czech in addition to English; state law provided for what was essentially bilingual education in the public schools if a sufficient proportion of parents requested it.[6]

Cather seems to have loved the ambience of ethnic communities like Wilber, and she noted with disappointment in 1923 that " 'Americanization' has doubtless done away with all this" ("Nebraska" 237). During the First World War, Nebraska's ethnic communities came under challenge from a surge of enforced Americanization that carried over to the postwar period. German books were destroyed. The legislature prohibited the use of foreign languages on the public streets or on the telephone and prohibited schools from using or even teaching foreign languages below the eighth grade. Wartime patriots initiated both official and vigilante action against German immigrants, something Cather describes with disapproval in *One of Ours* (204–07; Rodgers 1–22).

Although Cather wrote extensively about immigrants in her fiction set in Nebraska and published before 1922, Webster County did not have concentrations of immigrants as high as in eastern parts of the state. Only 13 percent of the total population of that county were foreign born in 1890, and nearly all of them came from just four groups: Germans comprised about 5 percent of the county's population; immigrants from the British Empire (Great Britain, Ireland, Canada) were nearly as numerous, with 4.5 percent; Scandinavians—Swedes, Norwegians, and Danes—accounted for under 2 percent; and Czechs constituted about 1 percent (U.S. Census Office, *Eleventh Census: 1890*, 1: 641–44).

Cather had never encountered European immigrants before coming to Nebraska, and she found cultural significance in the immigrants that belied their small proportions in Red Cloud or Webster County. She studied piano with a German-born music teacher, practiced Greek and Latin with an English-born storekeeper, and borrowed books from the large library of a French-born neighbor (Brown and Edel 25–27; Bennett 119, 153–54). In 1923, the editors of *The Nation* asked her for an essay on Nebraska.

Her contribution, "Nebraska: The End of the First Cycle," provides important insights into her understanding of the significance of immigrants for Nebraska:

> When I stop at one of the graveyards in my own county, and see on the headstones the names of fine old men I used to know: '*Eric Ericson, born Bergen, Norway . . . died Nebraska*,' '*Anton Pucelik, born Prague, Bohemia . . . died Nebraska*,' I have always the hope that something went into the ground with those pioneers that will one day come out again. Something that will come out not only in sturdy traits of character, but in elasticity of mind, in an honest attitude toward the realities of life, in certain qualities of feeling and imagination. . . . It is in that great cosmopolitan country known as the Middle West that we may hope to see the hard molds of American provincialism broken up; that we may hope to find young talent which will challenge the pale proprieties, the insincere, conventional optimism of our art and thought. (237–38)

In the same essay, Cather criticizes old-stock Americans as "seldom open-minded . . . cautious and convinced of their own superiority . . . provincial and utterly without curiosity" (237).

Cather looked to European immigrants to redeem America from its provincialism, and her works set in or near Red Cloud imply a larger proportion of immigrants than was the fact. No one expects statistical accuracy in fiction, but Cather extends her exaggeration of the proportion of immigrants to her essay for *The Nation*, a nonfiction piece. In that essay, she claims that foreign-born Nebraskans and their children totaled "900,571, while the entire population was 1,192,214," that is, just over 75 percent ("Nebraska" 237). In fact, the census shows that in 1910 this group constituted 538,218 in a total population of 1,192,214, equivalent to 45 percent (U.S. Bureau of the Census, *Fourteenth Census: 1920*, 3: 590). Apparently Cather's deeply held convictions regarding the cultural significance of European immigrants led her to accept erroneous census data.

Red Cloud, where Charles Cather moved his family in 1885, was like many of the small towns that dotted the plains. Regardless of the name she gave them or the state in which she placed them, the small towns in Cather's works all derive closely from Red Cloud, which she describes in detail in *The Song of the Lark*. The largest of the three towns in Webster County in 1890, Red Cloud grew from fewer than 700 people in 1880 to more than 1,800 ten years later (U.S. Census Office, *Eleventh Census: 1890*, 2: 30). In such a place, size imposed a sense of community. Most permanent residents knew each other, at least by reputation. Residents constantly encountered the same people in different social or economic roles. Such a town held few secrets; one wag claimed that small-town residents could hear gossip about their sins while on the way home from committing them (Atherton 39–40, 67).

In 1890, Cather left small-town life behind and moved to Lincoln to attend the University of Nebraska. Lincoln's 55,000 residents made it a far larger place than any Cather had previously known. At the university and in

Lincoln, Cather met people with broad cultural interests who stimulated her developing creative impulses, for she began to write long before moving East in 1896.[7] After Cather left Nebraska, she returned regularly to visit her family and friends, both in Red Cloud and in the surrounding farm country.

During the early years of the twentieth century, as Cather was acquiring a reputation as an editor and author, Nebraska's farms and small towns prospered. Grain prices rose and the weather was unusually cooperative. From 1910 to 1914, the ratio between prices for farm produce and farmers' costs showed the greatest advantage to farmers of any peacetime period in the twentieth century (Thomsen and Foote 94). When Cather returned for her occasional visits, she could not have missed the outward signs of this prosperity. The pioneers' soddies gave way to substantial frame houses and barns, just as brick commercial buildings replaced wooden storefronts in town. Trees planted as seedlings a decade earlier began to reach full growth. By World War I, steam-powered threshing machines became nearly as common as Model-T Fords among Nebraska's farmers.

After the war, however, prices for farm products fell, and agriculture entered the Great Depression nearly a decade before the rest of the nation. Many farmers replaced their horses with tractors in a vain effort to gain income by increasing productivity. Unfortunately, the more they produced, the lower prices fell. The postwar years also saw an increasing homogenization of life in most of rural America, as the automobile, the motion picture, and the radio combined with enforced Americanization and the passing of the immigrant generation to erase many of the unique characteristics of prewar rural and ethnic communities.[8]

Cather's fictional treatment of Nebraska before 1925 falls into three distinct phases, each corresponding with a phase in the state's social and economic development. In "My First Novels [There Were Two]," an essay published in 1931, Cather implies she first wrote about Nebraska in *O Pioneers!*, published in 1913 (92). While *O Pioneers!* was her first novel set in Nebraska, it was by no means the first time she used the state as a setting for her fiction. Before *O Pioneers!*, she had written more than a half dozen short stories about Nebraska, including "The Sculptor's Funeral" and "A Wagner Matinée," both published in *The Troll Garden* in 1905.

Cather's early portraits of life in Nebraska were almost uniformly negative, often harshly so. Nebraska, she wrote in "On the Divide" (1896), was "parched by drought, . . . sogged by rain, beaten by hail, and swept by fire, and in the grasshopper years . . . eaten as bare and clean as bones that the vultures had left" (37). In "A Wagner Matinée," it was "the black pond with the cattle-tracked bluffs; the tall, unpainted house, with weather-curled boards, naked as a tower; the crook-backed ash seedlings where the dish-cloths hung to dry; the gaunt, moulting turkeys picking up refuse about the kitchen door" (226). The barren landscape drove men to madness or suicide in "On the Divide," and the drudgery of farm life in "Eric Hermannson's Soul"

(1900) caused a man to "grow more and more like the clods among which he labored" (104). Small-town businessmen in "The Sculptor's Funeral" were knaves and scoundrels, fixated upon making money, with no understanding of art or culture (247, 248, 250). In her writing about Nebraska through the publication of *The Troll Garden*, Cather seems to have drawn largely upon her experiences during the 1880s and 1890s, when she witnessed the privation and distress of pioneer life and the narrowness of the small town. These works posed no challenge to what she described later as the prevailing notion in 1913 that "Nebraska is distinctly déclassé as a literary background; its very name throws the delicately atuned [sic] critic into a clammy shiver of embarrassment" ("My First Novels" 94).

O Pioneers! reveals a different attitude toward Nebraska, an approach that continued through the publication of *My Ántonia* in 1918. This second phase reflects the prosperous years preceding the war, years that also marked the high point for ethnic diversity. A successful magazine editor in New York, Cather now based her treatment of Nebraska on occasional visits. In her work during this period, she made immigrant women her central characters and provided a view of family and community life in Nebraska that balanced struggle with success, tragedy with fulfillment. In *O Pioneers!*, Alexandra Bergson suffers through the hard times of the 1890s, but she treats the land with "love and yearning" and in the early years of the century it repays her by making her one of the richest farmers on the Divide (65, 83). In *The Song of the Lark* (1915), Cather depicts the plight of those who, like herself, have aspirations for creative achievement. While suggesting that they could not fulfill their goals in Nebraska, her treatment of Nebraska (for Moonstone is, in fact, Red Cloud) is very different from that in "A Wagner Matinée"; she now points to the family and the community as providing an important basis for eventual success in the metropolis. In *My Ántonia*, she presents a hard-working, unlettered immigrant woman who triumphs over the destitution and hardships of pioneer life, the narrowness of the small town, and repeated misfortune; who makes serious mistakes but overcomes scandal and wins acceptance within the community by her hard work on behalf of her family; and who ultimately fulfills her destiny to become "a rich mine of life, like the founders of early races" (353). Cather seems to have used Ántonia at one level to personify the hard-working immigrant farm families, especially the women overcoming great obstacles to achieve a good life, and on another level to symbolize the fertility of the land itself in response to hard work and compassion.

The early 1920s witnessed a third phase in Cather's treatment of Nebraska. The subtitle of her 1923 essay in *The Nation* announces "The End of [Nebraska's] First Cycle." "The splendid story of the pioneers is finished," she asserts, and "no new story worthy to take its place has yet begun" (238). Americanization had suppressed immigrant cultures: "our lawmakers have a rooted conviction," she writes, "that a boy can be a better American if he speaks only one language than if he speaks two" (237). Furthermore, "materialism and showy extravagance" had overwhelmed hard work and love for the land. The new generation was infatuated with automobiles and moving pictures. They were transforming the university into "a gigantic trade school" where students studied "salesmanship and dressmaking" rather than the classics (238). For Cather, the culture of the West was in decay.

This theme of decline appears in *One of Ours* (1922), and it dominates *A Lost Lady* (1923) and *The Professor's House* (1925). The theme is stated clearly in *A Lost Lady*:

> The Old West had been settled by dreamers, great-hearted adventurers who were unpractical to the point of magnificence; a courteous brotherhood, strong in attack but weak in defence, who could conquer but could not hold. Now all the vast territory they had won was to be at the mercy of men . . . who had never dared anything, never risked anything. They would drink up the mirage, dispel the morning freshness, root out the great brooding spirit of freedom, the generous easy life of the great land-holders. (106)

Like Ántonia, Marian Forrester symbolizes the Western land, as Cather traces her passage from wife of a bold pioneer who conquered the wilderness to mistress of a cruel and conniving small-town lawyer, "trained in petty economies by hard times" (107).

These three phases in Cather's treatment of Nebraska are related not just to changes in her personal life, as critics and biographers have indicated, but also to real changes in the nature of life in the rural communities of Nebraska, where the hardships and struggles of the first settlers, depicted in Cather's short stories between 1896 and 1905, gave way to material success in the midst of a patchwork quilt of thriving ethnic communities, patterns celebrated by Cather in *O Pioneers!* and *My Ántonia*. Then, during World War I and the 1920s, Americanization and the passing of the pioneer generation coincided in time with the transition from the farmers' prewar "golden age" to a depressed economy and a more homogenized culture, criticized in *One of Ours*, *A Lost Lady*, and *The Professor's House* (which may be considered a Nebraska novel because Godfrey St. Peter's university is so closely patterned after the University of Nebraska; compare *The Professor's House* 140 and "Nebraska" 238). Thereafter, Cather abandoned Nebraska as a setting until after the death of her parents.

Cather's accounts of the decline and decay of the American West also coincide in important ways with patterns of thought among intellectuals after the war. The first volume of Oswald Spengler's *The Decline of the West* did not attract attention in this country until then, and the second volume appeared in 1922; an English translation published in the United States appeared in 1926, but Spengler's general argument was well known by then. He held that Western civilization was in decline and nearing its end; his thesis that history moves in cycles rather than as a vector may have influenced Cather's choice of subtitle—"The End of the First Cycle"—for her essay in *The Nation*. Also, *The Education of Henry Adams* won the Pulitzer Prize for autobiography in 1920; in it, Adams suggests that Western civilization had reached an apex of spiritual unity in the Middle Ages and that this spiritual unity had been shattered by technology (esp. chs. 25, 32–34). In 1921 William Butler Yeats published the poem "The Second Coming," with its vision of the imminent end of the "gyre," or cycle, of Western civilization.

Cather's work in the early 1920s echoes these themes of cultural decline and imminent destruction. In *One of Ours*, Cather draws a critical portrait of Claude Wheeler's brother, who is infatuated with more and better technological gimmicks; she suggests that Claude himself, the optimistic romantic, is better off for having died in the war, for he could not have adjusted to the materialistic postwar world. Claude's death may signal the death of Cather's own prewar optimism regarding life in the farming communities of Nebraska. Marian Forrester provided Cather with a metaphor for the subversion of the glorious opportunities of the West into mere money grubbing. In *The Professor's House*, as in Cather's depiction of the University of Nebraska in her 1923 essay, a great university abandons the classics of Western civilization in favor of business administration. Godfrey St. Peter, exemplar for the Western academic tradition, completes his great intellectual work and finds little reason to live. Whether Cather intentionally used the American West as a metaphor for the decline of Western civilization, her work during the early 1920s nonetheless reflects influences similar to those who thought Western civilization had run its course and was doomed.

—San Francisco State University

Apparently home to a family with three children and another on the way, and perhaps to two other adults, this Nebraska pioneer home seems to have been constructed by digging a hole in the ground and putting a roof of sod over it. Cather described a similar dwelling in *O Pioneers!*: "But for the piece of rusty stovepipe sticking up through the sod, you could have walked over the roof of Ivar's dwelling without dreaming that you were near a human habitation" (36).

Solomon Butcher took this photograph of a "soddie" in 1892. Butcher left a valuable pictorial collection of life in central Nebraska during the period from the 1880s through the first decade of the twentieth century; most of his photographs are from Custer County, north of Webster County.

By the early years of the twentieth century, those farmers who survived the hardships of the pioneer years and the hard times of the 1890s began to construct homes more befitting their success. Butcher took this picture of a family's new home in 1904.

Courtesy of NSHS

In 1903, Butcher's camera captured this farm woman caring for her chickens, in Buffalo County, north of Webster County.

Louis Bostwick photographed this Nebraska farmer taking a break during a wheat harvest, 1912.

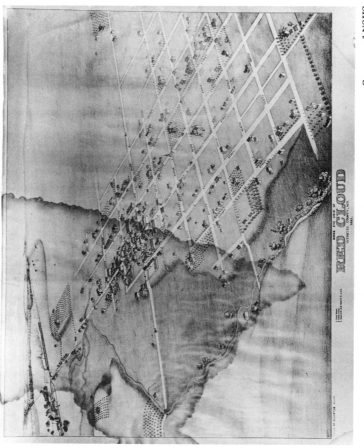

Bird's-eye views, such as this, were popular in the late nineteenth century. This one presents Red Cloud in 1881; the cluster of buildings near the center is the main business district. The train station is in the upper left, the courthouse and school in right center.

Downtown Red Cloud as it appeared about the time Cather left Nebraska to live in Pittsburgh. This is the intersection of 4th and Webster streets, the center of the business district.

Cather family home in Red Cloud, described in detail in *The Song of the Lark* and "The Best Years."

The home of the Miner family, a block west of the Cather home in Red Cloud. This house and family provided the model for the Harlings in *My Ántonia*.

Downtown Lincoln as it looked when Cather lived there as a university student. The large building at the end of the street is part of the university.

NOTES

1. This essay is a shortened version of the paper presented at the BYU Cather symposium. The longer version incorporated significant portions of an essay since published as "Willa Cather's Nebraska," *Approaches to Teaching Cather's MY ÁNTONIA*, ed. by Susan J. Rosowski (New York: MLA, 1989) 31–36. The material published in that volume has been removed from this essay, except where information was necessary to provide continuity. The paper presented at the conference was illustrated by eighty-five slides, of which only a few are reproduced here.

2. The most detailed treatment of the relationship between locations in Nebraska and Cather's fiction is by Mildred R. Bennett in *The World of Willa Cather*.

3. For pioneer farm life in the central plains, see Everett Dick, *The Sod-House Frontier, 1854–1890*. For photographs of sod houses and dugouts, see John E. Carter, *Solomon D. Butcher: Photographing the American Dream* (Lincoln: U of Nebraska P, 1985).

4. The generalizations that follow regarding social patterns in Nebraska in the late nineteenth century derive from Everett Dick; Lewis Atherton, *Main Street on the Middle Border*; Joanna L. Stratton, *Pioneer Women: Voices from the Kansas Frontier*; autobiographies and reminiscences; local histories of southern Nebraska; and conversations with people born in Nebraska in the 1880s and 1890s and with their children.

5. For a general treatment of the immigration experience, see Alan M. Kraut, *The Huddled Masses: The Immigrant in American Society, 1880–1921* (Arlington Heights: Harlan Davidson, 1982); for prohibition, see Joseph R. Gusfield, *Symbolic Crusade: Status Politics and the American Temperance Movement* (Urbana: U of Illinois P, 1963), and Luebke, *Immigrants and Politics*, chs. 5, 7.

6. For Nebraska Germans, see Luebke; for Czechs, see Rose Rosický, *A History of Czechs (Bohemians) in Nebraska* (Omaha: National Printing, 1929); and Vladimír Kucera, ed., *Czechs and Nebraska* (Ord, Neb.: Quiz Graphic Arts, 1967); for other groups, see Paul A. Olson, ed., *Broken Hoops and Plains People* (Lincoln: Nebraska Curriculum Development Center, 1976).

7. For Lincoln and the university, see Andrew J. Sawyer, ed., *Lincoln, the Capital City, and Lancaster County, Nebraska*, 2 vols. (Chicago: S. J. Clarke, 1916); Robert N. Manley, *Centennial History of the University of Nebraska: I. Frontier University (1869–1919)* (Lincoln: U of Nebraska P, 1969). For Cather's experiences there, see E. K. Brown and Leon Edel, *Willa Cather*, ch. 3; Phyllis C. Robinson, *Willa: The Life of Willa Cather*, ch. 2; Sharon O'Brien, *Willa Cather: The Emerging Voice*, ch. 6.

8. For general patterns of agriculture and society during the period from 1900 to the mid-1920s, see James C. Olson, *History of Nebraska*, chs. 20, 23; and Atherton, *Main Street on the Middle Border*, chs. 7, 9, 10.

BIBLIOGRAPHY

Adams, Henry. *The Education of Henry Adams: An Autobiography*. Boston: Houghton, 1961.

Atherton, Lewis. *Main Street on the Middle Border*. Bloomington: Indiana UP, 1954.

Bennett, Mildred R. *The World of Willa Cather*. Rev. ed. Lincoln: U of Nebraska P, 1961.

Brown, E. K., and Leon Edel. *Willa Cather: A Critical Biography*. New York: Avon, 1980.

Cather, Willa. "The Best Years." *The Old Beauty and Others*. New York: Vintage, 1976. 75–138.

———. "Eric Hermannson's Soul." *Willa Cather: 24 Stories*. Ed. Sharon O'Brien. New York: New American Library, 1987. 92–117.

———. *A Lost Lady*. New York: Vintage, 1972.

———. *My Ántonia*. Boston: Houghton, 1918.

———. "My First Novels [There Were Two]." *Willa Cather on Writing*. New York: Knopf, 1949. 89–97.

———. "Nebraska: The End of the First Cycle." *Nation* 5 September 1923: 236–38.

———. *O Pioneers!* Boston: Houghton, 1913.

———. "On the Divide." *Willa Cather: 24 Stories*. 35–49.

———. *One of Ours*. New York: Vintage, 1971.

———. *The Professor's House*. New York: Vintage, 1973.

———. "The Sculptor's Funeral." *Youth and the Bright Medusa*. New York: Vintage, 1975. 229–50.

———. *The Song of the Lark*. Boston: Houghton, 1937.

———. "A Wagner Matinée." *Youth and the Bright Medusa*. 215–26.

Dick, Everett. *The Sod-House Frontier: 1854–1890*. New York: Appleton, 1937.

Doctrines and Discipline of the Methodist Episcopal Church: 1896. New York: Eaton and Mains, 1896.

Hays, Samuel P. *American Political History as Social Analysis*. Nashville: U of Tennessee P, 1980.

Kleppner, Paul. *The Cross of Culture: A Social Analysis of Midwestern Politics, 1850–1900*. New York: Free, 1970.

Luebke, Frederick C. *Immigrants and Politics: The Germans of Nebraska, 1880–1900*. Lincoln: U of Nebraska P, 1969.

O'Brien, Sharon. *Willa Cather: The Emerging Voice*. New York: Oxford UP, 1987.

Olson, James C. *History of Nebraska*. 2nd ed. Lincoln: U of Nebraska P, 1966.

Parsons, Stanley B. *The Populist Context: Rural versus Urban Power on a Great Plains Frontier*. Westport: Greenwood, 1973.

Robinson, Phyllis C. *Willa: The Life of Willa Cather*. Garden City: Doubleday, 1983.

Rodgers, Jack W. "The Foreign Language Issue in Nebraska, 1918–1923." *Nebraska History* 39 (1958): 1–22.

Smith, Timothy L. *Revivalism and Social Reform in Mid-Nineteenth Century America*. New York: Abingdon, 1957.

Spengler, Oswald. *The Decline of the West*. 2 vols. Trans. Charles Francis Atkinson. New York: Knopf, 1926–28.

Stratton, Joanna L. *Pioneer Women: Voices from the Kansas Frontier*. New York: Simon, 1981.

Thomsen, F. L., and R. J. Foote. "Parity Price." *Agricultural Policy in an Affluent Society*. Ed. Vernon W. Ruttan, Arley D. Waldo, and James P. Houck. New York: Norton, 1969. 90–95.

U.S. Bureau of the Census. *Fourteenth Census of the United States Taken in the Year 1920: Composition and Characteristics of the Population by States*. Vol. 3. Washington, D.C.: Government Printing Office, 1922. 11 vols.

_____. *Special Reports: Religious Bodies: 1906*. 2 vols. Washington, D.C.: Government Printing Office, 1910.

U.S. Census Office. *Report on the Population of the United States at the Eleventh Census: 1890*. 2 pts. Washington, D.C.: Government Printing Office, 1895.

Willa Cather and Francis Parkman: Novelistic Portrayals of Colonial New France

WILBUR R. JACOBS

There is no question that Willa Cather avidly studied the early Canadian histories written by the nineteenth-century New Englander Francis Parkman. These volumes formed a kind of casement, opening a window on early Quebec, the lonely North American setting for *Shadows on the Rock*. Cather's friend and companion Edith Lewis tells us in her recollections that Cather found Parkman "the most interesting of American historians." Cather, moreover, had "long been" a reader of his books, and during a summer's visit to Quebec in 1927, she came upon his works while browsing in the Chateau Frontenac library. Here, in the atmosphere of the picturesque old hotel, she eagerly reread them with new interest (Lewis 151–56).[1] Her father's death that summer in Red Cloud and her mother's painful illness and death in Pasadena, California, shortly thereafter complicated but did not interrupt her study of Parkman and other sources on colonial New France.[2]

Cather and Parkman shared romantic views and ideas about old-regime Quebec, although he was a nineteenth-century Boston Brahmin from an old patrician family and her parents, middle-class Virginians, moved west to make their home in a Nebraska farming community. At the time of Parkman's death in 1893, Cather was a twenty-year-old college student who was reading Henry James and many other writers. She seems to have found Parkman's biography of La Salle and *The Oregon Trail* in the University of Nebraska library about this time (Brown 25).

My paper is concerned, then, with the Cather and Parkman connection in *Shadows on the Rock* and centers on three main themes: first, general factors that show why Cather was indebted to Parkman; second, her uses of Parkman's concept of environmental determinism, that is, the impact of a hostile wilderness upon the isolated Quebec colony; and third, the influence of this theory and the use of selection on her characterizing of individuals and types of people. From the viewpoint of a historian, her novel has both virtues and shortcomings. We can commend her uses of the environmental frontier theme but question her racist characterization of Woodland Indians as savages.

o   o   o   o   o

Cather was indeed indebted to Parkman. In turning to him, she had selected a historian who had a dominating sway over the writing of early Canadian history. The case can be made that the heroes and martyrs of those pioneering days became world famous largely because Parkman wrote about them. In the decades following Parkman's death, his *France and England in the New World* was increasingly accepted as the true story of Canada's colonial past by the majority of Canadians and other Americans. One recent Jesuit historian went so far as to argue that Parkman's legendary chronicles of missionary heroics were a key factor in canonization of the martyrs.[3]

Cather, it appears, could do no wrong in consulting Parkman. By the time she was writing *Shadows on the Rock*, she was a mature novelist of fifty-six who knew how to take what she needed from reference works. She had just completed a brilliant novel on French missionaries in the Southwest, *Death Comes for the Archbishop*, and here demonstrated that she was already a student of French culture and its spread to the New World. The bulk of her fiction, completed before she began *Shadows on the Rock*, shows that she wrote poetic novels about people who, as Leon Edel has stated, either revolted from or conquered their environment in the last phase of "an heroic era" (305–08). It is reasonable to assume that Cather found Parkman's histories especially appealing because his work, in a sense, was similar to hers. He, too, wrote about "an heroic era" with poetic feeling. His main "actors," and he called them "actors," were brave survivors who battled against or overcame their environment.

When we compare Cather and Parkman on the subject of New France, it becomes clear that in setting up her historical chronology for *Shadows on the Rock* Cather deferred to him because his accounts are clearly set forth, year by year and sometimes month by month.[4] Cather was undoubtedly aware that in addition to his text Parkman's footnotes are a source of a thousand fascinating details, although here her selectivity is revealed. For instance, these notes might follow the captivity of Massachusetts families in the Indian wars, specifying their birth and breeding and their descendants among prominent Bostonians such as the Winthrops and Derbys, but Cather passed over the chance to weave exciting captivity narratives into her story, even though English prisoners rescued from Indians lived in Quebec during the time span of her book. Her plot sequence might have been skewed by the intrusion of the prisoner issue, and this would have involved recasting her characterization of Count Frontenac as generally good-natured. He was in fact one of the most arrogant, tempestuous, and brutal of French leaders, noted for permitting the torment and burning of Indian captives. But in fairness to the count, he was more restrained than some of his contemporaries, who clamored for even more torture and burnings (*Count Frontenac* 459).[5]

I'm not sure Cather can be faulted for this kind of distortion. Still, what seems a harmless twisting of colonial times in a powerful novel serves as false history, and history has been used as a political weapon in Quebec's turbulent past and is being used in her turbulent present. Yet we must acknowledge that it is difficult to prove Cather entirely wrong in her benign characterization of Count Frontenac, for the count no doubt had his better moments. Contemporary readers and critics liked what Cather wrote, but recent scholars insist upon accuracy; similarly, historians have escalated their fault-finding in dissecting Parkman's writings.[6] Yet Parkman lives on, probably for the all-important reason that his books are never dull, and Cather would have nothing to do with dull histories, which she once told Mary Hunter Austin were sheer "agony" (Cather to Austin 1928).

There remains to be considered, however, the manner in which Parkman and Cather resorted to a kind of fiction to avoid inflicting the "agony" of boredom on their readers. Parkman's characters are recognizable human beings and perhaps appear much as they actually were. In my judgment, his portraits of seventeenth-century figures like Frontenac, Laval, and La Salle, and eighteenth-century figures like Amherst, Montcalm, and Wolfe are reasonably factual, although sometimes exaggerated to make them proponents, allies, or rivals. On Indians, as ethnographers generally agree, Parkman is accurate in details, but he greatly exaggerated in reporting on Indian "character" and behavior as barbarian (he relied on biased missionary and frontiersmen reports in portraying Indians). Cather also gives us this same stereotype, but she was not writing history and did not claim she was. She would form historical characters as her story dictated and confided to her friends Zoë Akins and Mary Austin that each novel had to have a certain drive or specific plan. Without such planning, there was a lack of pace, a low level of vitality (Cather to Akins 1935, and Cather to Austin 1927).[7] Thus her characters had to conform to her literary scheme. What did it matter if Bishop Laval was a quarrelsome busybody whose behavior at times was loathsome? Cather saw Laval as a kindly old priest who shepherded his sheep. When Cather was on the prowl for material that would lend vitality to her story, she grabbed it, regardless of historical accuracy (Bloom 216–17).[8]

Edith Lewis tells us that besides reading Parkman, Cather cultivated friendship with a French-Canadian priest at a village near Quebec, Abbé Henri Scott, who had written a pious biography of Laval. Here was a source for the French-Canadian ecclesiastical tradition. She went to the home of the abbé, admired his beautiful Latin library, and read his book (Lewis 154–55). She read, of course, a great deal more than Scott and Parkman. She surveyed missionary reports (like *The Jesuit Relations*, which were already translated) and exploration reports, and found at the Louvre, according to Mildred Bennett, the diary of an apothecary who had served under Frontenac (*World of Willa Cather* 133–34, 245). Visiting and revisiting Quebec, Cather immersed herself in the traditions of the city. She frequented Laval Seminary, the Ursuline Convent, and the marketplace in the lower town. As Lewis says,

Cather was "overwhelmed" by the Norman appearance of Quebec and the intensity of its French character (151ff.).

While acknowledging that many factors influenced Cather as she involved herself in the atmosphere, history, culture, and lifestyles of seventeenth-century Quebec, I find distinct particulars of Parkman's imprint on *Shadows on the Rock*. Cather, for instance, could scarcely overlook Parkman's skill in designing literary devices to grip the attention of his readers, which is nowhere more obvious than in the beginning scenes of *Pioneers of France in the New World*, the first part of his series. Here is an example of Parkman's manner of making his readers eyewitnesses of a historic panorama:

> The French dominion is a memory of the past, and when we evoke its departed shades, they rise from their graves in strange, romantic guise. Again their ghostly campfires seem to burn, and the fitful light is cast around on lord and vassal and black-robed priest, mingled with the wild forms of savage warriors. . . . A boundless vision grows upon us, an untamed continent; vast wastes of forest verdure; mountains in silent primeval sleep; river, lake and glimmering pool; wilderness oceans mingling with the sky. (*Pioneers* 1: xcviii)

One cannot readily imagine the impression such rhetoric had on Cather the novelist. We can more readily understand the influence on her of his representations of Canadian nuns. Here is Parkman's sympathetic portrayal of the hospital sisters:

> The nuns died but they never complained. Removed from the arena of ecclesiastical strife, too busy for the morbidness of the cloister, too much absorbed in the practical benevolence to become the prey to illusions, they and their sister community were models of that benign and tender charity of which the Roman Catholic Church is so rich in examples. (*The Old Régime* 2: 158)

Cather's depiction of the nuns in *Shadows on the Rock* is similar.

> Courageous these Sisters were, accepting good and ill fortune with high spirit. . . . They never vulgarly exaggerated hardships and dangers. . . . The Sisters' prayers could do much,—no one might say how much. . . . A Sister said pleasantly: "I hope we shall meet in heaven," . . . a happy appointment. (97–98)

Cather's words are not the same, but she stresses, like Parkman, the courage, charity, and willingness of the nuns to accept hardship and death without complaint.

But let us consider an additional sample of the prose that made Parkman's pages pleasing to Cather. Take for instance this description of Bishop Laval's school in which Parkman employs Catholic tradition and imagery to create memorable similes:

From the vast meadows of the parish of St. Joachim, which here border the St. Lawrence, there rises like an island a low flat hill, hedged round with forests like the tonsured head of a monk. It was here that Laval planted his school . . . where, athwart the gaunt arms of ancient pines, the river lies shimmering in the summer haze, the cottages of *habitants* are strung like beads of a rosary along the meadows of Beaupré. (*The Old Régime* 2: 164–65)

How similar is this in spirit and technique to Cather's celebrated description of Quebec in springtime:

It was the first day of June. Before dawn a wild calling and twittering of birds in the bushes on the cliff-side above the apothecary's back door announced clear weather. When the sun came up over the Île d'Orléans, the rock of Kebec stood gleaming above the river like an altar with many candles, or like a holy city in an old legend, shriven, sinless, washed in gold. (169)

We can, I believe, safely assume that Cather found Parkman a fascinating writer. She could not overlook the lifelike and poetic reconstructions of New France that abound in his volumes. It is no wonder that she, like generations of readers, ignored his sometimes offensive social ideas to bask in the romantic beauty of his prose.

o   o   o   o   o

The major common ground that becomes apparent as I compare Cather's and Parkman's portrayals of New France is a certain environmental determinism. There is good reason to believe that Cather adopted Parkman's concept about the influence of a hostile wilderness on the lonely colony on the rock at Quebec. The isolated rock was a strikingly appropriate setting for the story of the apothecary, his daughter, and historical figures such as Count Frontenac and Bishop Laval. This environmental theme, stressing the effect of the frontier as a conditioning factor in the lives of pioneers, is also present in *My Ántonia*, where during the long cold winter in Black Hawk human life was "shrunken and pinched, frozen down to the bare stalk" (181). Happily, Cather found it clearly expressed in Parkman's *Count Frontenac* and in his other books.

The title and opening of *Shadows on the Rock* create a hostile environmental mood with the apothecary Auclair sadly bidding farewell to "the last of the summer ships" as they begin their voyage back to France. Auclair and his family now face "the stern realities of life." "For eight months," Cather tells us, "the French colony on this rock in the North would be entirely cut off from Europe, from the world" (3). From October until July there would be no supplies, no letters. The only possible communication from France might come by couriers to Montreal, dispatched by Dutch traders. Across "from the proud rock of Quebec," Cather continues, the forest stretched no living man knew how far. That was the dead, sealed world of the vegetable kingdom, an uncharted continent choked with interlocking trees, living, dead, half-dead, their roots in bogs and swamps, strangling each other in a slow agony that had lasted for centuries. The forest was suffocation, annihilation; there European man was swallowed up in silence, distance, mould, black mud, and the singing swarms of insect life. . . . The only avenue of escape was along the river . . . that lived, moved, glittered, changed,—a highway along which men could travel, taste the sun and open air, feel freedom . . . reach the open sea . . . reach the world, even! (6-7)

Such memorable scenes of the solitude of Quebec's forests resemble Parkman's wilderness settings. Cather's descriptions evoke feelings of death, suffocation, and blackness that invite comparison with his in *The Old Régime*. Here are phrases from his descriptions of the forest flanking Quebec:

The gleam of sunlit waters dances in quivering light . . . ancient trees . . . their forlorn and savage ruin . . . some grisly with decrepit age, nightmares of strange distortion, gnarled and knotted . . . like serpents petrified in an agony of contorted strife . . . the impotence of rottenness . . . like mouldering reptiles . . . the forest devouring its own dead . . . the sheen of sparkling lakes. (2: 114)[9]

Note that both writers describe the waters in the forest as "glittering" or "quivering." Both have contorted trees in "agony" killing each other. Cather speaks of "mould," and Parkman describes trees as "mouldering reptiles." Both writers, it is evident, produce a feeling of overwhelming apprehension that the formidable woodland might well devour the infant colony if it does not struggle to survive. Both stress the immensity of the threatening natural world, dwarfing human endeavor. For Cather, the crude Harnois family, living on an island on the edge of the forest, reveals the harsh, dirty life of those exposed to the wilderness (*Shadows* 188-96).

Yet Cather and Parkman saw the hardy bush ranger as a product of the wilderness frontier, a robust figure capable of moving over the waterways to enjoy the freedom of the forest as well as the dog soup of the Indians (*Shadows* 187-88). In a burst of enthusiasm Parkman traces the whole evolution of New France from the wilderness frontier that produced the *coureurs de bois*. "Canada," he writes, "was at the very portal of the great interior wilderness. The St. Lawrence and the Lakes were the highway to that domain of savage freedom; and thither the disfranchised, half-starved *seignior*, and the discouraged *habitant* who could find no market for his produce naturally betook themselves. Their lesson in savagery was well learned, and for many a year a boundless license and a stiff-handed authority battled for the control of Canada" (*The Old Régime* 2: 198). It is this overall environmental safety-valve interpretation, the impact of the frontier upon the Europeans, so ably expressed by Parkman, that influenced Cather as well as the historian Frederick Jackson Turner, progenitor of the frontier theory in American history.[10] Cather idealizes the tough frontier trader–woodsmen in the character of Pierre Charron. The historical Canadian traders, friends of Frontenac and led by La Salle, Cadillac, and their bush rangers, were enemies of the Jesuits and Laval and engaged in a battle to control the rich interior brandy trade with the Indians. As Parkman tells us, the drunken brawls and violent behavior of the *coureurs de bois* at the far western posts gave impressionable warriors sordid models for behavior.

o   o   o   o   o

The environmental theme can result and has resulted in stereotyping people. Parkman sees Indians as "savages," drunk or sober; and Cather, though she left us sympathetic references to Indians in other writings, readily stresses Indian barbarity in *Shadows on the Rock*. She tells tales of Indians eating dogs and cooking human hands in pots of boiling soup. Although I can't readily locate the hand in the soup incident in Parkman's voluminous writings, there is something like it in his *The Jesuits* (1: 229).[11] Cather's account is in a tale told in "The Long Winter" by Father Hector Saint-Cyr, a missionary of "good breeding," "strong and fearless and handsome" (146–47). He knew the "dirty kettles" of the Indians and told of Father Chabanel, a missionary prisoner who, after swallowing a portion of his bowl, saw the Hurons pull "a human hand out of the kettle to show him that he had eaten of an Iroquois prisoner" (151–52). Chabanel "became ill at once, and they followed him into the forest to make merry over his retchings" (152). Without giving names of chiefs or attempting to describe cultures and lifestyles of the Huron–Iroquois people, Cather paints them all as cannibal–barbarians. She did these native people a great disservice in neglecting to do her homework. At the time she was writing her novel there were Huron–Wyandott people living in Quebec City and Six Nations Iroquois occupying a large reserve in Brantford, Ontario, who had oral history traditions and family histories.

Additionally, there was a superb corpus of cultural anthropological literature she should have taken the trouble to use. Cather must have known about the work of the illustrious anthropologist Lewis H. Morgan, founding father of Iroquois studies, whose books on the Six Nations even had an impact on Friedrich Engels, the colleague of Karl Marx.[12] Anthropologists were then beginning their culture area studies, describing and analyzing aboriginal nuclear and extended family and kinship bonds, subsistence patterns, religious traditions, and remarkable accomplishments in domesticating plants and in agriculture. Cather never tells us that the brutal Huron–Iroquois had developed a confederation government and a system of subsistence farming that rivaled the old nation-states of Europe. Morgan and his followers were saying such things before Cather was a freshman in college. But she shut them out to create her cruel world of forbidding forests and man-eating barbarians surrounding little Cécile and her father.

Cather, in short, oversimplifies. The historical period covered in her novel was one, as Parkman and his successors have written, of fierce intercolonial warfare, incredible atrocities, and the butchery of both Indian and white families.[13] *Shadows on the Rock* is limited in being told largely through the childlike vision of Cécile, who views Indians as a threat to civilization. Even the biased Parkman is fairer to the Indians, informing his readers about Woodland Indian societies in two learned essays.[14] He explores ritual cannibalism, the grand council of the Iroquois, tribal leadership, Iroquois and Huron self-interest, the terrible effects of smallpox on the tribes, and he writes about Indian response to the dwindling resources of beaver. Cather overlooks all this and more. She appears to have selected only the historical episodes, incidents, and facts that would serve her story.

Selection also defines her historical characterizations. She saw at once, for instance, how Parkman's description of Bishop Laval's face would suit her purposes. Parkman described Laval from extant portraits in this fashion: "a drooping nose of portentous size; a well-formed forehead; a brow strongly arched; a bright, clear eye; scanty hair, half hidden by a skullcap; thin lips, compressed and rigid." Parkman depended on this huge nose to suggest the nosiness that marked "the priestly type." Cather deflates the negativity of Laval's "drooping nose." Cécile, Cather tells us, "had never been intimidated by [the bishop's] deep-set, burning eyes or his big nose." The inference here, I believe, is that the child enjoyed special treatment from the powerful bishop with the threatening nose (*The Old Régime* 1: 163; *Shadows* 230–31).

The figure of Count Frontenac as it emerges in the novel is Parkmanesque in that Cather's general account of his career is accurate. From time to time she refers to his two administrations, his hostility to the Jesuits, his victories over the Indians, his vanity and extravagance. But her additional characterization of the count as amiable and benign is invention. Cather follows Parkman's detail in incidents such as the count's specific desire to have his heart sealed in a lead or silver container to be sent back to Paris to be buried in the family tomb, but she leaves out an enticing tidbit—the additional story that the count wanted his wife to have his heart in the silver container. As Parkman explains, it was said by Frontenac's critics that his wife said "she had never had it when he was living, and did not want it when he was dead" (*Count Frontenac* 451–52).

o   o   o   o   o

The novel's greatest virtue, from the viewpoint of the historian, is its *ancien régime* vision of Quebec in the era of Frontenac, with nuns, missionaries, miracles, and church ceremonies. A minor drawback, readily noted by historians, is that the novel has a certain flatness and banality in the artificial talk of historical individuals such as Laval, Saint Vallier, and Frontenac. At best, their conversations with Cécile and her father are only occasionally believable. However, the dialogue of the nonhistorical figures has genuine overtones of Quebec in the 1690s. A major drawback is Cather's stereotyping of the Woodland Indians: she dehumanizes them. The facts are that no Indian savagery surpassed the savagery and brutality of the Europeans—French or English. Cather's persistence in denigrating the Indians in her novel demonstrates how an author can stumble when anthropology is ignored. Where other fiction writers such as Helen Hunt Jackson went to great lengths to correct racist stories about American Indians, Cather resorted to exaggeration in *Shadows on the Rock*. She paralleled her dark and light visions of the forbidding forest with dark and light characterizations of people. The French are light and good, the Indians are dark and bad—a melodramatic view of the past.

Such racial stereotyping could be used as a political weapon against a minority people. It is regrettable that Cather relied on Parkman when such a wealth of anthropological data was available to her. There is the additional regret that she overlooked Parkman's occasional favorable portrayal of Woodland Indians as a society with a developed culture and admirable lifestyle. She ignored Parkman's descriptions of articulate Woodland Indian leaders and spokesmen at treaties and conferences with the French. In short, Cather took the worst of Parkman without understanding that his portrayal of Indians, based upon extensive research, was also an attempt to portray Indians as people of the forest who had their own objectives and policies in dealing with the French.

Yet another criticism of Cather can be made. Her emphasis on mutilation and torture to stimulate reader interest seems unnecessary. She was one of the best and had no real need to rely on her own fascination with tales of mutilation and Indian brutality to keep her audience.[15] She had, of course, the example of Parkman, who, as we have noted, tinctured his narrative with missionary torture accounts, many of them exaggerated.

Cather took much from Parkman's historical structure—his bias against Indians, his image of the forest, his chronology of events, his descriptions of historical characters. These emerge through the eyes of thirteen-year-old Cécile, undoubtedly a reflection of Cather's own girlhood. One can conclude that Parkman was, in many respects, a silent partner in the writing of *Shadows on the Rock*.

—Huntington Library and
the University of California, Santa Barbara

NOTES

1. Cather's biographers merely mention Parkman, using as their source Edith Lewis, Cather's intimate friend and living companion. See, for instance, James Woodress, *Willa Cather: A Literary Life* 431. Sharon O'Brien in *Willa Cather: The Emerging Voice* passes over Parkman in long but perceptive discussions of lesbianism (see 87 ff.). The lesbian theme is expanded in another book neglecting Parkman, Robert James Nelson's *Willa Cather and France*, which appears to be almost entirely concerned with "phallocentrism" and "transvestite males" in Cather's writings (see, for instance, 51ff., 141–45). Nor does Nelson give significant attention to *Shadows on the Rock*, the volume that most clearly demonstrates the impact of French culture on Cather.

2. A basic theme in Cather biographies is the close relationship that Cather had with her father, a relationship reflected in the father–daughter intimacy in *Shadows on the Rock*.

3. The late John Bannon, S.J., who wrote an introduction for a reprinting of Parkman's *Jesuits in North America in the Seventeenth Century*, made this point to me in conversations in the 1960s.

4. Chapter headings have specific dates, and each page shows in brackets the year or years covered.

5. See also Canadian historian William J. Eccles, *France in America* 95–99; *Frontenac, Courtier-Governor* 18–50; David Griffin, " 'The Man for the Hour': A Defense of Francis Parkman's *Frontenac*."

6. One of Parkman's most tenacious modern critics is Francis Jennings, who argues his case in "Francis Parkman, A Brahmin among Untouchables" and in *Empire of Fortune, Crowns, Colonies, and Tribes in the Seven Years War in America* (xvii, 126n., 171, 480). Also, Eccles summarizes his view that "Parkman's interpretation was marked by a strong anticlerical prejudice and an inability to see in New France much more than the reverse of the vices and virtues of New England in his day" in *Canada under Louis XIV, 1663–1701*, 265. This book gives a more Parkmanesque view of Frontenac than Eccles's earlier Frontenac biography and provides an excellent overview of early Canadian history. This said, one can examine Eccles's histories for echoes of Parkman. For instance, the "character" of Frontenac in Eccles's *Canada* (78–79, 241) lists Frontenac's shortcomings; many of these are given by Parkman in *Count Frontenac* (451–60). One criticism Parkman makes that is not stressed by Eccles is "the barbarity of the warfare that he waged" in permitting "Indian captives to be tortured" (459).

7. Cather argues to Zoë Akins that *Shadows on the Rock* had to be read at a slow pace as if by the fireside. Yet, as she told Austin, the novel still had to have pace and planning. Cather letters at the Huntington Library (the Zoë Akins Collection of 87 letters and the Mary Hunter Austin Collection of 13 letters) provide biographical data about Cather and her tastes, literary ambitions, and personal life. Cather letters in this paper are paraphrased and not quoted, in accordance with the restrictions of the Cather will. See the restriction statement in the Zoë Akins Collection, Huntington Library.

8. Edward and Lillian Bloom point out that Cather would make up Navajo gods for Cañon de Chelly to shape her narrative.

9. Parkman's best descriptions of Eastern forests were based upon his visits to what he called the "primeval" woodlands of New Hampshire, which in the 1880s he valiantly tried to save from clearcutting.

10. Although Frederick Jackson Turner was an admirer of Parkman and read his books with care, Turner never acknowledged that the frontier theory had a basis in *The Old Régime*. See Turner's review of Parkman's works in *The Dial* 16 December 1897: 451–53.

11. Parkman cites an old edition of Father Jerome Lalemant's Huron relation of 1693, reprinted in *The Jesuit Relations and Allied Documents* 17: 76–77. Lalemant's account is substantially repeated in Parkman, a typical example of Parkman's use of sources.

12. Lewis H. Morgan's classic *League of the Ho-Do-No-Sau-Nee or Iroquois* was in every major library when Cather was writing *Shadows on the Rock*.

13. This warfare, atrocity by atrocity, is told by Parkman and is summarized by William H. Eccles in *France in America* 95–99.

14. Parkman's ethnological treatises appeared as introductions, first in *Pontiac* and later in the *Jesuits*.

15. Cather, surprisingly, had a streak of hardness, even cruelty, which may have attracted her to Parkman. O'Brien argues that Cather found "perfect happiness" and "favorite amusement" in "vivisection" and "amputating limbs" (87 ff.). Her vivisection experiments were carried on in a makeshift laboratory during her late teens, when she called herself "William Cather M.D." According to O'Brien (87 ff.) and Bennett (*World* 115–18), Cather cut up frogs and toads and then dogs and cats. A friend advised Cather to keep her laboratory in a private place so the screams of the animals could not be heard. The inference here is that the animals were mutilated without a painkiller. Mildred Bennett recalled in a conversation at Brigham Young University in 1988 that Cather even took a "family dog" away from her sister and experimented with it and later made a rug from the dog's skin. Parkman, likewise, found "amusement" in seeing animals suffer. He found pleasure in shooting off heads of chickadees and in the seemingly endless slaughtering of buffalo (*Letters of Francis Parkman* 1: 12 and *The Oregon Trail* 402–33). Bennett in her introduction to *Willa Cather: Collected Short Fiction, 1892–1912* xxxviii refers to Lewis's suggestion that Cather was preoccupied with mutilation because a half-witted boy once threatened to cut off her hand. My feeling, however, is that Cather never got over her fascination with mutilation and, for instance, took a certain satisfaction in recounting incidents like Jim Burden's cutting up a fat old rattlesnake in *My Ántonia*.

BIBLIOGRAPHY

Bennett, Mildred R. Introduction. *Willa Cather: Collected Short Fiction.* By Willa Cather. Rev. ed. Ed. Virginia Faulkner. Lincoln: U of Nebraska P, 1970. xiii–xli.

──────. *The World of Willa Cather.* Lincoln: Nebraska UP, 1961.

Bloom, Edward A. and Lillian D. *Willa Cather's Gift of Sympathy.* Carbondale: Southern Illinois UP, 1962.

Brown, E. K. *Willa Cather: A Critical Biography.* New York: Knopf, 1953.

Cather, Willa. Letters to Mary Hunter Austin. 27 February 1927; 9 March 1928. Mary Hunter Austin Collection. Huntington Library, San Marino, Calif.

──────. Letters to Zoë Akins. 24 October [1924]; [19 April 1935]. Zoë Akins Collection. Huntington Library, San Marino, Calif.

──────. *My Ántonia.* Boston: Houghton, 1961.

──────. *Shadows on the Rock.* New York: Knopf, 1931.

Eccles, William J. *Canada under Louis XIV, 1663–1701.* New York: Oxford UP, 1964.

──────. *France in America.* New York: Harper, 1973.

──────. *Frontenac, Courtier-Governor.* Toronto: McClelland and Stewart, 1965.

Edel, Leon. "Willa Cather." *Notable American Women, 1607–1950: A Biographical Dictionary.* Ed. Edward T. James. Vol. 1. Cambridge, Mass: Harvard UP, 1971. 305–08.

Griffin, David. " 'The Man for the Hour': A Defense of Francis Parkman's *Frontenac.*" *New England Quarterly* 42.4 (December 1970): 605–20.

Jennings, Francis. *Empire of Fortune, Crowns, Colonies, and Tribes in the Seven Years War in America.* New York: Norton, 1988.

──────. "Francis Parkman, a Brahmin among Untouchables." *William and Mary Quarterly* 42.3 (July 1985): 305–28.

The Jesuit Relations and Allied Documents. Ed. Reuben Gold Thwaites. Vol. 17. Cleveland: Clark, 1898.

Lewis, Edith. *Willa Cather Living.* New York: Knopf, 1953.

Morgan, Lewis H. *League of the Ho-Do-No-Sau-Nee or Iroquois.* New York: Dodd, 1901.

Nelson, Robert James. *Willa Cather and France.* Urbana: U of Illinois P, 1988.

O'Brien, Sharon. *Willa Cather: The Emerging Voice.* New York: Oxford UP, 1987.

Parkman, Francis. *Count Frontenac and New France under Louis XIV.* Boston: Little, 1907.

──────. *The Conspiracy of Pontiac and the Indian War after the Conquest of Canada.* Boston: Little, 1907.

──────. *The Jesuits in North America in the Seventeenth Century.* 2 vols. Boston: Little, 1907.

──────. *Letters of Francis Parkman.* Ed. Wilbur R. Jacobs. 2 vols. Norman: U of Oklahoma P, 1960.

──────. *The Old Régime in Canada under Louis XIV.* 2 vols. Boston: Little, 1907.

──────. *The Oregon Trail.* Boston: Little, 1907.

──────. *Pioneers of France in the New World.* 2 vols. Boston: Little, 1907.

Woodress, James. *Willa Cather: A Literary Life.* Lincoln: U of Nebraska P, 1987.

Death Comes for the Archbishop:
A Novel Way of Making History

TED J. WARNER

A skillful writer and wonderful teller of tales, Willa Cather produced a work in 1927 that is eminently readable, fascinating, alive with detail and description of people and places. *Death Comes for the Archbishop* is a classic example of the novel accepted as history. It is prominently displayed in bookstores in Santa Fe, inviting tourists and the general public alike to read what is advertised as an accurate and sympathetic description of nineteenth-century New Mexico. To this day, high school teachers and university professors in both American literature and history assign this book to their students. It is probably the most-admired and best-known Southwestern novel and after more than sixty years continues to evoke profound emotions about the Catholic church, the Hispanos, Mexicanos, Native Americans, and Anglo-Americans of Territorial New Mexico. It is an enormously impressive work. Still it does some violence to historical accuracy and in fact does considerable damage to the reputation of one of New Mexico's greatest native sons.

Throughout her history New Mexico has touched responsive chords in inhabitants and visitors. For many years the New Mexico automobile license plate has proclaimed her "The Land of Enchantment." Tourists, artists, writers, and dudes invariably succumb to her charms and become "enchanted" with the landscape, the capital city Santa Fe, and Old Town Albuquerque. Some are moved to write a book or paint a picture. Many adopt Western clothing complete with squash blossom necklace or turquoise belt buckle and bola tie. Still others write letters to editors or feature articles for hometown newspapers proclaiming the beauty and wonders of the exciting new place they have just "discovered." Willa Cather must have been similarly impressed. She visited there in 1912, 1914, 1915, 1925, and 1926, and she wrote a book. Her vivid imagination, her sensitivity towards people and places, and her feeling for time and space admirably equipped her for the task. Her novel is compelling and riveting, and her talent makes it seem plausible, genuine, and true, based as it is on historic figures, places, and events.

At the time of Cather's first visit to New Mexico, lawyer-turned-historian Ralph Emerson Twitchell had just published a multivolume history of the new state. His *Leading Facts of New Mexico History* in six volumes was a sweeping account of the Native American, Spanish, and Mexican heritages through the American conquest and struggle for statehood. Although it reads like a lawyer's brief, Cather, a voracious reader, doubtlessly devoured it. She was fascinated by the long sweep of history and the many persons of diverse culture who contributed to the development of the new state, and all this may have implanted the germ for a novel.

During her 1925 visit to New Mexico, Cather stayed with friends Tony and Mable Dodge Luhan at their home in Taos, where no doubt she was regaled with stories of the local culture and perhaps had the opportunity to read Twitchell's latest book, *Old Santa Fe: The Story of New Mexico's Ancient Capital.* She became further acquainted with one of the best-loved and most highly respected men in all the Southwest, Bishop—later Archbishop—Jean Baptiste Lamy. In the cold, hard, factual narrative of his life as related by Twitchell, Cather saw the hero of a new story emerging. She thereupon decided to relate the epic struggles of Father Lamy during his episcopal labors in New Mexico at a critical time in church–state history. Thus, with her pen she helped create the "Lamy Legend." Based on the facts of Bishop/Archbishop Lamy's life, as well as the lives of other historical persons, *Death Comes for the Archbishop* became one of Cather's finest works. Her story caught the attention and imagination of the public and quickly became a national best-seller. Her feel for geography and grasp of the four conflicting cultures combined with her sympathetic understanding of human nature to strike responsive chords in the readers of her day, and they continue to do so in readers of ours.

For some reason, Cather used pseudonyms for her two main characters while retaining correct surnames for others. Father/Bishop/Archbishop Jean Baptiste Lamy became Father/Bishop/Archbishop Jean Marie Latour. His Vicar General and later Bishop of Denver, Joseph P. Machebeuf, was called Father Joseph Vaillant. (Perhaps she called Lamy "Latour" because this French priest was the tower of strength, and Father Machebeuf was indeed *vailant* [valiant] in the faith.) Kit Carson, however, and Father Antonio José Martinez, the priest of Taos, retained their given names. Latour and Vaillant emerge from her pages as devoted, selfless churchmen larger than life. Kit Carson received generally heroic treatment as a frontier American in New Mexico. But Padre Martinez is treated with contempt, and thus, unfortunately, the "Martinez Myth" was launched. Despite the book's other strengths and well-deserved plaudits, herein it is flawed.

Father Martinez was, and remains to this day, a controversial figure in New Mexico history. But Cather accepted as fact the worst accounts of his character and reputation. Because *Archbishop* is still so widely read, Martinez, despite some excellent attributes, remains in the minds of most readers one of the villains of fiction. Yet he is not a fictional character; he is a historical personage whose reputation has been sullied by a popular novel. Willa Cather describes Padre Martinez of Taos as "an old scapegrace" (an incorrigible rascal) and asserts that he had children and grandchildren in almost every settlement in northern New Mexico. She writes that he was a powerful old priest who was ruler in temporal as well as in spiritual affairs. She calls him a "dictator" to all the parishes in the area and says that even "the native priests in Santa Fe were under his thumb" (139). She accuses Martinez of instigating the Taos Indian Revolt of 1847, which resulted in the murder of Governor Charles Bent and a dozen other Americans. She claims that no attempt was made to bring Martinez to account for these deeds and that the priest even managed to profit personally from the affair by acquiring the property of the seven Taos Indians who were later arrested, condemned, and hanged for their role in the uprising. This, she asserts, made him "quite the richest man in the parish" (140). All this may make an excellent literary foil for her book's heroes, but, unfortunately for Cather, as a reflector of history it is just not true!

Nor did Padre Martinez impress Cather by his physical appearance. She describes him as "an enormous man. His broad high shoulders were like a bull buffalo's, his big head was set defiantly on a thick neck, and the full-cheeked, richly coloured, egg-shaped Spanish face . . . was so unusual . . . a high, narrow forehead, brilliant yellow eyes set deep in strong arches, and full, florid cheeks,—not blank areas of smooth flesh, as in Anglo-Saxon faces, but full of muscular activity, as quick to change with feeling as any of his features. His mouth was the very assertion of violent, uncurbed passions and tyrannical self-will; the full lips thrust out and taut, like the flesh of animals distended by fear or desire" (140–41). Father Latour did not even care much for Martinez asleep, for he "snored like an enraged bull" (149). Cather did admit that he sang the mass impressively in a beautiful baritone voice, that he drank from some deep well of emotional power, and that he "was not a man one would easily forget" (140). Anyone who passed him on the street, she allowed, would feel his great physical force and imperious will.

Bishop Latour was scandalized that Padre Martinez did not consider celibacy an essential element of a priest's condition. Even though this had been thrashed out many centuries before, Martinez retorted to the bishop that "nothing is decided once for all" (146). Martinez believed that celibacy was all very well for the French clergy (like Latour and Vaillant), but not for the Spaniard or Mexican. Cather charged that Padre Martinez lusted for women the way Padre Lucero of Albuquerque lusted for money. He paid a filial respect to the Holy Father, yet he also claimed that Rome had no authority in New Mexico and that the church there resented the Pope's interference in its affairs. Ultimately the split between Latour and Martinez became so bitter and nefarious that the bishop had no alternative but to excommunicate the recalcitrant and unrepentant priest. Martinez continued to lead his parishioners in Taos at the head of his schismatic church until his death in 1867. Such is the way Martinez has come to us through the pen of Willa Cather. Such is he considered since 1927 by those who have read *Archbishop*. Such is the Martinez Myth. The truth is, however, that Cather fictionalized the facts.

It should be remembered that even though Cather cast him in the role of Bishop Latour's (Lamy's) great antagonist, historically Father Martinez's conflict with the bishop came toward the end of an otherwise praiseworthy career that straddled three periods of New Mexico history—the Spanish, Mexican, and American. Martinez was involved in virtually every important event during fifty years of significant transition, but Cather and other writers have limited his actions to irresponsible resistance to Roman dominance and a self-serving struggle for personal power and wealth. Three opposing camps in New Mexico have a vital interest in seeing the conflict this way. English-speaking Americans have a confirmation for their position that the Hispanic people submitted peacefully, even eagerly, to their conquest. Protestants doing missionary work in the once solidly Catholic region welcomed any sign of inner readiness on the part of the people to break away from the church of Rome. And Catholic historians have found vindication for the course taken by Bishop Lamy and his successors (Francis 265–66). But modern scholarship strongly disagrees with this twisted image of Padre Martinez, and many present-day historians, Chicano leaders, Rio Arribans, and New Mexicans have banded together to rescue him from his unfortunate reputation.

One of the first attempts was by the New Mexico writer, Erna Fergusson. Writing in 1941, she proclaimed that "Martinez probably still ranks as the outstanding New Mexican." Recognizing but not dwelling on his spiritual qualities, she notes that they "were entirely overshadowed by his energy and his versatility in practical affairs" (307). He was a forward-looking priest who printed textbooks as well as a newspaper he called *El Crepusculo de Libertad* (The Dawn of Liberty). He established schools for boys and, unusual in that day, a school for girls. Whatever his priestly derelictions, he was "a strong character, a fascinating man, a true liberal" (*Our Southwest* 306–08). Fergusson calls him "the first New Mexico gringo" and claims that as a result of his part in the 1847 Taos Revolt he may have seemed a patriot to Mexico while a traitor to the United States. Ten years later Fergusson again defended Father Martinez, describing him as "New Mexico's most brilliant and controversial figure" (*New Mexico* 260). She calls him New Mexico's first modern and wonders if he may simply have been the last unreconciled Mexican. She also says that he never lost the confidence of his people.

Other writers have risen to the padre's defense. Stan Steiner claims that Martinez was "a man of obstinate and strong beliefs" and a leader of the independence battles in New Mexico (348). He believes the conflict between Lamy and Martinez was one that echoed and reechoed through the years between the poor priests of the villages and the opulent bishoprics. The native-born Spanish-speaking clergy and the Anglo and English-speaking hierarchy were united in the Mystical Body of Christ that was the church, but they were divided in every other way, including their way of life and cultural inheritance and their religious ritual and practice. In *The Proud Peoples: The Heritage and Culture of Spanish-Speaking Peoples in the United States* (1972),

Harold J. Alford calls Martinez "a pioneer educator and socially conscious leader" (238–39). As early as 1830 Martinez was preaching and writing on topics such as religious freedom, tolerance of other sects, and the necessary separation of church and state, all of which were considered extremely radical ideas in New Mexico at the time. The good padre also advocated an equitable redistribution of land to check the exploitation of the small farmer by the large landowner. "He gave his own lands to his servants and to his relatives and devoted all of his earnings to the enlightenment of the people of New Mexico. He urged education for all of the people, and a reduction of the civil powers of the church and clergy." He died "a poor man financially but one rich in the regard of his people, for his lifelong efforts to break down the barriers of ignorance and bigotry" (238–39). This does not sound like the Padre Martinez who emerges from the pages of *Archbishop*. Matt S. Meier and Feliciano Rivera explain that when Bishop Lamy was given the task of reforming and reorganizing the isolated and corrupted New Mexican church at mid-nineteenth century, church influence was at an all-time low. Lamy, they assert, was a man of great dedication and drive, but totally unfamiliar with the Hispano-Mexicano culture, and soon became involved in a quarrel over tithing with Father Martinez. But in spite of this conflict with the bishop, Martinez remained an important religious and political leader until his death (110).

Perhaps the most angry of the Chicano writers is Rudolfo Acuña, who writes that in the clash between the Anglo-Americans and the New Mexicans subsequent to the American takeover of the Southwest, the Catholic church—the most important institution in New Mexico—limited its function to tending strictly to the spiritual needs of the people, worked to "Americanize" the New Mexicans, and with few exceptions did not champion the rights of the poor. When, after 1850, control of the church passed from the Spanish/Mexican clergy to an Anglo-American hierarchy, "it became an alien clergy that related more to the power establishment and a few rich Anglo-American parishioners than to the masses. It became a pacifying agent, encouraging Mexicans to accept the occupation" (55). The undisputed leader of the Mexican clergy at that time, says Acuña, was Padre Antonio José Martinez. His devotion to the Catholic church was deep and abiding, but he saw it as an institution to benefit, not enslave, mankind. Acuña calls Martinez "one of the most important figures in New Mexican history, as well as one of the most beloved." In Taos, "Martinez took a progressive religious stand, refusing to collect tithes from the poor and opposing large land grants, claiming the land should go to the people. He criticized the church for its policy of allowing the clergy to exact excessive and oppressive tithes and fees for marriages, funerals, and like services" (55). He was also a staunch advocate of the separation of church and state. This does not sound like Cather's Martinez either!

The historical records reveal that Padre Antonio José Martinez's family was typical of the many Spanish colonial families who pushed into northern

New Mexico in the late eighteenth century. His father, Don José Manuel Martinez, secured a large land grant at Tierra Amarilla on the Upper Chama River. Four of the don's sons were placed there and four others were located in the Taos Valley. "Don Manuel's progeny were as prolific as they were able, and by the 1830s and 1840s the Martinez clan, by virtue of size and holdings, was called the 'big family' in Taos" (Lamar 38–39). Geographical isolation restricted marital opportunities, and the Martinez family soon spread throughout the Rio Arriba, "knitted together in a complex web of consanguinity" with other local clans (the Valdez, Vigil, Jaramillo, Lovato, and Trujillo families) "more characteristic of an old paternalistic society than of a frontier one. And in true patron tradition they and their relations controlled scores of devoted peons, domesticated Indians, and retainers. Though there were many feuds and personality conflicts between rival families, they felt a common bond of blood and environment which made them truly provincial" (Lamar 40). (John Nichols's *The Milagro Beanfield War*, made into a film in 1988 directed by Robert Redford, faithfully depicts the family life and ties of this region.)

The foremost member in this "big family" and the history of Taos was Antonio José Martinez. Born in Abiquiu in 1793, he entered the priesthood after his young wife died, and chose Taos as his parish. Trained in the seminary in Durango, Mexico, he was his community's well-traveled and learned man, and many thought him a legal expert. He selected the promising sons of prominent families as his students, and historian Howard R. Lamar credits him with "training at least a dozen future political leaders and priests of territorial New Mexico." Padre Martinez was shrewd and observant and a born leader with sizable ambitions, and Lamar recalls that to Twitchell he was "one of the most brilliant men of his time." Martinez recognized early that the Mexican rebellion against Spain in 1821 signified the beginning of a new era, but he was also a traditionalist who wielded great local power through his priestly offices, his family, and the Taos Indians who admired him. He became their spokesman in civil as well as religious matters (Lamar 40).

It has been suggested that by usual church standards Martinez was not a good defender of the faith and that he renounced few, if any, physical pleasures of the world. This, however, can be vigorously denied, it being pointed out that in his own lifetime he was "never openly attacked by even his bitterest enemies on grounds of immorality" (Francis 272). The archives of the Archdiocese of Santa Fe, which hold voluminous documents bearing on Martinez's conflict with Lamy, contain no records attesting to charges of immorality or licentiousness. Had such documents existed they surely would have been filed there to bolster the bishop's case against the padre. Bishop Lamy indeed found many irregularities among the priests laboring in New Mexico in 1851, but the record reveals no charges against Martinez. Several writers have claimed that Martinez was ultimately excommunicated because of an immoral life and illegitimate children, but it is possible that such charges arose simply because of the many Martinezes who lived in Taos and Rio Arriba—Martinez is a very common surname. Father Martinez, indeed, had two married brothers, Antonio and José Maria, with large families living in Taos. It would be easy to confuse Father Antonio José Martinez with either of these two, especially if there were motives to discredit him for political or religious reasons. In any case, no such charges were ever filed in his lifetime. Fray Angelico Chavez, a distinguished native New Mexican historian, scholar, novelist, and poet, emphatically denies any such immoral conduct on the part of Father Martinez (Francis 273).

Martinez seems at first to have looked with favor on the Texas Revolution of 1836, thinking that New Mexico might also gain independence from Mexico. He was probably active in the Taos Rebellion of 1837 (when the unpopular government in Santa Fe was overthrown) and perhaps approved the deposition and even the murder of Governor Pérez—an unpopular nonresident appointee—who was succeeded briefly by Taos buffalo hunter José Gonzales. "By such actions Padre Martinez illustrated the active and powerful role that he and many other local church leaders . . . played in New Mexican life" (Lamar 40–41). All this, however, led Americans to decry that "priest-ridden country" and persuaded Governor Pino to beg for a bishop. A bishop they got—Jean Baptiste Lamy, who promptly locked horns with the padre of Taos in a great power struggle.

The clash between Lamy and Martinez was primarily a head-on collision between two strong-willed personalities. Martinez believed Lamy was disregarding established precedence in New Mexico by enforcing the collection of church tithes. Lamy announced on 14 January 1854 "that the priests were to exclude from the sacraments all household heads who refused to pay tithes, and to demand triple fees for baptisms from other members of such families" (Francis 277). Martinez naturally objected to this and refused to collect such tithes from his impoverished parishioners. He thus placed himself in direct opposition to the new bishop, and the result was a schism. It was strictly a local affair, however, with only Martinez and one other priest excommunicated, and with the death of Martinez, most of his followers returned to the traditional Catholic fold. Martinez always declared "with great dignity and conviction that he was forever unto death a priest of the Christian, Catholic, Apostolic and Roman faith despite certain differences of opinion between him and the present bishop" (Francis 283–84).

Throughout his life, Martinez was in many things a liberal at heart, although his liberalism was of the eighteenth- rather than the later nineteenth-century variety. He was among the first to agitate for New Mexico's admission to the Union, believing that democratic institutions extended to New Mexico would benefit his people (Francis 269). He repeatedly emphasized that under a republican government everyone had a right to speak his mind for the enlightenment of the people. He believed it was his duty as a citizen, a native, an active member of the community, a Christian, and a priest to speak for people who were ignorant and intimidated. He favored religious tolerance, and he entertained friendly relations with Protestants.

His published writings contain references to "pure religion," to which, he explained, various kinds of believers adhered. His "sins" were not heresy or immorality; they amounted to difficulties with the bishop and pertained only to the realm of church government and discipline (Francis 284). He believed that the foreign prelates (French) were prejudiced and hostile to the native Spanish-Mexican clergy. But he "never attacked the Roman Catholic church as such or any of her doctrines. He did not even question the legitimate authority of Bishop Lamy. He was fighting against what he [honestly considered to be] the error not the institution" (Francis 288).

It is true that the old pastor of Taos exercised ecclesiastical functions without the necessary authority, publicly criticized his bishop without due moderation, failed to submit to his proper superiors, and caused a short-lived schism. Jean Baptiste Lamy, however, emerges as not quite the kindly, gracious prelate Cather painted as Bishop Latour. He refused to argue the case with the old and respected native priest, but insisted on invoking the authority of his office. "He was a practical man who wanted to get things done, and done his way." Perhaps his course was the proper one, "but it left a wound in the side of the Catholic church in New Mexico which was long to heal, and the scar can yet be felt" (Francis 289).

It is not my purpose to denigrate Willa Cather or criticize her too severely for damaging the reputation of one of New Mexico's greatest sons. We must remember that her book discusses only the last years of Martinez's life, when he was engaged in his power struggle with Bishop Lamy. Cather did not consider his earlier career as friend and protector of his people, and she used her novelist's right to literary license with the things she did consider. The difficulty lies in the fact that Cather's novel is so well written and still so widely read that her account of the sensual, corrupt priest of Taos is all most readers ever learn of a historical figure of some consequence. His true character and greatness remain unknown to all but the initiated and those willing to go beyond *Archbishop*. Cather's novel-become-history, therefore, has maligned Martinez, and the result has been a tragic distortion of history in the popular mind.

What is needed, of course, is another wonderful but more historically sound book about Martinez and Lamy in the same genre as Cather's—one that will be read by generations of students and accepted as history just as readily. As it is, the popular image of nineteenth-century New Mexico has been virtually set in concrete by Cather, and it will take more than an article or two in a professional journal to educate the public about the injustice done to the memory of the Padre of Taos.

—Brigham Young University

BIBLIOGRAPHY

Acuña, Rudolfo. *Occupied America: A History of Chicanos*. New York: Harper, 1981.

Alford, Harold J. *The Proud Peoples: The Heritage and Culture of Spanish-Speaking Peoples in the United States*. New York: Mentor, 1972.

Cather, Willa. *Death Comes for the Archbishop*. New York: Knopf, 1927.

Fergusson, Erna. *Our Southwest*. New York: Knopf, 1941.

————. *New Mexico: A Pageant of Three Peoples*. New York: Knopf, 1951.

Francis, E. K. "Padre Martinez: A New Mexican Myth." *New Mexico Historical Review* 31 (October): 1956. 265–89.

Lamar, Howard R. *The Far Southwest, 1846–1912: A Territorial History*. New Haven: Yale UP, 1966.

Meier, Matt S., and Feliciano Rivera. *The Chicanos: A History of Mexican Americans*. New York: Hill and Wang, 1972.

Nichols, John. *The Milagro Beanfield War*. New York: Holt, 1974.

Steiner, Stan. *LaRaza: The Mexican Americans*. New York: Harper, 1972.

Twitchell, Ralph Emerson. *Leading Facts of New Mexico History*. 6 vols. Cedar Rapids, Iowa: Torch P, 1911–1915.

————. *Old Santa Fe: The Story of New Mexico's Ancient Capital*. Chicago: Rio Grande Press, 1963.

Cather's Controversial Portrayal of Martinez

LANCE LARSEN

In 1925, Willa Cather happened upon *The Life of the Right Reverend Joseph P. Machebeuf*, an obscure diocesan biography, which proved to be the necessary catalyst for her writing a novel about the Southwest. Edith Lewis, Cather's friend and traveling companion, explains: "There, in a single evening . . . the idea of *Death Comes for the Archbishop* came to her, essentially as she afterwards wrote it" (139). Written by William Joseph Howlett, a priest who knew Denver's Bishop Machebeuf personally, *The Life of the Right Reverend Joseph P. Machebeuf* (1908) not only outlines Machebeuf's missionary experience in New Mexico but treats in some detail his friendship with Father Lamy and contains translations of several letters Machebeuf wrote to his sister Philomene, a nun in France. Referring to Howlett's book, Cather says:

> At last I found out what I wanted to know about how the country and the people of New Mexico seemed to those first missionary priests from France. Without these letters in Father Howlett's book to guide me, I would certainly never have dared to write my book. (*On Writing* 8)

Certainly these letters as well as Howlett's commentary did guide her, more than most Cather critics have suspected. She borrowed not only ideas, but specific episodes, even phrasing. One of her more controversial borrowings concerns the recalcitrant priest Padre Martinez, a chief opponent of Fathers Vaillant and Latour, Cather's twin protagonists. In fact, two recent critics, Thomas J. Steele and Ronald S. Brockway, have referred to her depiction of Martinez as "unfair," even "savagely libelous" (450). Surprisingly, no one has explored the parallel between Howlett's Martinez and Cather's Martinez in significant detail. Such a comparison reveals two things: Cather's indebtedness to Howlett and, more importantly, her creative process of narrative reshaping.

Cather follows Howlett rather closely in presenting biographical information about Martinez. Howlett records that "in his younger days Antonio José Martinez was married and had one child, a girl, but death early robbed him of both his wife and daughter" (227–28). Cather merely adds specifics, saying that Martinez was twenty when he married and twenty-three when he lost his wife and child (152). After suffering this loss, Howlett's Martinez "began his preparation for the priesthood in a seminary in Mexico, and made very brilliant studies" (228). Cather includes a few details here to particularize her narrative: "Taking his clothes and the little money he got from the sale of his household goods, he started on horseback for Durango" (153). And to dramatize the difficulty of taking up scholarly pursuits at so late an age, Cather's Martinez does not learn to read until after he is married (152). Howlett tells us that after being ordained, Martinez "entered the Concursus for the parish of Taos, recently vacated by the Franciscans, and received the appointment" (228). Here Cather introduces a minor difference, having Martinez return, not to Taos, but to Abiquiu, where he serves as the parish priest (153). So far, Cather's changes and additions seem of little consequence; they improve the readability of the events but do not alter them significantly. But then her account diverges somewhat.

Though Cather is true to Howlett's depiction of Martinez as "a man of great learning," she fails to mention that he established a school in his own home, opened the first printing office in New Mexico, and printed *El Crepusculo*, the first newspaper in New Mexico (Howlett 228). Cather purposefully suppresses these acts of community service because they would be inconsistent with the self-interested priest she wants to create. She can, however, develop Martinez as a scholar, one "deeply versed, not only in the Church Fathers, but in the Latin and Spanish classics" (153), for his academic inquiries can easily be presented as self-serving. For example, he uses St. Augustine's writings out of context to support his own rebellious views on celibacy.

Howlett and Cather also differ in the specific charges they level against Martinez. Edward and Lillian Bloom explain that Howlett "was cautiously convinced of Martinez's guilt" in the Taos revolt, though he never implicates Martinez directly (214). Instead, Howlett merely repeats rumored accusations:

> It was said that [Martinez] had much to do with the uprising of the Indians and Mexicans at Taos, when Governor Bent and about fifteen Americans and their Mexican sympathizers were massacred on Jan. 19, 1847. He at least shared with the Indians and Mexicans in hatred for the Americans, and, in their ignorance of events and conditions outside of their little valley, they imagined that they were but beginning a patriotic war which would result in freeing their country from the foreigner, who was supposed to be an enemy to their race and to their religion. (228)

Howlett concludes that suspicion of Martinez "is probably well founded, although the U.S. Government did not find Father Martinez guilty of direct complicity in the unfortunate insurrection" (228–29).

For Cather's purposes these charges against Martinez are not damning enough. To portray him as truly reprehensible, she makes him not just a political renegade, but a murderer, an unfeeling materialist, a liar, a betrayer of friends. She takes the rumor of Martinez's involvement in the 1847 massacre and presents it almost as fact, alluding to it as early as the Prologue, through the persona of Bishop Ferrand, a missionary in America:

"Only last year the Indian pueblo of San Fernandez de Taos murdered and
scalped the American Governor and some dozen other whites. The reason
they did not scalp their Padre, was that their Padre was one of the leaders
of the rebellion and himself planned the massacre. That is how things stand
in New Mexico!" (10)

As the Blooms point out, Cather delays a detailed account of the uprising
until some 130 pages later, when she introduces Martinez and elaborates
somewhat on his rebellious and immoral behavior (214). Cather begins with
mere insinuation: "It was common talk that Padre Martínez had instigated
the revolt" (139–40). But then she ignores her own label of "common talk"
and repeats the results of the massacre as if factual:

> Indeed, Padre Martínez had managed to profit considerably by the affair.
> The Indians who were sentenced to death had sent for their Padre and
> begged him to get them out of the trouble he had got them into. Martínez
> promised to save their lives if they would deed him their lands, near the
> pueblo. This they did, and after the conveyance was properly executed
> the Padre troubled himself no more about the matter, but went to pay
> a visit at his native town of Abiquiu. In his absence the seven Indians were
> hanged on the appointed day. Martínez now cultivated their fertile farms,
> which made him quite the richest man in the parish. (140)

Cather further blackens Martinez's character by ignoring Howlett's statement
that "the U.S. Government did not find Father Martinez guilty of direct
complicity" (228–29). Instead, she replaces it with an accusatory summation
that "no attempt had been made to call the plotting priest to account" (140),
which implies that if a court had been held, Martinez would have been
found guilty.

Certainly the Blooms are right, then, in concluding that Cather "accepted
Father Howlett's suspicion, and then manipulated the evidence to conform
to the shape of her novel" (215). They contradict themselves, however, in
saying that "the parallel between historical reality and Miss Cather's theme
is so close that her embroidery is imperceptible and the conflicts stand forth
with dramatic rightness" (216). Though the conflicts may be dramatically
right, Cather's embroidery is far from imperceptible. We are perhaps
chagrined at Howlett's Martinez, but when we read of Cather's Martinez
letting seven Indians die so that he can inherit their land, our chagrin turns
to contempt.

Cather colors our view of Martinez in other ways as well. She makes him
as sensual as a beast: "His mouth was the very assertion of violent, uncurbed
passions and tyrannical self-will; the full lips thrust out and taut, like the flesh
of animals distended by fear or desire" (141). To this she adds his boasts
of concupiscence. He is the avowed father of "a gawky lad of ten or twelve"
(142), the likely father of Trinidad, and the debaucher of a fifteen-year-old
girl whose virginity for seven years had been preserved "by a succession

of miracles" (157). And to justify himself in his sins, Martinez dismisses church rules and even morality, claiming that "celibate priests lose their perceptions" and that the soul "must be broken by mortal sin to experience forgiveness" (146). These additions are typical of Cather's embroidery, which creates a notorious antagonist. However, they do not, as the Blooms claim, mirror historical reality.

A comparison of how each author treats Martinez's schism yields further differences. Howlett records that "in 1856 Father Martinez offered his resignation of the parish of Taos to Bishop Lamy, giving as his reasons old age and infirmity." He was succeeded by Father Taladrid, a Spanish priest whom Machebeuf "brought from Europe in 1854." Taladrid "entertained the idea that, as [a Spaniard], he was upon a somewhat higher plane than his Mexican brethren." The problem came to a head when Martinez, who still "said mass, and occasionally officiated" after his resignation, disagreed with Taladrid "over the marriage ceremony between some of the relatives of Father Martinez" (229). Cather's account mentions Taladrid as well, but instead of blaming this young Spanish priest for the disagreement (she says nothing about his racism), Cather absolves him. She takes Howlett's objective statement of fact—that Martinez "said mass, and occasionally officiated solemnly at the parish church" (Howlett 229)—and makes it the basis of the disagreement with Taladrid: "Not only did [Martínez] avail himself of this privilege, but he continued to perform all marriages and burial services and to dictate the lives of the parishioners" (Cather 159).

In both accounts this misunderstanding between the priests results in a major schism. In Howlett's account, Taladrid and Martinez, both bullheaded in their pride, refused to settle their differences through Bishop Lamy, and finally came "to an open rupture, and Father Martinez set up an independent church" (229). When Martinez ignored Lamy's "fatherly advice and admonitions," there was nothing left to do but "suspend Father Martinez from the exercise of every priestly function" (229). This, however, failed to settle the problem, for many of those "who had always known and respected" Martinez followed him in his rebellion, including Mariano de Jesús Lucero, a Mexican priest at nearby Arroyo Hondo, "a former pupil and great friend of Father Martinez" (230). Neither Martinez nor his followers would admit their error. As Martinez and Lucero continued to oppose Lamy, Machebeuf pronounced excommunication upon them on succeeding Sundays. Howlett gives the following summary of these two priests and their followers:

> The friends of the rebellious priests kept up the opposition and the opposition church until after the death of Martinez, who died and was buried by Lucero in schism. A mission given by the Jesuits, in 1869, brought back the Martinez family, and the return of the others was easy. (233)

As we might expect, Cather's version of the schism is more dramatic and entertaining. Take, for example, the formation of the new church under Lucero and Martinez. Cather designates Howlett's "opposition church" (233) as "the old Holy Catholic Church of Mexico" (159), which raises the dispute from a local squabble to an ecclesiastical protest of some significance. And in fine Lutheran tradition, Martinez draws up a "long and eloquent Proclamation . . . giving an historical justification for his schism, and denying the obligation of celibacy for the priesthood" (159–60). Cather's commentary that the celibacy clause would do neither Martinez nor Lucero much good underscores the mock-heroic quality of their actions. But Cather ends her discussion of the churches by saying that "Father Martínez continued at the head of his schismatic church until, after a short illness, he died and was buried in schism, by Father Lucero" (162), a conclusion that echoes Howlett's account in both content and language.

As I have shown, Howlett's account suggested the framework for Cather's portrayal of Martinez. But Cather, anticipating the final themes and design of her novel, knew where to edit and embellish his character. What she creates is not merely a rascal, but a foil who, with his rebellious companion priests, Lucero and Gallegos, encompasses a cosmic representation of evil balanced by one of virtue in Vaillant and Latour. In fact, D. H. Stewart considers Dante's *Divine Comedy* as an influence on Cather's novel in this respect (249–59). He notes, for example, how the deaths of Martinez and Lucero serve as opposites to the deaths of Vaillant and Latour:

> Martinez [dies] disobediently in schism, Lucero shriven but howling obscenities at his enemy; Vaillant's funeral, on the other hand, is a solemn festival undimmed by his recent fiscal irregularities, and Latour passes away silently, crowned with virtues, lost in a vision of immortal youth. (255)

As in Dante's *Divine Comedy*, Cather represents the seven deadly sins through individuals—one of them Martinez, the type of lust (253–54). Cather's technique, then, is expansive; she takes what is historical and literal in Howlett and gives it epic and symbolic dimensions within a literary tradition.

Some readers are not pleased with Cather's portrait of Martinez because she uses his real name while greatly altering aspects of his character. Too many have assumed, as Cather claimed, that *Archbishop* "was accurate where accuracy was needed" (Small 19). One disgruntled reader, E. A. Mares, the great-great-nephew of José Martinez, has started a campaign to educate audiences about her inaccuracy. Upset at the distorted picture many have of his historical relative, Mares has been performing (since 1985) a forty-five-minute monologue in which he attempts to rescue the reputation of his ancestor. Dressed in the traditional cassock and speaking as if he were Martinez, Mares addresses a contemporary audience:

> "I knew it would come to this someday, that I would have to speak for myself, to answer what is written about me by esa mujer, by that woman, Willa Cather. . . . What was the book she wrote—'Death Comes for the Archbishop'? Where she says I stole from my people and have yellow teeth?" (qtd. in Peterson 6)

Mares concludes his monologue: "As we continue our cosmic journey, I hope I will meet this Willa. . . . I have a few words I would like to say to her" (6). Though Mares's monologue is, in a sense, a rebuke of Cather's scholarship, it is also an ironic tribute to her skill in characterization; if she had not done a superb job in *Death Comes for the Archbishop*, very few would now know of Martinez at all.

—University of Houston

BIBLIOGRAPHY

Bloom, Edward A., and Lillian D. Bloom. *Willa Cather's Gift of Sympathy.* Carbondale: Southern Illinois UP, 1962.

Cather, Willa. *Death Comes for the Archbishop.* New York: Vintage, 1971.

———. *Willa Cather on Writing.* New York: Knopf, 1949.

Howlett, William J. *Life of Bishop Machebeuf.* Ed. Thomas J. Steele, S.J., and Ronald S. Brockway. Denver: Regis College, 1987.

Lewis, Edith. *Willa Cather Living.* New York: Knopf, 1953.

Peterson, Iver. "Priest Willa Cather Assailed Finds a Defender." *New York Times* 29 June 1985: 6.

Small, Harold. "Willa Cather Tells 'Secret' Novel's Title." *San Francisco Chronicle* 26 March 1931: 19.

Steele, Thomas J., S.J., and Ronald S. Brockway. Afterword. "Willa Cather's Use of History and Especially of Howlett's *Machebeuf* in *Death Comes for the Archbishop*." *Life of Bishop Machebeuf.* By William J. Howlett. 1908. Denver: Regis College, 1987.

Stewart, D. H. "Cather's Mortal Comedy." *Queen's Quarterly* 73 (1966): 244–59.

The Family Affair at Mesa Verde

DAVID HARRELL

Their only acknowledgment by name is unfavorable—and misspelled—but the Rickner family at Mesa Verde National Park played significant roles in the formation of Willa Cather's impressions of the area and subsequently in the composition of "Tom Outland's Story" in *The Professor's House*. Their roles are so significant, in fact, that as a family the Rickners are second only to the Wetherills, whose importance to the story is already well known. The Rickners' influence was accidental, as literary influences so often are, but it can be seen in both the general atmosphere at Mesa Verde, to which the family certainly contributed, and specific events and character traits that reappear, sometimes in reverse, in Tom Outland or another of the characters. One of the lesser influences, evidently, was the patriarch of the family, Thomas Rickner; but it is with him nonetheless that this discussion should begin.

A former rancher, realtor, and butcher from Mancos (Torres-Reyes 28; Jeep), Thomas Rickner was the park superintendent when Cather and Edith Lewis visited Mesa Verde in August 1915. Called "the last of the political appointments" (D. A. Smith, letter), he lost his position in 1921 with the advent of a new administration intent upon appointing to the superintendent's position someone with a background in archeology (Jeep). While in office, Rickner had attracted some unfavorable attention because of nepotism (D. A. Smith 97), a condition that Professor St. Peter would surely have disdained. Even so, Rickner's correspondence, which is voluminous, indicates that the superintendent did have the welfare and improvement of the park uppermost in mind. It was during his tenure, in fact, that the first automobile road up the Mesa Verde was opened to the public, on the Fourth of July, 1914. Mr. Rickner bought a Model T himself that year, but he seems to have shared Cather's dislike for automobiles. The car "didn't last long," his son says. "It never understood 'whoa' and 'get up' " (J. E. Rickner).

As superintendent, Rickner was responsible for disseminating information about the park, a service from which Cather surely benefitted. For instance, in February 1915, responding to the increasing number of tourists, Rickner ordered twice the number of brochures as the season before. To a writer intensely interested in her subject, this brochure must have been a godsend. It tells the story of Richard Wetherill's discovery of Cliff Palace, quotes extensively from the early pages of Gustaf Nordenskiold's

The Cliff Dwellers of the Mesa Verde, describes the features at Cliff Palace and several other ruins, and enumerates forty-seven other publications about Mesa Verde. Cather doesn't acknowledge this document as a source—after all, it was neither as significant nor as picturesque as Nordenskiold's book or as the Howlett biography of Bishop Machebeuf that was the inspiration for *Death Comes for the Archbishop*—but it is unlikely that she could have missed it and quite improbable that, having seen it, she failed to use it.

Another way Rickner disseminated information during those early days of the park was by answering queries from prospective visitors. Eager but somewhat cautious, these people from such places as Chicago and Milwaukee wrote ahead of time to find out just what they would be getting into when they came. (If Cather or Lewis inquired beforehand, the letter must be lost.) In his replies, Rickner tends to wax enthusiastic about the "good accommodations" offered at the only overnight facility in the park, a tent camp across the canyon from Spruce Tree House, just below the present park headquarters on a site still identifiable by a single gnarled tree (J. E. Smith). What Rickner does not mention in these replies is that the Mrs. Jeep who runs the camp is his daughter Oddie.

This little omission notwithstanding, Rickner seems to have been fairly truthful about conditions at the camp. Photos from the day show not simple tents staked directly to the ground but seemingly permanent wooden walls with tents as roofs. Men would sometimes sleep in the open in their sleeping bags, but women generally used the tent structures (T. Rickner). Most of the furnishings that Oddie's son Fred T. Jeep recalls from about 1918 were probably in place by 1915: a double bed; a dresser; a wash basin, pitcher and stand; a throw rug; chairs, and a kerosene lamp. Whatever they were at the time, Cather found the accommodations quite to her liking at what she called this "very comfortable tent camp on the mesa" where "anyone can be very comfortable . . . for several weeks" (Rosowski and Slote 83). Less satisfied, however, was another guest two years later: "This is a family affair. The camp concessionaire being . . . a daughter of Supervisor Rickner. The meals are poor and the camp is more of a boarding house for road gangs who are served at the same time and in the same room with the guests, than a tent hotel for tourists" (Torres-Reyes 67).

Cather doesn't mention Oddie Jeep by name, but when she notes the "excellent food" provided at the camp by "the wife of the forest ranger" (Rosowski and Slote 83), she has Oddie unmistakably in mind; and she may have kept her in mind years later as she was creating Henry Atkins, the camp cook for Tom Outland and Roddy Blake. Mildred Bennett has identified the source of the fictional Henry as the real English cook of the same name employed by Cather's brother Douglass (37), but Oddie Jeep may have suggested a few of Henry's traits. Not only was she a good cook and housekeeper, giving Cather another firsthand experience with those skills, but, like the fictional Henry, she was also adept at exploring. According to an item in the *Mancos Times–Tribune* for 2 July 1915, Mrs. Jeep was "getting to be almost as skilled and daring a mountain climber as is Mr. Jeep himself and goes without hesitation over many places where the men's nerve fails when they assay to follow." An accomplished rock climber herself (see Woodress 8), Cather would have appreciated Oddie's abilities.

Cather's reference to the "wife of the forest ranger" points to another family connection, one that had provoked the notice and occasional comment of other guests. Oddie's husband was Fred Jeep, the park ranger whom Lewis praises as "a splendid guide, familiar with every foot of the Mesa" (95). That Jeep was the guide for Cather and Lewis may suggest that Cather's stature as a celebrity was growing: according to one park historian, Jeep tended to reserve his services for "important people, government officials in particular" (Torres-Reyes 191). Jeep was indeed an able guide; and, like his wife, he would also have been a convenient model. Two months before Cather and Lewis arrived, he and Clint Scharf (the Clint "Scarf" whom Lewis identifies as one of their "chivalrous" rescuers, incidentally) discovered a new ruin in Navajo Canyon about four miles southwest of Spruce Tree Camp. Like Tom Outland and Roddy Blake, they spent several days devising a way into the ruin, which had evidently not been entered since the days of its inhabitation.

In both cases, the real and the fictional, the explorers made ladders to enter the ruin but from different directions: Jeep and Scharf "built a ladder thirty-eight feet long which they swung over the cliff from above fastened securely to a cedar tree" ("New Cliff Ruin"); Outland and Blake "felled some trees and threw them up over the gaps in the path" that led to Cliff City (*The Professor's House* 207). Interestingly, Cather's two characters later devise a suspended ladder (211) similar to the one used by Jeep and Scharf. Another similarity is the size of the two ruins: the one discovered by Jeep and Scharf, named Daniels House, was said to contain about twenty-five rooms; Cather's Cliff City contains about thirty, far fewer than the roughly two hundred estimated for Cliff Palace in the park brochure for 1915. This smaller size is more conducive to the sense of intimate grandeur suggested by Tom Outland's "little city of stone, asleep" and "pale little houses of stone nestling close to one another" (201) than the more expansive view afforded by Cliff Palace. There is no gainsaying that Cliff Palace is the major prototype of Cliff City, but the fresh discovery of Daniels House by two men whom Cather actually met may well have influenced the story too.

In addition, certain characteristics of Fred Jeep may appear in Tom Outland in reverse. Unlike Tom Outland, whose archeological sensitivity is remarkably acute, Fred Jeep seems to have shared the prevailing attitudes of the day. Neither he nor Scharf could resist the temptation to inscribe their names in the ruin they had discovered (J. E. Smith). Historian Ricardo Torres-Reyes speaks of Jeep's "promiscuous pothunting" and his unawareness of the importance of notes and records, which he never kept (179–80). Moreover, as late as 1927 then-superintendent Jesse L. Nusbaum, who had tended to excuse Jeep's behavior in light of his enthusiasm, was still trying to reclaim for the park some of the artifacts that he said Fred and Oddie had removed (Nusbaum to Oddie Jeep). Perhaps in this aspect of Jeep's behavior (which, as noted, was not at all uncommon for the time) Cather saw a good negative example that she was careful to reverse in Tom Outland. Despite his own lack of training, Outland keeps careful notes and repudiates any sort of monetary gain from the ruins. And it would never occur to Tom to scribble "T. O." on the walls of Cliff City.

At any rate, knowledgeable though he was, Jeep was unable to guide Cather and Lewis on their final excursion because of the unexpected arrival of a large party of tourists, probably members of the Prairie Walking Club from Chicago (see "Walking Club Arrives"). In such circumstances he sometimes recruited Oddie as guide (Torres-Reyes 56), but this time he gave the job to another member of the family, his brother-in-law, the "young man named Richnor" whom Lewis mentions and who inspired some apprehension in his two new clients. However, as Lewis says, because Jeep made this arrangement "in Richnor's presence, we could hardly decline, and we started off with him" (95–96). The trek to this final ruin justified their apprehension but also led to one of Cather's most fruitful misadventures.

Thomas Rickner had three sons, James, Jack, and Charles (Ellis 161). Jack, the middle brother, who was twelve years old in 1915 and is at this writing "the last of the Rickner family living," seldom guided tourists and has no recollection of either Cather or Lewis. However, he does remember one occasion when his older brother James, who did serve as a tour guide, kept a party in the canyons long after dark and had to be rescued (J. E. Rickner). Moreover, on 22 May 1915 James had returned to Mancos after three years in medical school in Providence, Rhode Island, to spend the summer at home (*Mancos Times–Tribune*). For these reasons, it must have been James Rickner who led the two women along that "very rough trail" (Lewis 96) and later left them on a large rock while he went for help. The incident was fortuitous, of course, as it produced, for Cather at least, the four or five most rewarding hours of the trip (Lewis 97). Just how much of "Tom Outland's Story" was conceived during this time is, of course, impossible to know; but it is still pleasant to speculate upon the myriad impressions that entered Cather's creative consciousness during those few hours and remained stored there until needed. One can easily imagine Cather in the same attitude she attributes to Tom Outland: "I lay down on a solitary rock that was like an island in the bottom of the valley, and looked up" (250).

The two cheerful men whom Rickner sent to rescue Cather and Lewis were from the camp of Smithsonian archeologist Jesse Walter Fewkes, who was excavating Sun Temple at the time Cather and Lewis were there. In Fewkes, Cather had the opportunity for face-to-face exposure to the major archeologist at Mesa Verde. Precisely what, if anything, she gleaned from him is impossible to say now; but it was the Rickners who made the meeting possible. In fact, Southwestern archeologist Alden C. Hayes asserts, "Cather couldn't have avoided meeting him" (Hayes).

It was during his work at Sun Temple that summer when Oddie Jeep persuaded Fewkes to begin the series of campfire talks that continues even to this day. Each evening when any visitors were present, Fred Jeep would dig a fire hole not far from the tent camp and Fewkes would speak informally about the ruins and some of the archeological problems they posed (Torres-Reyes 189). "Somewhat of a romantic, he drove himself to make the 'mystical red man known to the literate public' " (D. A. Smith 71). It seems likely that during her week on the mesa Cather would have sat in on one or more of these sessions and later incorporated into "Tom Outland's Story" some of the material she absorbed around that primordial fire. It would have been a good opportunity to feel the excitement of modern discovery and to indulge in a wistful projection into a time long past. As the ranking scientific authority and an engaging talker to boot, Fewkes would have been a likely source to complement Cather's own powers of imagination.

Finally, beyond their influence as individuals, the Rickners and Jeeps at the tent camp may have suggested the family unit that Tom Outland forms on the mesa with Roddy Blake and Henry Atkins. Although they are hardly mirror images of each other and they pose no direct counterparts, the fictional and factual families have enough traits in common to suggest an influence, especially considering that Cather, like other guests at the camp, was surely aware of the Rickner family connections. In each case there are two men in a brotherly relationship, one several years older than the other (Fred and James/Roddy and Tom); someone who has made a significant discovery (Fred Jeep/Tom Outland); and an excellent camp cook who doubles as an explorer (Oddie Jeep/Henry Atkins). In addition, each group comprises three members on a more or less equal footing, a sort of fraternal unit rather than a conventional family of parents and children—"parenting displaced into male friendship," Susan Rosowski says of Tom's family ("Cather's Chosen Family" 74). In this sense, both families are atypical—or at least incomplete—but their members are united by the common bond of interest in, if not reverence for, the ruins of an ancient civilization. And for a while, at least, they both had the run of an idyllic setting. Jack Rickner has "fond memories of the park," and Tom says, "the three of us made a happy family" (198).

For Tom and his family, however, the happiness is short-lived, first through the tragic loss of Henry and then the heartbreaking disruption of the friendship between Tom and Roddy. With these losses Cather is clearing the way for the orphan Tom—"the quintessential modern man" (Stouck 208)—to make a second familial identification, this time with the mesa itself. As John Swift has pointed out, Tom "invests the Blue Mesa with the unmistakable language of specifically familial devotion." For instance, upon his return to the mesa he compares himself to "home-sick children when they come home," and later he finally recognizes that it was "filial piety" that he "felt for this place." Thus, "Tom Outland's Story" can be read as a quest narrative in which Outland searches for the family he never had (Swift 304–05), or what

Rosowski has called "ancestors we can all claim" ("Cather's Chosen Family" 72).

The Rickners, a true family, probably felt no such filial attachment to the ruins even though they took considerable pride in their work at the park (Jeep). There is, however, one more interesting parallel. The Rickners' presence on the real Mesa Verde is now hardly more substantial—more real— than Tom Outland's on the fictional Blue Mesa. Scarcely a trace of the tent camp remains at Mesa Verde; and letters, photographs, memories, and a single gnarled tree make as little impression upon the ruins as Tom Outland's nonexistent diary sealed up in nonexistent rock. What lingers, Cather reminds us, is the ruins themselves, the homes of other families whose existence is even more shadowy than that of the people who discovered their dwellings centuries later, whether in fact or in imagination.

—University of New Mexico

BIBLIOGRAPHY

Bennett, Mildred R. *The World of Willa Cather*. Rev. ed. Lincoln: U of Nebraska P, Bison, 1961.

Cather, Willa. *The Professor's House*. New York: Knopf, 1925.

Ellis, Fern. *Come Back to My Valley*. Cortez, Colo.: Cortez Printers, 1976.

Hayes, Alden C. Letter to the author. 6 May 1987.

Jeep, Fred T. Letter to the author. 11 November 1988.

Lewis, Edith. *Willa Cather Living: A Personal Record*. Lincoln: U of Nebraska P, Bison, 1976.

Mancos Times–Tribune. 22 May and 2 July 1915.

"New Cliff Ruin Found on Park." *Mancos Times–Tribune* 18 June 1915: 1.

Nusbaum, Jesse L. Letter to Oddie Jeep. 22 July 1927. History-General File, Mesa Verde Research Center.

The Prehistoric Cliff Dwellings: Mesa Verde National Park, Southwestern Colorado. Washington, D.C.: Government Printing Office, 1915.

Rickner, J. E. Letters to the author. 24 September 1987, 20 April 1988, and 26 August 1988.

Rickner, Thomas. Correspondence. Mesa Verde National Park Library, Vault.

Rosowski, Susan J. "Willa Cather's Chosen Family: Fictional Formations and Trans-formations." Paper presented at the Third National Cather Symposium, "Willa Cather: The Family and Community," Brigham Young University, 16 September 1988. See 67–78 of this volume.

———. and Bernice Slote. "Willa Cather's 1916 Mesa Verde Essay: The Genesis of *The Professor's House*. *Prairie Schooner* 58.4 (Winter 1984): 81–92.

Smith, Duane A. Letters to the author. 29 March 1987 and 15 April 1987.

———. *Mesa Verde National Park: Shadows of the Centuries*. Lawrence: U of Kansas P, 1988.

Smith, Jack E. Personal interview, Mesa Verde National Park. 4 August 1987.

Stouck, David. *"The Professor's House* and the Issues of History." Paper presented at the Third National Cather Symposium, "Willa Cather: The Family and Community," Brigham Young University, 16 September 1988. See 201–11 of this volume.

Swift, John N. "Memory, Myth and *The Professor's House." Western American Literature* 20.4 (February 1986): 301–14.

Torres-Reyes, Ricardo. *Mesa Verde National Park: An Administrative History, 1906–1970.* Washington, D.C.: United States Department of the Interior, National Park Service, 1970.

"Walking Club Arrives." *Mancos Times–Tribune* 22.16 (20 Aug. 1915): 1.

Woodress, James. *Willa Cather: A Literary Life.* Lincoln: U of Nebraska P, 1987.

Willa Cather reading to Jack and Elsie

Part Five:
Communities of Art, Families of Faith

This short section includes essays by Synnott, Monroe, and Murphy focusing on themes expressed or implied in several other essays: the family can be sacrificed and the home place left for a higher calling. That calling is usually art in earlier Cather, but in *Death Comes for the Archbishop* religion motivates painful separation. Higher callings in turn create communities of art-sharing and faith-sharing.

In "Conflicting Communities and Cather's Artists: The Absorbing Vision" Kevin A. Synnott analyzes Cather's resolution of dual allegiances—to East and West, Old World and New World, past and present, family and vocation—through a technique of the visual arts creating a community to participate in the artist's absorption. Thomas Cole's placing of the artist figure in his panoramic landscape *The Oxbow* helps us understand the success of Jim Burden, Thea Kronborg, and the narrator of "Two Friends" in creating communities to share the truth and visions they experience. Their success helps us understand as well the failures of Lucy Gayheart and Harry Gordon.

Where Synnott uses the painting model William Monroe sees stories as life patterns enabling us to survive real life's "flawed human congregations" in " 'Scripts and Patterns: Stories as 'Equipment for Living'—and Dying." Having found Tom Outland's story an inadequate one for midlife's weighty problems, Godfrey St. Peter in *The Professor's House* turns to Augusta and the transcendent hidden in the everyday life of our waste land world. As a community of readers we participate in the creation of Augusta's story and share its sustaining power. Her story becomes a communitarian spiritual vision.

John J. Murphy in "The Faith Community in *Death Comes for the Archbishop*" uses *My Ántonia. Shadows on the Rock*, "Neighbour Rosicky," "Jack-a-Boy," and "The Best Years" (which links the Nativity and the Redemption) to move the family ideal toward the supernatural and provide a background from which to explore the Southwestern novel. The cruciform tree at its beginning and the apricot tree near the end are juxtaposed to suggest the crucified Christ as the fruit of the tree, the nutriment of family and community. The novel becomes an attempt to establish and sustain community through the mass and the Eucharist, a missionary activity supported by image clusters of food, vegetation, and sunsets. The missionary heroes must sacrifice their own nuclear families and companionship to create a community that develops beyond sectarian and even Christian distinctions.

J. J. M.

Conflicting Communities and Cather's Artists: The Absorbing Vision

KEVIN A. SYNNOTT

When Jim Burden returns to Black Hawk in "The Pioneer Woman's Story" section of *My Ántonia*, he finally confronts the woman who has consistently challenged both his active imagination and his solidly middle-class values:

> "Do you know, Ántonia, since I've been away, I think of you more often than anyone else in this part of the world. I'd have liked to have you for a sweetheart, or a wife, or my mother or my sister—anything that a woman can be to a man. The idea of you is a part of my mind; you influence my likes and dislikes, all of my tastes, hundreds of times when I don't realize it. You really are a part of me." (321)

That "the idea" of Ántonia and what she might have been is what captivates Jim—and not her reality or the facts of their lives—emphasizes the preoccupation of Cather's narrator. Jim's verb forms alone are his unconscious admission that the significance of his relationship with Ántonia is centered in the past, allowing him to maintain an emotional distance from his now-disgraced friend. His utter conventionality is exposed when, even through imagination, he restricts Ántonia to utterly conventional roles, which, safely for Jim, she can never play in his life. The emotional presence she might represent in his life competes with the cumulative effect of a series of social influences represented in the course of the novel by his role as respectable town boy, his life at the university at Lincoln, his admiration for Gaston Cleric and the classics, his move to Harvard and New York—all defining a steady progression away from Ántonia and the frontier, even as they shape his developing social status and position as a successful lawyer.

The revelation of Jim's self-absorbed nature in the previously mentioned "confessional" challenges our sympathy toward him as a character, and we wonder how he can speak so insensitively to his "disgraced" friend. Jim's deliverance from this unseemly position comes in our recognition of the narrative ploy that makes him the teller of his own tale. By crafting the tale about Ántonia and himself, Jim effectively gains the advantage in dealing with his readers, giving lie not only to his prefatory apology in the Introduction for the manuscript's lack of form but also to the notion in the concluding sentence that the past he shares with Ántonia is "incommunicable." Jim's

"Ántonia" manuscript, despite the protestation that it is "pretty much all that [Ántonia's] name recalls to [him]," (Introduction) is really a persuasive demonstration of self-absorption in reconciling the conflicts and demands of his life, which he visually dramatizes around images of *his* Ántonia, who, though a "battered woman, . . . still had that something which fires the imagination, could still stop one's breath for a moment by a look or a gesture that somehow revealed the meaning in common things" (353). Through imagination, Jim can vivify his memories of the early days, his best years, perhaps, and transcend the social barriers that distance him both emotionally and physically from the real Ántonia. It is by the engrossing process of the retelling of his life's story that Jim finds his way back—"I had the sense of coming home to myself . . . " (371)—to the significant community of his youth.

The Ántonia manuscript frequently reveals that Jim, like other Cather characters, has been away from "home" for some time and that he is caught by the need, desire, and attempt to maintain dual allegiance to conflicting communities. In the most general sense, such dualities can be identified throughout Cather's work by a variety of tensions: East–West, old–new, past–present. Thea Kronborg, Niel Herbert, Godfrey St. Peter, Archbishop Latour, and Lucy Gayheart are but a few of a gallery of characters whose stories depict the internal struggle to reconcile the demands of conflicting communities—the dramatic confrontation between some ideal and an undeniably harsh, and perhaps unforgiving, reality. In confronting the apparently disparate and disjunctive elements of their lives, these characters develop a self-absorption or preoccupation that defines a unique dramatic tension within their narratives while challenging our understanding with significant complexity. Jim's farewell scene with Ántonia, Niel Herbert's disillusionment with Marian Forrester's will to live, Godfrey St. Peter's terror at the prospect of his family's return from Europe, and Lucy Gayheart's obliviousness to the financial sacrifices her father and sister make to keep her in Chicago are disconcerting because the behavior often seems selfish or petulant; and such situations are further complicated by our discomfort with the behavior of antagonists who prompt these unseemly reactions. The generally expected bonds of community—trust, mutual support, unconditional love—are apparently disregarded as strain and crisis invade the traditional familial, social, and communal bonds. Frequently, what emerges for Cather's main characters is the need to seek alternative communities, which are often, implicitly or explicitly in the narrative, communities of art, wherein the facts of a life may be imaginatively and successfully reorganized. Artists or not, many of Cather's characters share the artistic disposition to see, to understand, and to order, and they are endowed with what inevitably becomes a vision eventually reconnecting them to the larger human community. Moreover, the process of that vision's unfolding becomes for the community of Cather's readers a key to ambiguities and contradictions within the fictions. The absorbing vision, both a disposition and a technique derived by Cather from another region of her kingdom of art, reconciles conflict and community in her fiction, where its use can be found to varying degrees. Here, a somewhat eclectic group of works will serve to illustrate in some general sense how Cather uses the notion of absorption to create and re-create the sense of community in her fiction.

Absorption as both an artistic concept and a technique has a long tradition in the visual arts, where the "primacy of absorption . . . [has] always been tacitly at work in Western painting" (Fried 107). As a controlling device, the depiction of a figure engrossed in a singular activity reinforces "one primitive condition of the art of painting—that its objects necessarily imply the presence before them of a beholder" (Fried 4). This concept endorses the participation of each "beholder" and asks his or her involvement in the narrative aspects of the work. One participates, so to speak, in the idea of the painting—the story it tells—because of the demands of painterly composition and execution. The work of the seventeenth-century Dutch painters, which Cather acknowledges in discussing *The Professor's House*, provides an appropriate illustration of the significance of absorption. Vermeer's *Lace Maker*, for example, describes a visual intensity in the woman, who focuses all her energy on the point-lace she is working. Her sight line and all the lines of composition in this piece draw attention to her task and her complete involvement with it. There is little doubt as to where the beholder of this painting should be looking. The figure's absorption dominates the piece, even as the other carefully rendered details—the bright threads, the rich tapestry, the plush pillow, the wood-grained post—compete for some prominence. Works like this one complement the depicted involvement by focussing the beholder's attention on a specific object, task, or preoccupation. While there is no denying the integrity of the carefully detailed elements of such paintings—drapery, furnishings, architectural details—and their visual impact, attention is quickly drawn by overall composition to the contemplative figure. The composition creates the painting's narrative dimensions by forcing the viewer to understand the reason for the intensity of concentration and participate in the very act of absorption with the figure or figures depicted. Within the Dutch tradition and in subsequent European and American art movements, viewer participation is more directly acknowledged by the use of reflective surfaces and by the portrayal of figures casting their steady glances first toward the artist who is capturing them and then toward those who view them. Edouard Manet's famous *The Bar of the Follies Bergere* (1881) is a prime example.

A significant nineteenth-century American landscape, Thomas Cole's *The Oxbow* (1834) may illustrate the multiple dimensions of the absorbing vision as Cather came to practice it in narrative form. Within the broad scope of this canvas, a number of demands are placed on the beholder's attention by the strong diagonal lines of the composition, the tension of light and dark, and the dynamism of clearly articulated visual planes. But of compelling interest is the single, isolated human figure in the foreground dwarfed by the immense and unbounded natural world. This solitary figure—the artist—aided by the umbrella-turned-pointer, serves the compositional

The Oxbow. Thomas Cole 1801–1848.
The Metropolitan Museum of Art, gift of Mrs. Russell Sage, 1908

Detail from *The Oxbow*.

function of leading the eye from the turbulent, wild foreground toward the more serene middle distance where the human hand has tamed nature and then toward the distant, ineffable horizon. And at the same time, the backward glance of the artist figure toward the viewer challenges participation in and appreciation for the transcendent landscape. What Cole as artist defines visually here is the artist as creator or re-creator, alone and absorbed in confronting the world he seeks to know (in the Emersonian sense) and anxious to communicate with those who also seek to know through his work. In sum, the experience of the work of art is not simply the sum of its compositional elements—color, light, shadow, contrast, texture, line, and the like—but becomes, as Michael Fried suggests, "a singular, self-renewing, in important respects dialectical undertaking" (4).

Willa Cather seems to understand such complex dimensions of the dynamics of visual arts, as is evident by her comments on Jules Breton's *Song of the Lark* in the 1932 preface of the novel bearing its name. On one level, Cather sees the work as "a rather second-rate French painting in the Chicago Art Institute; a picture in which a little peasant girl, on her way to work in the fields at early morning, stops and looks up to listen to a lark" (Preface to *Song* v). On another level, she writes in a 1901 gallery review:

> You will find hundreds of merchants and farmer boys all over Nebraska and Kansas and Iowa who remember Jules Breton's "Song of the Lark," and perhaps the ugly little peasant girl standing barefooted among the wheat fields in the early morning has taught some of these people to hear the lark sing for themselves. ("The Chicago Art Institute" 843)

In her first comment, Cather is a more literal critic, concerned with what the painting depicts. In the other comment, she suggests the effect of the painting—the power it has to engage the viewer, setting up a particular relationship between the little peasant girl and those who see her caught up in the lark's song. Engaging with the work and understanding what occurs within it in a narrative sense seems the way Cather most enjoyed the visual arts. It is the way she most frequently tried to incorporate visual arts dynamics in her own work.

The Song of the Lark, the novel named after the Breton painting, depicts a voluntary and complete absorption in the kingdom of art and in the often opposing forces of life and art for its central figure, Thea Kronborg, who constantly struggles to overcome the limitations of her environment—the communal regimentation of a crowded house, a dull little frontier town, the Lily Fishers of the world—by pursuing her art with what seems at times heartless determination. Her first true insight into the meaning of art—the stream and the broken pottery in Panther Canyon—puts her on an unhesitating path toward what appears to be an expensive success, the neglect of family obligations, the rejection of love, the bare recognition that her art has taken her life. "Your work becomes your personal life," Thea explains to her friend Dr. Archie. "You are not much good until it does. It's like being woven into a big web. You can't pull away, because all your little tendrils are woven into the picture. It takes you up, and uses you, and spins you out; and that is your life. Not much else can happen to you" (546). That terrifying testimony is, of course, a clear, frank, and accurate explanation of the commitment she has made as an artist and of her choices, even as it may seem a harsh indictment of the world of art to Archie and to the reader. Yet there is no denying the exquisite consequence of Thea's devotion to art—the magnificent performance as Sieglinde, when she "came into full possession of things she had been refining and perfecting for so long," when "she entered into the inheritance that she herself had laid up, into the fullness of the faith she had kept before she knew its name or its meaning" (571). Moreover, the complete integration of her artistic success with the rest of her life is underscored with little subtlety by Cather's gathering of Thea's various influential friends—Archie, Ottenburg, Harsanyi, and even the volatile Spanish Johnny—the somewhat odd and eclectic community that recognized, nurtured, and developed Thea's art. All of them have made their way to the Met for her extraordinary performance, where they represent a new community, reconstituting elements of the past and joining them to the evolving present. In reuniting the influences of Thea's youth through her artistic success, Cather resolves, to some extent, the conflicts of Thea's life. The scene is another (and of course, earlier) way of seeing "what a little circle man's experience is" (My Ántonia 372).

Cather acknowledged the limitations of The Song of the Lark in her 1932 Preface. Nevertheless, the elaborate story of Thea Kronborg is a successful narrative depiction of the absorbing, and in this case, consuming, struggle of the "artist to [make] himself born" (Song 221). Within that narrative, the close involvement of Thea's benefactors and mentors—especially Dr. Archie and Fred Ottenburg—creates a community for the artist, a community that replaces the functions and supports traditionally provided by the family. For the reader, who, like those characters, must work to understand the challenges Thea confronts and the choices she makes, these characters create a sort of narrative middle distance. As readers, we participate on these characters' level—we sit at the novel's end among them at the Met to watch joyfully Thea's success and to wonder, at the same time, at the cost of it all. So much is forgiven Thea, it seems, by her friends when she finally comes magnificently into her own, that her "beholders" are able to do no less. Our enforced participation gives us the same perspective that the characters have, and like them we somehow see the reason for her behavior. In essence, we see Thea come "home" again.

In a later work, Lucy Gayheart, Cather again depicts the absorption of characters to the apparent exclusion of certain simple human relations one might reasonably expect. The relationship between Lucy Gayheart and Harry Gordon seems a much more somber examination of the consequences of self-absorption. Lucy is unable to integrate the worlds of Haverford and Chicago, and Harry cannot understand the path Lucy chooses to take. They parry with one another—he's ready to marry and she isn't; she wants to talk with him, but he hasn't the time to listen—until the novel's tragedy is realized. Lucy's artistic world and Harry's socially correct Haverford are communities in apparently unresolvable conflict. Lucy dies, her artistic success never fully realized, and Harry is left with only the image of her quick footstep. Harry comes to realize the folly of his hasty marriage to Miss Arkwright and redefines his sorrow at losing Lucy, in a manner reminiscent of Jim Burden:

> He is not a man haunted by remorse; all that he went through with long ago. He enjoys his prosperity and his good health. Lucy Gayheart is no longer a despairing little creature standing in the icy wind and lifting beseeching eyes to him. She is no longer near, beside his sleigh. She has receded to the far horizon line, along with all the fine things of youth, which do not change. (224)

As Jim has done with Ántonia, Harry transforms Lucy into an idea, and the only tangible images of her that remain are the "three light footprints, running away." Sadly unlike Jim's images of Ántonia, however, Harry's images of Lucy recede; they are neither cyclical nor self-renewing, a fact that lends poignancy to the novel. The opportunity to integrate conflicting communities is lost, and the sad consequence is the unfulfilled promise of both Lucy and Harry.

In "Two Friends," Cather works with another narrator, much like Jim Burden, who reminisces about the past and re-creates very particular vivid images to represent it. The narrator's absorption in the tale of the friendship between Dillon and Trueman results in a suspicious amount of precise detail. How could the narrator know, let alone remember, the daily schedules of the two men, the manner in which they spent their time in St. Joe, the amount of money Trueman carried with him, and what he did once he moved to San Francisco? The artifice of the tale is evident, and it is in the narrator's "idea" of the two men—referred to as "my heroes" and "my aristocrats"—that the real focus of the story lies, just as it had for Jim Burden and Harry Gordon in ideas of their heroines. We accept the inclusion of information beyond the narrator's ability to know because we parallel it with Cather's insight that "whatever is seen by the narrator as he speaks is sensed by the listener, quite irrespective of words" ("Two Friends" 218). We accept the controlling device, the creation of time and place and events that, like the occultation of Venus, we "might never chance to see again" in our lifetime. The absorption of the narrator in his work is the means whereby the unresolved conflict can be resolved. It is the reason for the telling—the need to remember and to capture in words and images "one of the truths we want to keep" (230).

Cather's final line in "Two Friends"—"the truths *we* want to keep"— underscores the interconnectedness of the figures within the tale with those who stand outside of it and speaks to some enduring sense of community. Such absorption becomes one of the techniques Cather uses to dramatize the essential conflicts of her leading characters, artists or not, and it underscores the costs and rewards of life. In its immediate sense, absorption can seem selfish, painful, and destructive, but with the distance of time and memory, and with the wholeness of vision, it serves to complete and sustain. It becomes the means of recapturing and re-creating the best of one's life, aligning past with present. Absorption leads to integration in Cather's work, even as it makes clear the hard facts of life, the choices one makes, and the consequences one suffers. It is not an escape to the memories of the past, but a bold act of imaginative reconciliation that endorses the wholeness of life and art, and the importance of aesthetic wholeness in the human community. Cather's work has much to say about the art of living, and it is for us, as it is for all the figures in the scene, to engage in the process with her and with her characters, to try to understand the truths in the fictions one creates from the facts of a life.

—Russell Sage College

BIBLIOGRAPHY

Cather, Willa. "The Chicago Art Institute." Rpt. *The World and the Parish.* Vol. 2. Ed. William Curtin. Lincoln: U of Nebraska P, 1970. 842–46.
_____. *Lucy Gayheart.* New York: Vintage, 1976.
_____. *My Ántonia.* Boston: Houghton, Sentry ed., 1961.
_____. *The Song of the Lark.* Boston: Houghton, Sentry ed., 1963.
_____. "Two Friends." *Obscure Destinies.* New York: Vintage, 1974. 193–229.
Fried, Michael. *Absorption and Theatricality: Painting & Beholder in the Age of Diderot.* Berkeley: U of California P, 1980.

'Scripts and Patterns: Stories as "Equipment for Living"—and Dying[1]

WILLIAM MONROE

In the recent PBS series "The Power of Myth," Bill Moyers related the advice Joseph Campbell regularly gave his liberal arts students at Sarah Lawrence College: "If you really want to help this world, you will have to teach people to live in it." Campbell, I think, would be pleased with *The Professor's House*, for even in this Eliotic, "waste land" novel, Cather develops scripts and patterns that help people live within the world's invariably repressive families and communities. Even within the sterile matrix of his university town, the professor finds the needed "equipment for living"; with the help of the sewing woman Augusta, he rediscovers sufficient material for a rehabilitative story. Cather, without papering over the sterile commercialism and pettiness of our modern waste land, is nonetheless committed to this world, and her storytelling helps us to live in it.

We participate in the professor's world—which is still, in essence, our world—through the professor's consciousness; and we discover his various qualities of mind, his characteristic attitudes, largely through his "use" and construction of stories. From *Medea* to *Le Mannequin d'Osier*, he imaginatively reconstructs narratives—actions performed by characters within particular scenes. These stories allow the professor to "strategize," as Kenneth Burke would say, to exercise a degree of freedom in his arrangement of narrative materials and thus in his approach to the world. More importantly, they offer him, and us, a limited but durable hope for an integrated life of healthy work and satisfying love.

Yet *The Professor's House* has frequently been understood as the beginning of Cather's withdrawal from modernity because of its negatives, and she certainly does not depict the world's congregations, its families, cities, and polities, as "nice" places full of happy people. Quite the contrary: Cather makes us as painfully aware of the sterility of modern civilization as Eliot does in "The Waste Land." Nor does she nostalgically proffer Tom Outland's Cliff City as a purer alternative to the commercialized technology, petty materialism, and conspicuous consumption of Hamilton and Washington, D.C. Many critics have missed the crucial fact that Mother Eve, Tom Outland's consciously adopted ancestor, is presumed murdered in the act of adultery. And if retributive violence, repression, and dangerous sexuality are endemic to the Cliff City, then it cannot represent, for Cather or for us, a prelapsarian world of pure harmony and untested innocence. If Cather is nostalgic, if she is a "mourner," as Alfred Kazin, Lionel Trilling, Leon Edel, and others suggest,[2] then she mourns not the loss of innocence, but the loss of a complex cultural context that includes suffering, sacrifice, and victimage. Such a culture lends weightiness to human conduct, a felt significance that modern commercial materialism has largely erased. But such weightiness, as opposed to what Milan Kundera calls "the unbearable lightness of being," can only be discovered or created within manifestly flawed human congregations. Hence the need for stories.

1. STORIES AS STRATEGIES FOR SURVIVAL OR DEMISE

Living, Phyllis Rose suggests in her provocative *Parallel Lives*, is an act of narrative creativity. "Each of us," she says, "in the ordinary process of living is a fitful novelist," and "at certain moments, the need to decide upon the story of our own lives becomes particularly pressing" (5–6). If so, then certainly the professor is in his own life at a point that demands an extraordinary manifestation of his storifying imagination. He has truly arrived at a crux. The world, broken in two, has undermined his understanding of life, the narrative pattern of beliefs, values, desires, and experiences that he has used to order and enrich his creatureliness. But when we examine Godfrey St. Peter's alienation from his family, his profession, and finally even from his memories, we can see that Cather gradually exposes his disengagement as a strategic response to a difficult professional and familial situation. The professor's growing self-pity and disaffection with the world seem parts of a compensatory narrative strategy, a psychological means of suppressing aspects of reality that he cannot control. His late-blooming hypersensitivity and withdrawal bespeak a new identity story of consolation through isolation. Unfortunately, this new plot includes a cessation of previous productive and reproductive ways. However great the cost, though, the professor's new story does allow him to endure the changes he observes in his friends and family (including the deeply felt loss of Tom Outland) and the normal and natural alterations that he reluctantly recognizes in himself. In short, the professor, by changing his life story, is dealing with what we have come to call a "midlife crisis."

Kenneth Burke's analysis of the human propensity to name situations strategically is especially helpful in understanding the professor's psychological responses and processes. According to Burke, works of art are social strategies "designed to organize and command the army of one's thoughts and images"; a person "tries, as far as possible, to develop a strategy whereby one 'can't lose.' One tries to change the rules of the game until they fit his own necessities" (298). We observe the professor developing and implementing just such a strategy, and not surprisingly, the strategy takes the form of a narrative. One dependable way to guarantee victory is by creating an identity story in which "success" is identified with worldly failure. "Success through defeat," the victim's characteristic victory, requires only renunciation and withdrawal—or even death. Such plots will always be ready and available, and, because they are not dependent on the capriciousness of persons or events, will prove efficacious if enacted. They have, moreover, proven irresistible to many thoughtful and high-minded persons in the twentieth century.

But Cather, herself gravely tempted by plots of alienation,[3] scrutinizes the professor's strategy of disengagement and finds it wanting. For instance, after returning from a buying trip to Chicago with Rosamond, a trip that turned into an orgy of acquisition, he is caught by Lillian "smiling—quite agreeably!" (156). It seems that the professor has been "amusing himself" by thinking about Euripides, who as an old man "went and lived in a cave by the sea" because "houses had become insupportable to him." He wonders if "it was because [Euripides] had observed women so closely all his life" (156). Some critics attribute such misogynistic rumblings to Cather herself, but I think that the author is demonstrating the destructive pleasure that can be taken in construing life materials into a negative story or narrative. In this particular story the professor casts himself as the discerning, uncompromising artist who, because he cannot tolerate the ways of women and the world, escapes to the cave of a hermit. Cather demonstrates the satisfactions achieved by such a narrative by having her central character take an obvious delight in what should be a painful recognition. In another moment of nostalgic despair, St. Peter wonders if Medea's solution—murdering one's children— is the only way to save them from the world (126). Such dark narrative fantasies are clearly products of a jaundiced attitude and point of view. Burke would say that the professor is not "keeping his weather eye open," not sizing up the situation properly so that the future can be anticipated (298).

If we were to specify St. Peter's temptation, we might say that it is toward a prideful story that manifests itself in gnostic despair. He thinks of his personal world as "small and tight and airless"; his life seems "insupportable, as the boat on which he is imprisoned seems to a sea-sick man" (150). Thus the dualistic impulse to conceive of the world as a prison-house appears in St. Peter's new story of revulsion and renunciation. But Cather's repetition of the key word *insupportable* to describe the professor's sense of his condition implies that this crisis is as much a function of his narrative imagination as it is of the world's iniquity. Further, she prepares us for St. Peter's final temptation in the garden by allowing the professor himself to describe despair as a personal response, an alteration of vision, a modification of plot: "Yes, it was possible," St. Peter tells himself, "that the little world, on its voyage among all the stars, might become like that, a boat on which one could travel no longer, from which one could no longer look up and confront those bright rings of revolution" (150). We recall that it was from another "little brig," called *L'Espoir*, that he had seen and accepted the design of his history, his great work: "St. Peter lay looking up at [the Sierra Nevada] from a little boat riding low in the purple water, and the design of his book unfolded in the air above him, just as definitely as the mountain ranges themselves" (106). The professor's voyage through the world, we must assume, has always been rough and hazardous. From the same vantage point, reminiscent of Stephen Crane's "The Open Boat," the professor had constructed his great narrative of contending and conquest, his life work. But that was then; this is now. The professor has given up the earlier story and is experiencing a Sartrean "nausea" in response to the life voyage. It is not so much the voyage or the world that has changed, but his capacity to enjoy its rich complexity and to delight in its bright possibilities. He seems to have lost, at least temporarily, the ability to find and utilize sustaining scripts and patterns.

2. THE PROFESSOR'S NEW STORY: RENUNCIATION AND *THANATOS*

While "Tom Outland's Story" certainly stands in judgment of the professor's family and the provincialism of his college and town, it would be a mistake to romanticize Tom and his story about the Blue Mesa, to see everything else in St. Peter's world as a mundane counterpoint to the seemingly perfect friendship represented by Tom and the supposedly ideal kinship represented by the Cliff City. Yet during the period of anguish and redefinition, St. Peter engages in just such a romanticizing and comes dangerously close to deifying Tom.

His recollections of his former student more and more resemble the adoration of his adolescent daughters who "used to live in [Tom's] stories" (131). Certainly there is nothing wrong with living in stories, if, as is my assumption, we all construct and make sense of our lives by utilizing narrative strategies. But "in the stories Tom told the children there were no shadows" (123), and St. Peter likens them to uncomplicated "adventure books." Like the stories told by Tom to Kitty and Rosamond, the story the professor tells himself about Tom Outland contains no shadows. He takes possession of the memory of his former student much as Kitty does: "Now that Rosamond has Outland," she tells her father, "I consider Tom's mesa entirely my own" (131). Surely Kitty's possessiveness is not unlike that which St. Peter himself has begun to feel, and its callow quality suggests the professor's misuse of Tom's story to plot his withdrawal from the world. "Our Tom is much nicer than theirs" (132), Kitty says, and while in one sense her observation is true, the use of *our* implies that there are now abroad several conflicting Tom Outland stories, each serving some strategic purpose for its author.

St. Peter would like to exonerate Tom Outland from any complicity with the world, and he reiterates the familiar Greek renunciation of mundanity— better to die young, best of all never to be born. Tom, by his early death, the professor muses, has enjoyed the "better" if not the "best" fate, avoiding "the trap of worldly success" (260). The professor enumerates the onerous duties that Tom would have had to perform:

His fellow scientists, his wife, the town and State, would have required many duties of [Tom's "fine long hand"]. It would have had to write thousands of useless letters, frame thousands of false excuses. It would have had to "manage" a great deal of money, to be the instrument of a woman who would grow always more exacting. He had escaped all that. He had made something new in the world—and the rewards, the meaningless conventional gestures, he had left to others. (261)

Thus the professor construes Tom as a Rousseauesque natural self that has avoided corruption by the world.

There is ample evidence, however, that Tom is cultivated and improved by his contact with the university community, that "the family" has indeed been crucial to the development of his identity story:

There was evidently something enchanting about the atmosphere of the house to a boy who had always lived a rough life. He enjoyed the prettiness and freshness and gaiety of the little girls as if they were flowers. . . . [The girls] were teaching Tom things that he needed more than mathematics. (124–25)

As the professor's melancholia deepens, he more often thinks of Tom reading Virgil alone on the mesa and strategically forgets those charming, chattering "groups of three he was always coming upon" in his house and garden (125). Tom Outland may be in the process of becoming for the professor what he is for Louie and Rosamond—an excuse for indulging appetites and private desires—or what he is for Scott McGregor: "Tom isn't very real to me any more," Scott says. "Sometimes I think he was just a—a glittering idea" (111). Toward the end of St. Peter's struggle, Tom ceases to be present to him even as a glittering idea. The professor's "gardening," a traditional symbol for cultivation and thus for order and culture, has become listless and is now suggestive of a less productive motive. As he begins constructing a new identity story for himself, he also begins "cultivating a novel mental dissipation—and enjoying a new friendship" (263). No longer a maker of scholarly narrations, he works through Tom's diary "in a desultory way" and begins to enjoy a "half-awake loafing with his brain" (262, 263). During the daydreams that threaten to become a premature senility, the professor rediscovers not his seasoned former student but the "original, unmodified Godfrey St. Peter," a boyish, narcissistic self: "Tom Outland had not come back again through the garden door . . . but another boy had: the boy the Professor had long ago left behind him in Kansas" (263). This mysterious and rather ominous child is very little like Tom Outland, whose gravity distinguished him from the jejune boys of the college. The "Kansas boy" with whom St. Peter spends the summer "was not a scholar. He was a primitive" (265). Unlike Tom, who always associated the Blue Mesa with a cultural tradition grounded in bonds of family and community, this boy "was only interested in earth and woods and water" (265).

St. Peter's decline has been marked by the employment of an imaginative script depicting the world as a prison. According to this story—a narrative of withdrawal, decline, and ultimately death—the demands of family and community become temptations to corruption. Now the mystical aspects of his narrative strategy personify themselves in the figure of this uncorrupted, unbounded and unbonded self, a boyish phantasm of uncomplicated and unenculturated innocence. Heroism, sacrifice, and risk, those elements that give weightiness to human conduct, are foreign to this child of St. Peter's imagination:

> He was not nearly so cultivated as Tom's old cliff-dwellers must have been—
> and yet he was terribly wise. He seemed to be at the root of the matter;
> Desire under all desires, Truth under all truths. He seemed to know, among
> other things, that he was solitary and must always be so; he had never
> married, never been a father. (265)

This other-worldly innocent, a construct of the professor's strategic story-telling, is wholly self-sufficient, indifferent to persons, families, communities, and cultures. He represents, I believe, what Walker Percy calls *thanatos*, the love of death.[4] Though he is a wild, undomesticated, unencumbered youth, the professor is falling in love with him—a narcissistic reflection of himself. And as the story of Book III unfolds, he begins to fall out of love with the world: "Falling out [of love], for him, seemed to mean falling out of all domestic and social relations, out of his place in the human family" (275).

3. AUGUSTA'S STORY: RECONCILIATION AND REHABILITATION

St. Peter may half believe that the "release from every obligation, from every form of effort" (272) the youth promises is devoutly to be wished, but we as readers recognize his narrative strategy as a life-denying story of renunciation and "deathiness." After all, in the past the professor has managed to construct livable narratives of inclusion by playing *all* his roles with vigor: "By eliminations and combinations so many and subtle that it now made his head ache to think of them, he had done full justice to his university lectures, and at the same time carried on an engrossing piece of creative work" (29). When St. Peter tries to contrast his research, his "own work" as we academics say, with his worldly allegiances, Lillian replies with an observation that carries incontrovertible authority: "I think your ideas were best when you were your most human self" (162).

The either/or dualism represented by the Kansas boy is overwhelmed by our memory of St. Peter's integrated past—a life of harmony and significant enterprise, of *"lieben und arbeiten,"* that Cather presents allusively and lyrically as a Christmas morning recollection:

> When he was writing his best, he was conscious of pretty little girls in fresh
> dresses—of flowers and greens in the comfortable, shabby sitting-room—of

his wife's good looks and good taste—even of a better dinner than usual under preparation downstairs. All the while he had been working so fiercely at his eight big volumes, he was not insensible to the domestic drama that went on beneath him. His mind had played delightedly with all those [homely] incidents . . . so, to him, the most important chapters of his history were interwoven with personal memories. (101)

Even the architecture of the old house itself, with the solitary intellectual struggle going on in the midst of the family drama, evinces a story of inter-dependence that has proven livable and sustaining. His study is located *above* the family drama, to be sure, but it is significant that only through and by means of the family space does St. Peter have access to his work; there is no private "scholar's entrance." For many years, then, the professor plays scholar and teacher, husband and father in a satisfying integrated life story.

Perhaps of even more importance is the fact that within his study itself St. Peter had admitted Augusta, the sewing woman who represents the practical life of service to one's fellows. After she has rescued the professor from asphyxiation, suggestive of the airlessness of a hermit's cave, St. Peter "lay watching her— regarding in her humankind, as if after a definite absence from the world of men and women" (279).[5] It was Augusta who created the "fresh frocks" and inspiriting evening dresses for the professor's wife and daughters. And her powers to transform extend beyond the superficial and cosmetic: St. Peter "had grown to like the reminders of herself that she left in his work-room—especially the toilettes upon the figures. Sometimes she made those terrible women entirely plausible!"[6]

Moreover, St. Peter's brush with death is not the first time that his stories and "manuscripts" have found Augusta's "patterns." The box-couch, the site of St. Peter's near-suicide, has in fact been shared with Augusta for years:

At one end of the upholstered box were piles of notebooks and bundles of manuscript tied up in square packages with mason's cord. At the other end were many little rolls of patterns, cut out of newspapers and tied with bits of ribbon, gingham, silk, georgette; notched charts which followed the changing stature and figures of the Misses St. Peter from early childhood to womanhood. In the middle of the box, patterns and manuscripts interpenetrated. (22)

The professor himself recognizes his attachment to the sewing woman, commenting, "I see we shall have some difficulty in separating our life work, Augusta" (22–23). So Augusta, representing humankind and worldly responsibilities—"Seasoned and sound and on the solid earth she surely was" (281)—has insinuated her work into St. Peter's since the beginning.

It is appropriate, then, that in the end it is Augusta who rescues St. Peter from the death that would have been the climax of his *thanatos*-story and his final renunciation of the world. But St. Peter's own intention was to change his plot of despair; Augusta has merely increased the efficacy of his belated attempt to return to the human family. Though some critics miss the point, St. Peter does attempt to save himself. Augusta hears the body fall after he gets up from the couch. Moreover, the professor has already begun the construction of a new life story, a script based on Augusta's "patterns": "if he had thought of Augusta sooner, he would have got up from the couch sooner. Her image would have at once suggested the proper action" (279–80). Augusta's intervention, then, can be seen as a narrative contribution to the professor's reentry to the world: their lives and their work have "interpenetrated" once again. Certainly St. Peter has come to see the petty and spiritless modern world as a waste land, yet even in his little borough of Hamilton there is Augusta to function as the transcendent made manifest in the everyday. For the professor, she re-presents, like the Virgin in *Death Comes for the Archbishop*, the story of "greatness returning to simplicity" (50). With Augusta's help, St. Peter is now perceiving and ascribing more value to his family and community. If he must move from his old house, change his *point* of view, he can nonetheless develop a narrative of survival and affirmation, now that his time of grief and despair is passing. Rescued from both death and from a death-in-life identity story by Augusta, St. Peter now thinks he can "face with fortitude the *Berengaria* and the future" (283).

In St. Peter's new story, his family and his larger communal situation (collectively represented by the *Berengaria*) no longer seem insupportable. Thus the interpenetration of spirituality and domesticity represented by Augusta proves twice productive of major narrative works: before, *Spanish Adventurers in North America*, and now, the professor's fresh "attitude of mind," his renewed strategy of life (282). In Book I, "The Family," Augusta is introduced early and shares the novel's first dialogue with the professor; moreover, she has been latently present throughout the novel, as "a corrective, a remedial influence" (280). She has a "story," just as Tom Outland does, and both function for St. Peter as miracles do for Father Latour in *Death Comes for the Archbishop*. Miracles, Latour says, "seem to rest not so much upon faces or voices or healing power coming suddenly near us from afar off, but upon our perceptions being made finer, so that for a moment our eyes can see and our ears can hear what is there about us always" (50). Cather's novels suggest that stories themselves, like the miracle reports, can teach us to look anew at the world. They can *rehabilitate*: restore to us faculties and quicken in us abilities that had seemed forever lost. Not always, but sometimes they manifest a power to refine perceptions, and thus to redeem and transform.

So *The Professor's House* can be seen as a story about deterioration and rehabilitation, about St. Peter's letting go of one exhausted story and his attempt to shape another, more effectual, one. The professor's need, in the terms of Burke, is to find a story that is gratifying and true enough to the facts so that the future can be anticipated and the world lived in. He finds such a "story" in the character of Tom Outland and his account of the Cliff City; but "Tom Outland's Story," though gratifying, is romanticized by ⌐t. Peter. Eventually the sentimentalization and deification of Tom Outland make it more difficult for the professor to live in the world, and Tom's story eventually loses its power to motivate and sustain him. When he forgets that Outland's story is essentially like the *Aeneid*, one celebrating Roman values of allegiance to family, to community, and to polity, Tom disappears and the unsocialized *thanatos*-child takes his place.

Augusta, however, eventually displaces the uncultivated child, just as he, the imaginary Kansas boy, had displaced Tom. Tom's story is certainly richer and more compelling for us as readers, and it remains so even after critical analysis, simple but beautiful, "a turquoise set in dull silver" (from Cather's epigraph). Yet Augusta's "story" also proves efficacious for St. Peter, suggesting that there is always in the world enough "material" for a sustaining story; one must simply, like Henry James and Willa Cather, emphasize the "treatment." Cather's stylistic restraint forces us, as always, to participate in the creation of this communitarian story, to imagine, as readers, possibilities other than the obvious. The professor may still be an old man in a dry month, but that dry season includes August and it brings a rebirth, albeit difficult and "cruel," by mixing memory and desire. St. Peter's new vision includes a world of simple people, of "fatheaded boys," ⌐s he now thinks of them with affection, to be lived with and taught, "a world full of Augustas, with whom one was outward bound" (281). *The Professor's House* thus contemplates the possibility of a life of affection and productivity, of weightiness, in the midst of conspicuous consumption and ordinary people—certainly an inauspicious and potentially barren cultural context. Perhaps another remarkable mind, another Outland will appear; perhaps not. But we and the professor have learned from Augusta's story no less than from Tom Outland's that a cultural regeneration can occur in a waste land and that while we wait for that rebirth a stoic reserve and the use of stories, a belief in art and in artifacts, may help us to live *in* the world, with its burdening but sustaining, confining but engendering, families and communities.

—University of Houston

NOTES

1. The quoted phrase comes from Kenneth Burke's frequently anthologized essay "Literature as Equipment for Living," originally published as a chapter in *The Philosophy of Literary Form*.
2. The charge that Cather became an escapist, that she withdrew from modernity, and that she began practicing a kind of literary denial (a charge often traced to *The Professor's House*) was lodged by some of the most distinguished critics of the

twentieth century, including Hoffman (189), Daiches (185), and Zabel (268–69), as well as Kazin (169), Trilling (49), and Edel (*Paradox* 2–12).

3. In his famous essay on the psychological aspects of *The Professor's House* in *Literary Biography*, Edel makes the proper connection between Cather's "loss" of her friend Isabelle McClung, who married Jan Hambourg (to whom the novel is dedicated), and the professor's grief over Tom Outland's death (56–80). But Burke's essay specifically addresses this sort of disappointment. "One tries to change the rules of the game until they fit his own necessities," Burke says. "Does the artist encounter disaster? He will 'make capital' of it" (298). Willa Cather, it seems to me, has done this very thing, and the "capital" made is the novel itself.

4. See McCombs's conversation with Percy.

5. This "turning" at the end of the novel is often taken for the final indication of St. Peter's decline; as evidence critics cite the passage in which Augusta is likened to "the taste of bitter herbs; she was the bloomless side of life that [St. Peter] had always run away from" (280). Yet surely this description of Augusta, like so many others that can be taken out of context in this reticent novel *démeublé*, incompletely represents the character.

6. Both the professor and Cather, as Latinists, would think of *plausible* in its original sense of "deserving of applause." Thus Augusta's adornment of the women in St. Peter's life demonstrates her skill at the storytelling technique known as "characterization."

BIBLIOGRAPHY

Burke, Kenneth. *The Philosophy of Literary Form: Studies in Symbolic Action.* Baton Rouge: Louisiana State UP, 1941.

Cather, Willa. *Death Comes for the Archbishop.* New York: Vintage, 1971.

——. *Willa Cather on Writing.* New York: Knopf, 1949.

——. *The Professor's House.* New York: Vintage, 1973.

Daiches, David. *Willa Cather: A Critical Introduction.* Westport, Conn.: Greenwood, 1971.

Edel, Leon. *Literary Biography.* Toronto: U of Toronto P, 1957.

——. *Willa Cather: The Paradox of Success.* Washington, D.C.: Library of Congress, 1960.

Hoffman, Frederick J. *The Twenties: American Writing in the Postwar Decade.* Rev. ed. New York: Free, 1965.

Kazin, Alfred. *On Native Grounds.* New York: Reynall & Hitchcock, 1942.

McCombs, Phil. "Century of Thanatos: Walker Percy and His 'Subversive Message.'" *Southern Review* 66 (1988): 808–24.

Rose, Phyllis. *Parallel Lives: Five Victorian Marriages.* New York: Knopf, 1983.

Trilling, Lionel. "Willa Cather." *After the Genteel Tradition.* Ed. Malcolm Cowley. Carbondale: Southern Illinois UP, 1965.

Zabel, Morton D. *Craft and Character in Modern Fiction: Texts, Method, and Vocation.* New York: Viking, 1957.

The Faith Community in
Death Comes for the Archbishop

JOHN J. MURPHY

We all are familiar now with the quotable passages on family from
Cather's works: about the ego at once seeking and trying to pull away from
human relationships, in the Katherine Mansfield essay; about Ántonia
Cuzak's family members liking to touch each other; about the clan feeling
among the Ferguessons, in "The Best Years," Cather's last completed story,
and so on. This last story is especially significant for understanding the
meaning of family in Cather; it begins with a description of the mystical unifying power of the horizon, "a perfect circle, a great embrace" of corn and
wheat fields and pastures (*Five Stories* 114). Landscape is charged with similar
power in "Neighbour Rosicky," a story devoted to family integrity, to drawing
daughter-in-law Polly into the Rosicky family circle. Papa Rosicky watches
the snow falling over his barnyard and the graveyard, seeming "to draw things
together like," a drawing together that transcends his nuclear family: "they
were all old neighbors in the graveyard, most of them friends; there was
nothing to feel awkward or embarrassed about" (*Five Stories* 81). Where
Rosicky eventually sleeps in the prairie graveyard it is "open and free. . . .
Nothing but the sky overhead, and the many-coloured fields running on until
they met that sky" (111).

Beyond what we discover about earthly family and community during
these symposium days, about the Cather family itself, local Nebraska history,
Cather's fictional families—the Bergsons, Kronborgs, Cuzaks, St. Peters—
there is the mystery associated with terms like *incarnation*, *redemption*,
resurrection, elevating humanity beyond nature. Before these concepts are
dismissed as passé or sectarian, we should recall that Cather celebrates
the resurrection of Ántonia's family from the fruit cave in the final book of
My Ántonia only after we reverence Mary's family in the first book (Jim
decorates a Christmas tree with the traditional symbols surrounding a card-
board "Baby in the manger" [83]), that *Shadows on the Rock* extensively
honors Christ incarnate in the Holy Family ("The Infant . . . lay rosy and
naked in a little straw-lined manger. . . . The Blessed Virgin wore no halo, but
a white scarf over her head. She looked like a country girl, very naive, seated
on a stool, with her knees well apart under her full skirt, and very large feet.
Saint Joseph, a grave old man in brown, with a bald head and wrinkled brow,

was placed opposite her" [108]), and that in *Death Comes for the Archbishop* the Holy Family appears as a humble Mexican one whose child traces the cross on the forehead of Father Junipero Serra. What Cather is doing in all three novels through association with spiritual heritage is expanding family into a universal community beyond its nuclear, terrestrial nature.

A challenge in Cather is the making of family where there is no group of people sharing the same blood. "Jack-a-Boy," one of Cather's earliest stories, published in the *Saturday Evening Post* in March 1901, meets this very challenge; it concerns a group of scattered and rather joyless individuals in a boardinghouse, who in the course of the story are united, made into a family through the life, death, and memory of a special little boy, whom Cather very obviously associates with "the greatest Revealer [who] drew men together," for whom "the fishermen left their nets," to whom "Nicodemus . . . came . . . by night, and Mary, of Magdala, at the public feast, wiped his feet with her hair" (*Collected Short Fiction* 322). In *Shadows on the Rock*, thirty years later, Jack-a-Boy reappears as the Quebec prostitute's son, Jacques Gaux, whom Bishop Laval rescues in the snow and sees as the "Infant Saviour" directing the old priest to renew the spiritual fervor of his early life. The novel, like the early story, gathers together a motley group of individuals: a motherless girl, a widower apothecary, a waif, a lonely old bishop, a woodsman, a missionary priest, an ex-convict, a prostitute, a dying governor, a sea captain, a sister superior, and so on. Hardly a family in the ordinary sense, these individuals share the French culture Cather admired and its Catholic Christianity. Admittedly, Quebec is a military installation, a fortress for the French monarchy, but it is also a rock built over with churches, convents, gardens, a seminary, and a cathedral, and it resembles "one of those little artificial mountains which were made in the churches [in France] to present a theatric scene of the Nativity" (4–5). Of course, in the process, Quebec becomes the house on a rock and the city on a hill, a symbol of church community echoing Matthew 5:13–16 and 16:15–19.

Nativity is but the first step in humanity's pilgrimage toward a celestial community assembled in love and united with God through redemption. "The Best Years" clarifies this journey idea as clearly as any story can. In its shortest, fifth section Cather joins the Incarnation and Redemption and establishes young Lesley Ferguesson as a Christ figure. Lesley had worked very hard before her death to buy her brother Hector a new coat—a heavy, cheap coat but all she could afford. Pensive Hector, the "flower" of the Ferguesson family, touched by his sister's giving nature, studies the bright stars as he labors up the hill from the depot under the heavy coat (cross?), "wondering if there were angels up there, watching the world on [this] Christmas Eve. They came before, on the first Christmas Eve, he knew. Perhaps they kept the Anniversary. He thought about a beautiful coloured picture tacked up in Lesley's bedroom; two angels with white robes and long white wings, flying toward a low hill in the early dawn before sunrise, and on that distant hill, against the soft daybreak light, were three tiny crosses" (*Five Stories* 137). Cather does here what T. S. Eliot had done in his poem "Journey of the Magi," where the astrologers travel to Bethlehem only to discover "three trees on the low sky" and the white horse without its rider (the glorified Christ). The narrator gets confused:

> were we led all that way for
> Birth or Death? There was a Birth, certainly,
> We had evidence and no doubt. I had seen birth and death,
> But had thought they were different; this Birth was
> Hard and bitter agony for us, like Death, our death.

When the Christ Child in the Mexican family in *Death Comes for the Archbishop* "lifted his hand, and with his tiny finger made the cross upon Father Junipero's forehead" (282), it is a clarifying gesture of inclusion. Death, the cross, the birthright, extends and transfigures the human family beyond its nature. In Eliot's poem, dated 1927, the year he announced his conversion to the Anglican church and the publication year of *Death Comes for the Archbishop*, five years after Cather's own conversion to the Episcopal church, the narrator dwells on the difficulty of the conversion journey—sharp weather, lack of shelter—"A hard time we had of it." Then there is the discovery of a temperate valley with a running stream and the sight of the three trees—the three crosses of Calvary. Notice the similar pattern at the beginning of *Death Comes for the Archbishop* where Bishop Latour, lost among conical hills, discovers a tree/cross and then, after prayer, a fertile green valley with a running stream.

The organic image of the tree is the key—suggesting at once the cross of the Crucifixion and the bearing vine in John 15:1–13: "I am the true vine," Jesus announces at the Last Supper, adding, "you are the branches. Whoever remains in me, and me in him, bears fruit in plenty; for cut off from me you can do nothing. . . . Remain in my love. . . . This is my commandment: love one another, as I have loved you. A man can have no greater love than to lay down his life for his friends." In Matthew 26:26–28 Jesus blesses the bread and gives it to his disciples. "Take it and eat," he says; "this is my body." Then he gives thanks over the fruit of the vine and hands the cup around: "Drink all of you from this, for this is my blood . . . poured out for many for the forgiveness of sins." In John 6:26–58 Jesus calls himself "the bread of life. . . . come from heaven," the new manna, "food that endures to eternal life": "I am the living bread which has come down from heaven. Anyone who eats this bread will live forever; and the bread that I shall give is my flesh, for the life of the world. . . . If you do not eat the flesh of the Son of Man and drink his blood, you will not have life in you." Community living in Christian terms, then, becomes sustenance sharing, the foundation stone of connectedness. Three passages in "The Best Years" are significant in this context. For Lesley, "the feeling of being at home was complete, absolute. . . . That feeling was . . . being with, and being one with, her brothers. It was the clan feeling, which meant life or death for the blood, not for the individual. . . . Creatures wanted the blood to continue" (*Five Stories* 134). And Lesley was pale—"Hector . . . had the fair pink-cheeked complexion which [she] should have had and didn't" (126). Also, the Ferguesson house, a symbol of church, "stood on a steep hillside" (122).

All this is prefatory, a background for considering *Death Comes for the Archbishop* as Cather's ultimate family novel, depicting community nourishment through sacrificial death and offering a transcendent paradigm for family living. It opens with Father Latour's discovery in the desert of the cruciform tree and his contemplation of Christ's suffering; the thirsty priest "reminded himself of that cry, wrung from his Saviour on the Cross, '*J'ai soif!*' . . . [and] blotted himself out of his own consciousness and meditated upon the anguish of his Lord. The Passion of Jesus became for him the only reality; the need of his body was but part of that conception" (20). In the novel's final book, summarizing the archbishop's last years, the discovery of what will become his retirement farm recalls the discovery of the cruciform tree: "Once when he was riding out to visit the Tesuque mission, he had followed a stream and come upon this spot, where he found a little Mexican house and a garden shaded by an apricot tree of such great size as he had never seen before. It had two trunks, each of them thicker than a man's body, and though evidently very old, it was full of fruit. The apricots were large, beautifully coloured, and of superb flavour." The age of the tree cannot be determined. The old Mexican owner says it "had been just like this when his grandfather was a boy, and had always borne luscious apricots" (266). This tree symbolizes redemption as much as does the cruciform tree.

In linking the myths of the planting cultures to the Christian story, the late Joseph Campbell in his popular television interviews reminded us that the Christian story is vegetal: Jesus is the vine and we are the branches; also, he is on the tree (the cross) as life-giving fruit. "The individual isn't quite an individual, he is a branch of a plant"; neither is death quite death but "required for new life" (*Power of Myth* 102, 107). As in Latour's "mythology," the fruit of the tree (Christ on the cross) is what unifies the faithful; Christ is the sacrificial victim, the corn god we bury, cultivate and consume as nourishment. As Bill Moyers commented to Campbell, love of neighbor actually becomes love of self, for you and your neighbor are one—in both flesh and spirit in Christ (111). Cather's narrative concerns more than anything the bringing of this fruit of the vine to a fallen-away people. The journeys of Latour and Vaillant are undertaken to graft scion to stock through the sacramental life of the church, primarily through Communion in the mass, which Campbell describes as the "replication" of Calvary (109). Consider the many masses celebrated in *Death Comes for the Archbishop*. Latour says masses at Hidden Water and Laguna, Vaillant at Santo Domingo; Latour senses defeat saying mass at Ácoma; Padre Martínez devoutly sings the mass at Taos; Vaillant says mass after a Pima Indian takes him into a cave where the holy vessels are hidden; in Colorado, he says mass in the open air on the trunk of his episcopal carriage; Latour celebrates his last midnight mass in his cathedral in 1888. We might add to this list Vaillant's administering the Sacrament in Las Vegas, New Mexico, before falling ill from black measles; his struggle to give Communion to dying, miserly Padre Lucero; and also the mocking of the mass by the low-caste Smith family, their blaspheming the procession of the Sacrament on the feast of Corpus Christi, and Sada's lament about being deprived of the mass for nineteen years. The central action of this novel can be seen as bringing the Sacrament to the people, as the struggle to nourish them toward a loving community.

Cather employs several reflectors to emphasize the centrality of the mass in her novel. The significant attention given to eating and food is one of these; there is abundant food-sharing and community eating. The novel opens with an elegant dinner in Rome, and ten pages or so after that Latour shares a prayerful supper in the candlelight with Benito and his family at Hidden Water: "Their manners were gentle, their voices low and agreeable" (26). Vaillant then prepares Christmas dinner for himself and Latour, experiments with cooked salad, and makes his almost apostolic onion soup, "the result of a constantly refined tradition" (39). At Manuel Lujon's, where he "worries" his host out of two white mules, Vaillant cooks his own meat and shares a bottle of Bordeaux wine. Attention is given to benign old Padre Jesus de Baca's simple fare of "beans and cornmeal mush" (85). More suggestive is Latour's breaking bread with Jacinto at Pecos. Then there are the lavish supper parties at Antonio and Isabella Olivares's with their sherry and sparkling wines. We are told that Latour's housekeeper Fructosa has been instructed in cooking by Father Vaillant and that Vaillant's ample dinners were quickly translated into spiritual energy. The "Legend of Fray Baltazar" is Cather's orgy of food and eating, its sumptuous clerical feast duplicating the ecclesiastical dinner of the prologue and reversing through exploitation the unifying nature of sharing sustenance. Padre Baltazar "took the best . . . corn and beans and squashes for his table, and selected the choicest portions when [the Ácomas] slaughtered a sheep" (104). The fatal dinner he prepares consists of roast turkey, and hare *jardinière* with carrots and onions floating in rich sauce, and it parodies the mass when the Indian serving boy is sacrificed to the Padre's anger. While the detail about Father Vaillant's meals being translated into missionary activity spiritualizes food and eating, two equally strategic passages on meals relate directly to the mass. The second of these in the book is Vaillant's carving his roast mutton during supper at Manuel Lujon's, when the serving-girls "looked with horror at the delicate stream of pink juice that followed the knife" (58). This is an obvious reference to the sacrificial Lamb of God. The other passage begins on the novel's first page, where in the center of Cardinal Allande's garden the dinner table "stood in a sanded square, among potted orange and oleander trees, shaded by spreading ilex oaks that grew out of the rocks overhead." This is the altar table, confirmed a page later when the setting sun, a symbol of Christ crucified, climaxes "with a ruddiness as of much-multiplied candlelight, an aura of red in its flames. It bored into the ilex trees, illuminating their mahogony trunks and blurring their dark foliage; it warmed the bright green of the orange trees and the rose of the oleander blooms to gold; sent congested spiral patterns quivering over the damask and plate and crystal" arranged on the table (3–4).

The dramatic light here reminds me of the mystical woods in Flannery O'Connor's story "A View of the Woods," in which spiteful, old Mr. Fortune studies the woods he is attempting to block from view by selling his yard for a gas station: "The gaunt trunks appeared to be raised in a pool of red light that gushed from the almost hidden sun setting behind them. The old man stared . . . as if . . . held there in the midst of an uncomfortable mystery that he had not apprehended before. . . . as if someone were wounded behind the woods and the trees were bathed in blood" (*Complete Stories* 348). Emphatically redemption-centered in her fiction as she was, O'Connor never hesitated to be explicit in her letters about the sun-reddened woods, that the woods were cut out for the Christ figure "role," that "the woods, if anything, are the Christ symbol," and that "the woods alone are pure enough to be a Christ symbol if anything is" (*Habit of Being* 189–90). While Cather was never so direct in her comments on the allegory in *Death Comes for the Archbishop*, she nevertheless persistently includes the sun symbol of Christ as a mass reflector framing Latour's mission from beginning to end. He enters Santa Fe for the first time as "the sun sank lower, a sweep of red carnelian-coloured hills lying at the foot of the mountains" (22). During his final entrance, again at sunset, the old archbishop has a pointed conversation with his student Bernard Ducrot: "A fine sunset, Father," comments Bernard. "See how red the mountains are growing; Sangre de Cristo [Blood of Christ]." Latour reflects, "Yes, Sangre de Cristo; but no matter how scarlet the sunset those hills never became vermillion . . . not the colour of living blood . . . but the colour of the dried blood of saints and martyrs preserved in old churches in Rome, which liquifies upon occasion" (272–73). Between these references, the "sun set red in an atmosphere murky with sand" (89) on the road to Laguna; at Laguna the "whole western sky was the colour of golden ashes, with here and there a flush of red on the lip of a little cloud" (92); at Pecos, before the ruined mission church, the "sun was sinking, a red ball which threw a copper glow over the pine-covered ridge of mountains, and edged [an] inky, ominous cloud with molten silver" (119).

The third reflector of the mass involves the novel's dominant image cluster, vegetation. This imagery, as in the O'Connor story where the sun reddens the trees, is frequently in conjunction with declining sun, thereby associating sun with son (Christ, the Light of the World) on the cross/tree with the fruit of the vine and the meal of spiritual community. In *Hidden Water*, Latour sits by the life-giving spring while the declining sun pours its "beautifying light" over the "grass and trees [apricot and plum] and flowers and human life" (31). Released from its dark cave into the sunlight, the water (sterile in the darkness beneath Stone-Lips cave) becomes the living water of John 7:37–38: " 'Let the man come and drink who believes in me!' As scripture says: From his breast shall flow fountains of living water." "The Faith planted by the Spanish friars and watered with their blood was not dead," reflects Latour; "it awaited only the toil of the husbandman" (32). Latour and Vaillant are these husbandmen. Where priests have exploited their flocks, as at Ácoma, the trees decline and die: "In the grey dust of the enclosed garden two thin, half-dead peach trees . . . struggled with the drouth, the kind of unlikely tree that grows up from an old root and never bears" (102). In neglected and remote areas the faithful are "like seeds, full of germination but with no moisture," says Father Vaillant. "A mere contact is enough to make them a living part of the Church" (206). Fittingly, the tamarisks, "the tree of the people, and . . . like one of the family in every Mexican household," "had been so neglected, left to fight for life in such hard, sun-baked, burro-trodden ground, that their trunks had the hardness of cypress. They looked, indeed, like very old posts, well seasoned and polished by time, miraculously endowed with the power to burst into delicate foliage and flowers, to cover themselves with long brooms of lavender-pink blossoms" (201–02). In Navajo country, the venerable cottonwoods, scoured with sand and twisted from wind and insufficient water, "seemed to be of old, dead, dry wood" but are capable of a "thick coruscation of growth, like a crooked palm tree" (222).

In summarizing Father Latour's pastoral activities, Cather juxtaposes them with vegetal images. He "brought his fruit trees . . . from St. Louis in wagons, along with the blessed Sisters of Loretto, who came to found the Academy of Our Lady of Light. The school was now well established . . . and the trees were bearing. Cuttings from them were already yielding fruit in many Mexican gardens" (201). In retirement, Latour "grew such fruit as was hardly to be found even in the old orchards of California; cherries and apricots, apples and quinces, and the peerless pears of France—even the most delicate varieties. He urged the new priests to plant fruit trees wherever they went, and to encourage the Mexicans to add fruit to their starchy diet. . . . He often quoted to his students that passage from their fellow Auvergnat, Pascal: that Man was lost and saved in a garden" (267). When he sends Father Vaillant into Colorado it is because "nobody in Colorado planted gardens" (260). In the miracles of Father Junipero Serra, three trees marked the spot in the desert where the Holy Family appeared, and at another time the missionaries' thirst was relieved by a mysterious young horseman (Christ?) who gave the priests "three ripe pomegranates, then galloped away" (279). This fruit symbolizes resurrection, the fertility of the Word, and the richness of divine grace (*Christian Symbols* 63–64).

The conflict of Cather's priest protagonists is double-edged, involving the sacrifice of their own nuclear families and intimate friendship for service to the faith community; it also involves confrontations with those who would destroy that community by separating the branches from the living vine and violating fellowship. Latour and Vaillant struggle with the schismatic priests, Martinez (who instigates revolt and breaks his vows of chastity and obedience) and Lucero (who replaces God with gold and who hoards the money Martinez gives him for masses for his soul). Other villains in *Death Comes for the Archbishop*, like murderer Buck Scales, American hater and Indian hunter Manuel Chavez, even Kit Carson when he invades the Canyon de Chelly and drives the Navajo three hundred miles to the Bosque Redondo, are guilty of sins against community. The less dramatic conflict concerns, as Vaillant puts it in remembering his departure from France, "a betrayal of family trust for the sake of a higher trust" (204). Separation from their families marks the beginning of the missions of both priests, relived over and over again as a response to Christ's challenge in Matthew 10:37–39: "Anyone who prefers father or mother to me is not worthy of me. . . . Anyone who finds his life will lose it; anyone who loses his life for my sake will find it." The two young Frenchmen comfort each other by recalling the example of Saint Francis Xavier when he set forth as missionary to India. He had stolen away as they had, " '*passed the dwelling of his parents without saluting them*,' as they had learned at school; terrible words to a French boy" (284). This departure is more Vaillant's struggle than Latour's; Latour's greater struggle comes later when he must separate from his friend since boyhood and release him to the Arizona and Colorado missions. He marks his surrender by breaking off a spray of tamarisk blossom "to punctuate and seal, as it were, his renunciation" (209).

The success of both missionaries in advancing the concept of church beyond narrow sectarian orthodoxy is evident in Latour's reflection after Vaillant's funeral that his friend "aroused and retained" "extraordinary personal devotion . . . in red men and yellow men and white" (289). Latour's humanitarian concerns motivate his comment to his student Barnard: "My son, I have lived to see two great wrongs righted; I have seen the end of black slavery, and I have seen the Navajos restored to their own country" (291–92). The archbishop's own community achievement is obvious after his death, when the bell tolled, and "the Mexican population of Santa Fé fell upon their knees, and all American Catholics as well. Many others who did not kneel prayed in their hearts. Eusabio and the Tesuque boys went quietly away to tell their people; and the next morning the old Archbishop lay before the high altar in the church he had built" (299). Community expands beyond Christianity in the "enlightenment" that comes to the dying archbishop "apart from his religious life. . . . that came to him as a man, a human creature. And he noticed that he judged conduct differently now; his own and that of others" (290).

Community is without conflict at the end, yet the anguish necessary for achieving it shouts out at us in young Joseph Vaillant's anguished cry to his friend: "What shall I do, Jean? Help me! I cannot break my father's heart, and I cannot break the vow I have made to Heaven. I had rather die than do either. Ah, if I could but die of this misery, here, now!" (285).

—Brigham Young University

BIBLIOGRAPHY

Campbell, Joseph, with Bill Moyers. *The Power of Myth.* Garden City, N.Y.: Doubleday, 1988.
Cather, Willa. *Collected Short Fiction, 1892–1912.* Rev. ed. Ed. Virginia Faulkner. Lincoln: U of Nebraska P, 1970.
_____. *Death Comes for the Archbishop.* New York: Vintage, 1971.
_____. *Five Stories.* New York: Vintage, 1956.
_____. *My Ántonia.* New York: Houghton, Sentry ed., 1961.
_____. *Shadows on the Rock.* New York: Vintage, 1971.
Eliot, Thomas Stearns. *Collected Poems, 1909–1962.* New York: Harcourt, 1963.
Jerusalem Bible. Ed. Alexander Jones. Garden City, N.Y.: Doubleday, 1966.
O'Connor, Flannery. *The Complete Stories.* New York: Farrar, 1971.
_____. *The Habit of Being: Letters of Flannery O'Connor.* Ed. Sally Fitzgerald. New York: Vintage, 1980.
Rest, Friedrich. *On Christian Symbols.* New York: Pilgrim, 1982.

Index
of
Cather Fiction